ELEMENTS and PRINCIPLES of 4D ART and DESIGN

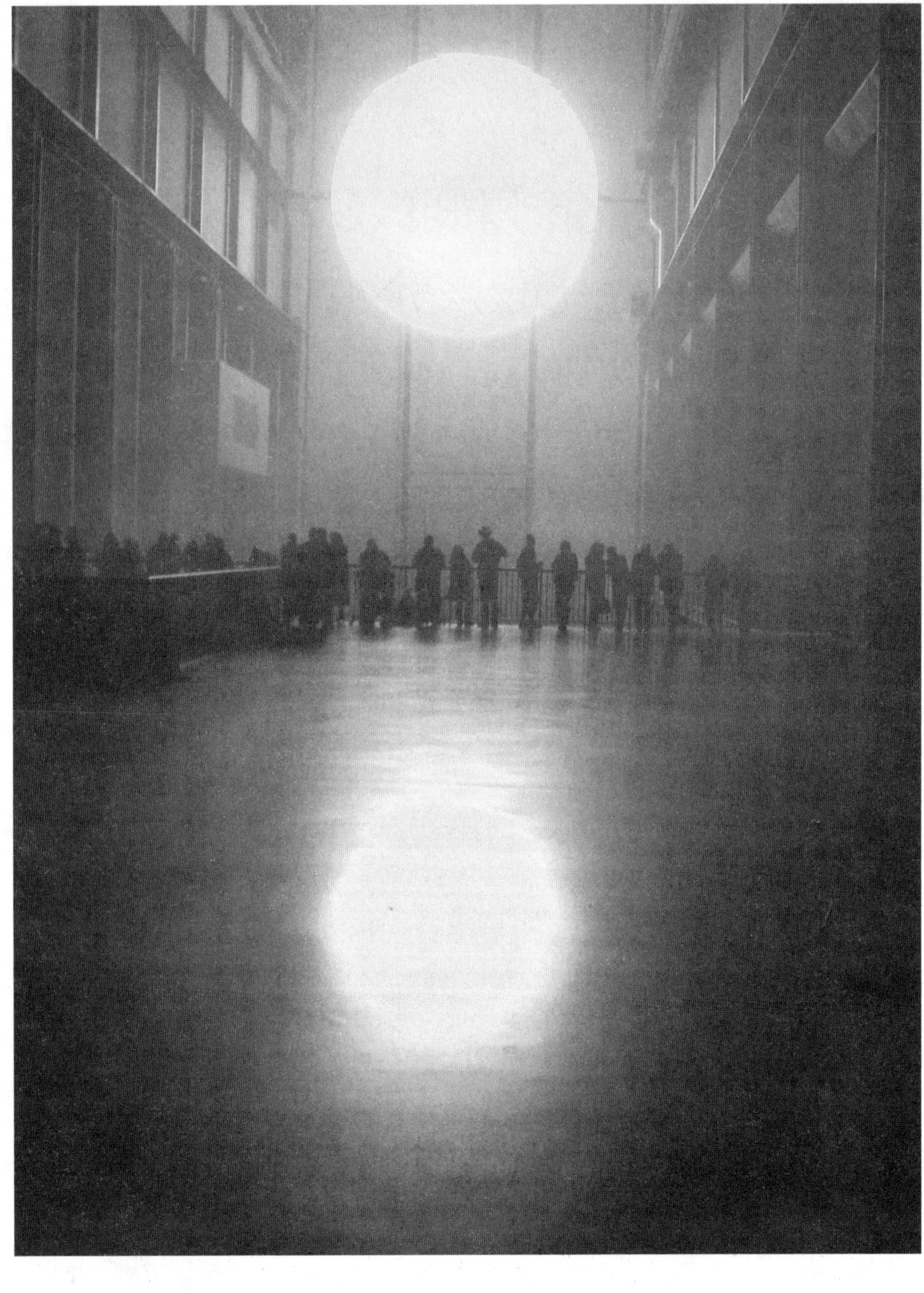

ELEMENTS and PRINCIPLES of 4D ART and DESIGN

ELLEN MUELLER

West Virginia Wesleyan College

New York   Oxford
OXFORD UNIVERSITY PRESS

Oxford University Press is a department of the University of Oxford.
It furthers the University's objective of excellence in research,
scholarship, and education by publishing worldwide.

Oxford   New York
Auckland   Cape Town   Dar es Salaam   Hong Kong   Karachi
Kuala Lumpur   Madrid   Melbourne   Mexico City   Nairobi
New Delhi   Shanghai   Taipei   Toronto

With offices in
Argentina   Austria   Brazil   Chile   Czech Republic   France   Greece
Guatemala   Hungary   Italy   Japan   Poland   Portugal   Singapore
South Korea   Switzerland   Thailand   Turkey   Ukraine   Vietnam

For titles covered by Section 112 of the US Higher Education
Opportunity Act, please visit www.oup.com/us/he for the
latest information about pricing and alternate formats.

Published by Oxford University Press
198 Madison Avenue, New York, New York 10016
http://www.oup.com

Library of Congress Cataloging-in-Publication Data
Mueller, Ellen, 1982- author.
  Elements and principles of 4D art and design / Ellen Mueller. -- First
[edition].
        pages cm
  Includes bibliographical references and index.
  ISBN 978-0-19-022514-8 (pbk. : alk. paper) 1. Arts, Modern--Themes,
motives--Textbooks. 2. Time in art--Textbooks. 3. Design--Textbooks.
I. Title.
  NX650.T5M84 2016
  709.04--dc23
                                                                2015033240

Printing number: 9 8 7 6 5 4 3 2 1

Printed in the United States of America
on acid-free paper

Contents

Color plate section follows page 140

List of Figures

Color Insert

Preface

Visual art programs in higher education are in the process of a foundational shift. There is a general move toward more four-dimensional (time-based) art and design, whether in motion graphics, film/video, performance art, social practice, sound art, installation, Internet art, game design, animation, and so on. Schools want to provide a foundation for these studies much like they have been doing for decades for two-dimensional (height and width) and three-dimensional (height, width, and depth) art and design. This book seeks to fill that void.

This text organizes and outlines the elements and principles of four-dimensional art and design in an effort to clarify the language used to discuss and critique four-dimensional works. To help readers fully understand these concepts, a variety of examples and interviews are included, adding useful context and demonstrated application. Instructors can choose from a selection of over 100 activities to help students apply these concepts to their art and design practice regardless of specific media or technology. There are tags assigned to every activity that enable instructors and students to quickly identify exercises that are best suited to their specific areas of study. The tags include:

SOUND: recording, editing, and presentation of sound

VIDEO/ANIMATION/MOTION GRAPHICS: recording, editing, and presentation of videos, animations, and motion graphics

PERFORMANCE/MOVEMENT/OTHER: –practice moving and performing live, as well as other exercises that do not fit into another category

INSTALLATION/SOCIAL PRACTICE: practice installing and organizing spaces for interaction

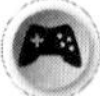 **GAMES:** practice creating, executing, and analyzing engaging games

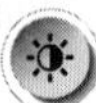 **LIGHT:** practice arranging and manipulating light

The accompanying website, **www.oup.com/us/mueller,** includes video and audio files for a selection of examples cited throughout the text; links and suggestions for online technical resources related to DSLR camera use, video editing, audio recording and editing, stop-motion animation; and links to additional resources on artists and art for more in-depth learning. Through use of these materials and critique of activities, students will become accustomed to assessing what works, what doesn't, and why. Students will be asked to articulate what they want to communicate, and how that reflects on themselves, others, and the world. The end goal is improved articulation of four-dimensional ideas.

These four-dimensional elements and principles are flexible, depending on instructor and program goals. Some instructors might choose to cover all of the text chapters at the start of the semester, and then practice utilizing those concepts via exercises for the remainder of the term. This approach allows for repeated and long-term recall of important concepts and ideas. Others might choose to alternate between reading and practice throughout the term, which allows for slowly building understanding. Others yet might opt for some combination of the two approaches. Flexibility is built into the text.

The concepts in this textbook are inspired by existing areas of study including film studies, sound design, motion graphics design, interactivity design, game design, lighting design, and the Viewpoints principles of movement.[1] This book aims to introduce the four-dimensional commonalities among these fields, and certainly recommends further study in each field beyond this text.

This text emphasizes readily available materials, improvisation or play, and conceptual rigor. Many of the activities are limited to a specific amount of time and involve a great deal of brainstorming. This approach is meant to embrace the spontaneous and to help eliminate hesitation, self-consciousness, and self-censorship. Any technology suggestions are limited to those generally accessible via inexpensive cameras or phones, and open-source software that is supported with a variety of online tutorials and support forums. More advanced or specialized equipment and software may be substituted as desired according to programmatic and curricular needs (see Chapter 2 for details). Overall, this text aims to be as practical, useful, and succinct as possible in every way.

Acknowledgments

This book was written in part during a 2-month residency at Nes Artist Residency in Skagaströnd, Iceland, and a 4-week residency at the Virginia Center for the Creative Arts, which was made possible in part by a Mid-Atlantic Arts Foundation Creative Fellowship. Both residencies were partially funded by West Virginia Wesleyan College faculty travel support. Searching for and securing examples for this text was made possible with the help of innumerable Facebook friends who helped compile lists such as "Animations That Involve Screaming." Thank you to all of the generous artists who agreed to submit thoughtful interviews for this book. I would also like to thank Cesar Cornejo, Vagner Whitehead, Beth Warshafsky, Jonathan Rattner, Caroline Peters, Rachel Clarke, Taylor Hokanson, Duncan MacKenzie, Santiago Echeverry, Cyane Tomatzky, Glenda Drew, Mike Salmond, Julia Bradshaw, Kate Shannon, Aki Torii, and two anonymous reviewers, who all volunteered to review the proposal or book. Thank you to my editors. Thank you to my sister, Laura Schweitz, for her many hours of reading and analysis. Thank you most of all to Phil McCollam, who spent huge amounts of time on this project, whether it was creating illustrations, brainstorming video game examples, or proofing chapters. The book would not have been possible without him.

Introduction

Four-dimensional art and design refers to those practices that involve time, the fourth dimension, in some way. For the purposes of this book, we will define art as those practices whose products and experiences are to be appreciated mainly for their imaginative, aesthetic, or intellectual content, while design will be defined as practices that focus on users and work within constraints established by a client. Having noted this differentiation, it is important to immediately acknowledge the border between art and design is nebulous and overlaps a great deal in certain areas. Examples of 4D practices include motion graphics, film/video, performance art, social practice, sound art, installation, Internet art, game design, animation, and so on.

Historically speaking, the Bauhaus school of art and design (1919–1933) in Germany may have been the first to embrace rudimentary elements and principles of four-dimensional art and design by embarking on an experimental performance program. The Bauhaus stage, run by Oskar Schlemmer starting in 1920, focused on the study of the relationship between humans and space. This program embraced experiments with space, form, color, light, movement, sound, and language.[1] Given this approach, it is likely that if the Bauhaus were still functioning today, it would certainly have programs in four-dimensional practices that go beyond theatrical space to include all manner of video, sound, motion graphics, social practice, and so on.

However, some basic ideological shifts had yet to happen during the time of the Bauhaus. It would not be until the 1960s that a large contingency of artists fully embraced a variety of changes to their processes including improvisational nonhierarchical approaches, a pointed disregard for the previous limitations of various art forms, and a tendency to establish one's own rules and structures within which to work.[2]

Additionally, computer technology, a significant part of many 4D practices, has taken decades to arrive at its current state. One of the most life-changing examples of this technology, the Internet, grew for years as a variety of networks and protocols developed, eventually reaching an important point in 1991 when Tim Berners-Lee, also the inventor of the first web browser and webpage editor, created the first website of the World Wide Web.[3]

Fast-forward to the present day, and many of the most popular art and design practices—whether online videos, animated GIFs, the opening titles of a movie, flash mobs, video games, websites, and so on—embrace the use of time. The elements and principles of 4D art and design are central to our ability to create and critique contemporary art and design.

ELEMENTS and PRINCIPLES of 4D ART and DESIGN

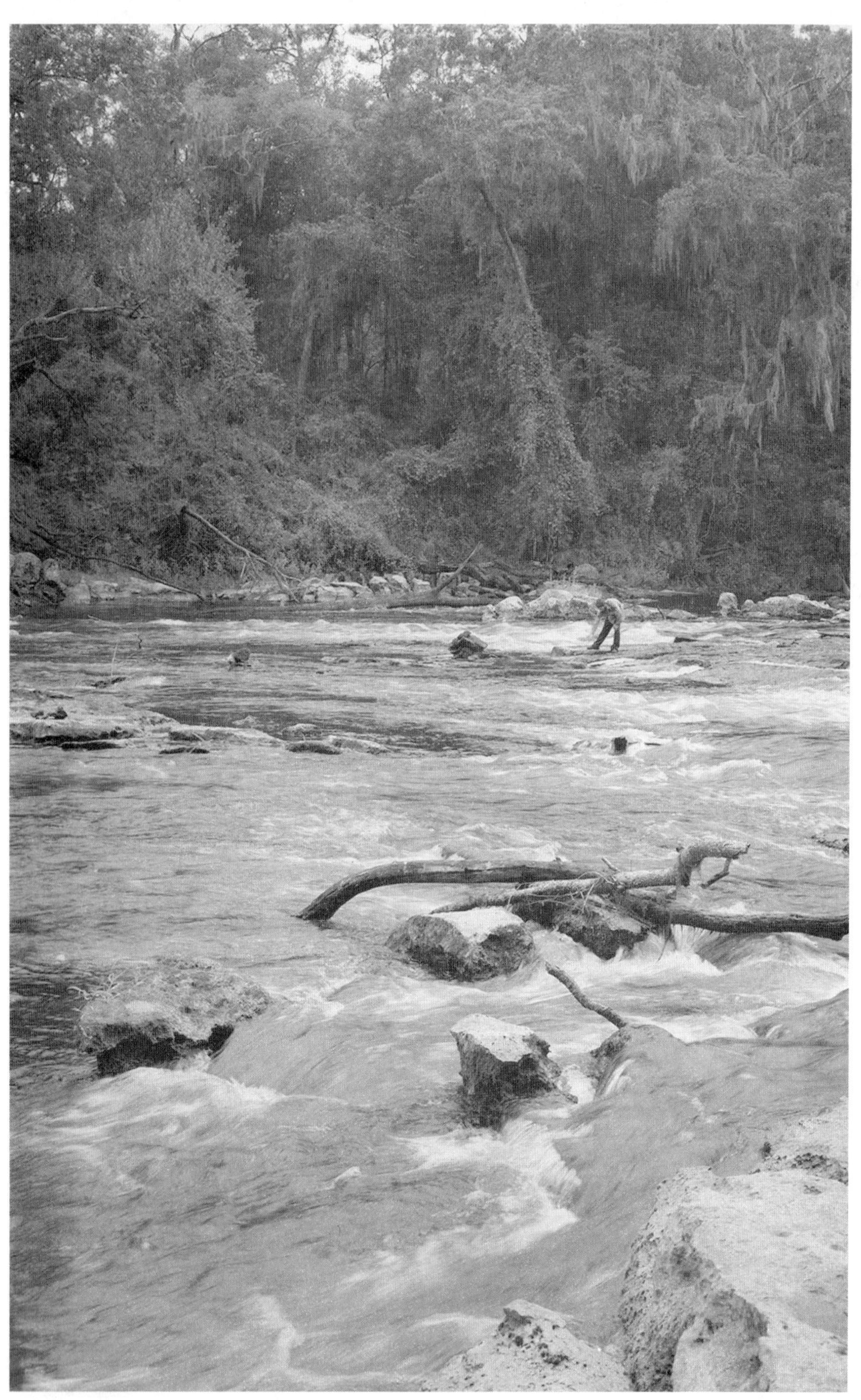

© Shawn Cheatham, Jeremy Chandler.

Components of a Work

All works of art and design—regardless of whether they are two-, three-, or four-dimensional—can be analyzed in terms of subject, form, context, and content. The **subject** is what the artist or designer is attempting to portray, the **form** is the sensorial experience of the work, **context** is the set of factors surrounding the creation and display of the work, and the **content** is the message the artist hopes to communicate. When taken in combination, the subject, form, context, and content of an artwork provide the overall experience for the viewer or participant. In this chapter, we will examine each of these components and how artists utilize them to create their works.

Subject

The subject is what the artist or designer is attempting to portray; subjects in a work can be people, places, and things. For example, in the movie *The Wizard of Oz*, the subject is Dorothy and the film follows her travels into the tornado, through Oz, and back home again.

The subject of a work is most often represented visually, but it can also be represented by invisible forms, such as sound or smell. Subject matter may be **representational**—meaning that it depicts a recognizable person, place, or thing, like Dorothy in *The Wizard of Oz*—or the subject may be **nonrepresentational**, which means the subject does not depict any particular person, place, or thing from reality. Nonrepresentational subjects instead put forth an abstraction, which is a collection of sensory elements such as shape, sound, color, or light. An example of a nonrepresentational subject could be a computer-generated artwork in which an algorithm is used to determine intricate digital patterns. This type of artwork is often called **generative art**. The patterns do not represent any specific, physical object; instead they display visually pleasing combinations of colors and shapes.

As an artist, when you select your subject matter, or as a designer, when you are given your subject matter, keep in mind that you have control over how simple or complex the subject will become. Will you focus on just one figure or a crowd? Will you focus on a long journey or a single encounter? Will you focus on just one part of a task or the whole task? Will you focus on just one application of a product or several applications? These choices about subject will affect how your audience connects with and understands your work.

Finding a Subject

If you have the freedom to select your own subject, and it is not assigned via client needs or other outside forces, you might find that it can be an intimidating or difficult task. There are endless possibilities for subject matter, and therefore it can be difficult or overwhelming to select an interesting subject off the top of your head. To help ease this challenge, it can be useful to focus on personal experience, which is a rich resource for subject matter. Jotting down lists or maintaining a journal of some form is an excellent way to collect potential subjects from your daily life. See Chapter 2 on brainstorming for additional ideas and approaches to generating subject matter.

Exercise

Keep a journal of your dreams. Every morning for a week, record everything you can remember from your dreams. After you have written as much as you can remember, examine the writing and make a list of subjects that may be useful in future work. Save this material for future reference. If this seems to be a fruitful approach, you might choose to continue the practice beyond just one week.

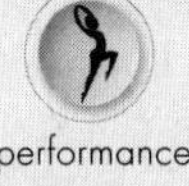

performance

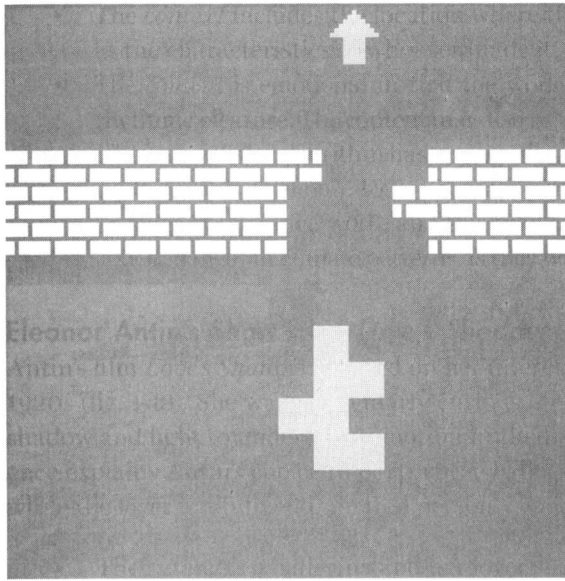

Fig. 1-1
Anna Anthropy, *Dys4ia*
(2012), video game.
© Anna Anthropy

Anna Anthropy's *Dys4ia*

An example of an artist using personal experience as subject matter is Anna Anthropy's online game *Dys4ia*, which takes as its subject specific struggles a transgendered person may encounter (fig. 1-1). The work also asks the participant to navigate these challenges through a variety of puzzles. Subject matter is the central component of this work, and, as Anthropy describes in her interview, this becomes a complication because the work focuses on her status as a minority, which can be both gratifying and challenging.

Interview: Anna Anthropy

For how little money it made me and how unreflective it is of my work as a whole, *Dys4ia* sure got way more press than any of my other work, got written up in newspapers, has been used by educators, inspired a lot of people (I'm told) to make the decision to start hormones. Got into a bunch of game design textbooks. It's pretty tokenizing to have the one game everyone knows me for be

(continued)

Interview: Anna Anthropy (*continued*)

the game about what minority group I slot into, you know? It also got me a lot of creepy messages on *Newgrounds* asking how I can be a girl if I have a girlfriend. Am I a lesbian?

—*Anna Antrophy*

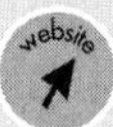
Visit the book's website to read the full interview.

Having explored subject as one of the four components of a work of art or design, you should be able to identify the subject and change the way it is represented by manipulating the form, content, or context.

Exercise

Go online and search for the generative artwork *MicroImage (Software 1)* by Casey Reas. After watching an excerpt from the work, write down what you think the subject is and then compare and contrast your answers with others'. How are your answers similar and different from those around you? Were there any trends in the answers?

video

Form

The form is the sensorial experience of the work; it is how we use our five senses to experience a time-based work. For example, we typically think of how a work of art or design looks, but in time-based work the form also encompasses how the work sounds, smells, tastes, and physically feels.

Medium

Form encompasses the material or media used to create a work, as well as the organization of the elements and principles of art and design within the work. When selecting a **medium** (**media** = plural), the artist or designer must consider how the medium will be experienced by the audience's senses. For example, some media, such as video or animation, are accessible only on a screen, and different screen sizes or viewing locations can affect how the work is experienced. Seeing a video or animation on a phone is a strikingly different aural and visual experience than seeing it projected on a movie screen with surround sound.

Additionally, each medium is accompanied by certain preexisting assumptions. If, for example, you consider the medium of video games, you might make various assumptions about perceived expectations, such as the audience associated with gaming, how the game will look, what the subject matter will be, where the game will be played, and so on. Moreover, some forms will lend themselves to specific groups of people. For example, commercial radio reaches a large number of car commuters who have to focus on the road, rather than look at a screen. Meanwhile, online video is more effective at reaching people who own mobile devices or computers. Based on creative goals, artists and designers can choose to work with or against preexisting associations and assumptions. Your choice of form will greatly affect the impact and reach of your work.

Exercise

Make a list of time-based media. For example, sound, video, animation, performance, motion graphics, installation, social practice, games, mobile apps, Internet art, and any other time-based media you can think of. Select two of the forms to compare and contrast. Brainstorm a list of attributes for each medium as well as a list of various groups of people who could be the audience for each medium. For example, video is screen-based and could therefore be targeted to people owning screen-based devices. Be specific in your lists. How are your two chosen media different or similar? What is the difference between each medium's potential audiences? See Chapter 2 for tips on brainstorming.

  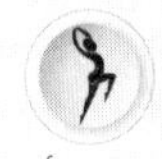  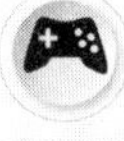

sound　　video　　performance　　installation　　games

Analyzing Form

One way to illustrate form is to examine a group of works with a common subject but different forms. For example, we can compare Yoko Ono's *Voice Piece for Soprano* (1961), Seth Boyden's *Hoof It* (2014), and Jillian

McDonald's *The Screaming* (2007). The subject of each of these works is screaming, while each one has a unique form.

To explain, Yoko Ono's performance work *Voice Piece for Soprano* was developed as a part of the Fluxus movement, which focused on ideas of chance, participation, experimentation, and ownership. Often, Fluxus works consisted of merely a series of instructions—also known as an **event score**—that the audience/participant was meant to carry out in order to experience the artwork. The instructions might be purposely absurd, involving actions that were not meant to be taken literally but hopefully would inspire an imaginative response. *Voice Piece for Soprano* consists of this set of directions: "Scream. 1. against the wind 2. against the wall 3. against the sky."[1] If you research videos of this work on the Internet, you will see people screaming in a variety of ways—screaming is clearly the subject, and live performance is the *form*.

In contrast, Seth Boyden's fairytale-themed animation *Hoof It* features a more literal representation of a scream at one point in its storyline. Upon meeting a talking tree stump, the main character screams in shock (fig. 1-2). Here the momentary subject is the scream of the main character, and the *form* is a digital animation. In both *Hoof It* and *Voice Piece for Soprano*, the subject is screaming, but the form of live performance is very different from that of an on-screen animation.

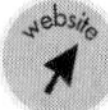 Visit the book's website to read an interview with Seth Boyden.

We can continue to build on this comparison with Jillian McDonald's 11-minute video work *The Screaming* (2007), which features the artist composited into horror films and screaming in a variety of ways. She

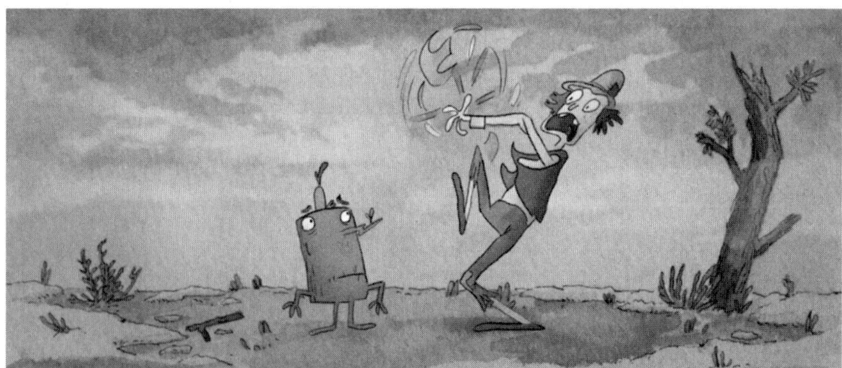

Fig. 1-2
Seth Boyden, *Hoof It* (2014), animation, 4 minutes. © Seth Boyden.

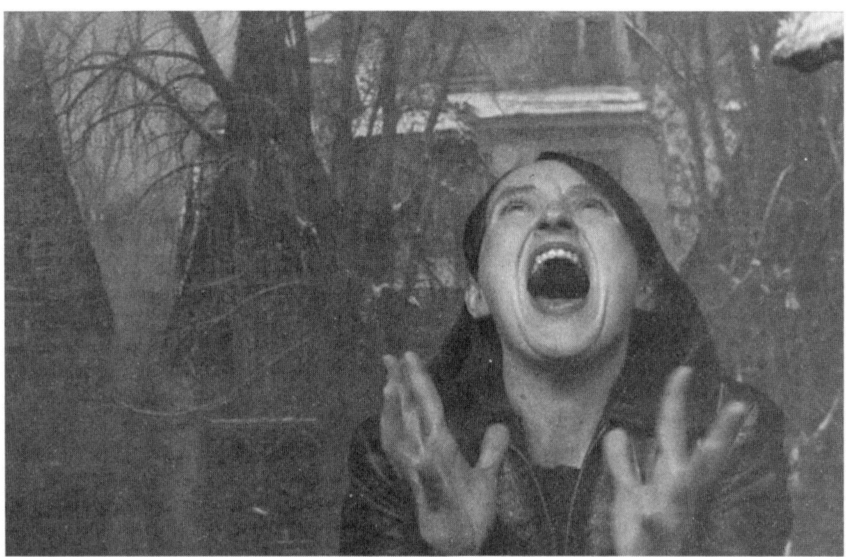

Fig. 1-3
Jillian McDonald, *The Screaming* (2007), video, 11 minutes. Courtesy of the artist.

utilizes a stylized screaming, which is recognized by the audience as an exaggerated expression of fear, almost a parody of the real emotion. In this video, the scream destroys or scares off well-known cinematic villains (fig. 1-3). Thus, we can continue to track the pattern of screaming as subject matter, and in this instance the *form* is a composited video work.

 Visit the book's website to read an interview with Jillian McDonald.

Exercise

In the works of Ono, Boyden, and McDonald, the subject is the same—screaming—while the form is quite different. Try to identify three works, each with the same subject, but with different forms. You will likely use the Internet and other research tools, such as library databases, to help you find these works. Report your results back to the class.

 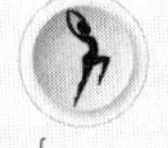 

video   performance   sound

Craft

Form can also be evaluated on the basis of **craft**, or the skill with which the media is manipulated. A very succinctly coded website or a cleanly edited video can be said to have excellent craft. On the other hand, an audio work in which the click of the record button at the start or end of the work can be heard might be said to exhibit poor craft (unless that extraneous sound somehow contributes to the meaning of the piece). As an artist or designer, it is through practice and research that you improve your craft. You must dedicate time and energy to honing your craft in order to avoid unintentionally distracting the audience with minor details or mistakes, such as prolonged loading time on a website, sloppy edits between video clips, or unintentionally uncomfortable interactions within an installation. As you analyze and critique works, be sure to keep the quality of the craft in mind.

Gestalt Theory

Gestalt theory is linked to form because it is a way of analyzing the arrangement, or **composition**, of the elements and principles of art and design. Visual psychologists developed Gestalt theory in the early twentieth century. *Gestalt* means "unified whole."[2] It refers to the human mind's tendency to interpret individual elements of an image as a unified whole (fig. 1-4). Gestalt theory offers some basic insight into this process. It illustrates how the mind creates new meaning that is greater than the individual elements have alone. This idea is summarized in the famous Gestalt expression "The whole is greater than the sum of its parts."[3]

Gestalt theorists formulated seven specific ideas about perception that are applicable to our understanding of form:

1. *Proximity:* When elements are near to each other, the human mind tends to group them. For example, say there are three performers standing in different spots on a stage. When you look at them you might see a triangle, even though the performers are not connected.
2. *Common fate:* The mind unites elements moving in the same direction. For example, in a video game, if a swarm of bees is flying toward a location on the screen, your mind will focus on the swarm rather than movement of the individual bees.
3. *Similarity:* The mind unites elements that are like each other in terms of shape, light, color, movement, and so on. For example, if the people facilitating a socially interactive work are all dressed in

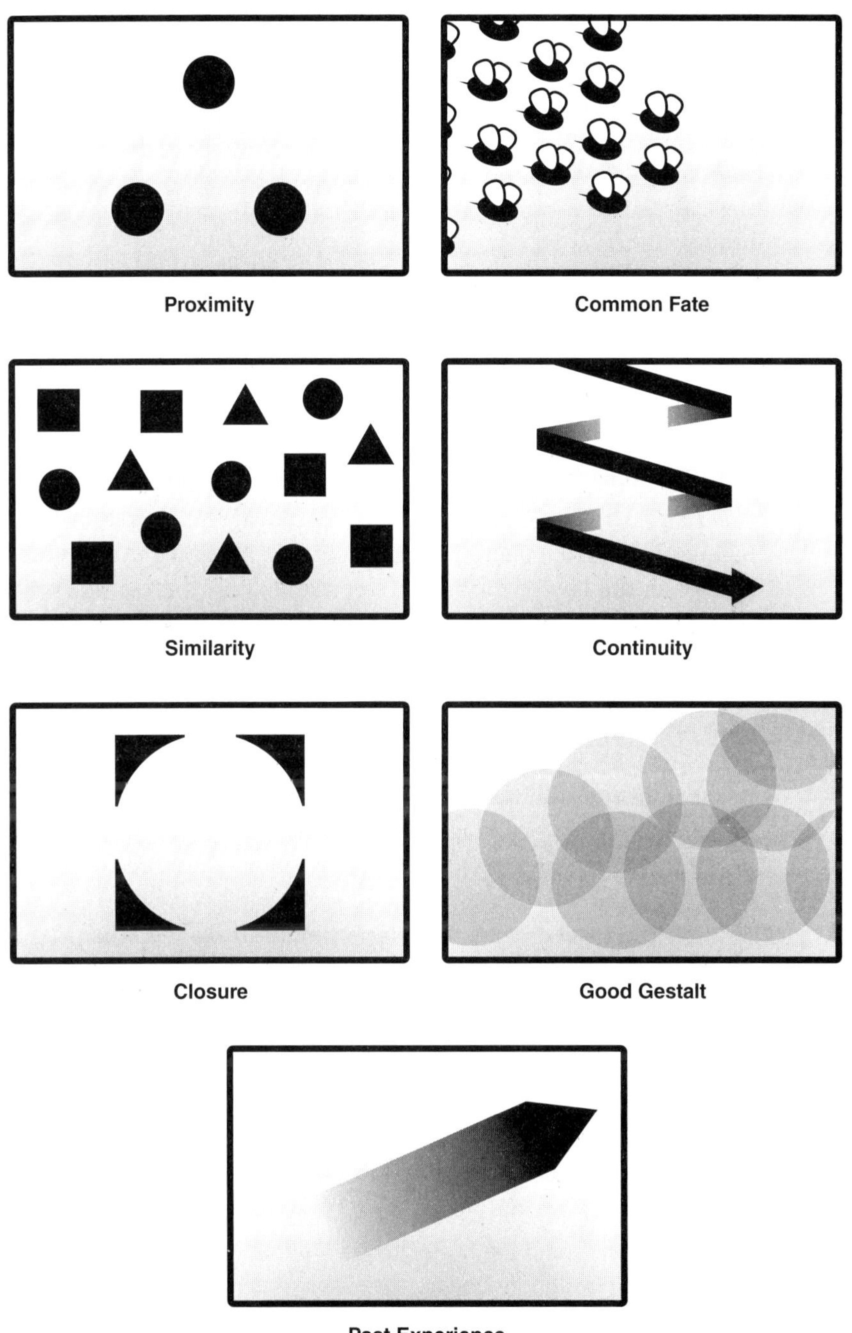

Fig. 1-4
Gestalt theory illustrations. © Phil McCollam.

the same clothing, you are more likely to think of them as part of a whole instead of as individuals.

4. *Continuity:* The mind unites elements along a path. For example, if a line is traveling across the screen of a generative artwork and is interrupted and then resumes, the viewer will automatically bridge the gap with his or her mind, continuing the path between the broken line.

5. *Closure:* The mind will unite elements that are part of a closed figure. For example, if an installation in a field includes a free-standing doorway, an armchair, and a standing lamp, the viewer or participant can infer that these elements are a part of a living room scenario, even though the space is not completely enclosed. This principle could explain why humans generally seek closure or a sense of finality in nearly all experiences.

6. *Good Gestalt:* The mind unites elements that are "as simple, orderly, balanced, unified, coherent, regular, etc. as possible."[4] This is also known as the law of Prägnanz. For example, if there are several overlapping shapes in the opening titles of a movie, the viewer will generally see the simplest shapes, rather than the smaller more complex shapes formed by the overlapping.

7. *Past experience:* The mind's experience with new elements is affected by past experiences with similar elements. For example, in the medium of animation, audiences have grown to understand that a blurred moving image implies that it is going very fast due to our previous experience of seeing objects move fast in real life.

As you consider the form of your four-dimensional work, keep the principles of Gestalt in mind as a means of creating work greater than the sum of its parts.

Exercise

Create two games whose objective is speed. One game must include a deck of cards, and the other game must include a ball of some sort. You can designate any number of players and any setting, but each game can have only three rules. You will have to play the games and make revisions before you arrive at the finished works. Once you have developed each game, compare and contrast how each game supports the objective of speed. Which game does it better and why? Out of everyone in the class, whose game supports speed best? How does the form of that game support speed?

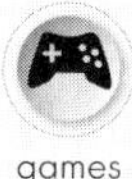

games

Altogether, choice of media, execution of craft, and compositional decisions are parts of form, which has a central effect on the reception of a work.

Context

Context is the set of factors surrounding the creation and display of the work. It is the collection of events and attributes that affect artists or designers and their audience as they develop and present their work. Context is present in all works, physical or virtual, because every setting, group of people, or individual has unique features, such as: class, race, gender identity, sexual identity, age, physical or mental ability, appearance, nationality, language, religion, culture (historical heritage, memes, traditions, shared learned behaviors, ways of life, ideals/values), scientific ideas, technological abilities, intellectual abilities, geographic and political associations, and so on.

Designers will sometimes use specific alternative vocabulary to describe contextual elements because their work is often restricted by business-related needs. Instead of talking about class, race, gender, and so on (although these are still present in design work), designers might use more business-oriented vocabulary including: clients/stakeholders, colleagues/teammates, problem/challenge/opportunity, brand considerations, technical constraints, timetable, deliverables, project objectives, business objectives, budget/resources, users, success metrics, and environmental factors. These attributes and circumstances (context) affect not only how a work is created, but also how it is received in terms of the environmental and cultural conditioning of the audience. For example, ancient Egyptians revered cats as being holy, whereas in contemporary Western culture, we use cats as fodder for humorous Internet videos. The context of ancient Egyptian religious art is obviously quite different from the context of our contemporary Western Internet culture due to the different geographic locations, the time periods, cultural and religious differences, and so on. Context influences our experience of the subject matter.

Privilege

Privilege is an element of context because every artist, designer, and participant is privileged in different ways. **Privilege** is an unearned benefit or advantage due to an aspect of your identity, such as race, religion, gender identity, sexual orientation, class/wealth, citizenship status, and so on. Privilege affects how works of art and design are understood. For example, in Anthropy's game *Dys4ia*, she carefully walks participants through the ways in which transgendered persons are not privileged and the struggles they face due to their gender identity (fig. 1-1).

Exercise

Take a moment to think about your own privilege by folding a sheet of paper in half, and on one side brainstorm all the ways you are *not* privileged—feel free to refer to the list of the four basic components of an artwork discussed at the beginning of this chapter to jog your thought process. Then, on the other half of the paper, brainstorm all the ways you *are* privileged. Finally, share your two lists with a partner to see how your lists are similar and different.[6]

installation

Context and Place

Context can be used as a tool to limit or expand the audience of a specific work because different people are located in different places. For example, Vanessa Beecroft's installation *vb35* (1998) takes place in a very specific context, in this case the Solomon R. Guggenheim Museum in New York City (fig. 1-5). This stylized arrangement of semi-naked women brings to light questions about female beauty as dictated by the fashion industry, as well as notions of individuality versus homogeneity. In any

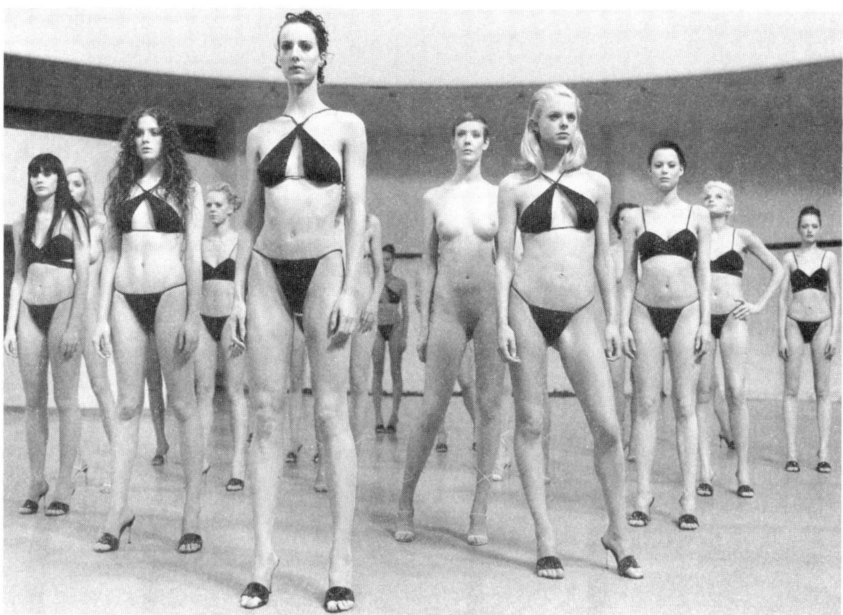

Fig. 1-5
Vanessa Beecroft, *vb35 performance* (1998), Solomon R. Guggenheim Museum, New York, NY. vb35.377.ms. Courtesy of the artist, © 2014 Vanessa Beecroft, photo by Mario Sorrenti.

other context this work would not only be received very differently, but an entirely different audience would encounter it. For example, if Beecroft had installed the same installation in a grocery store, the work would be understood very differently and encountered by an entirely different subset of people.

The collaborative group Fallen Fruit also works within a very specific understanding of context and place for their project, *Public Fruit Maps* (2004–ongoing), which involves mapping all the fruit trees that grow in or over public space in neighborhoods to which they are invited (fig. 1-6). Part of the context for this project is that the artists are invited guests in the spaces they work, and their work is collaborative and limited to spaces that produce fruit trees. After working with the community, the maps are distributed for free, and are downloadable from their website, which perpetuates and continues the project. Similar to Beecroft's work, Fallen Fruit's maps are potentially less engaging to audiences outside of the site for which they were originally intended.

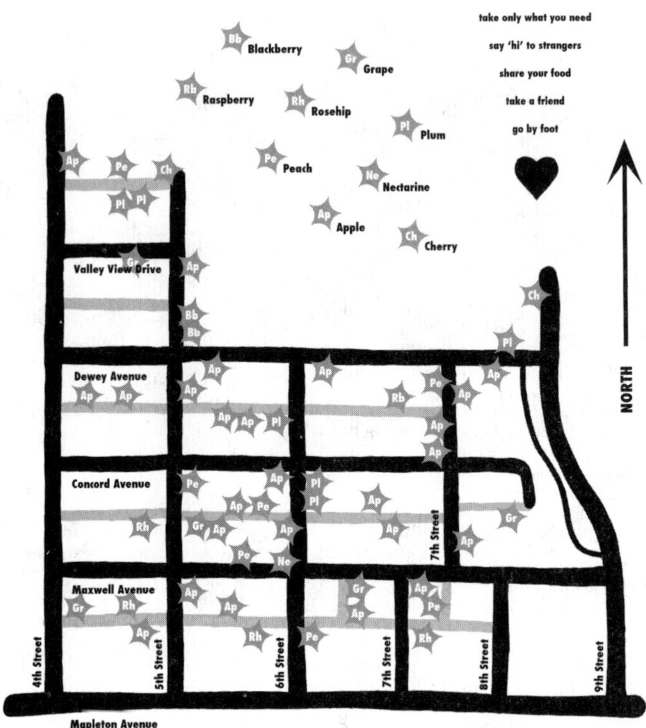

Fig. 1-6
Fallen Fruit (David Burns, Matias Viegener, and Austin Young), *Public Fruit Map, Mapleton Hill, Boulder, Colorado* (2010), digital file, dimensions variable. Courtesy of the artists.

Interview: Fallen Fruit

The *Public Fruit Maps* is an indexical system that references the real world. We carefully construct a map—first we make sure that [the locations] are approximately correct, meaning that they are accurate in types of trees and general geographical landmarks, street names, scale, etc. We make sure they are missing information so they behave like a treasure map—we do not put addresses or exact locations for the fruit trees and we expect people performing the map to use their imagination about the places they are exploring.

—*Fallen Fruit*

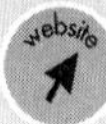
Visit the book's website to read the full interview.

To elaborate on this concept of place and context, take note that every context comes with an established framework of expectations, and therefore affects the starting mindset of the viewer or participant. Consider the physical and emotional differences of experiencing a work in a gallery versus on your home computer screen, versus on the street. In the gallery it is likely that participants are expected to maintain quiet and respectful behavior. At your personal computer you might give a work only a few seconds of your attention before browsing elsewhere on the Internet. When encountering work on the street you could be talking on your phone, carrying bags, and experiencing other distractions. In each scenario, context affects the way the participant experiences the work. Furthermore, when a work takes into consideration its context, it can become even more immersive and powerful by acknowledging additional layers of meaning, rather than relying on only subject and form to convey content.

Exercise

Select a space. Go be in the space, and write down at least five aspects of its context. Remember to take into consideration class, race, gender, political associations, and so on. Think about seeing the familiar in a new light with fresh eyes. What would a stranger notice about this site? Now design additions to, or subtractions from, the space that encourage people to stay in the space for as long as possible. Try shifting participants' expectations for the site. You might think in terms of an interactive installation like Thomas Hirschhorn's *Cavemanman* (Plate 11, color insert) or a social activity like Allora and Calzadilla's *Chalk* (fig. 1-17). Remember that you should use your analysis of the context to help inform your choices. Compare and contrast the success of each person's space and its ability to compel people to stay there. What was particularly successful and why?

installation

Context and Art History

Another aspect of context is the history of art and design. While each individual's knowledge of art or design history may vary, it is important to acknowledge that all works exist on this continuum and will be compared to those that came before them. Artists and designers should be aware of their intentions as they relate to existing traditions, and the ways in which they can challenge or subvert those modes if they desire.

For example, performance art and conceptual work were deeply influenced by artists' desire to subvert established gallery systems in the 1960s and 1970s. Artists used a variety of tactics to try to work outside established galleries. For example, for Claes Oldenburg's *The Store* (1961), the artist installed, promoted, and sold his sculptural work himself in a storefront on the Lower East Side of Manhattan, rather than engaging an art gallery to sell for him. Further, the art he sold included many mundane objects, such as a banana split or a pair of shoes, roughly rendered in painted plaster, which brought up questions about value, commodities, and artist self-promotion.

Allan Kaprow also attempted to disrupt the gallery system by creating performative works that included a great deal of change, disorder, and audience participation, thereby making it more difficult to commodify, or sell, the art experience. An example of this work is Kaprow's *Sawdust* (1970), in

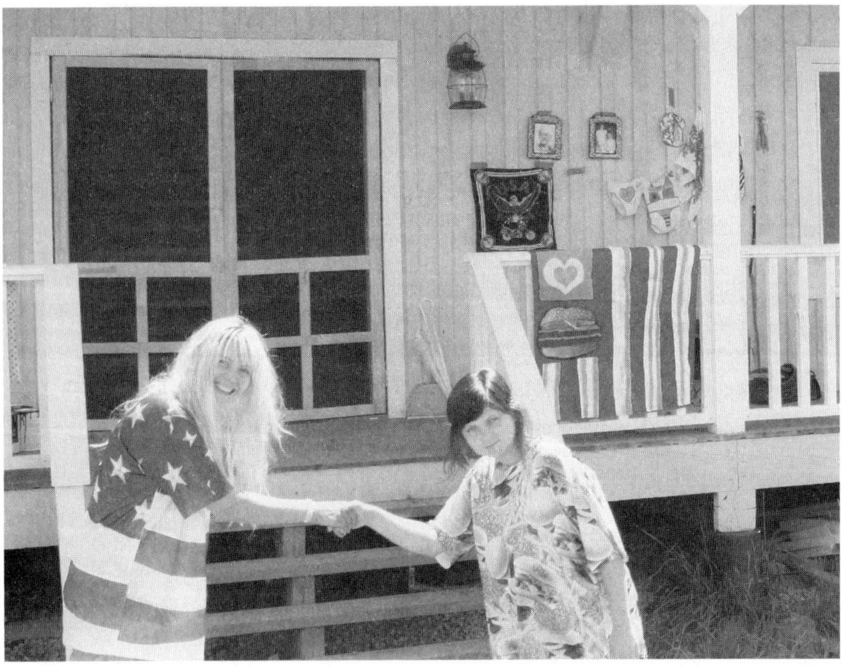

Fig. 1-7
Destineez Child (April Childers and Carmen Tiffany), *Destineez Child Sealing the Deal in Chesterfield, Ohio* (2012), performance still. Courtesy of the artists.

which he invited participants to shave a wooden beam into sawdust, one saw blade width at a time. He then collected the sawdust, combined it with glue, and cast a new reconstituted beam, which could be shown at a museum. Through this work, Kaprow was able to provide an experience for participants, while also mocking the museum system's need for objects, even if they are only crude imitations of originals, as is the case with *Sawdust*. These artists purposefully chose to work in opposition to the established norms of art history in order to strengthen their messages.

In contrast, if an artist today were to use the same approach as those pioneering artists, the result would be strikingly different in part because the art historical context continues to change. For example, *Destineez Child*, a collaboration between artists April Childers and Carmen Tiffany (fig. 1-7), holds live sales of a variety of handmade and modified goods that generate critique of commercialism, classism, and ideas of quality and craft, much like Oldenburg's *The Store* or Kaprow's *Sawdust*. However, their work also references Internet gross-out culture and identity politics, which are issues that have been explored through contemporary art and design since the 1960s and '70s. The changing art historical context affects how participants understand and react to the work.

Changing Context

After a work's initial installation, single elements of the context may change. It may be relocated, or factors surrounding its creation could change, which can affect the work's meaning. An example of how a change in context can completely change a work is Melati Suryodarmo's performance, *EXERGIE-butter dance* (2000). In this work, Suryodarmo, wearing a tight black dress and red high heels, attempts to dance on 20 blocks of butter arranged in a square at a black box performance space with an audience looking on (fig. 1-8). She is exploring risk, the quality of the moment before one falls, and the will to get back up and continue. She dances and falls multiple times. After 20 minutes, Suryodarmo rises one last time, covered in butter, and leaves the stage.

A video of this live performance was shared on the Internet. However, someone online replaced the original audio with a popular song by the singer Adele. The video with the new soundtrack went viral, and an entirely different audience, those at home in front of computer screens rather than those at the live performance, viewed the work. Those at the performance space were prepared to see a work of performance art, and may even have had knowledge of the history of performance art. In contrast, the viewers at home may or may not be aware of what performance art can encompass, and may not realize that the performance was not originally

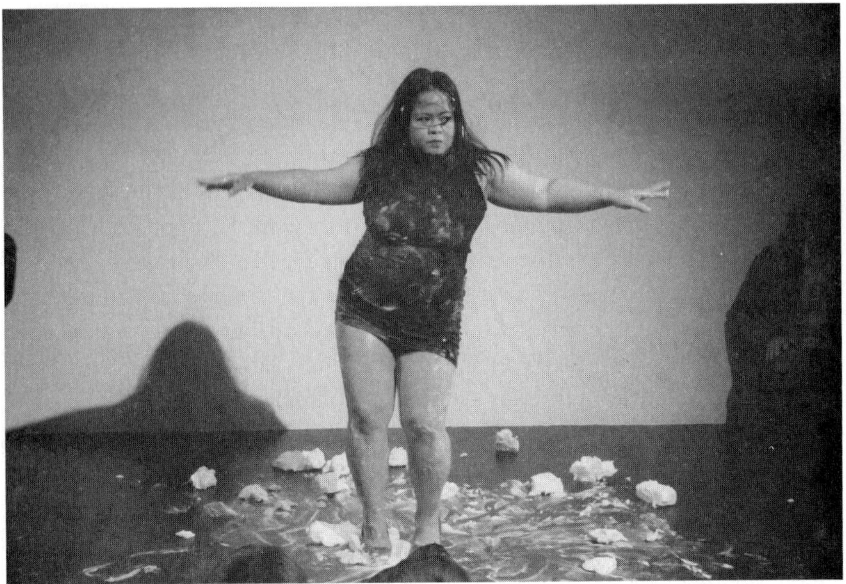

Fig. 1-8
Melati Suryodarmo, *EXERGIE-Butter dance* (2000), performance, 20 minutes. Courtesy of the artist.

intended to be juxtaposed with the Adele song. This shift in context led to a number of misunderstandings and misinterpretations because the new audience was unaware of the original context under which the work was developed.

Interview: Melati Suryodarmo

EXERGIE-Butter dance was inspired by my interest about time, especially how the human body relates to its biological, psychological, and physical time. I also believe that everything happens in this world does not stop, even when we die. What we can deal with is the time that our body can adjust to the whole conception of time, whether it is physical or biological. But in this piece, I was seduced to enter the specific moment, a moment where my body relates with a very specific delicate moment, like just before I fall down. This is a moment where all my consciousness controls my body, but at the same time the risk becomes unpredictable. I might lose the control, but the will to get up again is more important to me. It is about our attitude towards this very specific moment in life. As our perception of pain is produced within our education and cultural environment, I believe that everybody perceives the action and images of this work in many different ways.

—*Melati Suryodarmo*

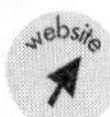
Visit the book's website to read the full interview.

Another example of a work that is entirely dependent on its specific context is Nancy Paterson's *Stock Market Skirt* (1998) (fig. 1-9). This installation consists of a blue taffeta and black velvet party dress surrounded by screens displaying online stock prices being continuously updated. A computer script analyzes stock prices and accordingly raises and lowers the

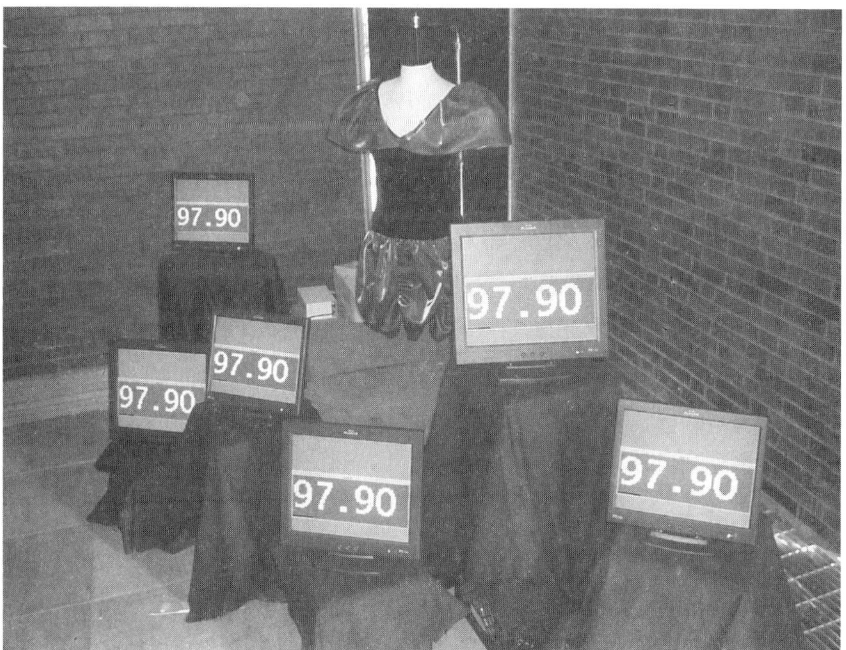

Fig. 1-9
Nancy Paterson, *Stock Market Skirt* (1998), fabric, monitors, step motors, computer script, dimensions variable. © Nancy Paterson.

hemline of the skirt: as prices go up, so does the hemline, and as prices go down, the hemline is lowered. This work is inextricably tied ideas of sexuality, economic excess, and infinite growth, as well as the very existence of the stock market. A change to any of these contextual elements can entirely change the meaning of the piece. For example, the work would cease to have meaning if the stock market ceased to exist.

Interview: Nancy Paterson

Stock Market Skirt was first started to be worked on in 1995 when I started sewing the dress—blue taffeta and black velvet—and also started working on the stepper motor. In 1995 I was looking forward to the time when stock market quotes would be available over the Internet. This happened around 1998 and Yahoo.com was the first to do this. Out of gratitude, *Stock Market Skirt* tracked YHOO as the first ticker symbol at start up.

—*Nancy Paterson*

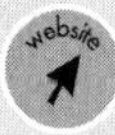 Visit the book's website to read the full interview.

Exercise

Remove an action from its stereotypical context, and place it in a totally different one, recording both instances on video. For example, take the action of preparing a cup of coffee in your home kitchen, and place it in a boat in the middle of a lake. How does context change the action? Compare and contrast your recordings with everyone in class.

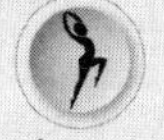
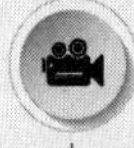

performance   video

Obscuring Context

While there is no such thing as a neutral space, sometimes the context of a given piece is not readily apparent. If this is the case, the artist or designer

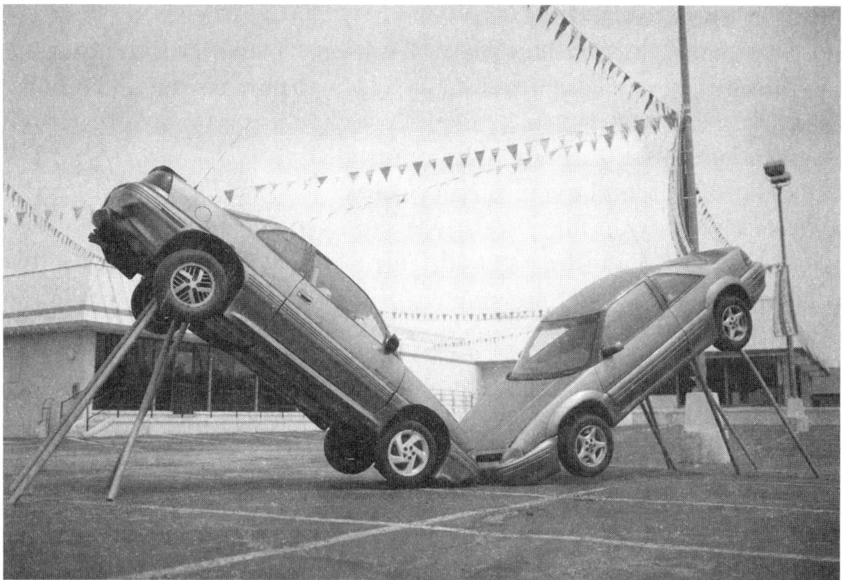

Fig. 1-10
Jesse Sugarmann, *We Build Excitement* (2013), production still, dimensions variable. © Jesse Sugarmann.

may choose to highlight or subdue contextual information according to the needs of the piece. Jesse Sugarmann's *We Build Excitement* (2013) is a video piece about the abandoned Pontiac car brand; the title comes from an advertising slogan used for many years to sell Pontiacs. In this video, Sugarmann places old Pontiac cars on top of long unstable pipes in an abandoned sales lot (fig. 1-10). He intersperses this footage of suspended cars with interviews of ex-automobile assembly line workers and car crash survivors.

While the work examines the various ways that the automobile has affected Americans, the context may not immediately present itself to the viewer. Thus, Sugarmann slowly reveals contextual elements one by one, first with a view of car lot flags flapping in the wind, then with the sales center emblazoned with a giant Pontiac sign, followed by a car crash survivor repeatedly acting out his crash, thereby helping to signal underlying information about this particular context. Slowly, the viewer realizes that all the footage is directly or indirectly related to the automobile industry and specifically the Pontiac brand.

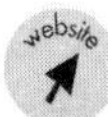

Visit the book's website to read an interview with Jesse Sugarmann interview.

Context and Ownership

Another aspect of context is whether the work may or may not be sold after its initial installation, and if it is sold, who purchases it and for how much. Typically, the person or institution who owns a work can alter the way it is perceived. In Fred Wilson's installation *Metalwork 1793–1880* (1992–1993), at the Maryland Historical Society in Baltimore, the artist arranged a display of fine silver vessels in alongside slave shackles from the same location and time period. This juxtaposition thus implied "the production of the one was made possible by the subjugation enforced by the other" (fig. 1-11).[5] The viewer's understanding of the sale and ownership of art and design becomes an important aspect of the work's context—the installation enhanced the implication that the original owners of the silver objects may have also owned the slaves who wore the shackles. While personal or private ownership of the vessels by an individual would instill a sense of importance or monetary success—based solely on the price of the vessels themselves—the ability of the Maryland Historical

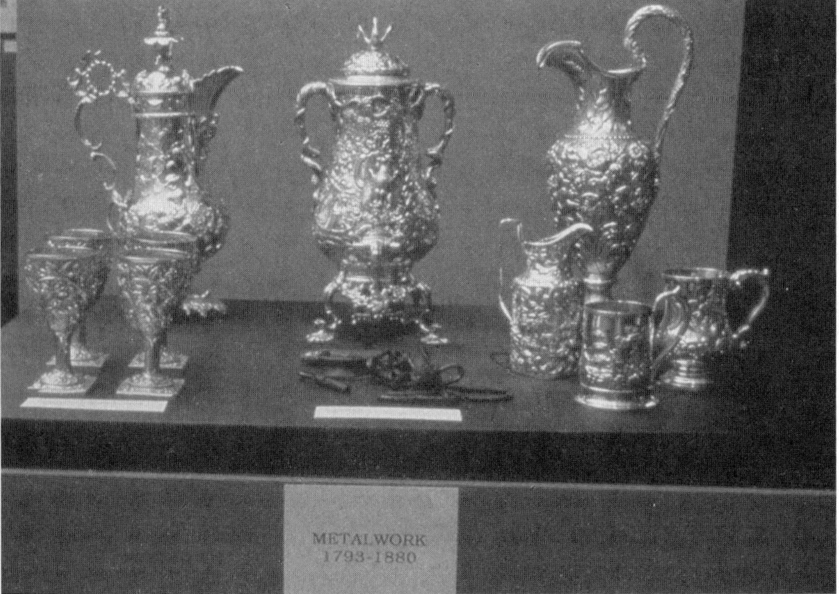

Fig. 1-11
Fred Wilson, *Metalwork 1793–1880* (1992–1993), from *Mining the Museum: An Installation by Fred Wilson*, The Contemporary and Maryland Historical Society, Baltimore. Silver vessels in Baltimore Repoussé style, 1830–1880, maker unknown; slave shackles, c. 1793–1872, maker unknown, made in Baltimore. Photograph courtesy of the artist and Pace Gallery. © Fred Wilson, courtesy Pace Gallery.

Society to display a public critique of the unethical cost of the vessels changes the context and value of the work.

Sometimes the ownership of a work is a more influential aspect of context than the actual monetary value of the work. For example, when Douglas Davis donated his interactive Internet project *The World's First Collaborative Sentence* to the Whitney Museum of American Art in 1995, the work gained a greater sense of prestige, in part due to the reputation of the museum. The work remained live on the Internet until 2005 when it was discontinued due to changes in web design. The work is now considered a "classic" of Internet art, and it even underwent a restoration effort in 2012 when the museum released a refreshed, live version of the work for new participants to engage with and compare to the historical version. In this case, ownership led to increased awareness of the piece, as well as preservation efforts that might not have otherwise occurred.

Point of View

Point of view is an important facet of context, and answers the question "Whose story is this?" Point of view is closely related to the concept of privilege because specific class, race, gender, political associations, and so on accompany any point of view. To illustrate this point, a pair of creative activists called the Yes Men performed their work *US Chamber of Commerce Goes Green* (2009) at a press conference at the National Press Club. In this performance, the Yes Men posed as US Chamber of Commerce [USCC] representatives and announced that the USCC would be reversing its position on climate change (fig. 1-12). Then, a *real* USCC representative interrupted the event to state that the Yes Men did *not* represent the organization. The ensuing chaos helped to awkwardly highlight the USCC's financial support of environmentally harmful policies. Through this performance, the Yes Men commandeered a much larger and different audience than if they had simply spoken out as themselves. By co-opting this specific point of view, listeners and viewers were more open to considering the Yes Men's ideas because they believed the message was coming from the USCC.

One of the most direct expressions of point of view is the testimonial, which is often used in film, video, and live performance. A testimonial consists of a person directly telling his or her story, whether on-screen or in live performance. For example, in Stan Maertens's short documentary *Norton Spirit* (2014), a testimonial helps shape our understanding of one man's lifelong passion for Norton motorcycles (fig. 1-13).

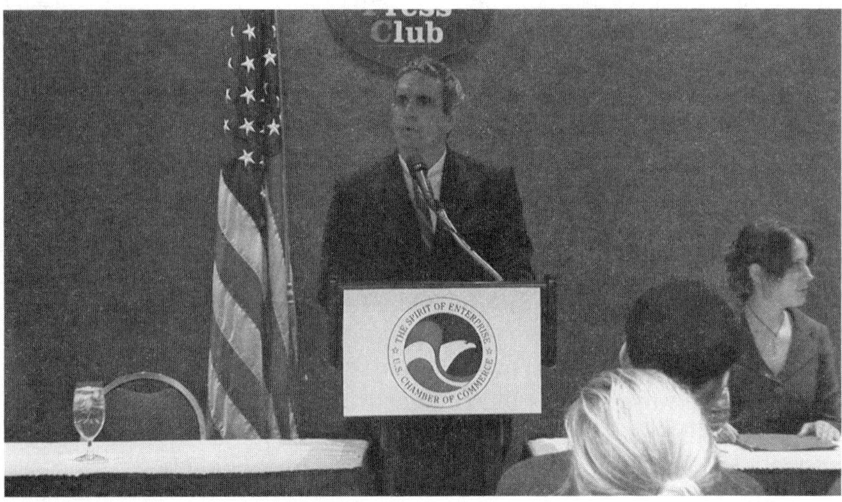

Fig. 1-12
The Yes Men, *US Chamber of Commerce Goes Green* (2009), digital still, dimensions variable. © The Yes Men.

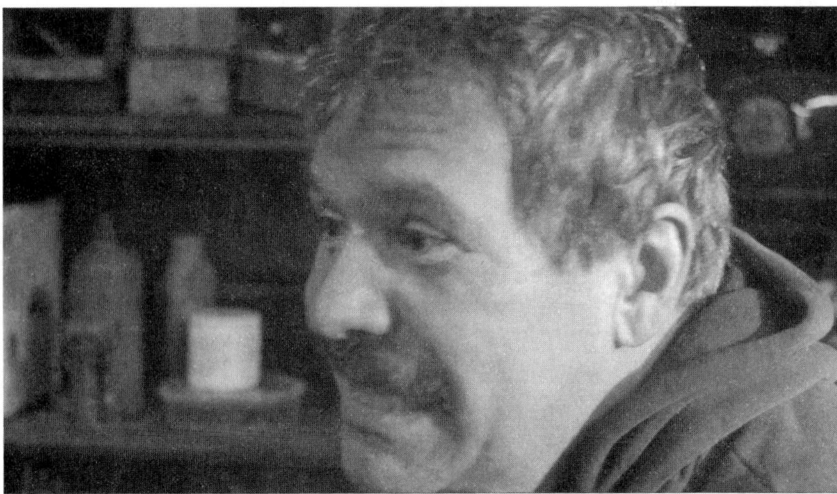

Fig. 1-13
Norton Spirit (2014), short documentary, 5 minutes. Director and Editor: Stan Maertens, Director of Photography: Robert Hoebeke. Courtesy of Stan Maertens.

Testimonials can be taken literally or can be used ironically. People's words can reveal a person's own prejudices or blind spots. In documentary filmmaking, testimonials are often used without further comment, with the filmmaker expecting the audience to decide whether the speaker is reliable.

A slightly different definition of point of view, sometimes also called **viewpoint**, is found in film and video, where the composition of each shot can express facets of a point of view. For example, a **crane shot**, in which the camera is mounted on a crane that can rise smoothly to a place far above the scene or can lower down to ground level, will present a different point of view, or viewpoint, than a **hand-held shot** that is intentionally unstable and shaky. When a camera shoots from above its subject, there may be a sense of potential, vastness, and domination. When a camera shoots up at a subject, there can be a sense of inferiority or smallness. These simple shifts in viewpoint can help reinforce power relationships within your work.

To illustrate this idea, Jeremy Chandler and Shawn Cheatham's 14-minute film *Coventry* (2011) depicts three men traveling through isolated north Florida terrain, gathering unidentified items (fig. 1-14). With camera shots aimed up into the trees, and down into rushing water, there is a clear sense of the dominance of nature in respect to humans. As the men traverse the land, their social interactions deteriorate and tensions become evident. At the end of the film, two of the men have singled out the third, and danger feels imminent. The viewpoint of the camera focuses tightly on each of their individual faces, helping to articulate the power relationships

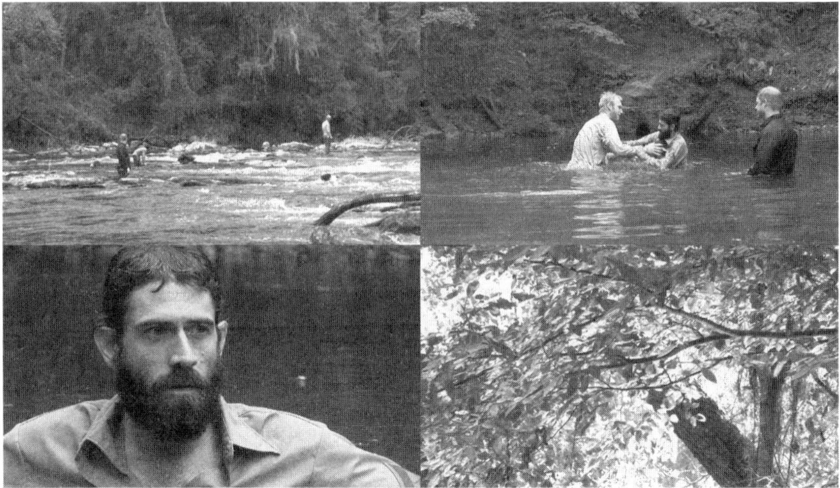

Fig. 1-14
Shawn Cheatham and Jeremy Chandler, *Coventry* (2011), digital still, 14 minutes. © Shawn Cheatham, Jeremy Chandler.

between the men. The viewpoint has changed from one in which the men are shown within a large natural surrounding, to tight close-ups that emphasize the men's emotions.

Interview: Jeremy Chandler and Shawn Cheatham

Shawn Cheatham: Jeremy is a photographer and I typically work with motion pictures, so we come from different perspectives when telling a story and tend to use different tools. I learned a lot from Jeremy in the process because he orchestrates ideas in a much different way. For example, he thinks through ideas using simple sketches in a notebook to define visual landscapes. I tend to be interested in visualizing the entire picture, which can sometimes be a detriment to the creative process in many art forms. I subscribe to the theory that a filmmaker or director has an overall vision for a film, and the success of that film depends on realizing that overall vision through the trials and tribulations of production. Jeremy had these incredible still images he wanted to animate and I did my best to help facilitate developing these images into motion pictures.

Jeremy Chandler: As Shawn or I would have initial ideas for shots or scenes, those ideas would be refined through discussion and even during shooting. We would typically start a shoot with general parameters of what we wanted to achieve, often make adjustments while on location, trying different versions of what we had in mind. I knew the area where we shot *Coventry* intimately having grown up and made many photographs there and was able to suggest spots that would be good for the scenes we had in mind. We were also able to recruit friends of mine that I had worked with previously, so I was able to contribute a great deal in regards to casting.

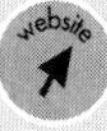
Visit the book's website to reader the full interview.

The Importance of Context

The impact and meaning of works of art and design are influenced by their context. Therefore, artists and designers need to ask themselves what they want their work to do. Creation comes with responsibility. Remember that context is affected by individual attributes, cultural influences, environmental qualities, business restrictions, and the history of art and design. Changing the context of a work can completely shift its meaning, audience, and effectiveness. When context is not immediately recognizable, artists and designers can use that to their advantage by creating anticipation or even discomfort.

Exercise

Refer back to the dream journal exercise. Select one dream as the subject for a work. Using this dream as your inspiration, brainstorm a sound-based work and a performance-based work about the subject (this does not have to be a performance that you will perform yourself; it could be a performance for someone else). For example, if you selected a dream in which your cat was talking to you about what he did when you were gone all day, you might create a sound work involving cat noises and a performance involving people trying to coax a cat to talk. When you have settled on an idea for the pieces, create a **storyboard**, a series of sketches describing planned actions in a work, for each piece that will clearly explain your idea to others (for a sample storyboard, see fig.1-15). Often, these sketches are **thumbnails**, or small rough sketches to communicate general ideas.

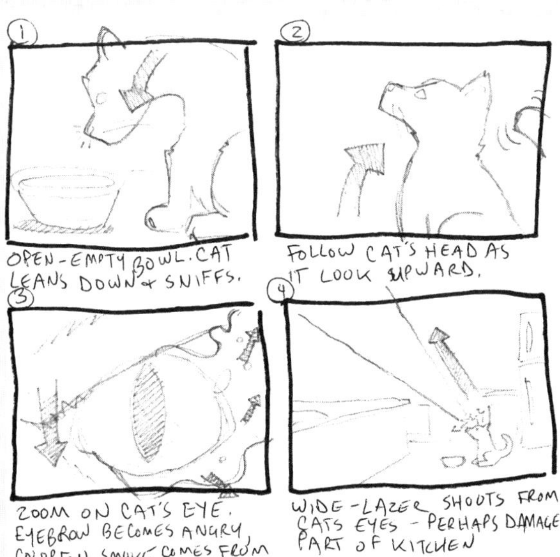

Fig. 1-15
Sample of storyboard with thumbnail sketches.
© Phil McCollam.

(continued)

> **Exercise** (*continued*)
>
> Then, ask yourself, in what context would each of these works would be best presented and why? Compare your proposed contexts to those of your classmates. See if there is a grouping of pieces that could be exhibited together, and plan for their exhibition. Remember that work does not have to exist in the locations we might expect (recognized gallery spaces, online videos, etc.)— try to think outside the stereotypical solutions. Once exhibition groupings have been established, everyone can execute their chosen work and display with the others in their chosen context. Technical tips are available in Chapter 2.
>
>  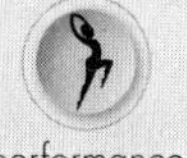
>
> sound   performance

Content

The content is the message or **concept** the artist or designer intends to communicate. It is the goal of the work, or the intended audience reaction or understanding. Content is created through the intersection of subject, form, and context. However, every individual participant brings his or her own context to a work, so artists and designers cannot completely control reactions. Nonetheless, artists and designers can help shape and direct participants by effectively executing subject, form, and context to create content that can be physical, emotional, intellectual, or a combination of these ideas.

Physical Content

Physical content affects our bodies or biological functions. For example, if a designer is creating seats for an airplane, the physical comfort of the passenger will be one of the primary goals of the design. Similarly, if a director is making a commercial for a fast-food restaurant, his or her primary goal is to incite a craving or hunger response in the viewer. Physical content can also exist in sound works that are meant to be physically *felt* as well as heard. Sound artist Maryanne Amacher often worked in this vein, creating works that were meant to be experienced at extreme volumes in order to cause physical sensations in participants. Peter Watrous wrote in the *New York Times* after a performance of her work at the

Kitchen in 1988 that "she used immense volume to make sound feel liquid, all-enveloping, as if it were pouring into ears, between fingers and through hair."[7]

Emotional Content

Emotional content is any element of the work that causes the participant to have an emotional reaction. Emotional content was used to great effect in the opening title sequence produced by Prologue, a visual effects company, for *Dawn of the Dead* (2004), a zombie horror film (fig. 1-16). Laying the groundwork for a zombie apocalypse, which is the backdrop for the film, the titles integrate quick, successive cuts between clips of zombies, faux-news reports, found-footage of social unrest, and the opening credits made of splattering and dripping blood, all set to the song "The Man Comes Around" by Johnny Cash. Combining motion graphics effects with clips of real-world violence and a haunting song referencing the Book of Revelation, the sequence instills the emotions of fear, desperation, and anticipation within the viewer, setting the tone for the upcoming film.

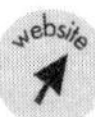

Visit the book's website to read an interview with Matt Normand, one of the designers who worked on the *Dawn of the Dead* titles.

Exercise

Watch the *Dawn of the Dead* titles on the book's website. After watching the work, write down what you think are the subject, form, content, and context for this work. Compare and contrast your answers with others'. How are your answers similar and different from those around you? Were there any trends in the answers?

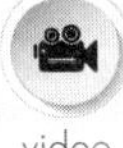

video

Intellectual Content

Intellectual content engages the participant's thought process. For example, a work might trigger confusion in the participant, cause a realization, heighten awareness, or encourage the viewer to ask a question. Allora and

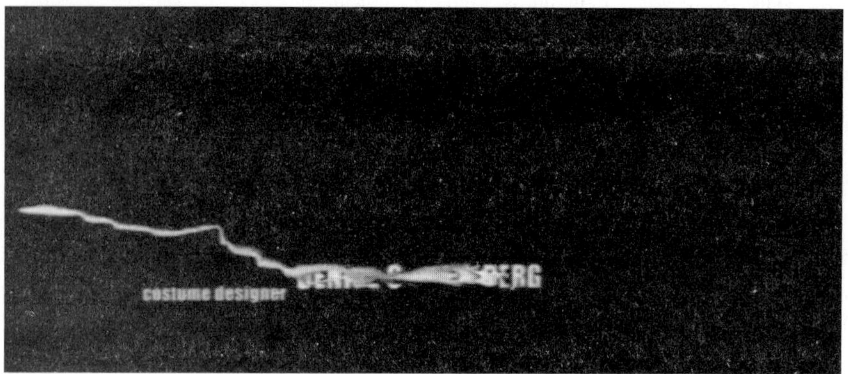

Fig. 1-16
Kyle Cooper, *Dawn of the Dead* opening titles (2004), motion graphics, 2:30 minutes.
Courtesy of Universal Studios Licensing LLC.

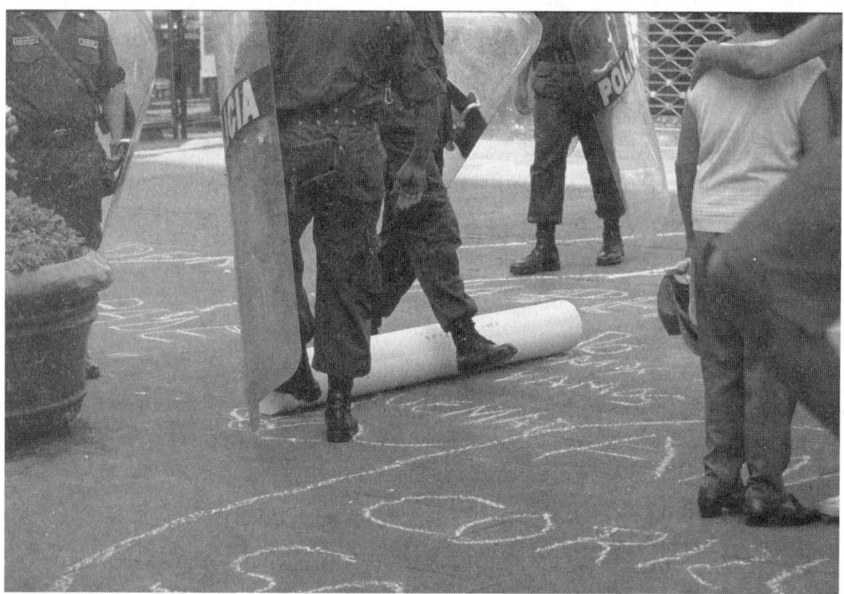

Fig. 1-17
Allora and Calzadilla, *Chalk* (2002), documentary still, dimensions variable. Courtesy of
the artists. © Allora and Calzadilla.

Calzadilla, a collaborative comprised of two artists, created an interactive
installation, *Chalk* (2002). The subject of this work is people writing on the
sidewalk with chalk, and then getting stopped by the police (fig. 1-17). The
form is six-foot-long pieces of chalk laying on a sidewalk available to

participants to collaboratively draw with or break apart into chunks for single-person use; the context is a public plaza adjacent the parliament building and the president's mansion in Lima, Peru.

This social artwork began with benign chalk doodles, but street protesters later arrived at the plaza and expressed more political statements, accusing the government of corruption and unjust labor practices. The event lasted 3 hours before officials shut it down by breaking up the chalk and trucking it away. The officials also sent in a crew to wash away all the chalk messages and imagery.

Taking all these attributes together, the viewer can infer that the content of this work is showing "the limits of free speech in a so-called democratic society," in Calzadilla's words. [8] This content is intellectual because it asks us to think and consider these ideas. That being said, be aware that intellectual content does not preclude emotional or physical content; a work can have multiple types of content.

Interview: Allora and Calzadilla

Chalk (2002): Succession of events, April 17, 2002

- 12:00 pm: 24 chalks were positioned on the Pasaje, some were broken and written with as to suggest their function
- 12:10 pm: [Passersby] begin writing and drawing with the chalk, the Pasaje transforms into a giant outdoor chalkboard, a surface of inscription, communication, and dialogue.
- 1:00 pm: The daily demonstrators, pressing various social and economic demands, make their way from Plaza de Armas to the Pasaje Santa Rosa. They begin using the chalks as a vehicle to write down their petitions. The scale of the writings is large due to the enormous size of the chalks. They wrote a variety of statements such as Toledo Dictator, Andrade Assassin, to statements about government lay-offs and months of work without pay, along with other statements about government corruption.
- 1:30 pm: The writings continue to grow in size and variety. The activity on the street begins to get noticed by government officials who show their dissatisfaction with what is being written. A heated debate ensues over who has access to the public space of the Pasaje. Who has the right to speak, write, and lay claims there? Whose voice can, should, and does get heard? This debate was registered through the inscriptions on

(continued)

Interview: Allora and Calzadilla (*continued*)

the plaza as well. Phrases such as "Toledo Es Del Pueblo" (Toledo is of the people) began to appear.

- 2:00 pm: The National Police along with some government officials go into the Biennale office, which is located on the Pasaje.
- 2:15 pm: We are informed that the work is going to be removed from the Pasaje.
- 2:30 pm: The chalks are broken up and placed on a large truck.
- 2:40 pm: A cleaning squad arrives and begins to wash away the writings with buckets of water, brooms and water hoses. The government officials direct the cleaning squad as to which writings to erase first, namely, those which make accusations against the government.
- 7:00 pm: After the Pasaje was clean of any writings that questioned or interrogated the government's policies publicly, Government Officials make their inaugurating speeches at the Mayor's house located on the Pasaje Santa Rosa. The inaugural speeches celebrated the liberating potential of art as a unique form of expression vital to society.

—*Allora and Calzadilla*

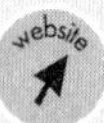

Visit the book's website to read the full interview.

Exercise

Find one clip from two different movies, each with different content or messages. For example, you could select a clip from *The Wizard of Oz*, in which the message is finding home, and *Gone with the Wind*, in which the message is the pursuit of unrequited love. Edit these two clips together using any editing techniques you like; however, the result must convey a new and different message from either of the original clips. If you were to continue following the example, the content for the edited work could not be "finding home" or "unrequited love"; it would instead have to be something completely different.

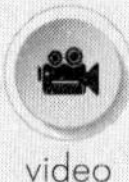

video

Content in Socially Engaged Art

When creating a socially engaged work, an artist or designer is working in tandem with a community. Take for example Fallen Fruit's public fruit park in Del Aire, California. In 2012, the artists worked with Los Angeles County, the Los Angeles County Arts Commission, the Department of Water and Power, the Department of Parks and Recreation, the neighborhood council, and the park's staff in order to bring this public fruit park to realization (go to the book's website to view this video). This example illustrates how artists and designers must strive to communicate openly and honestly with the community about the components of the work, especially the work's content. The artist or designer must explain how this work is art, which will help avoid miscommunications during and after the execution of the work. Fallen Fruit had to explain that the fruit trees would act as their artistic medium, and they would be addressing ideas related to public space, ownership, healthy foods, and childhood obesity through their work.

Clear and constant communication of responsibilities will help both parties (the artist and the community) from feeling used by the other. Fallen Fruit had to explain to the various community representatives that fruit trees would not become a nuisance or create the potential for a lawsuit (any more so than non-fruit-bearing trees). The work would instead present an opportunity to display the community's values, which included combating childhood obesity.

When entering into such a working relationship, it is the artist's responsibility to clearly share his or her goals, which must be realistic given the community's availability. With Fallen Fruit's public fruit park, there already had been a plan to add additional trees to the park, which made the proposal to change those trees to fruit-bearing trees somewhat easier. The collective may have had a harder time convincing the community to dedicate their time and resources to the project if they had not previously expressed interest in planting additional trees in the park. It is also the artist's responsibility to understand the context of the community, including the community's needs and interests, which in turn will affect content.

Finally, the artist or designer must also be ready to deal with changes in interests and needs as the project progresses. Think of Allora and Calzadilla's chalk piece, in which participants expressed unpredictable thoughts and opinions, from declarations of love to political outcry (fig. 1-17). Know that it is possible (and likely) that your interests and the community's interests may come into conflict. Be ready with conflict resolution approaches to ensure that the intended content can continue to be clearly communicated.[9]

In the case of *Chalk*, a heated debate took place about who has access to public space. This debate, as well as the police presence and their actions, underscored the artists' intent in creating the work by reinforcing the idea that free speech was being restricted.

It is important for artists and designers to be mindful as they select content because it can affect the thoughts, mood, physical body, and behaviors of those who witness the work. It is the artist or designer's responsibility to wield that manipulation thoughtfully.

Exercise

As a class, brainstorm at least 10 subjects, 10 forms, and 10 contexts and write each one down on a slip of paper. Randomly select one subject, one form, and one context. Using these group-determined criteria, each person will come up with a message for a work, and will not share their chosen message or finished work with anyone until critique. At critique, discuss the similarities and differences between all the works. How was it different to start with the subject, form, and context, rather than a message?

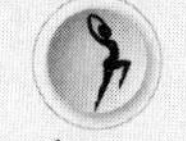   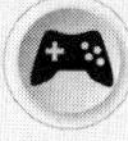

Identifying Subject, Form, Context, and Content

When taken in combination, the subject, form, context, and content of an artwork provide the overall experience for the viewer or participant. Let's look at a few examples and identify the subject, form, context, and content of each one.

A Generative Artwork

Let's return to the example of a computerized generative artwork that can display intricate digital patterns controlled by algorithms.

- The colorful arrangement of shapes is an example of a nonrepresentational *subject*.
- The *form* of the generative artwork is a digital display created by underlying algorithms.

- The *context* includes the location where the work is viewed, as well as the characteristics of whoever made it, owns it, and views it.
- The *content* is emotional in that the work simply evokes visual and rhythmic pleasure. The content may also be intellectual if the data running through the algorithm has any significance. For example, an artist or designer may choose to use climate pattern data points to create his or her generative work, and this may cause participants to think about changes in climate patterns as they watch the work develop.

Eleanor Antin's Short Film, *Love's Shadow* (1986)

Antin's film *Love's Shadow* is based on her interest in the silent films of the 1920s (fig. 1-18). She was particularly curious about how filmmakers used shadow and light to underscore emotion in their works. This area of influence explains Antin's choice to portray the ballerina of her film in shadow, while the lover is a fully illuminated person.

- The *subject* is a ballerina and her lover.
- The fact that the ballerina is depicted only in shadow while the lover is a fully represented person, and that the piece was shot on 16-mm black-and-white film and lasts 2½ minutes, are all aspects of *form*.
- The *context* of the work includes a variety of factors such as the date of creation (1986, the fact that the artist is a woman, and that the work was intended for show in galleries and museums.

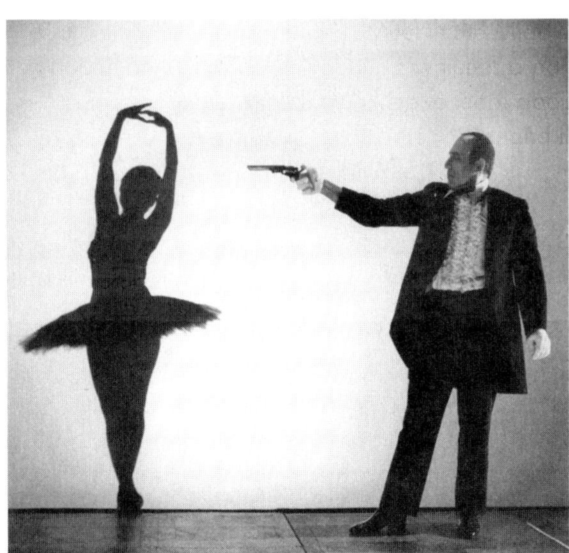

Fig. 1-18
Eleanor Antin, *Love's Shadow*, from *Loves of a Ballerina* (1986), 16-mm black-and-white film, 2:30 minutes. Courtesy of Ronald Feldman Fine Arts, New York.

- The *content* of *Love's Shadow* is complex and includes both emotional and intellectual content by critiquing a romantic trope about the unattainability of beauty and love. The work makes the you feel sadness for the ballerina; however, it also makes you think about beauty and love.

Interview: Eleanor Antin

Love's Shadow was originally part of a group of short films I made to look like old silent films for a large gallery installation (*Loves of a Ballerina*). Through the doors of a life scale, constructed theatre facade, the viewers looked at the films over the heads of the people supposedly watching inside. (The "people" were life scale and dark, made of cardboard, and they got smaller towards the front to give the proper perspective). You could hear strains of the music through the doors. It was a melancholy atmosphere of times gone past, specifically the early 1930s. . . .

The story is pretty simple. The lover yearns for the unattainable ballerina (danced by me) and when he can't have her, shoots her, and then falls over the body weeping in anguish. This is obviously, a romantic trope about the unattainability of beauty and love. Think of the line repeated endlessly in Oscar Wilde's poem *The Ballade of Reading Gaol*: "all men kill the thing they love." It's a long-standing romantic trope, certainly going back at least as far as the ancient Greeks (think of Orpheus looking back at Eurydice and losing her forever.)

—*Eleanor Antin*

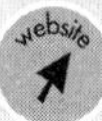

Visit the book's website to reader the full interview.

Daniel Sousa's Animated Film *Feral* (2013)

In *Feral*, Sousa uses hand-drawn animation to tell the story of a young boy who grew up in the wild (fig. 1-19). A hunter finds him and brings him to the city where he struggles with the structures of city life.

- The *subject* is a wild boy in the woods brought back to civilization by a hunter.
- The *form* is a 12-minute hand-drawn animated film.

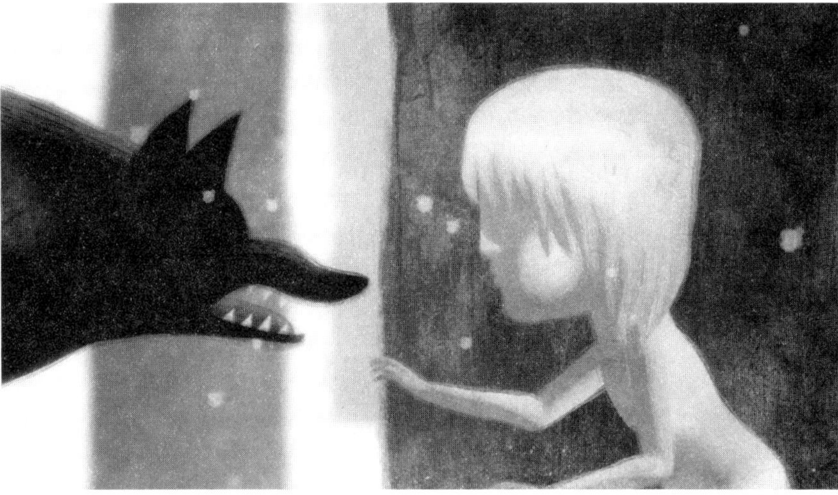

Fig. 1-19
Daniel Sousa, still from the film *Feral* (2013, animation, 12 minutes. © 2012 by Daniel Sousa.

- The *content* is both emotional and intellectual, touching on ideas of wilderness versus civilization, alienation, safety, identity, instinct, and the nature of being human.
- The *context* includes the fact that the work was created over the course of 2008 to 2013, the animator is a man, and the intended venues were film festivals with large-scale projection and online viewing, which involves a significantly smaller screen.

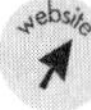 Visit the book's website to read an interview with Daniel Sousa.

Exercise

Search online for a four-dimensional work in a medium of your choice and view it. After watching the work, write down what you think are the subject, form, content, and context for this work. As you practice this skill, it should become faster and easier to identify these components in any work.

 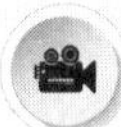 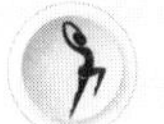   

sound   video   performance   installation   games   light

Exercise

Execute three self-portraits. In each self-portrait the subject is the self; however, by changing the form, content, or context, you can change how participants understand you as a multifaceted person. None of the self-portraits may contain your face, and all of them must utilize time. They could be sound works, videos, animations, performances, interactive installations, games, apps, and so on. For inspiration, revisit Anna Antrophy's free online game *Dys4ia* (fig. 1-1), which functions as a type of self-portrait from a specific time in Antrophy's life. This assignment could be short, lasting only a class period, or very extended, lasting all term. After completing the three self-portraits, reflect on how you used the same subject for each work but managed to create three unique works. What does this say about you as the subject? What does this say about how subjects are portrayed in general?

  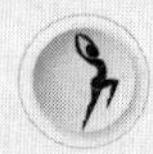   

Exercise

Set a timer for 2 minutes. Next, brainstorm and write down 24 subjects for a 10-second stop-motion animation: 8 subjects must be people, 8 must be places, and 8 must be things. (As you practice brainstorming, the process will move more quickly and will feel more natural. For more tips on brainstorming, see Chapter 2.) **Stop-motion animation** is a series of still images shown in quick succession to imply movement. The images are created using a camera to capture a subject; then the artist or designer moves the subject a little and takes another shot, and so on until a complete movement or set of movements is made. (See Chapter 2 for more information about stop-motion animation.)

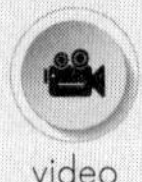

Summary

In this chapter we have learned what constitute the subject, form, context, and content of any given work of art or design. We have learned how to identify these components in several different four-dimensional media and practiced this skill of analysis and identification.

Key Terms

composition   The arrangement of the elements and principles of art and design

concept   The message the artist or designer intends to communicate

content   The meaning or impact of the work created through the intersection of subject, form, and context

context   The set of factors surrounding the creation and display of the work

craft   The skill with which media is manipulated

crane shot   The camera is mounted on a crane that can rise smoothly to a place far above the scene, or can lower down to ground level

emotional content   Content that causes the participant to have an emotional reaction

form   The sensorial experience of the work; it encompasses the material or media used to create a work, as well as the organization of the elements and principles of art and design within a work

generative art   Computer-generated artwork that is algorithmically determined

Gestalt theory   visual illusions created to highlight the human tendency to establish continuity between various arrangements of objects or partially obscured objects

hand-held shot   A video shot that is intentionally unstable and shaky

intellectual content   Content that engages the participant's thought process

medium (media = plural)   The material and process used to create a work

nonrepresentational   When a work does not depict a recognizable person, place, or thing, and the subject is purely the quality of arranged sensory elements, such as shape, sound, color, light, and so forth

physical content   Content that affects one's body or biological functions

point of view   A facet of context answering the question "Whose story is this?"

privilege   An unearned benefit or advantage due to an aspect of your identity, such as race, religion, gender identity, sexual orientation, class/wealth, citizenship status, and so on.

representational   When a work depicts a recognizable person, place, or thing

stop-motion animation   A series of still images shown in quick succession to imply movement

storyboard   A series of sketches describing planned actions in a work

subject   What the artist or designer is attempting to portray; the depicted people, places, and things

thumbnails   Small, rough sketches to communicate general ideas; often they are completed in large batches as a brainstorming technique

viewpoint   A term from film and video studies describing how the composition of each shot can express facets of a point of view

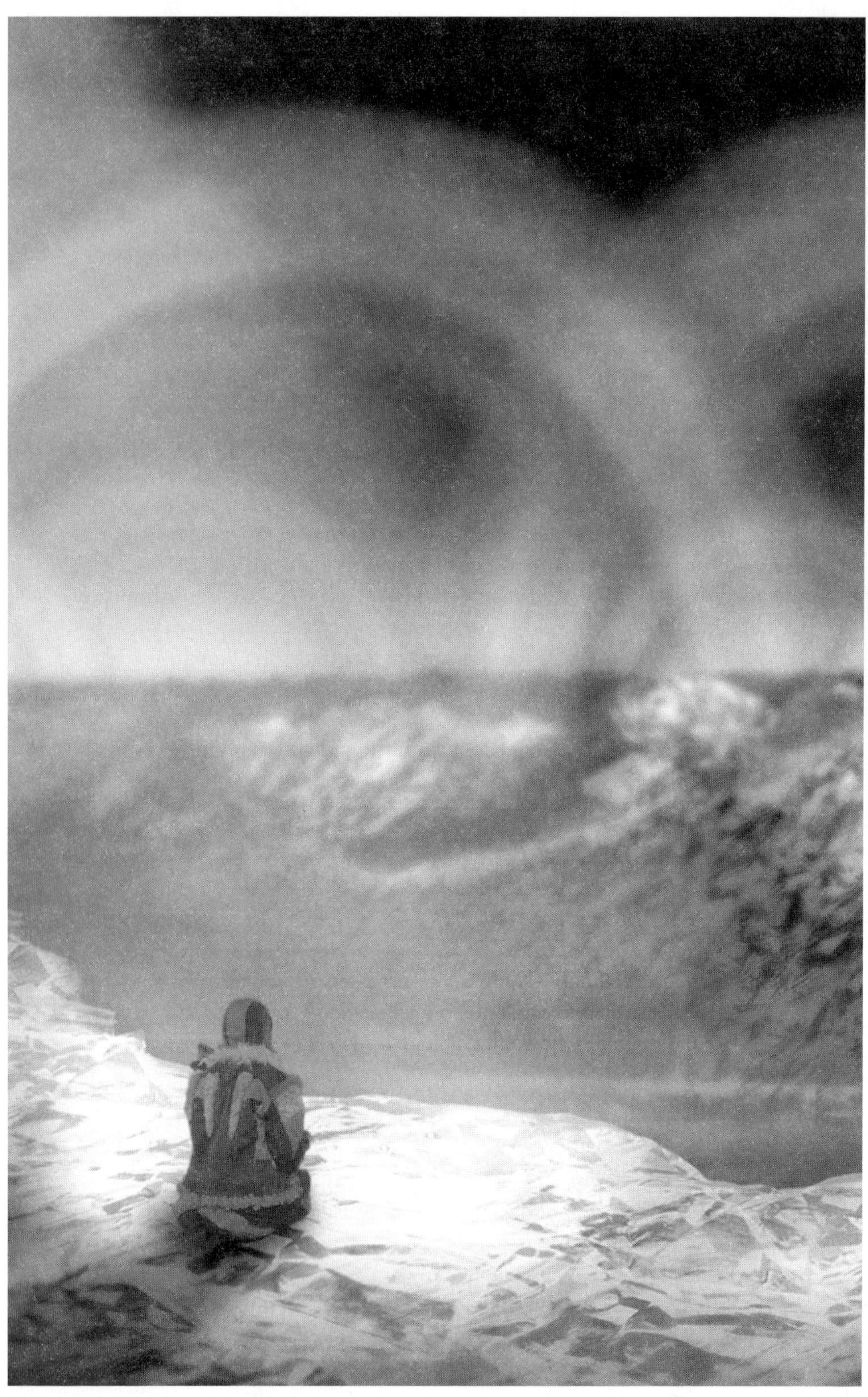

Courtesy of the artist. Commissioned by The Banff Centre, Canada and The Collective Gallery, Edinburgh. Funded by Creative Scotland.

2

Getting Started

n this chapter, we'll go over some basic concepts that we will be working with throughout the text, including brainstorming, researching, creating a narrative, and critiquing your own work and the work of your classmates. These four concepts will be involved in all of the exercises that you will be completing as part of the process of understanding 4D art and design. Then, we'll look at some theories of gaming and play that have influenced 4D artists in developing their own ideas for their works. We'll next describe some organizing concepts that you might use in creating your own 4D works. Finally, we will then go over some basic technical tips that will help you make the best use of the basic equipment and software that you will be using.

Brainstorming and Serious Play

As artists and designers develop their work, they will start with an idea. Coming up with ideas can be active, involving effort, or passive, allowing ideas to surface when they will. **Brainstorming** is an active approach to producing ideas and solutions in a noncritical environment with emphasis on quantity over quality. Brainstorming allows an artist or designer to move beyond their initial impulses to create a pool of potential ideas or solutions. This approach is meant to help artists and designers embrace the spontaneous and eliminate hesitation, self-consciousness, and self-censorship.

One way to achieve this objective is to incorporate serious play. Professor Gay Lemons states, "Laughter provides a train wreck for the mind, suspending thought and being in the moment, which opens the channels for innovative, creative thinking. You can't think while you are laughing. Try it. Try doing a calculus problem (or moving a couch) while in the throes of laughter. It can't be done. But what it does do is metaphorically open the cranial channels and allow for creative, innovative thinking to emerge."[1]

Before you start brainstorming, you will need to schedule enough time to let your ideas incubate. You will brainstorm, then take a break, and then return to the brainstorming process. These breaks allow your subconscious to work on the new material you have generated, and eventually arrive at new solutions, or move you toward one. The length of these breaks can vary depending on the individual, the level of difficulty of the problem, and the overall amount of time you have for the project.[2]

As you start the brainstorming process, you will want to find a good place to do it. Look for an environment where you can feel relaxed (skip the room with giant windows where passersby might stop to check out what you are doing). When you brainstorm, you want to remove any serious consequences for your ideas so that you can make mistakes without a second thought; onlookers can inhibit risk-taking. Next, set a time limit for yourself or your group, depending on your project.

A simple way to implement play is to start with a silly, imaginative exercise to loosen up, much like you would do a warm-up before launching into a strenuous workout. For example, you could do a quick timed word-association exercise, or a timed drawing exercise based on a subject related (or not) to your brainstorming subject just to get your brain working. Two of my favorite exercises for group brainstorming are "Clams Are Great" and "Purse."[3]

Exercise Clams Are Great

In this exercise, one person occupies the center of a circle formed by the rest of the group. The person in the center has the task of brainstorming, as fast as possible, three ways that clams are great (any object could be chosen in place of clams). He or she does this by repeatedly completing the sentence "Clams are great because __________." There is no wrong answer, and anything can be said to fill in the blank. After the person in the center finishes, another person must jump in, until everyone in the circle has gone. Players cannot repeat each other's phrases. Because you can say anything to complete the phrase, this exercise helps people to feel confident and supports the rapid acceptance of ideas. This exercise is intentionally silly, which may be the biggest hurdle for artists and designers who are sometimes encouraged to take themselves very seriously.

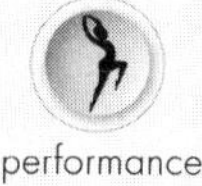

performance

Exercise Purse

In this exercise, the group forms a circle, and participants work their way around the circle, one person at a time. It is very similar to "Clams Are Great" except this time people brainstorm different items to put in a purse. Everyone performs the exercise while clapping to a beat, to maintain a steady tempo throughout. This again encourages participants to go with their first idea in a nonjudgmental way. The artificial rhythm set by these exercises pushes students out of their comfort zone while providing a safe structure or system within which to fail.

performance

Once you have warmed up, you can start thinking of ideas. Remember: there are no bad ideas during brainstorming, and you should record all the ideas. You want to generate the largest possible volume of ideas within your allotted time. It can help to get up and move around: bounce a ball, play with a toy, walk around the perimeter of the room, and so on. Changing your physical location can help you change your mental perspective, opening the door to more ideas. As author Jesse Schell states in *The Art of Game Design*, "Play is manipulation that indulges curiosity." Be curious in your brainstorming; indulge what-if scenarios, and don't be afraid of seemingly crazy ideas.

If you have stray thoughts that are distracting you from the brainstorming process, record them and then set them aside for later. As Schell reminds us, "Play is about having fun . . . and escaping from reality, and a play world is simpler than the real world, but you have much more power."[4] You want to use that power to focus on generating new ideas rather than how much you want to check your email, go grab a quick coffee, check on that other project you're working on, or take a nap. Speaking of sleep, make sure you get plenty of it: being well-rested will help your brain function at optimum level and speed.

As you are coming up with ideas, you'll want select a way to record them all. You could type them, or you could write them down on any number of surfaces, such as index cards, sticky notes, giant sticky notes, lined paper, or plain copier paper, which may be friendlier to spontaneous sketching. Some people like having physical paper they can move around once the brainstorming is over. You may rely on a combination of writing and thumbnail sketches. Others like to make a specific collection of sketches and imagery such as a **collage** or **photomontage**. Still others might like to employ small rough models made from paper, clay, or other readily available materials. Make sure you have more than enough materials for the brainstorming session: be prepared for anything.

If you find yourself getting stuck, there are several tactics you can try. First, you can try broadening the definition of your challenge. Try to think beyond the ordinary solutions to the problem. Sometimes simply changing your perspective to view the issue from the outside will help generate new ideas. Another approach is to try numbering your lists; this may give the items on the list more importance and can jog your brain into producing more. You might also try creating categories into which you will brainstorm. Categories give you the opportunity to later mix and match from the varied lists. A sample set of categories could be verbs, adverbs, and adjectives associated with your challenge, or people, places, and things related to your subject.

Sometimes it can help to list facts related to the challenge and evaluate that list for truthfulness. This can help you sort out what is actually foundational to the issue versus what you perceive to be fact. You might also actively seek out the opposite of what you think you're working on. For example, if you are examining a social issue in your work, you might try taking the opposing stance on the issue to unearth new ideas related to your own point of view. If you are having a hard time brainstorming, try getting a partner to help. Likewise, if you are finding group brainstorming suffocating, try brainstorming alone. You can also try talking to yourself. Sometimes engaging the sense of hearing can help an idea click in your head.[5]

Research

Zelda Fichandler, founder of Arena Stage, once said, "Imagination is what is there after you know everything."[6] Research can be very useful for informing your decisions as an artist or designer. Some research can be integrated into your daily routines: you may engage with popular culture through social media, television shows, movies, news, games, books, and radio. Other research is much more pointed and specific, involving learning more about your audience, your own biases, the subject and context of your work, and methods of execution. Here are some general guidelines for conducting research, many of which are inspired by Dan Saffer's book *Designing for Interaction*. Some steps will prove more meaningful and useful for some projects rather than others; pick and choose those that seem most pertinent to your work.

First, *examine yourself.* Do an inventory of your personal biases, hopes, beliefs, fears, attitudes, and so on. Become aware of how these factors can and will affect your research and your work. Keep this inventory with you and refer to it often.

Identify the central subject(s) in your work. Your work might deal with any number of subjects from farming to space exploration. Whatever your subject, take the time to do traditional research at a library. Learn the foundational knowledge of your subject area from experts – take note of the information that is repeated in several sources. Another spin on this foundational research is to do an image search online. Enter keywords related to your subject, and scan through the pages of images that turn up. Look for visual trends; print out or save particularly striking images and add them to your research materials. Take note of how your subject is typically represented or framed, and examine whether you want to continue or break with those trends.

Go to your participants and observe them in the same context in which your work will occur. Find out what they expect when they encounter a work like yours (a film, animation, performance, installation, website, etc.). You might simply watch them and take notes, and/or you could ask to shadow one or two of them to find out what they are doing and the choices they are making. You might ask questions while shadowing them.

Afterward, you might choose to talk to them to find out whether they have tendencies toward certain behaviors such as problem solving, exploring, socializing, or performing. Learn about their interests and histories. Be sure to let them tell their stories in their own way, and refrain from judging anything that you learn during this time.

Keep in mind that anytime you work with people, you need to be ethical in your approach. Make sure to get informed consent from those you are studying, and explain any risks or benefits (if they exist) before you begin your work. Respect privacy, and compensate your research subjects for their time. This doesn't have to be in the form of money, but it should be something meaningful to those with whom you are working. Also, if they ask, be willing to share your research with the participants.

Write everything down. You can do this by hand or type it, but you'll want a written record of all your research. Having a physical record will help you with the final step, which is *looking for patterns in your observations.* If you were in these participants' shoes, what would you want to see in your work, and what would you like or dislike about the project?

You may also want to do a historical survey. Research artists and designers who have addressed this issue before you. Dissect their solutions. Ask how you could improve on their work. Figure out what they did in their own research to arrive at their final piece.

Narrative

Narrative is another name for storytelling. Narratives, or stories, are built with specific literary elements such as plot, **characters**, **setting**, beginning/middle/end, conflict, resolution, and causality. Generally, a narrative contains characters with goals they care about, a series of obstacles that cause conflict, and an examination of how the conflict is resolved. Conflict can be territorial, economic, knowledge-based, and so on. Even the most seemingly fragmented narratives, such as Rachel Maclean's *Over the Rainbow* (2013), contain these basic elements (Plate 1, color insert). In this video, we encounter a variety of colorful characters threaded together by tenuously related sound clips from popular culture. The characters overcome bizarre conflicts and transform throughout the work.

Characters can be separated into **protagonists**, the heroes we root for and who undergo transformation, and **antagonists**, the villains we root against. All characters, regardless of their status as protagonists or antagonists, have defining traits such as being outgoing or timid, brooding or agreeable, and so on. Generally, it is good to ensure your narrative includes a variety of characters, and to be clear about how the characters feel about one another. This tactic will maintain participants' interest.

Testimonial performance works such as Spalding Gray's *Swimming to Cambodia* (1987) or Tim Miller's *My Queer Body* (1992) use traditional storytelling. They convey a narrative that includes conflict, resolution, and causality. We see narrative frequently utilized because it can be useful for forging emotional connections with viewers or participants. We are accustomed to taking in narratives because we are bombarded with them daily through various forms of advertising. Narratives have also been used for centuries as both entertainment and a means of passing on history. They are a central part of the human experience.

In film, the idea of narrative is divided into scenes and sequences. "A scene is "defined by the unity of time, space, and action. . . . A sequence, on the other hand, maintains one or more of these unities while introducing a discontinuity."[7] Keep in mind that narratives may or may not be presented in chronological order. Typically, a narrative begins with a hook, or something to grab participant's' attention. Then the narrative will gradually rise in intensity, with moments of rest scattered throughout, until the climax of the conflict, and finally a resolution of some sort.

Narrative is also often an integral part of activism. As Doyle Canning and Patrick Reinsborough point out, "Sometimes the best response to a powerful enemy is a powerful story."[8] For example, the activist group Billionaires for Bush (2000–2009) used the humorous narrative of a group of wealthy funders publicly campaigning for then-candidate George W. Bush. Using costumes and minimal props, Billionaires for Bush engaged in street theater and creative media actions to expose inequality and the influence of the super-rich. This simple, strong narrative was purposefully designed to encourage participation across the country.

When creating an action, you must identify the conflict being addressed. You must be aware of all the "characters" involved. You will likely rely on some narrative imagery to get your point across. As you make your argument, you must foreshadow the resolution to the conflict. All of these literary narrative devices are a necessary part of nearly any activist action.

Advertising also employs narrative. Television, print, web, and radio ads all use narrative—even if only momentarily—to grab listeners and viewers' attention and hold it. For example, consider the famous *1984* commercial that was developed to introduce the Apple Macintosh personal computer. The ad, which borrowed the narrative from George Orwell's dystopian novel of the same title, begins with people marching while we hear a big brother figure's praise of information purification. Intercut with the marching people is the image of a woman running with a hammer. We then see the speaker's face projected on a giant screen. She is pursued by a group of helmeted men as she runs through the now-seated figures who are mesmerized by leader's speech. Toward the end, the woman throws the hammer into the screen, and everyone watching the screen looks shocked. That image fades away as the Mac logo appears. The *1984* ad closed with the quote "On January 24th, Apple Computer will introduce Macintosh. And you'll see why 1984 won't be like '1984.'" Without the familiar narrative of human individuality overcoming repression, this commercial would not have been nearly as effective.

It is important to note that not all 4D works utilize narrative. Some artists and designers purposefully subvert narrative conventions to create interest or to focus on a particular concept. For example, many postmodern films attempt to subvert familiar conventions of narrative structure by manipulating the audience's suspension of disbelief. In the feature film *Synecdoche, New York* (2008), written and directed by Charlie Kaufman, the narrative starts out in a conventional and recognizable way, introducing a main character with a challenge. In this case it is an ailing theater director who is working on an elaborate stage production with an exaggerated commitment to recreating the real world. As the film progresses, the boundary between the theater director's fictional world and the actual world begins to blur, creating narrative confusion. By subverting traditional narrative approaches, this film is able to bring further attention to themes of delusion, decay, and death.

Exercise

Select a postmodern film. If you are unfamiliar with postmodern film, you may have to do some quick online research to find one. Watch the film. Identify the subject, form, content, and context of film. Write an analysis of how the film embraces or discards traditional narrative elements as previously described.

video

Critique

Thorough and frequent **critique**, or the act of discussing an artwork, helps you practice seeing, experiencing, interpreting, and articulating. Critique can take place while work is in process or after it is finished, or both. Through the practice of critique, you will learn that not all interpretations of work are of the same quality. Some interpretations are less cohesive or supported in specific observations than others. A good interpretation makes sense, is grounded in observations of the work, and acknowledges the entire work, not just selected aspects. Additionally, critique helps reveal that interpretations are not necessarily right or wrong: instead, they are strong or weak based on how compelling they are.

Here are a few reminders of the ground rules for useful critiques:

- It is the artwork, not the artist, that is being discussed.
- Feedback should be honest and respectful.
- Critique requires participation; it fails unless everyone engages in the discussion.
- Groups should decide beforehand whether members will be making suggestions for changes, or if the group will be offering only observations.
- If participants in the critique are going to offer a judgment (whether the work is "good" or "bad"), they must also offer supporting reasons and criteria, as well as provide a description of their personal artistic preferences.

Sample critique questions might include:

- What do you see, hear, smell, taste, and feel?
- What are the prominent elements and principles of 4D art and design utilized in this work? Do they complement one another or clash?
- Does the artist/designer use the elements and principles of 4D art and design well? If not, how could he or she have better utilized them?
- Could this work be improved by enhancing a specific element or principle?
- Are the components of the artwork (subject, form, content, and context) immediately clear to the participant? Is that good or bad? Could it be improved?
- Does the work have enough variety, or is it too chaotic? What changes might you make?

- What do you think the content of this work is? (Consult with the artist/designer only after you have taken a guess.) How does this work communicate its content? Is the content or goal clear?
- Where do you focus first? Second? Why? Does this focus support or hinder the content of the work?
- If you constructed a triangle with physical, emotional, and intellectual content at its points, where in the triangle would this work land? What do you think about its placement within this triangle?
- What do you think the artist's/designer's intent was? Do you think he or she achieved the perceived intent? After answering this question yourself, ask him or her what the actual intent was. Do you think it was achieved? Was the actual intent a good idea, or could it be improved? How?
- Describe the audience for this work. What must participants understand to "get" the work? What skills must participants bring to the work? (Do they need their imagination, a specific physical ability, etc.?) What does this artwork assume about participants?
- Is there anything in this work that could be eliminated?
- How do participants know how to interact with this work? Some media, such as film, have recognized rituals, while others require participants' discovery. Where does this work land on that spectrum, and is it working well?
- Are there any parts of the work that distract participants from the content or goal? If so, can the distractions be better tied into the work to help enhance content/goals?
- How does context affect and alter this work?
- What experience do you think the artist/designer intends? Begin by discussing the possibilities before asking the artist/designer what experience was intended for the participants.
- What is essential to this work's success? Could it be strengthened in any way?
- What, if anything, is surprising about this work? Is there anything fun about this piece? Could it benefit from more surprises or fun? Clearly, this question may not apply to some projects.
- What questions does the work raise? Does the piece do anything to make participants care about the questions?
- Do any aspects of the work remind you of other artists' work? Who?
- Could the artist have used any visual or symbolic metaphors to enhance the work?
- Is the audience for the work too narrow? Is the audience too broad?

Sample critique approaches could include:

- Select three to five questions from above, and use them to approach each work. This method tends to create a tempo and time limit for the critique, which can be helpful in promoting participation.
- Work in pairs, critiquing two works that are not your own, and then report your findings back to the class as a whole. I recommend using guidelines to help structure the critique, such as: find three things that are working well and three things that could be improved. Allow artists and designers to respond to the feedback after each pair has reported, which may result in further discussion.
- Give each participant a block of sticky-note paper and tell them to stand in front of a work that is not their own. They will have 1 minute to write a constructive critique of the work on the sticky note and then stick it next to the work. After each minute, they should rotate to a new work. They cannot repeat a critique that has already been left by the work (this is what pushes them to use their new vocabulary). After all works have been addressed, the participants should take time to read through the feedback and respond to the class as a whole.
- This approach needs a little bit of extra preparation. Have each student examine and respond to one or two pieces of professional art or design criticism. Next, when it is time to critique a project, have each student select a work that is not their own, and write a piece of art criticism that could be published in a professional magazine or blog. This approach will not only force students to be thorough in their critiques, but it will also help them see how critique relates to professional practices.
- Give students five index cards, and tell them to write a phrase starting with "When I see this piece, . . . " On the back of each card, have students write the name of the artist they are critiquing.[9] After a minute or two, have everyone rotate to the next work and repeat the exercise. Repeat five times. Then have everyone sort the cards into piles according to artist names and redistribute back to the artists for feedback.

Critique Cheat Sheet

It may be helpful for students to have a sheet listing the elements and principles of 4D design as a reminder of what they are looking for during these critiques. We will be covering these elements and principles in greater detail in the remaining chapters.

CRITIQUE CHEAT SHEET

Components of an Artwork

Subject

Form

Content

Context

Continued from 2D and 3D

Balance

Color

Contrast

Direction/Reflection

Repetition

Scale

Shape

Value/Brightness

Space

Elements of 4D

Architecture/Topography

Light

Movement

Sound

Time

Principles of 4D

Causality

Duration

Energy Dynamics/Intensity

Interactivity

Musicality

Simultaneity/Juxtaposition

Spatial Relationships

Tempo/Speed

Transitions

Sample Critique Breakdown
Daniel Sousa's *Feral* (fig. 1-19)

CRITIQUE CHEAT SHEET

Components of an Artwork

Subject: A feral boy

Form: Animation

Content: Ideas of wilderness versus civilization, alienation, safety, identity, instinct, and the nature of being human

Context: The work was created over the course of 2008–2013, the animator is a man, and the intended venue was film festivals with large-scale projection. The work is also available for online viewing, which involves a significantly smaller screen.

Elements and Principles from 2D and 3D Design

Balance: In the opening scene of the trailer, the frame is asymmetrically balanced by the deep shadow of the tree trunk on the left and the boy and background on the right.

Color: This is a nearly monochromatic animation relying on creams and browns with moments of color such as the red in the wolf's mouth or the pale yellow of the sun.

Contrast: As the cityscape floats into position, the contrast of dark buildings against a light background helps create focus.

Direction/Reflection: The clockwise rotation of the boy turning into different animals at the end of the trailer helps to create a hypnotic effect.

Repetition: The repetition of the imagery of the boy's mouth helps tie together the trailer from beginning to end.

Scale: The larger scale of the man versus the boy emphasizes the boy's youth.

Shape: The rectangle shapes, such as windows and doorways, in the opening scene of the city help establish this man-made environment.

Value/Brightness: The brightness of the sun helps emphasize the open spaces of nature, whereas the dark interior spaces help emphasize the containment the boy feels near the end.

Space: The repetition of tree trunks in the woods helps create a sense of ongoing infinite space in nature.

Elements of 4D Design

Architecture/Topography: The rectilinear architecture of the cityscape is pronounced in contrast with the organic forms of the woods.

Light: Sunlight helps foster a sense of openness when the boy is in the woods.

Movement: The movement of the rearing horse creates rising tension.

Sound: The sound of droning music helps move the piece forward, while the sounds of schoolchildren and the horse and growling emphasize the boy's struggle to integrate himself in this new world beyond the forest.

Time: We see edited time, because the boy goes from living in the forest to attending school in only 1:20 minutes of reel time.

Principles of 4D

Causality: When the boy bites the man's hand, it causes the man to slap the boy.

Duration: The duration of the trailer is 1:20, but the duration of the full animation is 12 minutes.

Energy Dynamics/Intensity: The energy builds throughout the trailer and peaks as the boy imitates the gnashing of wolves' teeth.

Interactivity: This work does not rely heavily on interaction beyond the viewer's commitment to watch the entire work from beginning to end.

Musicality: Throughout the work, music is playing. The rhythm of the piece helps hold the viewer's attention and build tension throughout.

Simultaneity/Juxtaposition: The juxtaposition of a wolf and a naked boy in the woods at the very start of the trailer helps pique the viewer's interest and create curiosity because this is not an everyday occurrence.

Spatial Relationships: Being very near to the boy (we see only his knees to shoes) when he is in the schoolyard and a ball is kicked his way helps create a sense of intimacy and sympathy when he drops his book.

Tempo/Speed: The speed of the cuts increases as the tension builds throughout the trailer.

Transitions: The use of floating geometric shapes to create the cityscape is a striking and creative transition that emphasizes the foreignness of the city to the boy.

Game Theories as Inspiration for Creativity

Several theorists have developed their own ideas about key objectives for both the creators and the participants in 4D works. These can all serve as key objectives for your own works, whether or not you are designing a game.

LeBlanc's *The Taxonomy of Game Pleasures*

In his book *The Taxonomy of Game Pleasures*, leading game designer and educator Marc LeBlanc proposed eight types of pleasure that participants derive from games:

1. *Challenge:* A compelling struggle, or challenge, is central to games: they all have at their core a challenging problem to be solved. It is up to the artist or designer to decide how hard or easy the challenge is. Challenge is a unique organizing concept because it could be the content or the form of your work.

2. *Discovery:* Many games rely on discovery, the act of exploring and finding or revealing, as a driver for game play.

3. *Expression:* Participants allowed to express themselves within a work will be able to customize aspects of the experience. When playing a video game, you might have the option of selecting a costume or avatar. In Yayoi Kusama's installation *Obliteration Room* (2012), participants could choose where to apply their sheet of colorful dot stickers in the formerly white room (Plate 15, color insert).

4. *Fantasy:* Games allow people to engage their imagination in ideas or situations that are impossible in reality. It is the act of immersing oneself in an imaginary world.

Exercise

Art21 has an episode on fantasy (season 5). It features the work of Chinese artist Cao Fei, in which she explores ideas of alter egos in video and Second Life, an online community. Write a descriptive analysis of one of Cao Fei's works. Discuss the subject, form, content, and context. Identify and explain the use of any elements or principles you feel are central to this work.

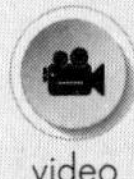
video

5. *Fellowship:* A shared experience of community is at the heart of many social practice works. For example, in Tom Marioni's *The Act of Drinking Beer with Friends Is the Highest Form of Art* (1970–present), participants drink beer served by Marioni, or a designated bartender, and converse.
6. *Narrative:* The art of storytelling is central to games; we have discussed its importance in art and design.
7. *Sensation:* The senses—lush visual, auditory, smells, tastes, and tactile experiences—play a major role in many works in the field of social practice, especially those that involve food or eating, or those that involve participants making something with their hands.
8. *Submission:* The act of giving yourself over heightens the game experience. In some works it is easy to suspend disbelief or skepticism to participate, whereas in others it takes a great deal of effort to engage and submit to the parameters of the game world.

Sutton-Smith's *The Ambiguity of Play*

Brian Sutton-Smith was one of the leading authorities on gaming and play. His book *The Ambiguity of Play* defines seven rhetorics of play:[10]

1. *Play as imaginary:* This type of play is the core of play because it involves intense creativity to bring new ideas into the world.
2. *Play as power:* This type of play is a means of establishing and maintaining status among those who control the play or are looked at as leaders/heroes. The type of games that embody this type of play include athletic competitions or contests.
3. *Play as progress:* This type of play is utilitarian, in that the process of playing helps children develop into adults.
4. *Play as fate:* This kind of play is governed by a force other than free will, such as fortune, gods, luck, and so on.
5. *Play as frivolity:* This type of play is the polar opposite of work ethic. In other words, it is playing for the sheer enjoyment of it.
6. *Play as identity:* This is a means of establishing and validating the identity of a group of people. This type of play occurs in ritual celebrations and festivals.
7. *Play as self:* This is a way of developing oneself through experiences of amusement or unwinding, which could include any number of game-like hobbies completed in one's free time.

A Selection of Organizing Concepts and Techniques

Here is a selection of common organizing concepts and techniques and approaches used by 4D artists and designers that can help get you started in creating your own works. The distinction between a concept and technique may be somewhat arbitrary, but the point is to separate out underlying inspirational themes and ideas from practical approaches and techniques that artists use to express them. Undoubtedly, you could think of many more, so use this list as a springboard for further brainstorming. A selection of the exercises in this section ask you to go online to view episodes of PBS's series *Art21, The Art Assignment,* and *New York Close Up.* These are all available for free viewing online.

Concepts

THE ABJECT. The abject encompasses all the elements of being human that society would like to keep concealed: everything disgusting, shameful, taboo, and degrading. It could include corpses, excrement, vomit, menstrual blood, internal organs, mold, any expression of sexuality not condoned my mainstream culture, sewage, beautiful things made ugly, pus, the homeless, genocide, disease, infection, and so on. The artist collective Destineez Child embraces the abject in much of the materials it offers for sale (see fig. 1-7).

BOUNDARIES. Boundaries can be physical, intellectual, emotional, ideological, and so on. Boundaries make an interesting conceptual focus for many works because they are influenced by those who establish them and those who disregard them. Fallen Fruit's *Public Fruit Maps* help illustrate the controversial nature of boundaries by raising questions about what fruit is public versus private (see fig. 1-6).

COMPASSION. Because human beings are emotional, concern for the suffering of others frequently inspires works of art and design works. Anna Anthropy's *Dys4ia* aims to cultivate compassion by revealing the struggles of a transgendered person (see fig. 1-1).

Exercise

Art21 has an episode on compassion (season 5). It features the work of Colombian artist Doris Salcedo, in which she develops a large-scale installation, *Shibboleth*, at the Tate Modern in London, which reflects on violence, racism, and border crossing. The episode also focuses on South African artist William Kentridge's stop-motion charcoal animation, which focuses on issues of apartheid and identity politics.

Write a comparative analysis of these two creators. Discuss the subject, form, content, and context of one work by each of them. Identify and explain the use of any elements or principles you feel are central to the work.

video   installation

CULTURE/SOCIETY/COMMUNITY. Culture is the collection of various customs, habits, and ways of life for a group of people. Society is a name for that collection of people. A community is a group of people within a society, or sometimes community is a term for a specific area or neighborhood. An example of culture and society being foregrounded in a work is Shana Moulton and Nick Hallett's multimedia opera *Whispering Pines 10* (2010). In this performative work, Moulton and Hallett explore how American culture and society react to physical and psychological discomfort by showcasing a variety of fad cures and New Age kitsch that unfolds in a live-animation environment (see fig. 3-1).

Exercise

Interview a member of your community and make a short video documentary of the interview. Collect the entire class's interviews together to create a portrait of the community.

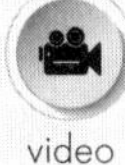

video

DEATH/MORTALITY. Because death is a guaranteed, shared experience, this concept easily translates into a common theme of art and design works. Artists and designers may address the anxiety that often accompanies approach of death, or daily manifestations of death and mortality. This use of death, mortality, and anxiety for dramatic effect is evident in the opening titles of *Dawn of the Dead*, which include images of blood and zombies (see fig. 1-16).

DREAMS. A dream is a vision experienced during sleep, or during a waking moment when the mind is allowed to wander, also known as daydreaming. Dreams can be fantastical, horrifying, confusing, or mundane. Nearly everyone experiences dreams and can easily identify them as an inspiration for, or subject matter of, a work of art or design. In Zachary Zezima's animation *Cruising* (2014), the main character daydreams at the edge of a cruise ship (Plate 2, color insert). The subject of dreaming is reflected in the formal choices; colors, shapes, and movements take on a fanciful look as the main character imagines himself at the bottom of the ocean. An excellent resource for learning more about dreams is PBS's NOVA program, *What Are Dreams?*

THE EVERYDAY. Many contemporary artists and designers choose to make work about the mundane, ordinary, and often overlooked aspects of daily life, which is called "the everyday." One's natural instinct might be to focus on spectacular or amazing events or ideas, but creating a work about the everyday can be an effort to showcase a specific dignity that comes with the small, underappreciated details of living. For example, in Joelle Dietrick and Owen Mundy's generative artwork *Anemophilous Formula for*

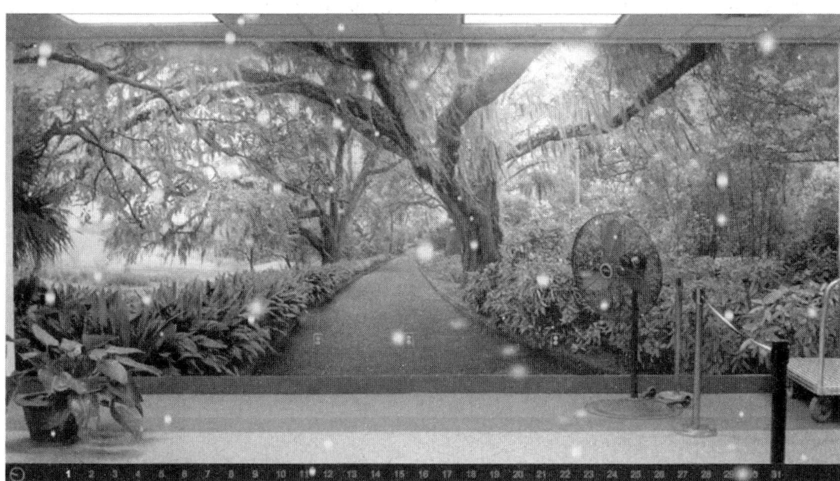

Fig. 2-1
Owen Mundy and Joelle Dietrick, *Anemophilous Formula for Computer Art* (2007), single-channel video and custom software, 3 minutes. Courtesy of the artists.

Computer Art (2007), a series of floating yellow-green dots increases or decreases according to the pollen counts at different times of the year (see fig. 2-1). Pollen counts are rather mundane, but in this work they are highlighted as a detail worth participants' attention.

FAILURE. Humans spend their lives seeking and striving. Inevitably, we have to deal with failure on many levels, from the mundane details of everyday life to the philosophical struggles of human existence. As Lisa Le Feuvre states in her book *Failure*, failure can consist of dissatisfaction, rejection, doubt, error, incompetence, or the result of experimentation. Failure is an interesting concept because it is a universal human experience. In Melati Suryodarmo's *EXERGIE-butter dance*, the repeated failure to dance on the butter bricks can act as a metaphor for struggles in daily life and the capacity or will to overcome them (see fig. 1-8).

FOOD. Food is a necessity for human survival, and therefore frequently appears as the focus of art and design works. The subject of food can manifest as the physical and emotional sense of taste, issues of scarcity and abundance, social functions and rituals associated with food, growth and decay, food as comfort, explorations of indulgence versus restraint, the physical process of eating and digesting food, various sexual associations, as well as the packaging and advertising of food. Siqi Song's animation *Food* (2014)

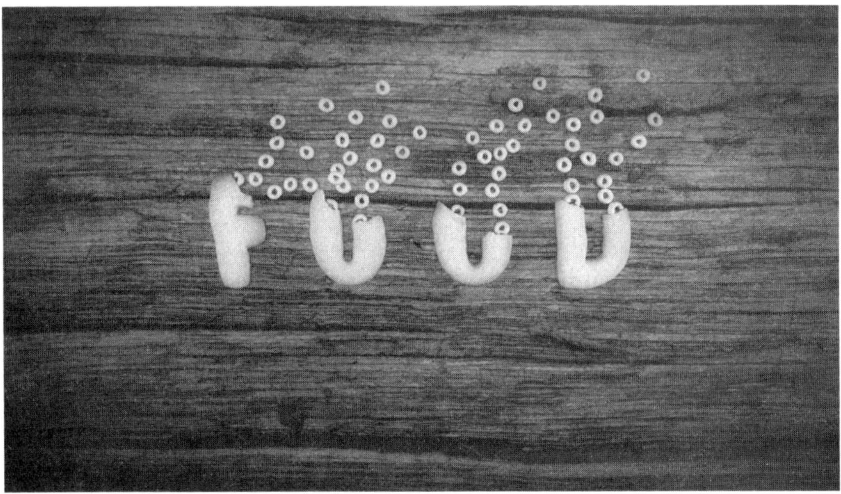

Fig. 2-2
Siqi Song, *Food* (2014), stop-motion animation, 3:30 minutes, dimensions variable. Courtesy of the artist. © 2014 Siqi Song.

not only uses food as the stop-motion objects being animated, but also addresses conceptual concerns related to food, such as vegetarianism, animal rights, and agricultural concerns (fig. 2-2).

HISTORY. History is the study of the past. Art and design have long embraced history by establishing and promoting specific histories. Fred Wilson's *Metalwork 1793–1880* shows the use of history as a central concept by focusing on the relationships between the production and display of historical artifacts (see fig. 1-11).

Exercise

Art21 has an episode about history (season 6). It features artist Marina Abromović, who discusses the importance of her personal history and legacy. The episode also focuses on artist Mary Reid Kelley's films based on historical feminist struggles. Write a comparative analysis of these creators. Research Abromović's work *Balkan Baroque* (1997) and Reid Kelley's *The Syphilis of Sisyphus* (2011). Discuss the subject, form, content, and context of these works. Identify and explain the use of any elements or principles you feel are central to the works.

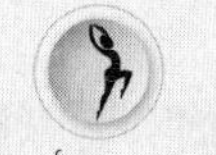 

performance   video

IMMIGRATION/EMIGRATION/MIGRATION. Emigration is the act of leaving your home country to live permanently in a new country. Immigration is the act of entering a new country to live permanently. A person in your home country would call you an emigrant, whereas a person in the new country would call you an immigrant. Emigration and immigration are controversial political topics in countries around the world. Similarly, migration—the movement of people or animals to new places to find better living conditions, whether permanent or not—is closely tied to many of the same concerns as emigration/immigration. These issues have proven to be rich ones for artists to explore in their 4D works. As an example, Cayla Skillin-Brauchle's performance *Certifying the Truth* (2013) touches on issues related to the difficulties of moving through a country different from your own by examining the continuous bureaucratic procedures necessary to maintain visas and affiliations in India (fig. 2-3).

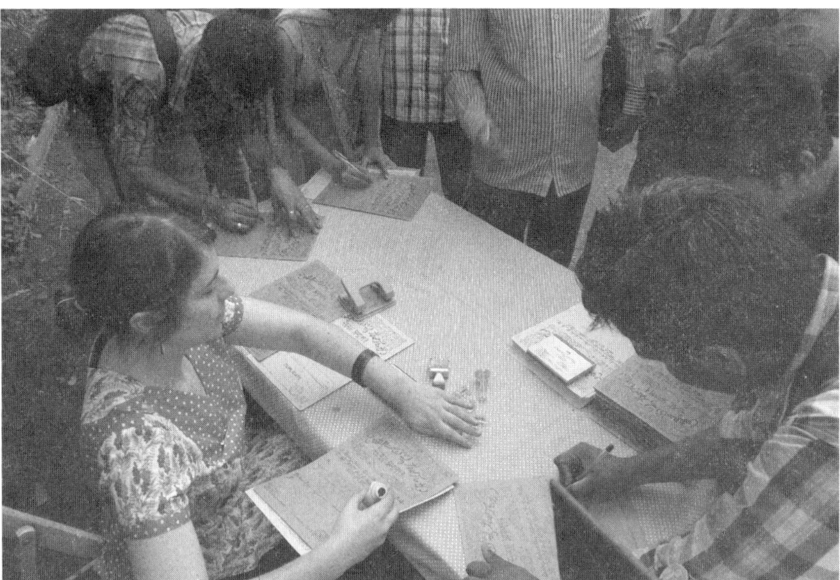

Fig. 2-3
Cayla Skillin-Brauchle, *Certifying the Truth* (2013), performance with printed book, dimensions variable. Photo Credit: JJ Gregg.

INTERPRETATION/SYMBOLS. Interpretation is the act of explaining something. Symbols are placeholders that represent something else. A person can interpret symbols. Artists and designers often rely heavily on symbols to convey meaning and create interest. Many games involve symbols. Think of a standard deck of cards, in which symbols designate the four suits: heart, diamonds, clubs, and spades. These symbols are interpreted differently based on the rules of whatever particular card game you are playing.

LOSS AND DESIRE. Loss is a feeling of grief when one is deprived of something or someone. Desire is the act of wanting or wishing. Through the cycle of life and death, these themes appear and reappear, making them a commonly understood idea at the center of many works. Janine Antoni's performance work *Lick and Lather* (1993) embodies these ideas. Antoni created the work by modifying seven portrait busts of herself in chocolate and soap by slowly licking away at the chocolate ones and washing down the soap ones to diminish their features. As the facial features were lost, the viewer is left with a physical embodiment of loss.

Exercise

Art21 has an episode about loss and desire (season 2). It features artist Gabriel Orozco's piece *Oval Billiard Table* (1996), which addresses desire as it relates to competition and games. It also features the work of Janine Antoni, including *Lick and Lather* (1993).

Write a comparative analysis of these two creators. Discuss the subject, form, content, and context of one work by each of them. Identify and explain the use of any elements or principles you feel are central to the work.

performance   installation

MEMORY/CHILDHOOD. Humans have an innate desire to return to home, whether that is physically, emotionally, or symbolically. Sounds, tastes, and smells can trigger particularly strong memories. Felix Gonzalez-Torres's *Untitled (Portrait of Ross in L.A.)* (1991) is an interactive installation consisting of 175 pounds of multicolored candies individually wrapped in cellophane, which participants are welcome to take. The pile of candy is an allegorical representation of the artist's partner, Ross Laycock, who died of an AIDS-related illness in 1991. The candy's weight, 175 pounds, corresponds to Ross's ideal body weight. As participants take the candy, the diminishing amount parallels Ross's weight loss and suffering at the end of his life. Gonzalez-Torres directed that the candy should be replenished as

Exercise

Artist Mike Kelley created a film, *Day Is Done* (2006), which pulled from Kelley's personal memories. Find and watch *Day Is Done* and write a descriptive analysis. Discuss the subject, form, content, and context. Identify and explain the use of any elements or principles you feel are central to this work, and describe how the work relates to memory.

performance

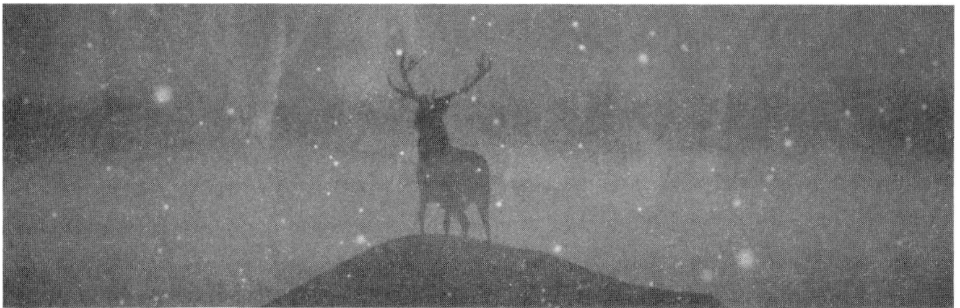

Fig. 2-4
Constantinos Chaidalis, *Beast* (2013), animation, 5:51 minutes. Courtesy of the artist.

long as the work is on display, which represents a symbolic immortality. The memory of the artist's partner drives the creation of this work.

MORALITY. Morality is the distinction between right and wrong. Some works hint at morality. In *Beast* (2013), an animation by Constantinos Chaidalis, the artist implies that the bullying of the main character is wrong (fig. 2-4). Morality is central to creating dramatic interest in this work. Other artworks set forth clear values without much narrative context or symbolism. Jenny Holzer's *Truisms* (1984) features a series of truisms, or moral claims, that are so obvious or self-evident that they act more as a reminder than as a revelation. These truisms are flashed one after the other on an electric display sign, broadcasting morality-based statements to anyone passing by.

NATURE/ECOLOGY. Nature consists of all non-human-made phenomena on earth. Ecology is a branch of biology dealing with organisms' relationships to one another and their environment. With the onset of climate change, these subjects are used more frequently in art and design. For example, in the Yes Men's performance *US Chamber of Commerce Goes Green*, climate change awareness is the main message of their work (see fig. 1-12).

Exercise

Find a location in a natural setting, and develop a 4D work that reacts to that space and its natural elements. Find a location in a human-made setting, and develop a 4D work that reacts to that

(continued)

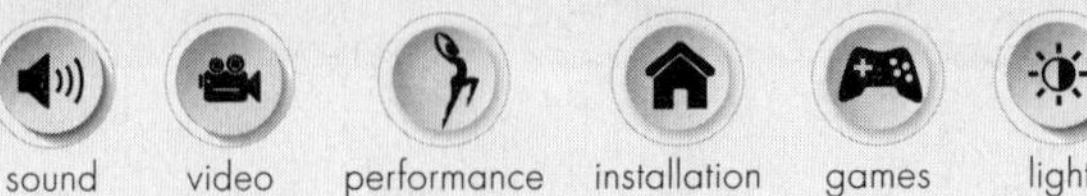

Exercise (*continued*)

space and its human-made elements. Both works should use the same medium (for example, if you did a game for the first work, you will do a game for the second work). Afterward, compare and contrast the two works. How did nature, or the lack thereof, affect the pieces?

PEACE/WAR. Peace and war have been, and continue to be, the subject of many works of art and design due to their seemingly ever-present nature. Peace and war are also closely tied to a variety of other subjects, such as money, religion, land rights, water rights, mineral rights, and so on, which are all closely related to the daily activities of people all over the world. For example, in the open-world video game *Fallout 3*, the cause of the nuclear fallout, which is the narrative foundation of the game, is a Sino-American war in 2077, caused by the scarcity of petroleum reserves (see fig. 2-5). This war-based narrative is a familiar one that allows players to immediately understand elements of this action role-playing game.

PLACE. A place is a specific point in space. Sometimes a place can be defined by specific architecture or other landmark. Places can be very important to people in terms of memories and a sense of home, and therefore they are often chosen as the focus of various works. An example is Pat Oleszko's parade performance and film, *Odds at Sea Bahian Odyssey* (2008), which is very specific to the Brazilian location in which it took place. The work would not have been the same without the place-specific ruins or the sea, which are used to bookend the beginning and the end of the work (fig. 2-6).

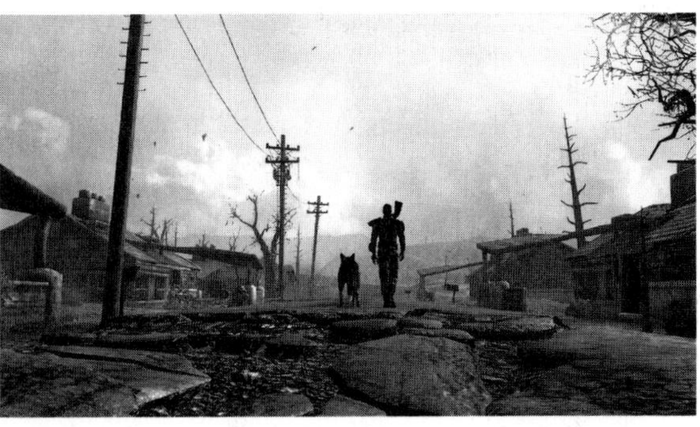

Fig. 2-5
Fallout 3, video game screen capture. Fallout® 3 © 2008 Bethesda Softworks LLC, a ZeniMax Media company. All Rights Reserved.

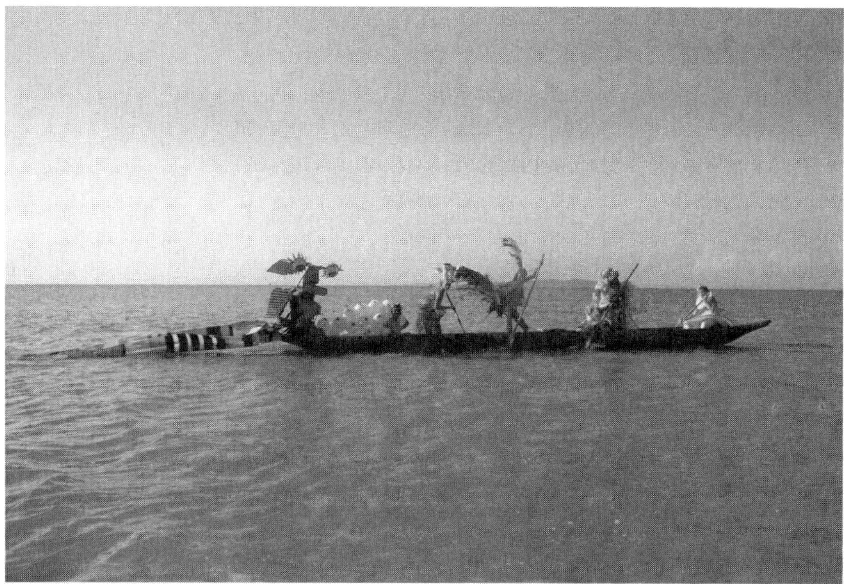

Fig. 2-6
Pat Oleszko, *Odds at Sea Bahian Odyssey* (2008), performance, 5-mile hike. Photo Credit:
Tamara Burlando.

Exercise

Go online and find the video "Meet in the Middle—Douglas
Paulson and Christopher Robbins," which is a part of PBS's *The Art
Assignment* series. Watch the video to learn about artists such as
Marina Abromović, Ulay, and Francis Alys, and then execute the
art assignment "Meet in the Middle."

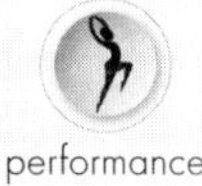

performance

POWER. Power is the ability to act in a specific way in certain contexts. For
example, the president of the United States has the capacity, or power, to
issue executive orders. Power, abuse of power, scarcity of power, and so on
are popular subjects to explore in art and design works because people
struggle with power and powerlessness on a daily basis. Stefan Prosky's

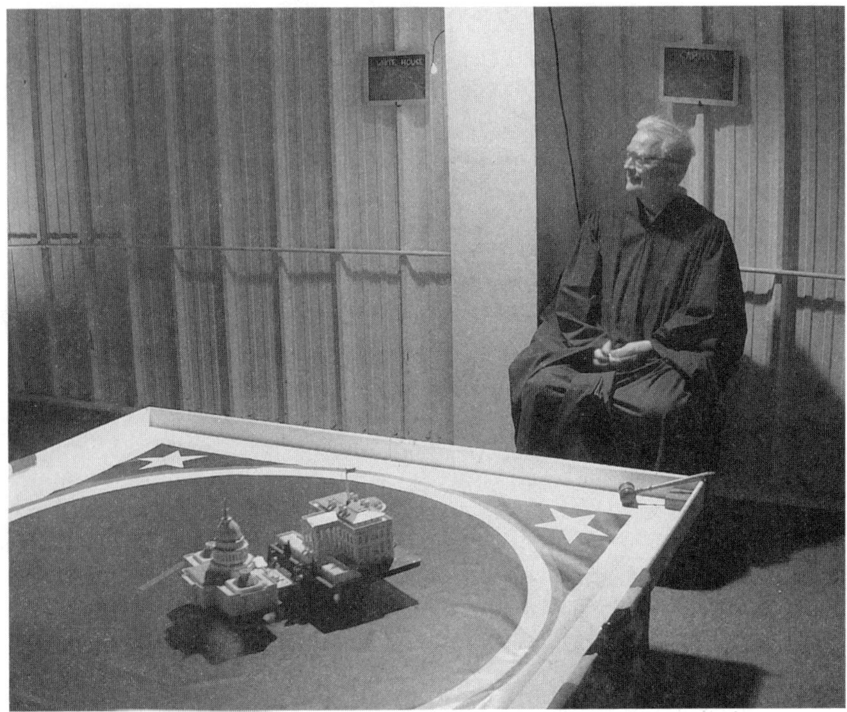

Fig. 2-7
Stefan Prosky, *Partisan* (2014), interactive robotic installation, 6′ × 6′. Photo courtesy of the artist; taken at Currents New Media Festival 2014 by Bill Mitchell.

interactive installation *Partisan* (2014) explicitly pits two power structures, the White House and the Capitol, against each other in the form of two equally equipped wheeled robots (fig. 2-7). The robots are programmed to attempt to push each other outside of a predefined ring. As they attack and shove each other, the robots embody the power struggles the actual White House and Capitol act out on a regular basis.

PROGRESS. Progress is forward advancement toward a goal. Humans strive for progress, whether it is financial, emotional, or physical, which makes this idea a common concept in art and design. Progress is the basis for many games including Tarn Adams's video game *Slaves to Armok: God of Blood Chapter II: Dwarf Fortress* (2006–ongoing)—better known as simply *Dwarf Fortress* (fig. 2-8). In this game, players control a group of dwarves who build a fortress. Progress toward a completed and thriving fortress is the central goal of the game.

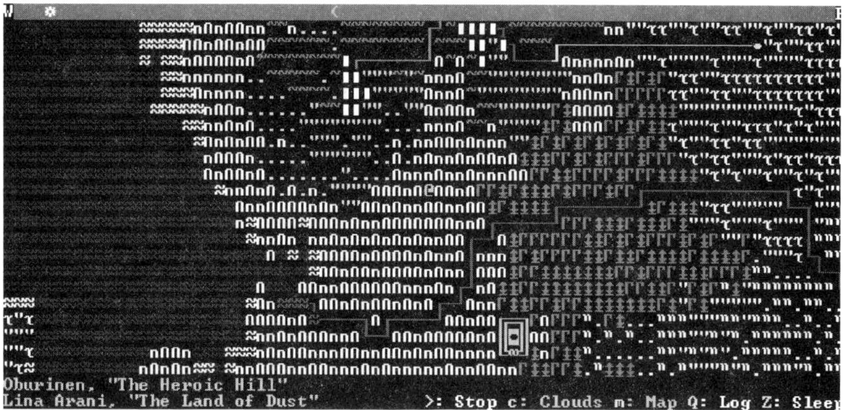

Fig. 2-8
Tarn Adams, *Dwarf Fortress* (2006, ongoing), video game, dimensions variable. Courtesy of the artist.

ROMANCE. Romance is a feeling of delight and mystique associated with love. Romance is one of the most common narratives used in art and design because people enjoy being in love, and people will expend huge amounts of time and energy to fall in love or maintain loving relationships. Love is a central theme in Eleanor Antin's short film *Love's Shadow* (fig. 1-18) in which the ballerina is shot by her lover.

Exercise

Find and watch artist Laurie Simmons's film *The Music of Regret* (2006), which involves live actors and puppetry acting out a narrative. Identify the subject, form, content, and context of the work. Describe how romance operates as a central theme in the work.

performance   video   performance

SPIRITUALITY/FAITH/BELIEF. Spirituality is everything related to the human spirit or soul, rather than the physical experience of being human. Faith is total trust in something or someone. Belief is the act of accepting something as true. All three of these ideas intertwine and can run parallel to

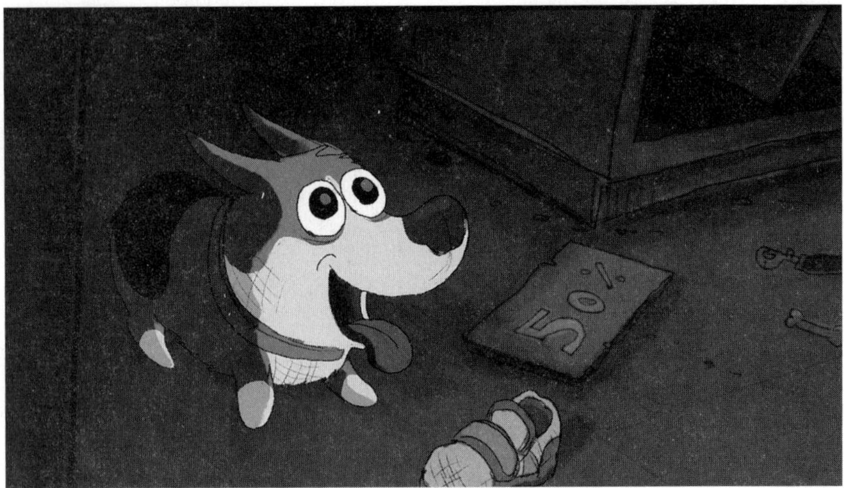

Fig. 2-9
John Kim, *Steadfast Stanley* (2014), animation, 4:11 minutes. Courtesy of the artist.

one another at times. For example, the dog in John Kim's animation *Steadfast Stanley* (2014) remains faithful to its owner despite a zombie apocalypse, and this causes the viewer root for the dog as it searches for its owner (fig. 2-9).

Exercise

Art21 has an episode on spirituality (season 1). It features the work of artist Ann Hamilton, in which she discusses a number of works tied to spirituality including *Volumen* (1995). The episode also focuses on artist James Turrell and his work on his light and space installation, *The Light Inside* (1999), at the Museum of Fine Arts in Houston, Texas.

Write a comparative analysis of the two creators. Discuss the subject, form, content, and context of one work by each of them. Identify and explain the use of any elements or principles you feel are central to the work.

installation

THE SUBLIME. The sublime is that which inspires awe. Things that go on infinitely and cannot be fully comprehended by the human mind, such as the nature of the universe or natural wonders of huge or microscopic scale, can cause this awe. The sublime brings participants to a place where logic and reason seem out of place, and transformation takes place. The mind is altered by the impact of this profound experience. Paul Pfeiffer's video work *Morning After the Deluge* (2001) shows both a sunrise and a sunset simultaneously with the horizon aligned in both. The work lasts the actual length of a sunrise/sunset and draws attention to a daily natural wonder (see Plate 3, color insert).

UTOPIAS/DYSTOPIAS. Utopias are imagined better places than current circumstances provide. The idea of a utopia comes from the human desire to make this world a better one in which to live. Utopian ideas can take the form of proposed living guidelines, city plans, proposed solutions to social problems, and so on. Proposed utopias magnify the problems in our society to ask whether we have the ability to change them. In contrast, a dystopia is an imagined place that is seemingly worse than current circumstances provide. Dystopias are often representative of innate fears or concerns shared by a culture. Ernesto Neto's *Walking in Venus Blue Cave* (2001) is a surreal utopian vision with emphasis on sensuality (see Plate 4, color insert). The nylon stocking fabric filled with Styrofoam beads creates large squishy forms into which participants can sink. This utopian environment seems void of the trials and tribulations of reality.

Techniques/Approaches/Media

ACTIVISM/PROTEST. Activism implies campaigning to bring about political or social change through the promotion of empowerment, criticality, and sustainability. Andrew Boyd and Dave Oswald Mitchell's book *Beautiful Trouble*, which calls itself "a toolbox for revolution," examines the many diverse practices that blur the boundaries between artist, activist, hacker, and dreamer. In an increasingly globalized and conflicted world, this is a growing segment of the art and design world. These works pose arguments for the viewer's or participant's consideration.

By incorporating activism into your art, or vice versa, it is assumed that you have a **message** and an **audience** you wish to reach. Therefore, it is imperative that your message is clear, and that your group (even if it is a group of one) is clearly branded. To **brand** yourself means that you distinguish yourself from others by creating your own narratives and designs to describe your identity. If you do not brand yourself, the media will brand you according to their interests. Accordingly, make sure you select tactics that reinforce your brand and message, and that are suited to your audience. Activism in art and design requires a lot of research and groundwork to execute well.

Often this approach to art and design incorporates much more communication, in a variety of forms and with more numerous groups, than other approaches. You will have to consider "staying on message" and "making your actions both concrete and communicative."[11] Your work may become tactical as you consider the people/groups that you are trying to activate, as well as those that may want to oppress your activism. At times you may consider taking up allies or using the law to reinforce your position.

An excellent example of this type of art is Reverend Billy & The Church of Stop Shopping, a performance artist and activist group that has created works such as *Seven Brides for Seven Corporations* (2013). This work protests "Citizens United," a Supreme Court ruling that states that independent political expenditures by corporations and unions are protected under the First Amendment and not subject to restriction by the government.[12] This performance consisted of ceremoniously marrying women to corporations to illustrate how unlike people corporations are.

Politics and nationalism are often closely tied to activism. Politics can encompass any activities linked to the governance of an organization, city, state, or country. Nationalism is a feeling of patriotism toward a specific country, and it often involves a sense of superiority over countries other than one's own.

Exercise

Watch *LaToya Ruby Frazier Takes on Levi's* (2011) in PBS's series *New York Close Up*. Analyze the work in terms of activism, and write at least three sentences explaining the work's relationship to activism.

performance

APPROPRIATION. Appropriation is the act of borrowing and transforming works created by others. One pivotal example is Marcel Duchamp's *Fountain* (1917) in which he signed a prefabricated urinal and submitted it as an artwork to an exhibition. A more four-dimensional example is Mike Kelley's *Mechanical Toy Guts* (1991/2012). In this installation, several mechanical toys have been deconstructed down to their mechanical cores, and have been strewn on the floor, writhing and squeaking, propelling themselves nowhere. This work seems to embody absurdity and emptiness.

Appropriation can often involve **recontextualization**, meaning that the artist or designer juxtaposes a familiar element—such as an image, movement or sound, and so on—with a context that is not typically associated with it. For example, Guy Trefler's short motion graphics work *Not Mine* (2014) is a reorganization of hundreds of popular culture icons. In each other's context, these images and animations take on new meaning.

Fair use is a concept closely tied to appropriation. It is a section of US copyright law that allows the use of published materials as long as a specific set of criteria are met. Fair use considers four points: the purpose of the new work; the nature of the original; the amount of the original that was borrowed; and the effect the new work has on the market value of the original work. While artists and designers have incorporated the work of others as part of their own work for centuries, it's generally better to be safe than sorry, and you should always ask permission to appropriate works when possible.

If you are going to appropriate work without asking permission, you should avoid uses that do not generate new artistic meaning. Changing the medium of a work is likely not enough to change its meaning. Always be ready to justify your new and specific objective that necessitated this appropriation. Artists and designers should avoid suggesting that the appropriated material is their own; instead, cite your sources. Again, if you do not do so, you must be able to articulate an aesthetic reason for not doing so.

Creative Commons (CC) licenses are closely related to fair use. Creative Commons is a nonprofit organization that enables the sharing and use of creativity and knowledge through a series of six free and easy-to-use copyright licenses. These licenses are simple and standardized in order to give the public permission to share and use licensors' work according to conditions of their choosing. The biggest benefit of CC licenses is that a licensor can state "Some rights reserved" rather than "All rights reserved," which is the default for standard copyright law. CC licenses are not an alternative to copyright; instead, they work alongside copyright to enable licensors to modify their copyright terms to best suit their needs.

ARCHIVES/ARCHIVING. An archive is a collection of items related to a specific person, place, thing, idea, or experience. An archive can be intimate, meaning it is meant for a single person's interactions, or it can be a place that you visit to see a sprawling collection. The term can also be a verb, as in "She was archiving the artifacts." Archives' meaning can change depending on how they are organized, where they are located, whose materials are in them, and who did the archiving. Archiving as a methodology has gained popularity with contemporary artists such as Mark Dion, who travels the world creating archives in many different environments.

Exercise

A **dérive** is an unplanned experimental walk through an urban space. The walker is guided by the subtleties of the architecture and topography, with the goal of a new and unexpected experience. Find a place where you can take a dérive, and while you are out walking, collect small mementos of your time. At the end of your dérive, arrange what you have collected into an archive that describes your experience. Think about the archive's presentation.

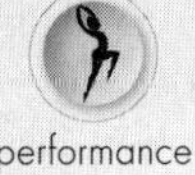

performance

CHANCE. Chance is the possibility of something happening. It is the uncertainty of a specific outcome. Some might refer to it as fate or luck. Many contemporary artists and designers rely on chance in the development of their work. In Paul Souellis's social practice inspired book *530 (Sá veldur sem á heldur)* (2013), he began by documenting a series of chance encounters with people, places, things, stories, and data in a remote Icelandic fishing village. The sections of the book were also arranged by chance. It was printed as a limited edition of 50, and many of the books were given away in a series of encounters within the village, some known, while others were chance encounters in the town's public spaces.

Chance is also closely tied to games. Uncertainty is a central element of all games; it implies that the participant could have an impact on the outcome. If a game is pure chance, some participants will disengage because they see they have no effect on it. Therefore, chance can lead to a sense of chaos or futility for some depending on the point of view of the participant(s).

Exercise

Go online and find PBS's *The Art Assignment, What, How, Where—Florian Rivière & Jim Walker.* This episode explains how to interact with an online chance-operating game, while also touching on works by the early surrealists. Execute a round of *What, How, Where.*

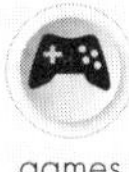

games

CHANGE. Change is the act of altering or becoming different. The world is full of constant change, so it seems natural that artists and designers would take up the idea of flux in their work. Artists and designers can also act as agents of change by articulating poignant ideas. Lighting Design Collective embraced change in their responsive light installation *Silo 468* (2013) (fig. 2-10). The piece includes algorithms that transform data into beautiful patterns of light by tracking a variety of ever-changing environmental parameters.

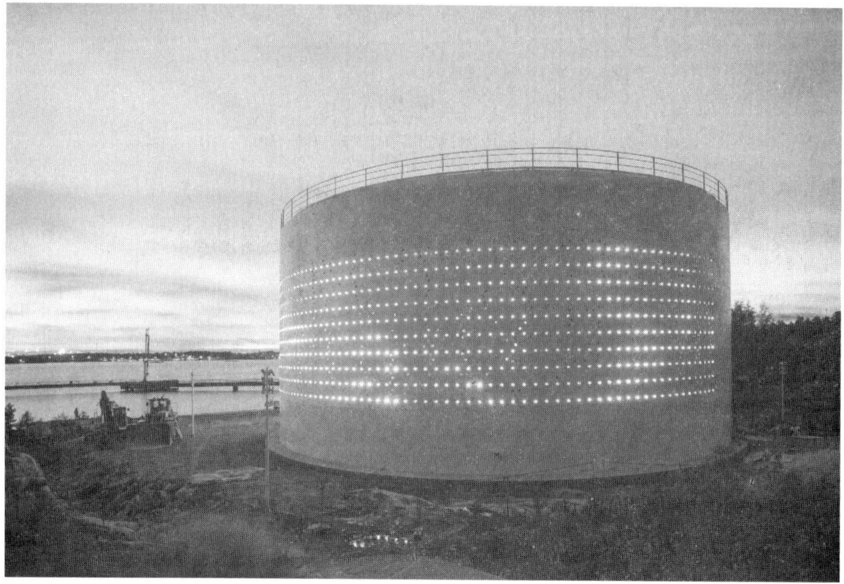

Fig. 2-10
Lighting Design Collective, *Silo 468* (2013), lighting installation. Courtesy of Lighting Design Collective. Photographer: Hannu Iso-Oja.

Exercise

Think of a change you recently experienced. Use that change as the inspiration for a 4D work. You can pick the media of your choice.

Hold a critique of all the works in the class. See if you can correctly identify the change that inspired each person's work. What led you to the correct guess, and what led you astray? Which works were more interesting to experience—the ones you were able to guess correctly, or those you guessed incorrectly? What do you think this means about creating works of art and design? Does it have any significance?

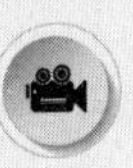
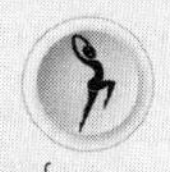

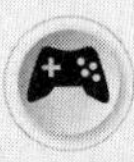

CONSUMPTION. Consumption is the act of using up a resource. It could be human consumption such as eating or drinking, or it could be monetary consumption, dealing with money and transactions. Mel Chin's site-specific installation *Revival Field* (1991–ongoing) explores a method of using plants to reclaim harmful metals from the soil. The site is located on a landfill where various types of garbage were disposed of and never adequately covered. The work underscores the harm that has been created by human consumption of natural resources.

Exercise

Think of a problem that is caused by consumption; no two people should choose the same problem. Develop a solution to that problem that does not involve money (think about alternatives to money; you may have to do some research). Create a short video commercial for your solution to present to the class. (This exercise is inspired by an exercise by Cesar Cornejo.)

COMMUNICATION/LANGUAGE. Language and communication are used on a daily basis. All art and design communicates, but some works take up communication as a central concept. Other works use language and narrative to convey meaning. Some works are made exclusively from text, which is closely tied to language. Fallen Fruit's *Public Fruit Maps* clearly communicate the location of fruit to participants, making the communication of this information central to the execution of this project (see fig. 1-6).

Exercise

ArtBabble.org has sections on both communication and language. View the short videos *Gu Wenda Describes His Artistic Process* and *Notice: A Flock of Signs*. Write a comparative analysis of these two creators and their use of language.

installation

THE HUMAN BODY. The human body affects how individuals create their identity. Humans can purposefully change their bodies through weight loss or gain, piercings, tattoos, clothing choices, hair color, and so on. The body can convey messages to others. Some artists and designers work with their body as a type of performative canvas. Performance artist Carolee Schneemann is well known for work involving her nude or semi-nude body in a variety of constructed environments, and designer Stefan Sagmeister has similarly featured his body in a variety of posters.

HUMOR/JOKES. Humor is the juxtaposition of a convention and an absurd treatment of it. Humor can act in many different ways: as a point of access for those outside the contemporary art world, as a salve, as a political tool, and so on. By engaging with people's sense of humor, some of their defenses can be let down, and important issues can be broached. Humans have been using this phenomenon for hundreds of years via political cartoons and theater.

Some of the main types of humor are:

- *Parody.* Parody is a mockery of a subject. It requires prior knowledge of the subject, as well as any meanings or impacts associated with the subject. Therefore, it is in the artist's interest to provide some signals of what you are referring to, so participants can effectively engage.

- *Frivolity.* Historically, this type of play has been embodied by characters such as the Trickster or the Fool, who indulge in foolishness and idle behaviors, but who are also privileged to speak the unvarnished truth. Therefore, on occasion frivolity can also be revolutionary.

- *Satire.* The basis of satire is juxtaposing a situation, person, or idea with its logical extreme, thereby humorously exposing its flaws. Satire is closely tied to the activist tactic of "hoax," which is defined as creating "a momentary illusion that exposes injustice through satirical exaggeration, or that demonstrates how another reality is possible."[13] The Yes Men regularly use this tactic to impersonate companies and expose important truths.

- *Slapstick.* Slapstick is a highly physical type of comedy including absurd high-energy situations, and over-the-top violent actions. Slapstick includes acrobatics and stunts, performed with impeccable timing. The name slapstick comes from a prop paddle that creates a loud slapping noise when a performer pretends to whack another performer with it.

- *Clowning.* Clowning involves identifying a specific point of view, as well as a sense of buoyancy and resilience. It is ridiculous and playful. Some clown categories include the simple clown, pathetic clown, tragic clown, and buffoon clown. Some forms of clowning will utilize the recognizable red nose.

IDENTITY/INDIVIDUALITY. Identity is the set of characteristics that define a person. Some artists engage with **identity politics**, which involves taking political action to promote the interests of an ill-treated or repressed group. These groups include those based on gender, race, ethnicity, sexuality, ability, and any other number of qualities that can build one's identity. Vanessa Beecroft's performative installation *vb35* can be interpreted as a critique of individual identity by posing a series of very similar looking, nearly naked women as a group (see fig. 1-5).

Exercise

Art21 has an episode about identity (season 1). It features artist Maya Lin, and her work to create an architectural and topographic installation in Grand Rapids, Michigan. The piece deals with the

identity of a specific location. Write a descriptive analysis of one
of Lin's interactive installations; it could be this one or another one.
Discuss the subject, form, content, and context. Identify and explain
the use of any elements or principles you feel are central to this
work, and describe her work with identity and place.

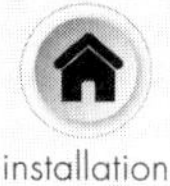

installation

METAPHOR. In literary terms, a **metaphor** is a comparison that does not use "like" or "as." One thing is another. For example, "Life is a journey" or "All the world's a stage" are literary metaphors.

A visual metaphor associates an image with a general concept or emotion. By putting a glowing halo over a person's head, it is implied that they are good, regardless of whether or not they actually are. The image of the halo is associated with angels through centuries of artwork and has therefore become a metaphor for "goodness." If you show a person with fire coming out of their mouth, it could be implied that they are angry. Artists can use specificity, or a lack thereof, to create visual metaphors that can be open to interpretation.

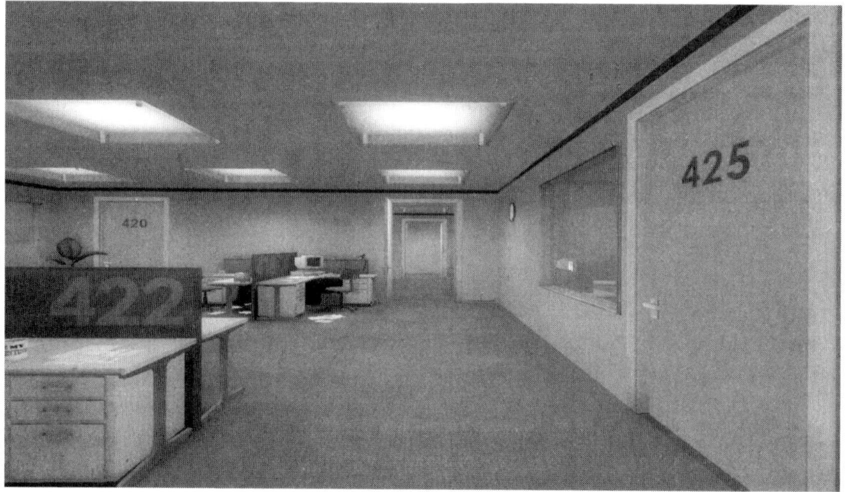

Fig. 2-11
Davey Wreden and William Pugh, *The Stanley Parable* (2011), game-play still, dimensions variable. © Davey Wreden and William Pugh.

PARADOX. A paradox is an apparent contradiction despite seemingly reasonable premises. Sometimes a paradox can express a truth in disguise. Davey Wreden and William Pugh's first-person exploration game *The Stanley Parable* (2012) engages the player with a series of paradoxical scenarios in which it seems you are making choices, but then you have no choice (fig. 2-11). The game will end, but it also seems to not have an ending. These paradoxes challenge the players to find meaning for themselves.

PERCEPTION. Perception is the ability to process or become aware of something through any of the senses. Many works involve the perception of light, such as James Turrell's "skyspaces." These are simply framed openings aimed at the sky, and rely on participants' perception of light and color. The experience of perceiving subtle changes to the skyspace is the aim of the work.

Exercise

Go online and find the video "What Is Something Repulsive That You Find Gorgeous?" on ArtBabble.org. Make your own list of five things you find both repulsive and gorgeous.

installation

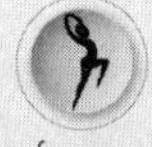
performance

SYSTEMS/STRUCTURES. A system is a set of connected things that form a more complex whole. A structure is an arrangement of parts that supports something larger or more complex. In a world bound by technology, systems and structures are central to the daily activities humans depend on for life. Therefore, it is no surprise that artists and designers often take up these ideas as the focus of their work. Cory Arcangel's video work *Paganini Caprice No. 5* (2011) was developed using a very specific system (fig. 2-12). The artist found hundreds of guitar instructional videos online and reassembled notes played in those videos to create a version of Paganini's Fifth Caprice. The work would not exist if the artist had not used this specific system of assembly.

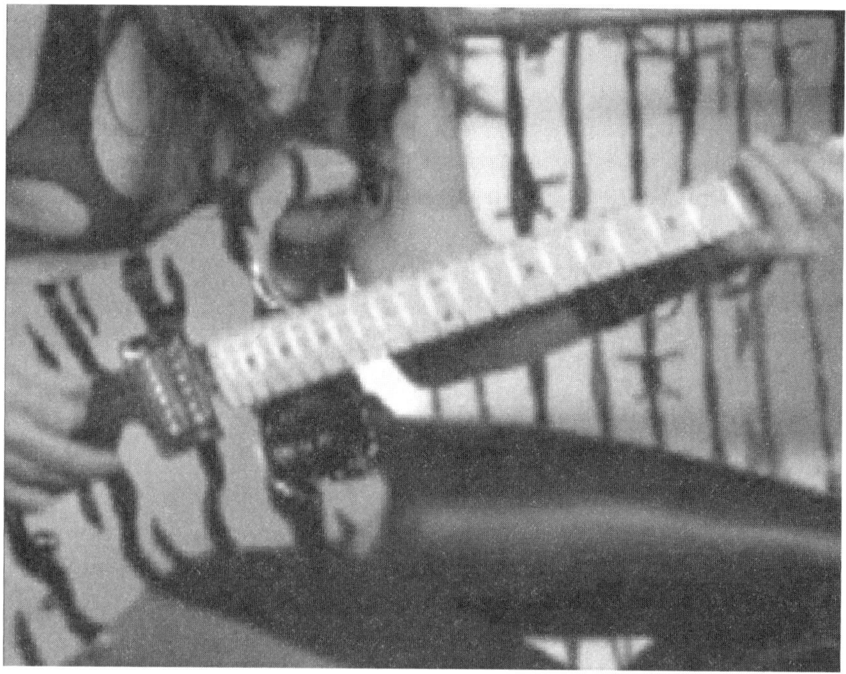

Fig. 2-12

Cory Arcangel, *Paganini Caprice No. 5* (2011), single-channel video. 3:41 minutes. © Cory Arcangel. Image courtesy of Cory Arcangel.

Exercise

Art21 has an episode on systems (season 5). It features the work of Kimsooja, who develops systematic ways of working, whether in video, performance, or installation. Also profiled is John Baldessari (see Chapter 4) whose work, especially the early work in video, is underpinned by a systematic approach. Compare and contrast the subject, form, content, and context of a work by two of the artists. Identify and explain the use of any elements or principles you feel are central to the work.

 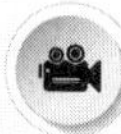 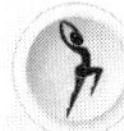

installation   video   performance

TRANSFORMATION. Transformation is a metamorphosis in structure, appearance, or ability. Every part of human life could be classified as a transformation, from birth to death. The human race has been transforming since it first came into existence, and similarly, the earth is always undergoing constant transformation. Artists routinely address this idea of transformation, including how humans transform the earth and vice versa. In Daniel Sousa's *Feral*, the adults attempt to transform a young feral boy into a socialized child (see fig. 1-19). The struggles associated with this attempted transformation create the necessary tension in the piece.

Summary

In this chapter, we've outlined some of the basic processes that are central to the creation of all artwork, including brainstorming, researching, building a narrative, and critiquing your work. We've also looked at some theories from gaming that are pertinent to the creation of 4D art, along with some organizing concepts and techniques employed by 4D creators.

Key Terms

antagonist   The villain we root against

audience   The people with whom you are communicating through your work

brainstorming   An active approach to producing ideas and solutions in a non-critical environment with emphasis on quantity over quality

brand   To distinguish an entity from others by creating specific narratives and designs to describe its identity

character   A person portrayed in a performance or work of writing

collage   A specific collection of sketches and imagery arranged by an artist or designer

critique   The act of discussing an artwork

dérive   An unplanned experimental walk through an urban space

fair use   A section of US copyright law that allows the use of published materials as long as a specific set of criteria are met

identity   The set of characteristics that define a person

identity politics   Taking political action to promote the interests of an ill-treated or repressed group

message   Your stance on a particular issue; relating to activism and protest

metaphor   A comparison that does not use "like" or "as"

photomontage   A specific collection photographs arranged by an artist or designer

protagonist   The hero we root for and who undergoes transformation

recontextualization   Juxtaposition of a familiar element, such as an image, movement or sound, and so on, in contrast with a context that is not typically associated with the element

setting   The location where a narrative takes place

testimonial   A statement referencing personal experience

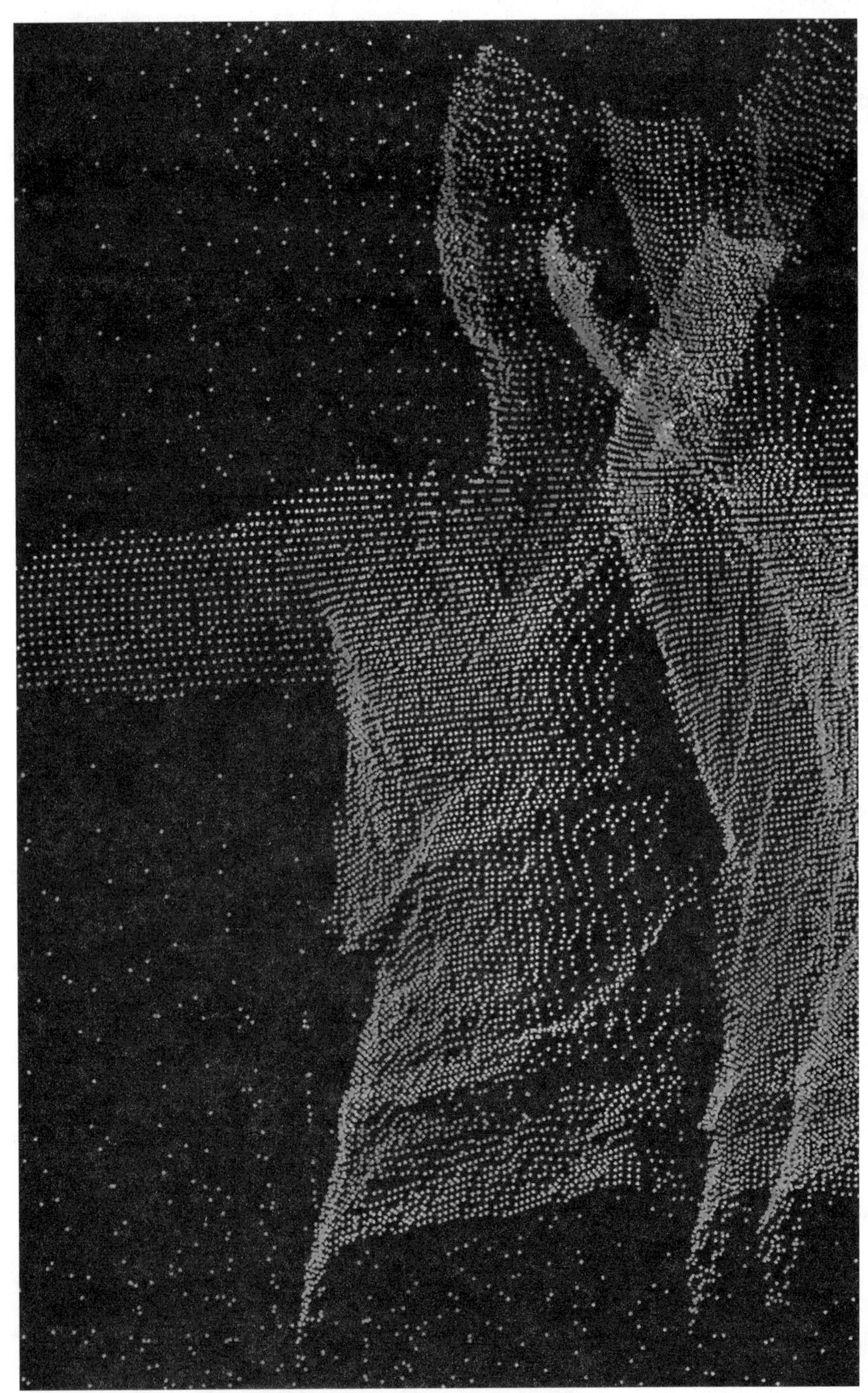

© Santiago Echeverry // Music © Felipe Ramírez Rodríguez.

Elements from 2D and 3D Art and Design

All works of art and design can be analyzed in terms of the elements and principles of design, which can change according to how many dimensions a work occupies: two (2D), three (3D), or four (4D). In this chapter, we will examine elements from 2D and 3D art and design that are also applicable to works completed in 4D.

Shape

In 2D and 3D design, **shape** refers to the outline of a form. Shape has the same definition when applied to elements of 4D art and design, such as architecture, topography, light, and movement. Thus, shapes can be stationary, moving, or formed by a temporary combination of the two. Some shapes are well recognized, such as squares and circles, while others, such as the outline of a spilled liquid, are more freely formed. Shape can be **organic**, meaning rounded and soft; **geometric**, meaning linear and angular; or a mixture of both. Shapes can work together harmoniously, or they can be purposefully contrasting. No matter what media you choose to work in, shape will likely play an integral role in defining and communicating content to your participants.

Exercise

Think to one of the first times you failed at something. Focus on as many details of that situation as possible. As you think about the event, try imagining any shapes you associate with this memory, both representational and expressive. During this process, brainstorm a list of at least 10 shapes. Evaluate your list. Do you notice any trends, such as similarities or differences, in these shapes? Using these shapes, plan and create a stop-motion animation that is no longer than 1 minute. See Chapter 2 for more information about stop-motion animation.

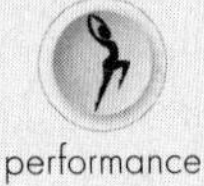

performance

Shape in Architecture

Shape appears in **architecture**, including buildings and other fabricated structures through and around which an individual can move. A wall could be rectangular, a window might be circular, or a doorway might have an arch. Shape in architecture can be used to reinforce, or work against, the audience's expectations. For example, Frank Gehry's organic architectural shapes contrast with our expectations of what a building often looks like. He uses flowing shapes to create this unique style and catch participants' attention rather than relying on more traditional shapes such as rectangles.

In contrast, some works will purposefully employ recognizably shaped architectural elements or spaces in order to direct your focus to other elements of the work, rather than the enclosure itself. For example, Shana Moulton and Nick Hallett's multimedia opera *Whispering Pines 10* (2010) was presented at the Kitchen in New York City, which is a formalized black-box stage setting. In this work, Moulton uses interactive projection screens to explore how people react to physical and psychological discomfort (fig. 3-1). The shape of the Kitchen is a very specific, enclosed shape that is instantly recognizable as a performance space. The shape of this space helps to direct the audience's attention to the movements and projections, rather than to the architecture that surrounds the performance.

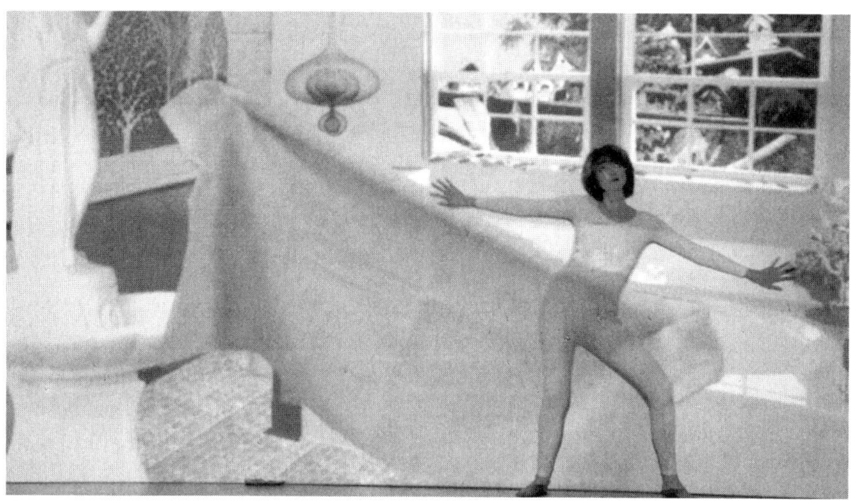

Fig. 3-1
Shana Moulton and Nick Hallett, *Whispering Pines 10* (2010), opera with interactive projections at the New Museum of Contemporary Art, dimensions variable. Courtesy of Art21.

Interview: Shana Moulton

My training is in music, but my career and practice encompass all sorts of time-based visual forms, including opera, lightshows, *son-et-lumières* in planetarium environments, soundtracks for film, live cinema, and installation. I like to call myself a composer rather than an artist, but there is not much of a difference in my mind between what those two things are. I'm ultimately interested in the quality of culture a work of art or performance creates and understand that music and sound are an essential element to activate 4D concepts. Within my collaborative projects, I tend to serve as a catalyst from the inception stage through development to a work's reception by an audience, taking on a greater creative role than would a traditional composer, engaging with concepts of dramaturgy, design, and integration of technology. I always work with the hope that the governing principles over the visual process are the same or connected to the ones I use to write the music. This incites the kinds of synesthetic responses I am very interested in.

—Shana Moulton

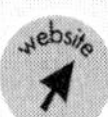
Visit the book's website to reader the full interview.

Topography

Shape is also present within **topography**, which is the physical nature or quality of the surface on which the work takes place. In Matthew Moore's earthwork *Rotations: Moore Estates* (2005–2006), he addressed suburban sprawl by recreating a map of a new division of homes being built on his family's farmland through the planting of crops (fig. 3-2). In this work, the shapes incorporated into the topography of the farm field are central to the content of the work. The 253 box-shaped homes were planted in green sorghum, and the winding roads of the development were planted in yellow wheat. Without this careful use of shape in combination with topography, the work would not have been as impactful.

Light (or its absence) can also be used to create shape. In the puzzle/platformer video game *Closure* (2012), the majority of the playfield is concealed in darkness (fig. 3-3). The player must use various light sources within each level to illuminate the environment and solve puzzles; areas that are within the light are structurally solid, while areas in shadow do not physically exist. Each light source creates a different shape, with its own spatial limitations. Light orbs illuminate circular areas but affect a small portion of the screen, while lamps can reveal areas at a distance—but only linearly—representing a small, spotlight effect.

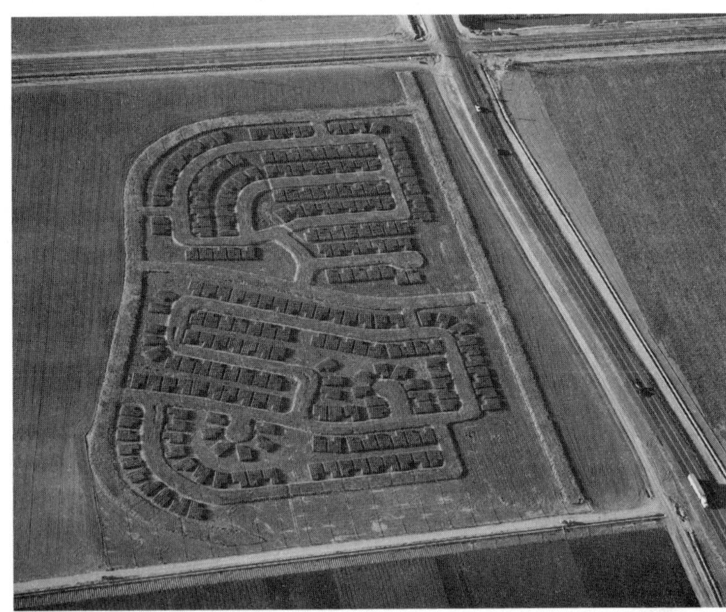

Fig. 3-2

Matthew Moore, *Rotations: Moore Estates* (2005–2006), sorghum and wheat on 35 acres of family farm, Phoenix, Arizona. Courtesy of the artist.

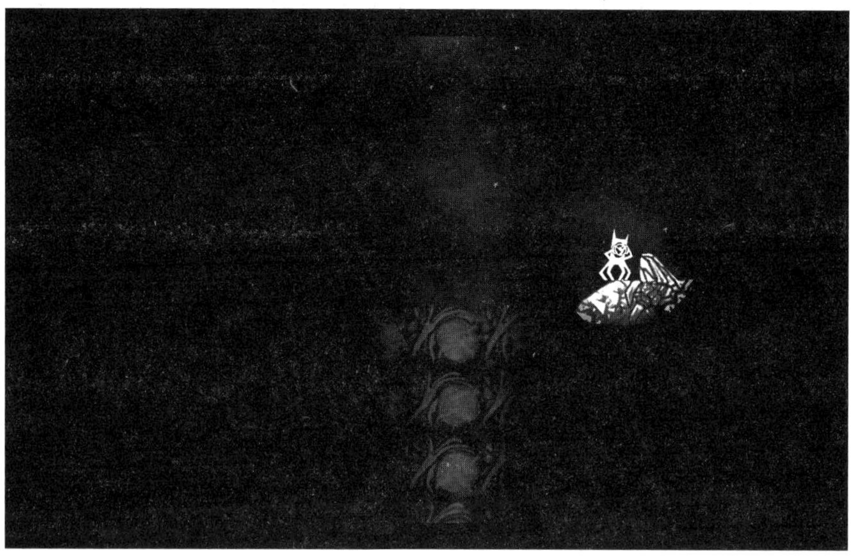

Fig. 3-3
Tyler Glaiel, *Closure* (2012), video game, dimensions variable. Copyright 2012 © Eyebrow Interactive. All rights reserved.

Interview: Tyler Glaiel

I am a programmer and a game designer. I work in very small teams, usually myself and an artist/animator and a musician, but I usually seek collaborators out after I have a prototype of a promising project ready. I have been programming since I was 11 years old. It's second nature to me now and I don't really think about the code much while writing it anymore; it's just like speaking a language. I work best when learning new things as I create though, so a lot of my work is based around my seeking out technical challenges. I don't make games that are just the same kinds of mechanics that are already in other games but with a different theme or story on top, I invent my own.

—*Tyler Glaiel*

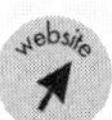
Visit the book's website to read the full interview.

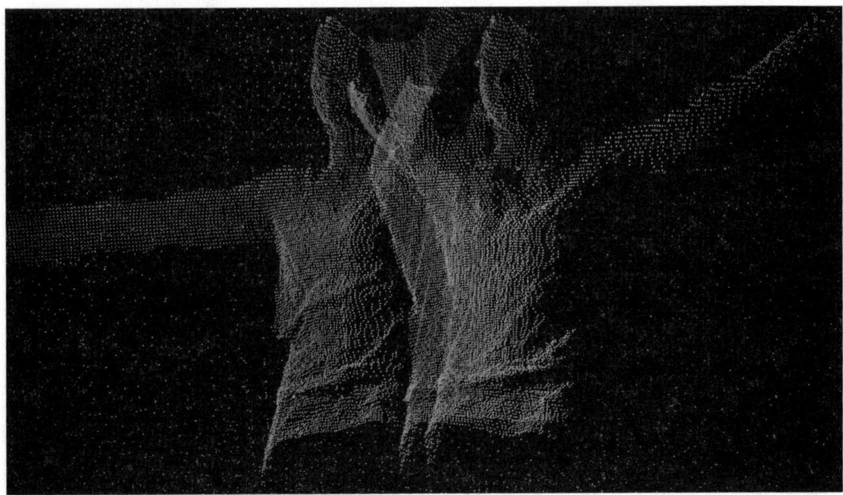

Fig. 3-4
Santiago Echeverry, *Orishas* (2014), digital video, 6:50 minutes. © Santiago Echeverry //
Music © Felipe Ramírez Rodríguez.

Movement

Movement also affects shape. In Santiago Echeverry's video *Orishas* (2014) he explores the Afro-Cuban water deities Yemayá and Ochún. He used custom code in Processing—a programming language—combined with motion sensors and a camera to transform movements of the choreographed dancers into a virtual representation of their actions (fig. 3-4). In this work, the specific shapes of the dancers' movements are key points of interest that create moments of transition that synch with the music.

Exercise

In this group exercise, begin by standing in a circle. One person will jump to the center of the circle and create a shape with their body. Next, a second person will jump into the center and add their body to create a joined shape. A third person will then jump in and add their body to the shape of the second person. Then the first person will exit, while the second person continues holding the pose.

People will continue to enter and exit in a specified order until everyone has participated. A shape made from two bodies is always in the center of the circle. This exercise encourages play and spur-of-the-moment brainstorming. The most challenging and important thing is to keep the momentum and rhythm continuous until every individual has participated.[1] After completing a cycle of the exercise, quickly execute a few sketches of the most interesting shapes you saw in the circle. Repeat several times, and keep this collection of shapes for future reference.

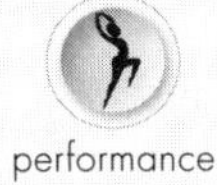

performance

Exercise

Start by finding a partner. Each of you will select an emotion but will not share your choices with each other. To begin, one of you will verbally tell the other how to move their body to express your chosen emotion. The face of the person being moved must remain neutral or unexpressive. You must have your partner move in terms of formal composition and shape rather than clichéd and overdramatic facial expressions. For example, if your emotion is despair, you might ask your partner to lie on the floor as if having just collapsed, and hide his or her face from view. Once you have arrived at a satisfactory body shape for your emotion, make sure your partner remembers the position for sharing with the class. Switch roles. After everyone has completed the exercise, compare and contrast poses and emotions. Whose body arrangements were most successful and why?

performance

Interview: Santiago Echevarry

Who are three artists that influence your work and why?

- José Alejandro Restrepo: He is one of my unofficial masters—he never was my professor—but he is an inspiring installation and video artist from Colombia who is able to see the world in powerful interpretations. He is a very intelligent, and a very generous human being.
- Leigh Bowery: He was the most talented performance artist in the UK. He died in 1994 of AIDS. He transformed himself into a work of art, and broke all stereotypes and barriers, modeling nude for Lucian Freud and scandalizing crowds giving birth to his own wife on stage. I admire his freedom, and "laissez-faire" attitude.
- Golan Levin (www.flong.com) is the perfect balance between an advanced knowledge of technology and art. He is S.T.E.A.M. incarnated (Science Technology Engineering Art and Math). I considered him as a pioneer in the field of interactive performance opening the door for a lot of us to follow his research.

—Santiago Echevarry

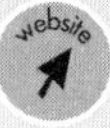 Visit the book's website to read the full interview.

Exercise

The artist Golan Levin is involved in coding and new media art. Go online, search for, and view Levin's collaboration with Zachary Lieberman entitled *Re:FACE, Anchorage Version* (2010). After watching the work, write down what you think are the subject, form, content, and context for this work. Also, analyze how the artists used shape. Compare and contrast your answers with others'. How are your answers similar and different from those around you? Were there any trends in the answers?

video   installation

Shape Defining Space

Different shapes can define space. The work of collaborative duo Luftwerk is an excellent example. In their interactive light and sound installation entitled *Luminous Field* (2012), they developed a rectangle-shaped projection field that was 80′ by 30′ in front of Anish Kapoor's highly reflective *Cloud Gate* sculpture located in Chicago (Plate 5, color insert). The projection field consisted of a grid of 384 animated, colorful tiles, which created a delineated, rectangular, playful space around and under *Cloud Gate*.

Interview: Luftwerk

Luminous Field was a response to the accessible and inclusive character of Millennium Park. We intended to create a piece that engages people to move and play with it. Taking inspiration from centuries-old Italian floor mosaics, the urban grid, pedestrian symbols, like crosswalks, and tessellation patterns of MC Escher, we began to animate geometric shapes into a colorful luminous field.

—Luftwerk

Visit the book's website to reader the full interview.

Another illustration of how the shape of a space can affect a work's content is given by the video games *Fallout 3* (2008) and *Passage* (2007). In *Passage*, the player is confined to a rectangle-shaped environment only 100 pixels wide by 12 pixels tall (fig. 2-5). Although the player can explore unseen areas above and below his or her current location, the experience is confined by the limitations of the rectangle and the steady, continuous advancement of the environment—from left to right—over time. In contrast to the highly limited environment of *Passage*, *Fallout 3* utilizes a vast, open-world model that encourages players to explore the virtual environments at their own pace and progression (fig. 3-5). By largely eschewing linearly arranged and clearly shaped spaces, *Fallout 3* places emphasis on exploration and discovery, allowing for a personalized—rather than a highly scripted—experience.

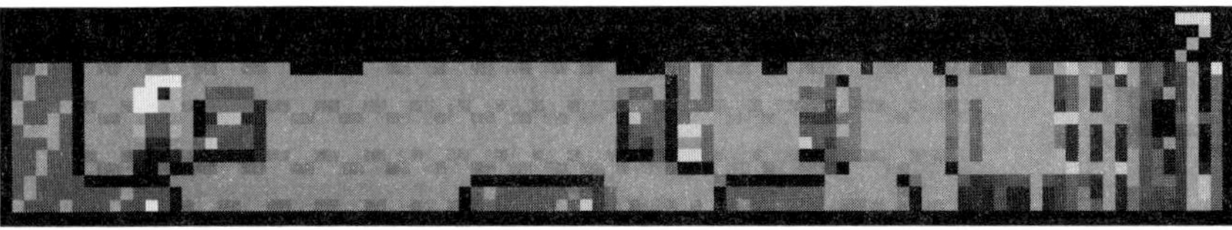

Fig. 3-5
Jason Roher, *Passage* (2007), video game, 5 minutes. Public domain.

Space

Space is a continuous area or expanse within which a work can take place. It can be digital or analog, occurring in two dimensions, such as a screen, or three dimensions, such as an architectural space. Space affects how the viewer or audience feels. For example, a crowded space will feel very different from one that is empty of people or objects. Similarly, a dark space will provoke different reactions than a very bright space, while loud spaces cause different experiences than spaces that are quiet. Nearly all the elements and principles of 4D art and design affect and define space, including architecture, topography, lighting, sound, and movement. Artists and designers must take all of these factors into consideration as they plan a work.

Exercise

Brainstorm a list of 10 memories that are important or powerful. Next, select one of those memories and analyze the space in that memory. Write down as many descriptive notes about that space as possible. Then, make a list of memories from the past 24 hours. Select one of those memories and analyze the space in the memory (do not physically visit the space to analyze it—just use your memory). Write down as many descriptive notes about that space as possible. Finally, analyze the space you currently are in, and write down as many descriptive notes about it as possible. Compare and contrast the three lists. Are there clear similarities or differences? Do your memories affect your ability to remember the spaces? Each student will present their findings to the class.

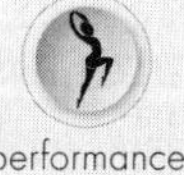

performance

The Base Plane

Space is often defined by the medium of the work. In time-based work—such as a performance, installation, videogames, or animation—it is interaction or activity in the work that generally helps define the space. This space of interaction or activity has a **base plane**, which is simply the horizontal field of space on which the action is taking place (fig. 3-6). The base

Base Plane

Elevated Base Plane

Depressed Base Plane

Overhead Plane

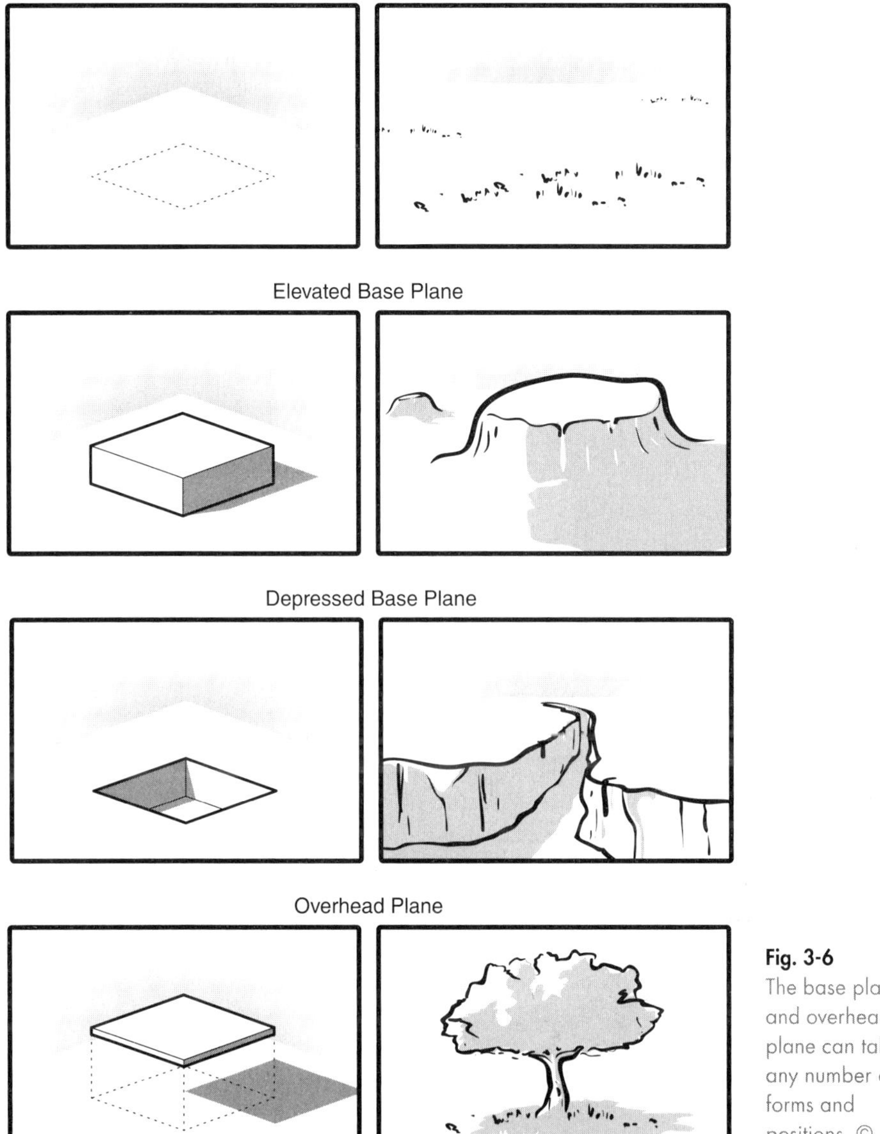

Fig. 3-6
The base plane and overhead plane can take any number of forms and positions. © Phil McCollam.

plane could be as simple as a blanket on grass or a pool of light shining on the floor, but some boundary will be implied, even if it is very imprecise such as "any paved street in North America."

The base plane might be elevated or depressed to further set it apart from the background or inactivated space. For example, some theatrical stages are elevated above the audience, while others are at the bottom of amphitheater-style seating. In natural settings, an **elevated base plane** might be a desert plateau, while a **depressed base plane** could be in a canyon or swimming pool. Additionally, spaces can be further defined by an **overhead plane**, which occurs above the base plane and further defines the boundaries of the space. Most commonly, a ceiling may represent an overhead plane. However, in outdoor settings, the overhead plane could be a bridge, a tent, or a tree with a large canopy.

An example of how planes are used in space is Dead Roman's animation *Spheres on a Plane* (2011). The planes of receding hallways and rooms create a mysterious and hypnotic environment within which spheres and other geometric figures hover and transform (fig. 3-7). The base plane is a central element of this sequence because it anchors all of the action and reveals the floating figures' relationships to each other. Another example of how planes are used in space, this time in architecture, is the collaboration between office furniture company Steelcase and Susan Cain. Cain is a researcher on introverted personalities. Together, this team has created a series of five spaces, *Susan Cain Quiet Spaces* (2014), to address the need for less distraction and more privacy in workplaces (fig. 3-8). These designs rely on semitransparent vertical planes as a means of creating quiet and focused spaces.

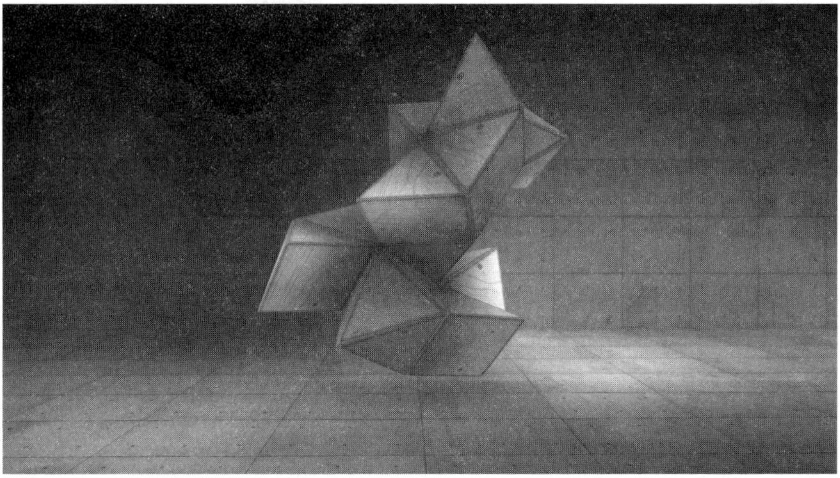

Fig. 3-7
Dead Roman, *Spheres on a Plane* (2011), motion graphics, 3:27 minutes. Courtesy of the artist.

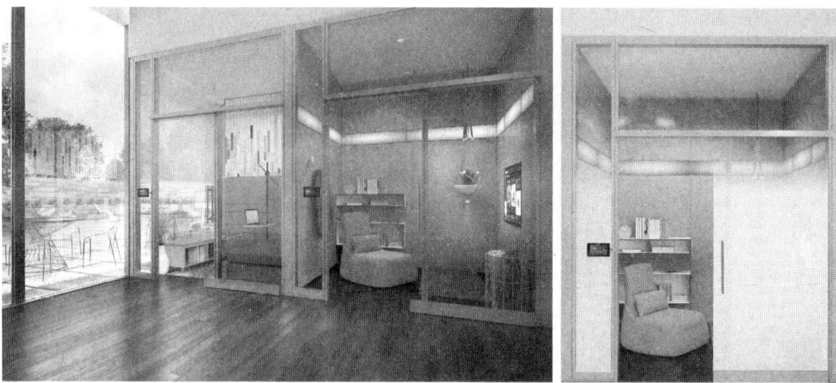

Fig. 3-8

Examples of *Susan Cain's Quiet Spaces*, including an illustration of the variable opacity film applied to the glass upon installation. Courtesy of Steelcase.

Exercise

Find a confined space in which you can do an interactive installation; the most basic examples might be a closet or a short hallway. While planning your installation, think about what advantages and disadvantages the space presents. How will the space affect the ideas you want to convey? Create sketches and descriptions for the installation that will help a stranger understand your plans. Do you need special lighting or sound? How will you entice participant interaction, and how will it affect this installation? Share your installation ideas and sketches in small groups. Give each other feedback on how you might improve each idea.

installation

The Rule of Thirds

Space can be divided in different ways, not only by adding or changing planes. One of the most popular methods for dividing space is using the **rule of thirds**. This rule states that a space can be divided into equal thirds by height, width, and depth (if you are working in a three-dimensional

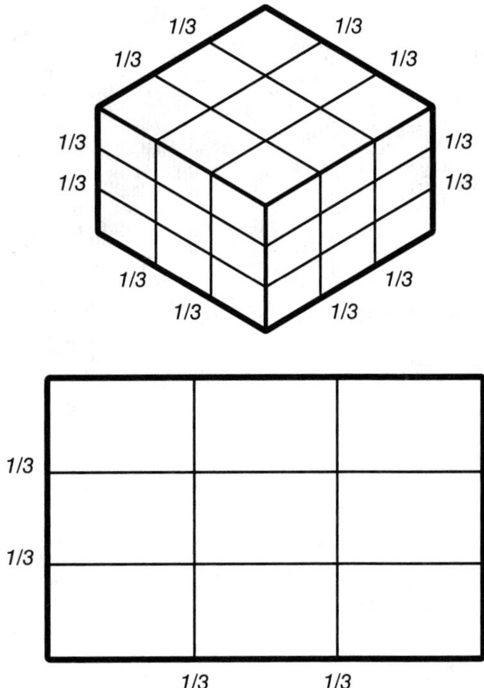

Fig. 3-9
You can divide a space into equal thirds by height, width, and depth. © Phil McCollam.

space). Where those thirds intersect are optimal locations to place your subject because it will often create a more interesting composition than centering the subject within the space (fig. 3-9). For example, in fig. 1-19, a still from Daniel Sousa's *Feral*, the boy's head falls exactly on the 1/3 mark of the frame, creating a scene that is more visually compelling for the viewer's experience.

Some artists intentionally break the rule of thirds. A good example is Bill Viola's video work *The Crossing* (1996) (see fig. 6-22). In this work, the performer is situated in the center of the frame on each screen rather on one of the 1/3 marks. This compositional choice reinforces symmetry between the two screens that could not be achieved as effectively with the rule of thirds.

Positive and Negative Space

Space can also be divided into positive and negative areas. **Positive space** is a form, or area of focus, within a larger environment; in contrast, **negative space** is the area surrounding the form or area of focus. In Joelle Dietrick and Owen Mundy's generative artwork *Anemophilous Formula* *for Computer Art*, pollen is represented by yellow-green dots animated in front of a wall-sized photograph of an idyllic forest (fig. 2-1). The work uses data from the National Allergy Board to parody computer art that simply crunches numbers to create random forms. The green floating dots are experienced as positive spaces, while the background is viewed as negative space.

Interview: Joelle Dietrick

I vividly remember how people reacted to *Anemophilous Formula for Computer Art* when I projected it in my studio. It was fascinating to watch people enter my studio at dusk and settle into the seats that I had across from the projection. Most seemed mesmerized by the projection and its bird sounds, allowing it all to put them into a sort of trance.

It seemed perfect projected at that scale (8 ft tall, 11 ft wide). Elements in the composition effectively extended the space: the photo of the photo helped them make a leap from the room into the artwork, the fluorescent lights in the projected ceiling stretched from the lights in my studio; the scene of nature echoed the lush Virginian landscape seen through my large studio windows. The path in the animation furthered deepened that illusion of space.

Another amazing moment was when my friend, an insanely clever woman with a fascinating past as an AP reporter in Beijing and Berlin, said I don't get it. We let her live with the piece for a bit, and she figured out everything in a few minutes, even down to the month represented. Having her watch the projection loop repeatedly through the month helped her to figure out, that the yellow flurry was not random, but followed a pattern, apparently linked to the days of the month. Furthermore, the colors, movement, and spatial illusions seemed to put her in a state that allowed her to meditate on the ideas. One of the biggest challenges with creating time-based work is getting people to spend time with the artworks.

—Joelle Dietrick

Visit the book's website to reader the full interview.

Using Sound to Define Space

Although we typically think of space as being defined by physical structures and boundaries, the arrangement of sounds can also create the sensations of being in and interacting with a space. If an artist places speakers around the perimeters of a specific location, it becomes immediately clear to a participant whether he or she are inside or outside of the space of the work based solely on the aural experience. By manipulating the sounds coming out of those speakers, an artist can imitate the feeling of various spaces, changing the perception of the space from a basement to a forest to a cathedral. Additionally, a sound can be made to sound farther away in space by lowering its pitch, and increasing the **reverberation**—also known as prolonging the sound—off walls and ground; the opposite is true for sounds that appear to be nearer to the listener. Through these and other manipulations of sound, a 3D or 4D space can be more clearly defined.

In 2D screen-based media, sound can help define space by implying what is happening off-screen on the right, left, top, bottom, or even behind the viewer. Sound can often be utilized in these situations to give a sense of distance. In John Kim's short animation *Steadfast Stanley* (2014), in which a loving and somewhat clumsy dog attempts to find his owner during a zombie apocalypse, we hear doors opening and closing off-screen, as well as hoards of zombies in the distance (fig. 2-9). Although most of the action focuses on the experiences of the dog, Kim uses sound to expand the space of his work beyond the edges of the screen, making the world of the animation seem to be much larger scale.

Visit the book's website to read an interview with John Kim.

Exercise

Sound is very closely tied to space. For this exercise, select some objects that can make sounds, like an empty water bottle, a bell, your phone, and so on. Select a partner, and find three different spaces in which to make these sounds. One of the spaces needs to have hard walls, one should have either soft walls or carpet, and the third space should be outdoors. With your partner, record your sounds in the three different spaces, and create sounds at a variety of distances from your recording device. These changes in location and distance will cause changes in intensity and timbre. **Intensity** is the amount and type of energy felt by the viewer or participant at any given moment. **Timbre** is the quality of sound as it is affected by the shape, size, and substance of any instrument creating the sound, including the human voice.

After recording, meet with your classmates in small groups to play back the sounds that you recorded. Use descriptive language, such as intensity and timbre, to describe where you think the sounds were recorded.[2]

sound

Using Light to Define Space

Light can also be an important tool for defining space. People are often guided through space by bright vertical surfaces (walls) in their day-to-day activities. Artists and designers can use these types of expected behaviors to their advantage as they create their work. In *The Stanley Parable* (2011), a first-person video game developed by Davey Wreden, set in a seemingly abandoned office building, the depiction of fluorescent overhead lighting is critical to creating a believable, relatable environment. In the game, the participant takes on the role of an office worker, Stanley, navigating a variety of choices and contending with consequences and recommendations from the narrator (fig. 2-11).

Lighting is also vital to establishing the mood of a space, which may attract or repel participants. Take for instance Olafur Eliasson's *The Weather Project* (2003) at the Tate Modern's Turbine Hall (Plate 6, color insert). This piece used light to emulate an indoor sun and to create a meditative mood. It attracted participants and set a mood where they felt comfortable engaging in faux sunbathing and other non-typical museum-going behaviors based on this artificial sun placed in a massive, vacuous space. It is clear that light is not only central to defining space, but also a key tool in setting the mood of a space.

Visit the book's website to read an interview with Davey Wreden.

Exercise

Download *Thirty Flights of Loving,* a nonlinear game by Brendon Chung (it costs $5) and play it (it lasts approximately 15 minutes). After experiencing the game, write down what you think are the subject, form, content, and context for this work. Analyze how the artist used space to guide the player or to evoke emotional responses. Compare and contrast your answers with others'. How are your answers similar and different from those around you? Were there any trends in the answers?

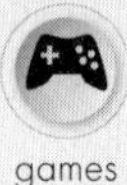

games

Altogether, it is clear that space can be defined and divided in numerous ways through the manipulation of light, sound, architectural, and topographical planes, as well as mathematical divisions, such as the rule of thirds. As artists and designers, your approach to space will be critical to the participant's interaction with and understanding of your concept.

Color

Color is our perception of different wavelengths of visible light. It functions in 4D art and design much like it does in 2D or 3D, acting as an expressive or descriptive tool. Keep in mind that colors can mean different things in different contexts. For example, black can symbolize death, power, or foreboding, just as white can symbolize purity, peacefulness, or cowardliness, depending on the context. The cultural context can also affect our understanding of color; in ancient Egypt, purple symbolized the earth, whereas in Japan a dark purple was considered an imperial color. Participants may consciously or unconsciously perceive these contextual connotations.

Color is still separated into three basic components:

1. **Hue,** also known as the name of the color (blue, red, green, yellow, etc.)
2. **Saturation,** also known as purity or intensity of a color
3. **Value,** which is the relative lightness or darkness of a color

In fact, in common image manipulation software such as Adobe Photoshop, it is possible to select and identify colors based on their hue [H], saturation [S], and value or brightness [V or B] using scales from 0 to 100 (Plate 7, color insert).

We can observe all three of these attributes at work in the opening scene of the animated series *Adventure Time*, season 2, episode 1. This series is set in the fantastical post-apocalyptic Land of Ooo, and it follows the adventures of a human named Finn and his best friend dog, Jake, who can magically change shape and size at will. In this episode, we see a variety of hues across the frame, with shifts in both saturation and value as space transitions from outside to inside the cave setting (Plate 8, color insert). Through these manipulations of color, the viewer gains details about the setting and mood of the scene.

Color is also a key descriptor of light, which is a central element of many four-dimensional works. White light is composed of a variety of wavelengths, each representing a different hue. When white light shines on a given object and we see a color, it means the object is absorbing all the hues except the one reflected back to our eyes. White objects reflect nearly all light; black objects absorb nearly all light. In situations where the lighting is very bright, colors appear more intense; in dimly lit environments, colors appear less saturated. This phenomenon can help direct focus in a work.

Color can also be added to white light by means of **filters**. These filters are generally placed in front of a white light source. They absorb all the colors of light except the color they are supposed to transmit. For example, a blue filter absorbs all light except blue. These color filters are often called **gels**, and are typically made of thin, transparent plastic sheets. Through the use of gels, an artist or designer can change the overall mood of a space using only colored light.

Primary and Secondary Colors

The **primary colors** of light are red, green, and blue (**RGB**). These three colors compose the tiny pixels of television screens, computer screens, and mobile devices (Plate 9, color insert). To create the different colors we see on these screens, the red, green, and blue lights in each pixel are adjusted to shine at different intensities, which causes our eyes to perceive different hues. This process is called **optical color mixing** because our eyes—rather than the displays themselves—mix the colors together.

When you mix two primary colors together you get a **secondary color**. For example, mixing red and green light makes yellow light; when red and blue lights are mixed together, you get magenta light; mixing blue and green light creates cyan light; and finally, when you mix the three primary light colors, you create white light. Therefore, when mixing the primary colors of light, we start with darkness and add colors that reflect into our eyes. This process of adding light in order to produce new colors or light mixtures is referred to as **additive color mixing**.

Additive color mixing is in contrast to **subtractive color mixing**, which subtracts the number of colors that reflect back into the eye. As pigment-based colors are mixed together, less and less light is reflected, eventually moving the perceived color of the mixture toward black. While additive color mixing is used to create colors of light, subtractive color mixing is used for mixing paints, inks, and pigment-based media. There are two sets of primary subtractive colors: red, yellow, and blue (**RYB**) for media such as paint; or cyan, magenta, yellow, and black (**CMYK**) for typical color printing, such as from a computer's printer.

Additive and subtractive color mixing can interact when colored light is reflected from a nonwhite surface. If you shine a red light at a green turtle, it will appear black because the green turtle is capable of reflecting only green light. A red light has no green in it, which means no light is being reflected back to the viewer's eyes. This results in the perception of blackness where the green should be (Plate 10, color insert).

White Light

White light has a **temperature**, which ranges from warmer (a hint of red/orange) to cool (a hint of blue). We encounter warm lights when we are in the sun in the summer, or exposed to a tungsten light bulb; cooler lights are typically linked to fluorescent bulbs or winter sun. Therefore, the temperature of the light you choose to work with can easily alter the mood of the work. In Thomas Hirschhorn's installation *Cavemanman* (2002–2006), he created an elaborate life-size series of cave tunnels and rooms—which participants can wander through—made of cardboard and packing tape, and illuminated with fluorescent lighting (Plate 11, color insert). A wide variety of books, cans, and photocopies are placed throughout the space creating a sense of chaos, hoarding, and paranoid plotting. The cold artificial glow of the fluorescent lights reiterates the artificiality and paranoia of the space, creating an environment that feels less relaxing or welcoming.

Exercise

Think of political topic that is important to you. Research the opposing viewpoint using online image searches, news sources, history books, and even dictionaries and thesauruses. Using these research materials, create a stop-motion animation that embodies and supports the opposing viewpoint. Use color to help illustrate this viewpoint. With a partner, view each other's animations and see if you can explain why various color choices were made and how those choices affect your perception of the topic. See Chapter 2 for more information about stop-motion animation.

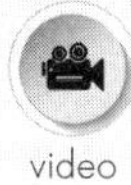
video

WHITE BALANCING. When you are shooting video or photography in a space with white light or natural daylight, you always have to adjust your camera to match the light's temperature. If you are in an area lit by tungsten bulbs, the light will be warmer, and if you are in an area with fluorescent bulbs, the light will be cooler. Similarly, if it is a bright and clear sunny day, the light produced by the sun and atmosphere will be warmer than on a cloudy, overcast day, which results in cooler environmental light. In Plate 12, the first image has an overly warm color cast; the second image has been properly white-balanced, making the objects appear more natural (see Plate 12, color insert).

White balancing is adjusting your camera to record a true white according the temperature of any given light source. Some cameras have a setting for automatically white balancing, or a collection of presets for tungsten or fluorescent lights, cloudy days versus sunny days, shade, or indoor versus outdoor photography. On many cameras you can adjust the white balance yourself by holding a piece of white paper in front of the camera and then adjusting the settings until the white looks correct. Making this adjustment to your camera will help you avoid a cool or warm color cast across your image.

CHROMA KEYING. Sometimes when you are shooting video, you want to insert a different background behind your subject. This can be achieved through **chroma keying**, a technique for compositing two images or video clips together by masking a particular color range. For example, weather forecasters on the news use chroma keying to display a variety of maps behind them. This method involves placing your subject in front of a highly saturated green or blue background, and then using software to make that color transparent, revealing another image or clip behind the first. This process allows an artist or designer to shoot one object or person—such as a person in a car—and insert moving imagery behind it—such as trees moving by at high speed.

The highly saturated, uniform background of blue or green is used because these colors are most different from human skin tones. When using chroma keying, nothing in the foreground, such as a person's clothes or skin, can match the color of the background you intend to remove. Anything that includes the keyed color will be made transparent. For example, if someone wore a bright green blazer that was similar to the green of the background, then that person's blazer would become transparent, creating a floating head effect.

Peter Campus in *Three Transitions* (1973) uses this phenomenon specifically for its surreal quality. In this video work, Campus slowly applies makeup to his face and uses the makeup color to chroma key his face out. As the image behind his face is slowly revealed, it becomes clear that the image is another clip of his face, creating a mask-like effect of his own face.

Relative Color

Color is relative, meaning that our perception of color changes depending on the surroundings. For example, colors can appear more intense when two complementary colors are placed next to each other; this creates an effect that is called **simultaneous contrast**. Simultaneous contrast often results in a sensation of the colors vibrating at the juncture where they touch. (See Plate 9 for an illustration of complementary colors.) There is a great deal of simultaneous contrast in Yayoi Kusama's immersive installation *Obliteration Room* (2012) (see Plate 15, color insert). As a part of this installation, participants were each asked to apply a sheet of colorful dot-shaped stickers to all the surfaces of a white room. As more and more dots were applied, more instances of simultaneous contrast arose in which red dots were placed next to green dots or blue dots were placed next to orange dots.

Additionally, when you mix two complementary colors *of light*, your brain will read the resulting light mixture as white. For example, if you mix blue and yellow, green and magenta, or red and cyan, you get white light. (See Plate 9 to see the additive mixing chart.) In fact, your brain reads this mixed white as more vibrant than a single white light because of the mixing of colors.

Another phenomenon is called **afterimage**, which is a "ghost image" that is visible after a participant looks away from the original object. It occurs when a participant looks at a bright color or light for an extended period of time then looks away. The ghost image will appear in the viewer's field of vision, even though the actual object may not be within sight. You can try this experiment by staring at Plate 6 (Olafur Eliasson's *The Weather Project*) for 10 seconds, and then looking at a white sheet of paper. You will notice the afterimage where the sun form was located.

Exercise

Brainstorm a list of 10 problems that you regularly encounter during your daily activities. For example, you might list finding a parking space or getting out of bed on time. Next, brainstorm three solutions to each problem: these do not have to be solutions based in reality; use your imagination. Select your favorite problem/solution pair and create a 15-second public service announcement (PSA) video related to the problem and its solution, using color to emphasize your message. If you need inspiration, do an online search for "The More You Know," which is a series of PSAs that have been running for over 25 years. At critique, ask which PSAs are most effective and explain why. For each PSA, determine how color affected its message and effectiveness.

video

Color Schemes

There are many rules and systems that can guide your choices when selecting color groupings, including a variety of color wheels (see Plate 13, color insert). Interior designers know that cool colors such as green, blue, and violet are often used for passive-activity spaces—like hospitals—while warm colors such as red, orange, and yellow are often used for more active spaces—such as fast food restaurants—because of their physiological effect on humans.

Color schemes, specific and pleasing groupings of color, have been created that provide guidance for designers and artists. For example, a **monochromatic color scheme** consists of a hue and its tints and shades, which are the hue mixed with white (**tints**) or black (**shades**). Plate 14 (color insert) shows a red monochromatic still from Glitter Chariot's music video *Should Have Been Blonde* (2012).

The 12-color RYB color wheel demonstrates a variety of established color schemes (Plate 9, color insert):

- An **analogous color scheme** consists of three colors that are immediately next to one another on a 12-color color wheel (such as red, red-orange, and orange).
- A **complementary color scheme** is a pairing of two colors that are directly across from each other on a color wheel (such as red and green).
- A **split-complementary color scheme** consists of a single color and the two colors on either side of the color's complement (such as red, blue-green and yellow-green).
- A **triadic color scheme** is composed of three colors that form an equilateral triangle on a 12-color color wheel (such as red, blue, and yellow).
- A **tetradic color scheme** is composed of a collection of 4 colors that are connected by a rectangle on a 12-color color wheel, and consist of two complementary pairs (such as red, orange, green, and blue).
- A **square color scheme** includes a collection of 4 colors that are connected by a square on a 12-color color wheel (such as red, yellow-orange, green, and blue-violet).

Artists and designers may choose to limit or expand the use of color and color schemes in their work for a variety of effects on participants. In Rachel Maclean's video *Over the Rainbow* (2013), she purposefully uses a full range of highly saturated colors, rather than selecting a specific, limited color scheme. This choice helps illustrate a surreal, psychedelic world that critiques notions of purity as portrayed by commercial children's television programming and pop culture, as well as highlights who does and does not have a voice in pop culture (Plate 1, color insert). The work follows a range of constantly changing, highly colorful characters through a fractured narrative created through sound clips borrowed from pop culture sources. The intensely saturated colors of the characters remind viewers of the overly saturated, puppet-populated worlds of children's media.

Interview: Rachel Maclean

Over the Rainbow was produced as part of a 6-month residency at The Banff Centre in Alberta, Canada, which is an arts complex within a national park. While I was there I became interested in ideas of natural omens or portents and the symbol of the rainbow became the focus of this. I was intrigued by the myriad uses of the rainbow and rainbow colors, as a natural phenomenon as well as appearing in children's television, psychedelic art, and as a symbol of gay pride. It appears to be an exclusively positivist representation, alluding to other worlds, childish utopias, altered perception, and ideals of an accepting and tolerant social space.

"Over the Rainbow" is the longest and probably the most ambitious video I've made to date and ended up taking about two years to finish. There are several characters within the film, which are all played by me and include a baby-blue dog, faceless clones and a talent show judge in 18th-century dress. Like most of my work, the film uses an array of found audio taken from a variety of sources, specifically horror films, children's television, Hollywood movies, and most notably several covers of "Over the Rainbow" from *The Wizard of Oz.*

—*Rachel Maclean*

 Visit the book's website to reader the full interview.

Exercise

Artist Paul McCarthy uses color as one tool to explore concepts of the grotesque. Go online, search for, and view McCarthy's video entitled *Painter* (1995). After watching the work, write down what you think are the subject, form, content, and context for this work. Analyze how the artists used color. Did color affect the meaning or interpretation of the work? Compare and contrast your answers with others', and determine how your answers are similar and different from those around you. Finally, determine whether there were any trends in the answers.

video

Changing Color over Time

In four-dimensional art and design, color can be dynamic, or capable of change over time. Ruairi Glynn and Alma-nac's *Balls!* (2014) is a light installation that acts as an architectural toy and a system of interaction and ownership of space (Plate 13, color insert). For the first half of the month-long installation, the balls responded to sound levels within the building: rising, falling, changing color, and clustering as they reacted to ambient noise and vibrations. For the second half of the month, the building's users learned how to manipulate the light installation through workshops that explained the open source system. The balls could be programmed to react to various inputs; to play a game on or with; or to display anything that could be translated into sound, color, and form. This work illustrates how artists and designers can use dynamic color changes to engage participants.

Overall, it is important for artists and designers to ask questions about color use, including: What colors and how many will be present in the piece? Will the work adhere to a specific color scheme? Do the colors work with or against one another? What are the contextual associations with the colors being used? Do I want the color to be consciously or unconsciously perceived? Thus, it is necessary to research and clearly establish the purpose of color in your work, making conscious decisions that render your work more effective.

Exercise

Brainstorm a list of five major changes that occurred in your life. For example, you might list the day a sibling was born or the day you graduated from high school. Then, create a self-portrait inspired by these five changes using a four-dimensional media of your choice. As you develop the work, allow color to take a central role in communicating your message. After completing the work, the whole class will critique the use of color throughout the piece. Ask how each artist or designer has most effectively used hue, saturation, and value. Would a specific color scheme have helped clarify the work? What color-based components of the work could be strengthened?

 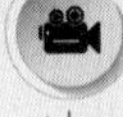   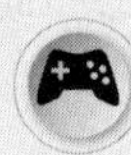 

sound   video   performance   installation   games   light

Summary

In this chapter, we've examined some elements of 2D and 3D design that are also found in 4D works:

- Shape, including its effect on architecture and movement, and how shape can be used to define space
- Space, including important concepts like the base plane and the rule of thirds, as well as using sound and light to define space
- Color, including understanding the difference between primary and secondary colors, how white light acts, how our perception of color changes depending on our surroundings (relative color), developing color schemes for a work, and how changing color over time can enhance a work

These elements have to be considered whether a 4D artist is dealing with architecture, topography, light, movement, sound, energy dynamics, interactivity, or spatial relationships. Having a working knowledge of each element will help you better conceive of and create your own 4D works.

Key Terms

additive color mixing   The process of mixing colors of light

afterimage   A "ghost image" that is visible after a participant looks away from the original object

analogous color scheme   Three colors that are directly next to one another on a 12-color color wheel

architecture   Buildings and other built structures through and around which an individual can move

base plane   The horizontal field of space on which action takes place

chroma keying   A technique for compositing two images or video clips together by masking a particular color range

color   The perception of different wavelengths of visible light

color schemes   Specific, pleasing groupings of color

complementary color scheme   Pairing of two colors that are directly across from each other on a color wheel

CMYK   Acronym for cyan, magenta, yellow, and black: the primary colors for printing processes

depressed base plane   A horizontal field of space on which action takes place below participants

elevated base plane   A horizontal field of space on which action takes place above participants

filters   Generally placed in front of a white light source to alter the quality of the light

gels   Filters made of thin transparent plastic sheets placed in front of a white light source to absorb all the colors of light except the color they are supposed to transmit

geometric shape   Linear and angular

hue   The name of a color (blue, red, green, yellow, etc.)

intensity   The amount and type of energy felt by the viewer or participant at any given moment

monochromatic color scheme   A grouping of colors that consists of only one hue and its tints and shades

negative space   The area surrounding the form or area of focus

optical color mixing   The process whereby the human eye mixes two or more colors together because they are physically close to each other

organic shape   Rounded and soft

overhead plane   A horizontal field of space that occurs above the base plane and further defines the boundaries of the space

positive space   A form or area of focus within a larger space

primary colors   The irreducible colors that can be mixed together to create additional colors; there are different primaries for light, pigment, and ink printing processes

reverberation   Prolonging a sound

RGB   Acronym for red, green, and blue: the primary colors of light

rule of thirds   A guide stating that you can divide any space into equal thirds, by height, width, and depth, and where those thirds intersect are good locations to place your subject

RYB   Acronym for red, yellow, blue: the primary colors of pigment-based mixing

saturation   Purity or intensity of a color

secondary color   The result of mixing two primary colors together to reach a hue exactly balanced between the two primaries

shade   The mixture of a pigment-based color with black

shape   The outline of a form

simultaneous contrast   The visual effect in which two complementary colors placed next to each other appear more intense

space   A continuous area or expanse within which a work can take place

split-complementary color scheme   On a 12-color color wheel, this is a single color and the two colors on either side of the color's complement

square color scheme   On a 12-color color wheel, this is a collection of 4 colors that are connected by a square

subtractive color mixing   The process of mixing pigment-based colors

temperature   The relative warmth (a hint of red/orange) or coolness (a hint of blue) of white light

tetradic color scheme   On a 12-color color wheel, this is a collection of 4 colors that are connected by a rectangle, and consist of two complementary pairs

timbre   The quality of sound as it is affected by the shape, size, and substance of any instrument creating the sound including the human voice

tint   The mixture of a pigment-based color with white

topography   The physical nature or quality of the surface on which the work takes place

triadic color scheme   On a 12-color color wheel, these are colors that form an equilateral triangle

value   Relative lightness or darkness (can refer to color or light)

white balancing   Camera adjustment to record a true white according the temperature of a given lighting situation

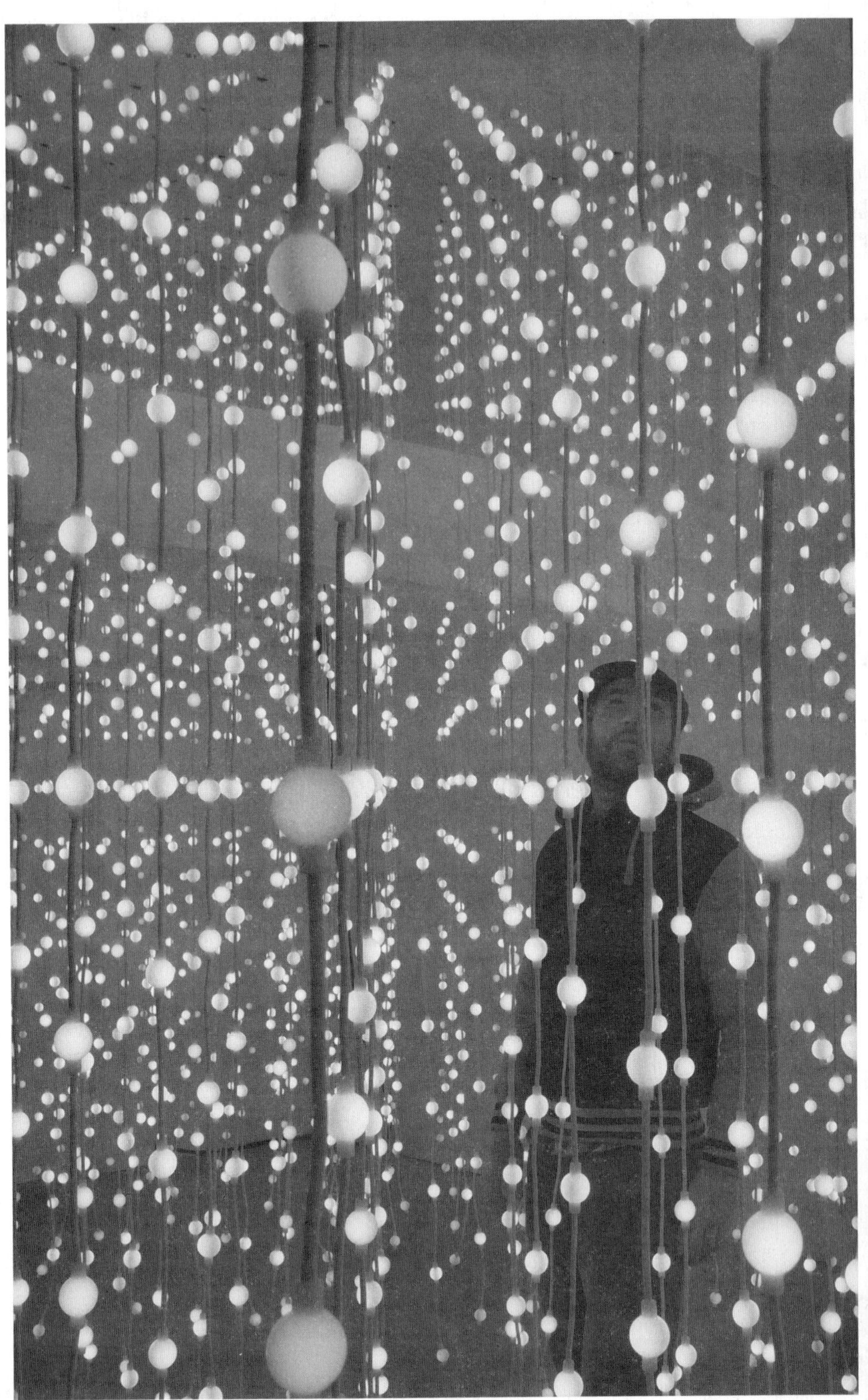

Courtesy of Anthony Rowe/Squidsoup. www.squidsoup.org.

4

Principles from 2D and 3D Art and Design

We discussed the elements of 2D and 3D design that are relevant to 4D design in Chapter 2. We'll now address the principles that carry over to 4D design: value/brightness, balance, contrast, direction/reflection, repetition, and scale.

Value/Brightness

Having already discussed value in relation to color (see Chapter 2), we will focus here on **value** or brightness in relation to the use of light. Intensity, luminance, and value are all descriptions of a light's **brightness**, which is relative to the physical surroundings. For example, the light from a small flashlight in a dark room may seem to be very bright, but the same flashlight would not appear nearly as intense in a sunny outdoor setting.

Another example of using relative brightness in a work is *Submergence* (2013), an interactive installation by Squidsoup, an international group of artists, researchers, and designers working with digital and interactive media experiences (fig. 4-1). This walkthrough experience uses thousands of points of light floating in space to alter participants' perceptions of space and presence. The points of light change brightness and color to create patterns and atmospheres, as well as a sense of presence and movement, in the physical space. Without these undulating changes in value, the work would not be as dynamic and immersive.

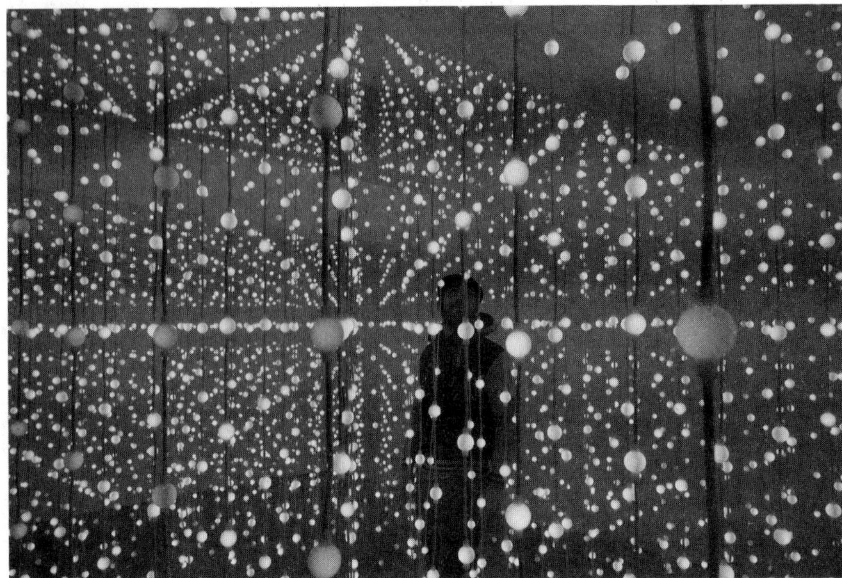

Fig. 4-1
Squidsoup, *Submergence* (2013), 8,064 individual points of suspended light and computer
controls. Courtesy of Anthony Rowe/Squidsoup. www.squidsoup.org.

Interview: Anthony Rowe of Squidsoup

Submergence is the latest in a series of experiments into the
possibilities of creating immersive experiences where the media
component occupies physical, three-dimensional space. We use
arrays of individually controllable suspended LEDs as voxels, or
pixels in space, to recreate abstract imagery that people can walk
through and be enveloped within. Exact roles within the conceptual
and technical development of the piece are hard to define, and
blur within the mists of time. The original idea was inspired by the
"penetrable" works of Jesus Rafael Soto, and the low resolution
video works of Jim Campbell (that I first saw in Japan in 2002),
and an ambition to combine the two.

—*Anthony Rowe of Squidsoup*

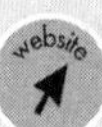

Visit the book's website to read the full interview.

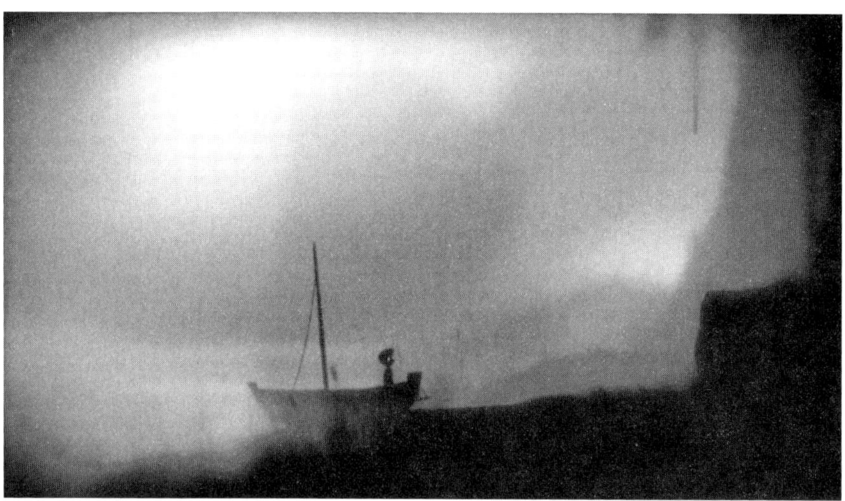

Fig. 4-2
Playdead, *Limbo* (2010), video game, dimensions variable. © Playdead.

The intensity of a light is also related to psychological and physiological aspects of participants. For example, if a person is not feeling well, a bright light may seem brighter and more irritating than if the person were feeling better. Also, if human eyes are in low light for an extended period of time, they become more sensitive to light, and even a small amount of light will seem brighter. It is important to note that as human eyes become more adapted to the dark, they also lose the ability to detect fine details.

This sense of loss of detail is utilized in the puzzle-platform video game *Limbo* (2010) by Danish game developer Playdead (fig. 4-2). This game employs a dark, blurred vignette around the frame of the screen, which emulates the loss of detail in darkness, helps create focus, and emphasizes the dark psychological game space. Throughout this game the player, appearing exclusively in silhouette against a dim, foggy background, is seeking his sister in a variety of seemingly abandoned settings. The brightest points are the boy's eyes, as they are pure white against the black of his silhouette. All other details are less distinguished, emulating the natural behavior of our eyes when confronted with low-value light.

Exercise

Brainstorm a list of at least 10 ideas for narratives that involve brightness or darkness. Create a storyboard of thumbnail sketches for one of your narratives (see figure 1-15 for sample storyboard). Thumbnails are small, rough sketches to quickly record an idea. Share the storyboard with a partner and have him or her guess what the story might be and how brightness and darkness relate to the story. Use your partner's feedback to revise your storyboard to better reflect your intentions and more clearly explain the use of brightness or darkness. Show the revised storyboard to a second partner and ask for the same feedback. Compare and contrast their feedback with your first partner's feedback. Have you improved?

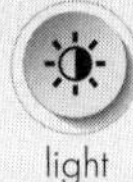

light

Scale of Brightness

Consider a scale of brightness, with one end total darkness and the other blinding white light. Environments or scenes with less brightness are often referred to as **low-key lighting**; those that are very bright are often called **high-key lighting**. An example that shows both high-key and low key lighting is *Adventure Time* (see Plate 8, color insert). The interior of the cave uses low-key lighting, while the outside of the cave uses high-key lighting. In between these two extremes are a range of direct, reflected, and diffused lights:

- **Direct light** is light pointed at a specific object or location.
- **Reflected light** is light bounced off of one surface onto an intended object or location.
- **Diffused light** is light that has passed through a material that scatters the light (clouds, haze, and precipitation diffuse light, as does a sheet of diffusion plastic).

Light can also be a combination of these three categories, producing any number of effects (fig. 4-3).

Direct Light

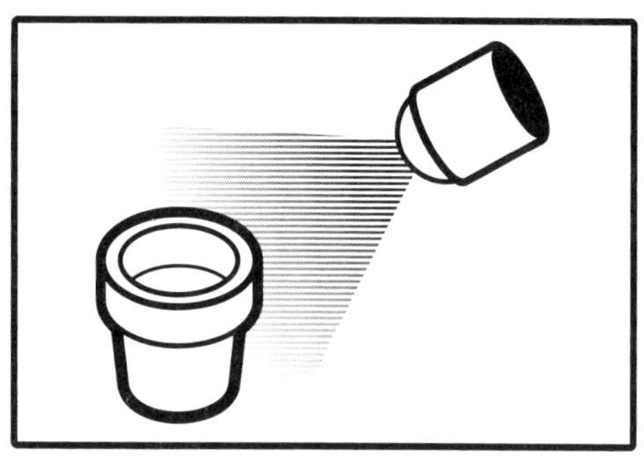
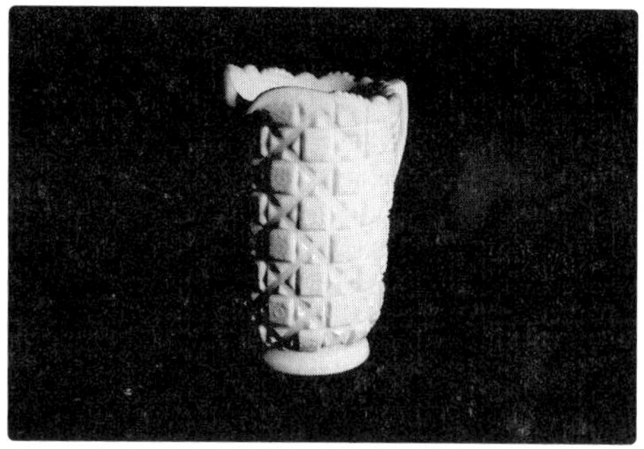

General tone is lighter, cast shadows have sharper edges, greater contrast between light and dark.

Reflected Light

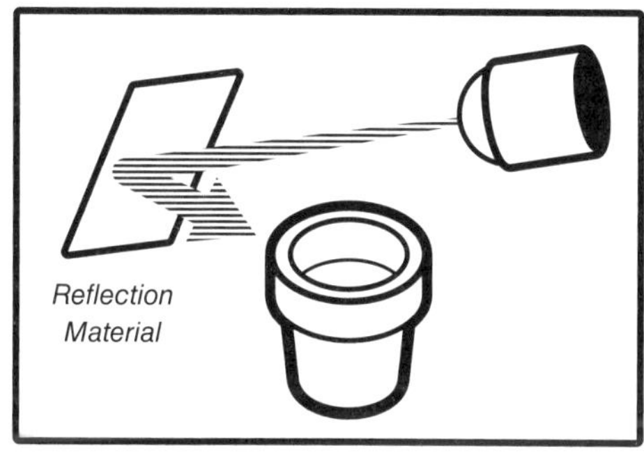

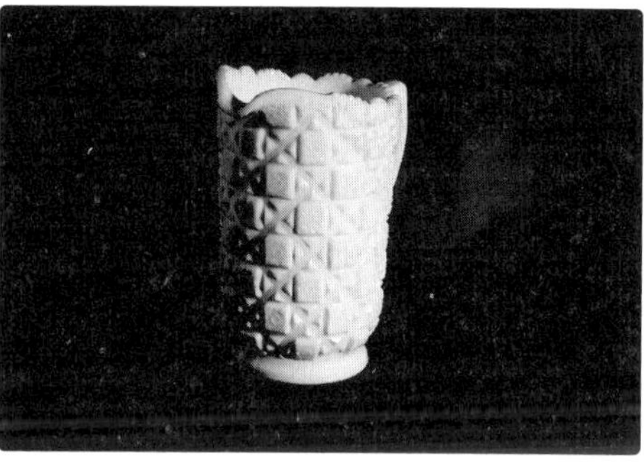

Reflection material can reduce shadows on or cast by the subject. Note the lighter left side of the pitcher.

Diffused Light

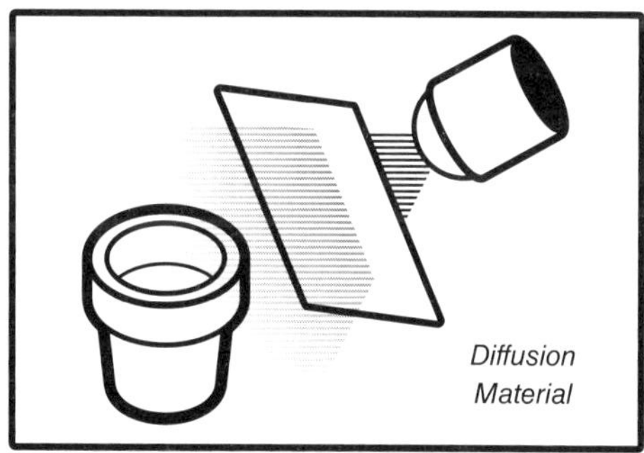

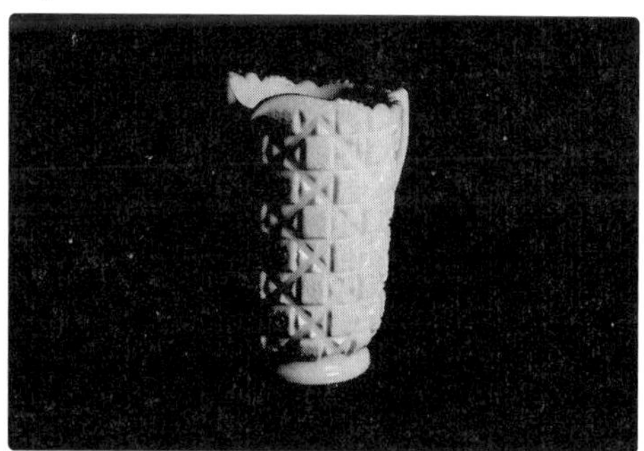

General tone is darker, cast shadows have softer edges, reduced contrast between light and dark.

Fig. 4-3

Illustration of the different effects produced by direct, reflected, and diffused light. © Phil McCollam.

Exercise

Brainstorm a list of the five best days of your life. Create a flipbook (a series of bound drawings that slowly change as the viewer flips through them to create a rudimentary stop-motion animation) inspired by one of these days. These do not need to be naturalistic drawings; they can feature rudimentary stick people if necessary. The flipbook should include variations in value of light. During critique, be ready to explain how these changes in value enhance your work.

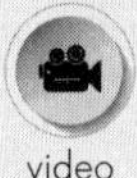

video

Diffused light from a reflected source can have the effect of reducing participants' sense of orientation, depth perception, and visual clarity because there will be few if any highlights or shadows.[1] In contrast, direct light will often provide a measure of reflected light, and will cast strong shadows and bright highlights. We can observe this direct-lighting effect in Justin Lee Martin's durational video work *Ten Feet Tall* (2012). In this video, Martin chops wood under strong work lights that cast sharp dark shadows from his arms as he swings the axe and adjusts the pieces of wood (fig. 4-4). The strong lights and darks, lending the piece a sense of foreboding, further emphasize the somewhat violent action of chopping wood. For the artist, the bright, stadium-like lighting recalled the college football games that captivated his hometown of Missoula, Montana. By substituting an even more masculine figure—a woodchopper—under these lights, he wanted to question the ideas of masculinity that both activities suggest.

Interview: Justin Lee Martin

The woodsman was a prominent figure throughout my youth. Mythical legends containing woodsmen seemed to be born in my backyard, the Rocky Mountains. In addition to this figure, my hometown, like many towns in America, is captivated by local sports; in Missoula, Montana it has always been college football. For *TEN FEET TALL*, I started to question how gender roles were constructed in these types of environments. I wanted to construct a video that incorporated elements of masculinity, which for me are identified with the lumber industry and football games. I wanted to see a lumberjack under stadium lights splitting logs in the middle of a forest. There is no climax to the performance, just me splitting wood. Although, I wanted to set the viewer up to feel as if something bad was about to happen even though nothing does.

One of my favorite 4D artworks is Francis Alÿs's *Paradox of Praxis (Sometimes Doing Something Leads to Nothing)* from 1997. There are many layers to his performance that interest me. One is how he reveals Mexico City and its workers through the poetic act of pushing a block of ice through the hot and dusty streets. Many of his works are about exposing some type of physical condition or regional temperament. The 5-minute video is not just documentation of Alÿs's performance but more or less a statement about place and its relationship to the people that inhabit it. In the end, the ice melts and nothing is left to show for it. This performance creates dialogue about human welfare and makes us question our stance as viewers.

—*Justin Lee Martin*

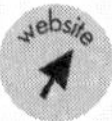 Visit the book's website to read the full interview.

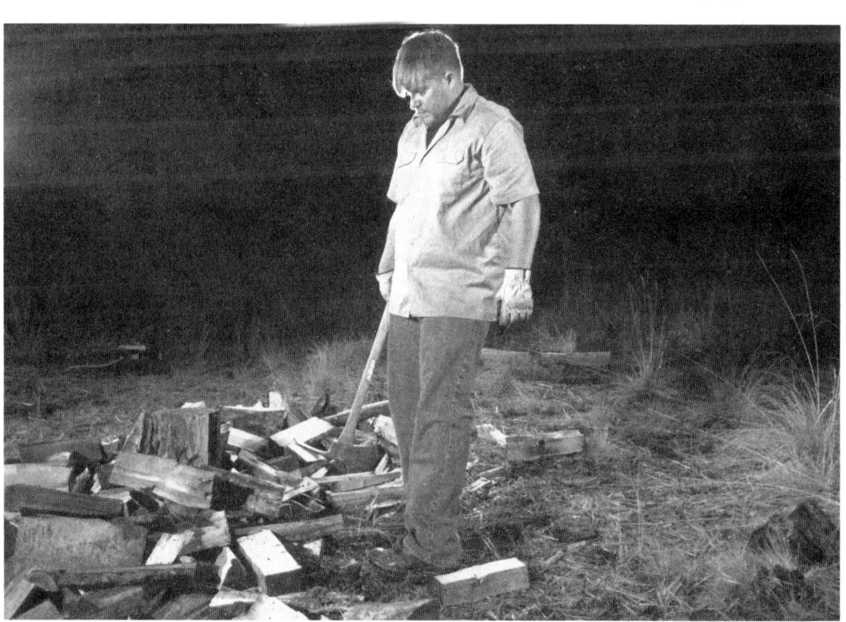

Fig. 4-4

Justin Lee Martin, *TEN FEET TALL* (2012), digital video, 9:22 minutes. Courtesy of the artist.

Exercise

Go online, search for, and view Francis Alÿs's *Paradox of Praxis (Sometimes Doing Something Leads to Nothing)*. Write down what you think are the subject, form, content, and context for this work. Analyze how the artist used value in terms of light. Compare and contrast your answers with others'. How are your answers similar and different from those around you? Were there any trends in the answers?

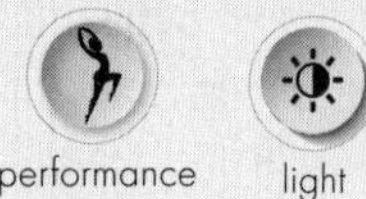

performance   light

When selecting the brightness of your lighting, keep in mind the areas and levels where you want to draw the viewers' focus. If the work is participatory, consider how you want participants to move through the space. It is helpful to remember that the human eye will always travel to the brightest area first. Use that to your advantage. Reflected light will illuminate at least two surfaces; make sure those are surfaces you need and want illuminated. Diffused light is less harsh than direct light and lights a larger area, but does not necessarily draw focus as readily as direct lighting. Avoid simply going with your first impulse or what is readily available in terms of light sources. Play with brightening and darkening the space as a whole. Think creatively about how to control the brightness of your space. For example, projecting light through plants or other sculptural objects can help soften a harshly lit interior space.[2]

Exercise

Create a list of 25 words you associate with the idea of money. For example, you might list spending, saving, working, and so on. Use that list to inspire a 30-second video work. Include emphasis on the value and brightness of light in this work. The work does not have to be narrative. After viewing everyone's videos, ask which videos made the most and least successful use of value and brightness. What worked well and what didn't?

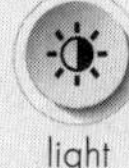

video   light

Altogether, value or brightness is relative, and can be manipulated using many different types of light including direct, reflected, and diffused. The luminosity of your work will affect where participants look and when, so it is important to spend time considering these choices.

Balance

Balance is the measure of the relationship among different elements in an artwork. It can affect movement, sound, light, architecture, topography, space, and time. Balance can be achieved visually, physically, aurally, or even through taste. Balance can be **symmetrical**, meaning that the balancing parts are the same on either side of a midline and feel very stable; **radial**, meaning the balancing parts radiate out from a central point; or **asymmetrical**, meaning the balancing parts are different on either side of a midline and feel like they could easily be thrown out of balance.

In Sparksight's overview video *10 Reasons to Go ShoreTel* (2014), animator Ryan Austin uses text and imagery with frequent radial and symmetrical balance as shots transition from one to the next, conveying reasons for businesses to invest in this company's services (fig. 4-5). This use of balance helps convey stability and reliability on behalf of the company.

Interview: Ryan Austin of Sparksight

There are a lot of really incredible artists and designers that develop their own unique style and are able to produce all their projects in that. There's definitely a place for that, but for what I do and what I'm interested in, I work in a different style for almost every project. Our clients always want something different from one another so the team at Sparksight really gets to play with something new almost every time.

I really enjoy this way of working since it forces me to research the look more and it's freeing. You're not stuck in the same color scheme or design so you're constantly working those creative muscles that don't always get exercise.

—*Ryan Austin of Sparksight*

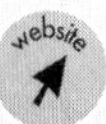

Visit the book's website to read the full interview.

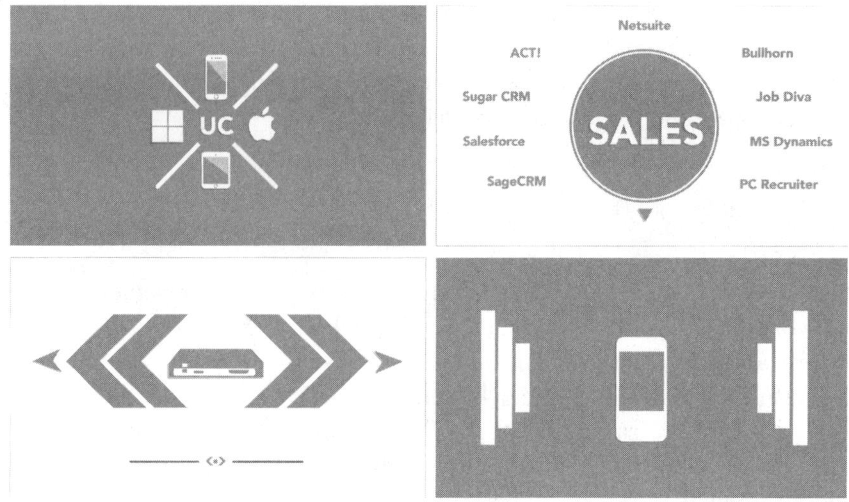

Fig. 4-5
Sparksight, *10 Reasons to Go ShoreTel* (2014), motion graphics, 2:22 minutes. Design & animation: Ryan Austin. Courtesy of Sparksight.

Exercise

Go online to find and view Phil Borst's animation *Wasichana Fund—Can Pads Save the World?* Write down what you think are the subject, form, content, and context for this work. Analyze how he used balance. Compare and contrast your answers with others'. How are your answers similar and different from those around you? Were there any trends in the answers?

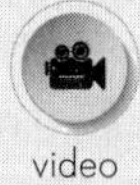
video

A work also can be **imbalanced**, meaning it is not balanced at all. If you are going to utilize imbalance in your work, be sure it is purposefully expressing your concept. Typically, imbalance expresses change or instability. For example, Melati Suryodarmo's performance *Exergie—Butter Dance* (Fig. 1-8) does an excellent job of utilizing physical imbalance as the performer slips and falls repeatedly, emphasizing perseverance in the face of difficulty.

Visual Weight

Balance within screen-based works largely depends on the **visual weight** of the objects on-screen. The dimensions of an object, its shape, its location on-screen, and color determine the visual weight. A large object will have more visual weight than a small object. A compact and simply shaped object will have more visual weight than an irregularly shaped object. Objects in the corner of the screen, the upper part of the screen, and the right part of the screen will all have more visual weight than those in the center, lower part of the screen, or left part of the screen. An object with a warm hue or a saturated color or a dark color will have more visual weight than an object with a cool hue, weak saturation, or light color.[3]

Exercise

Portray a memory in any four-dimensional media you like. The work could center on an object, feeling, location, social media post, toy, article of clothing, and so on, related to this memory. How can you utilize *balance* or lack thereof to emphasize the memory quality of this piece? In critique ask, "Could you feel the impulse behind the work? Was there a question that had to be asked or a statement that needed to be made? Could you feel necessity in the piece?"[4] If you had trouble identifying the statement of any piece in critique, work together to come up with ways to better articulate the work.

  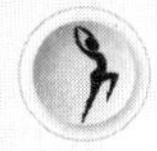  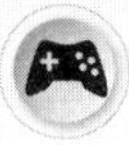 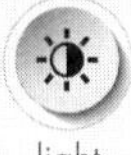

sound   video   performance   installation   games   light

Movement

Balance can also be expressed through movement, in the literal sense of maintaining your balance. Janine Antoni's video work *Touch* (2002) shows her maintaining a careful physical balancing act, walking a tightrope that is visually aligned with the horizon (fig. 4-6). This piece plays with ideas of the horizon as a representation of the world beyond one's home. Antoni's walking in this specific space, which was filmed at the beach outside her childhood home in the Bahamas, can represent walking into the unknown or a space of boundless possibility.

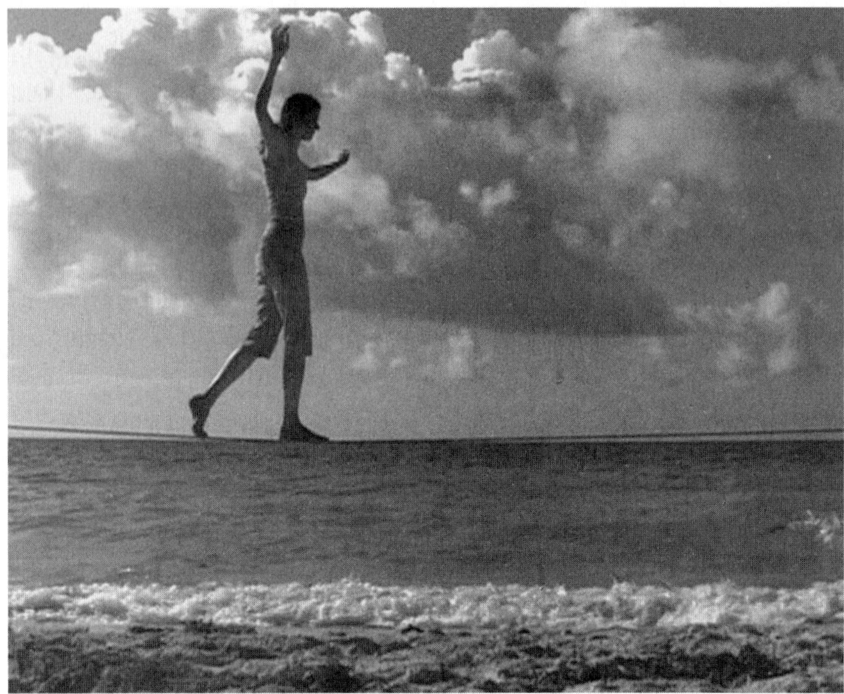

Fig. 4-6
Janine Antoni, *Touch* (2002), video installation, edition of 5 plus 2 APs, 132′ × 178′,
9:37-minute loop. © Janine Antoni; Courtesy of the artist and Luhring Augustine, New York.

Similar to the physical balance used in *Touch*, the video game *Super Monkey Ball* (2001) was one of the first games to utilize a balancing gyroscope as the game controller (fig. 4-7). In order to progress, the player had to physically tip the controller out of balance to move the ball on-screen toward its final objectives. In both Antoni's performance and *Super Monkey Ball*, physical obstacles to achieving balance helped create tension in the work.

Exercise

Find a partner. Take turns writing/sketching out a series of three movements that use all or part of your partner's body. Your first series should consist of *balanced* movements, and your second series should consist of *unbalanced* movements. Think about symmetrical balance versus asymmetrical balance in the body. It may be helpful to ask your partner to try a variety of your ideas before committing your two series to paper. Once everyone has completed their two series, the entire class should move through their balanced series together, and then the unbalanced series together. Students should step away from the movements one by one to observe the group's movement from outside the group. How does the room look and feel different during each set of movements?

performance

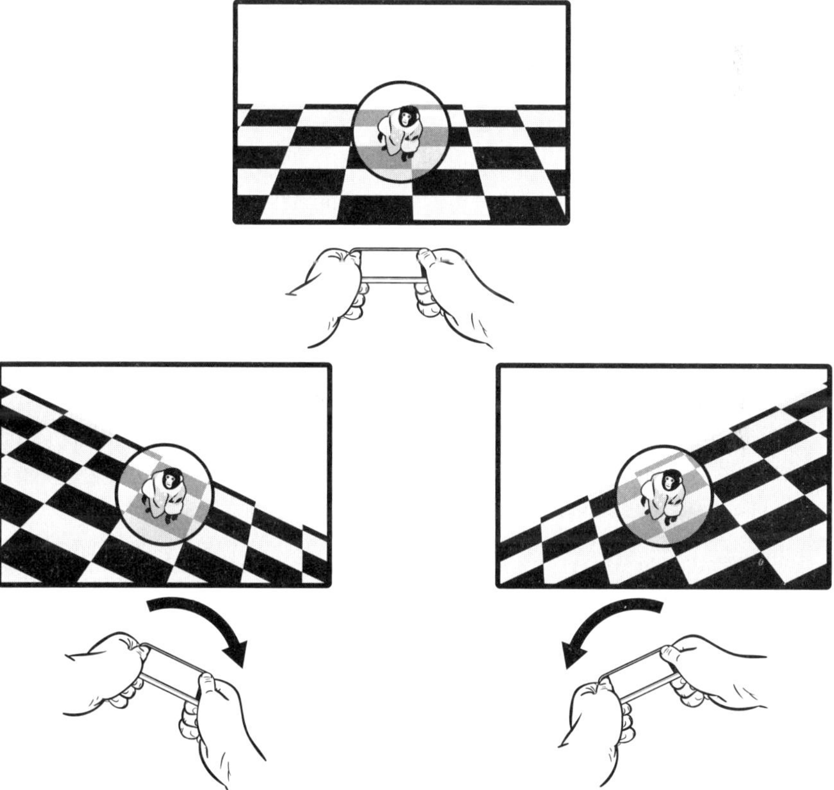

Fig. 4-7

Super Monkey Ball (2001) was one of the first games to utilize a balancing gyroscope as the game controller. © Phil McCollam.

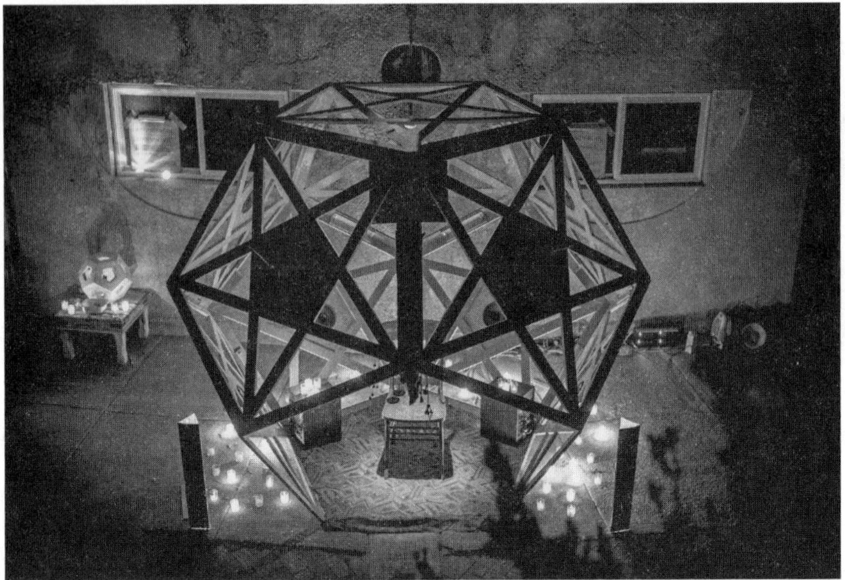

Fig. 4-8
Arjan Miranda and Matthew Morgan, *Hedron* (2014), 12 opposing planes 8′ apart, made of wood, bolts, speakers, and amps. © Arjan Miranda and Matthew Morgan.

Sound

Arjan Miranda and Matthew Morgan are sound artists. Their work *Hedron* (2014) involves a radially balanced construction (fig. 4-8). This work consists of an 8-foot dodecahedron at the center of 10 inward facing speakers and two subwoofers, which are speakers dedicated to bass, or low-pitched, audio frequencies. In this work, sound moves in all directions around the participant. This nontraditional, radially balanced setting helps focus listeners' attention on the audio.

Exercise

Find a partner. Select a space in which to install a sound installation addressing the idea of science. Science is a big umbrella term, and you can go in many different directions (experiments, chemicals, biology, etc). Your sound installation must have at least three speakers with different sounds coming out of each. Play with the arrangement of the speakers in the space to find different ways to *balance* the sound. If you don't have many speakers, you can play your sounds from any portable sound device: laptop, phone, tablet, and so on. When the sound in the space feels balanced, invite a different pair of people into the space and ask them to describe their experience of balance or unbalance to you. What changes could you make based on this feedback?

sound   installation

Lighting

Balance, or lack thereof, can also be used in lighting to add drama to a particular moment or space. By using unbalanced chiaroscuro lighting, in which only select items within a given space are illuminated, an artist or designer can build focus and emotion. The stop-motion animation *Chiaroscuro* (2012) by Vitùc documents the meandering of a day's events. The opening moments utilize a small desk lamp to achieve a chiaroscuro effect. The lamp is very bright, while everything else in the frame remains dark, creating a sense of drama (fig. 4-9).

Interview: Vitùc

Chiaroscuro is an experimental film . . . the third short of the hipstographic film series, after *YESTERDAY* and *LIFE FRAGMENTS*. It was shot with an iPhone with the wonderful Hipstamatic App and one specific effect included in the app (old photography burn effect). I wanted to create emotion through stop motion photography and through this effect. Playing with light and shadow . . . chiaro (clear) and scuro (dark), the pictures were taken in Italy during a vacation. I took over 5000 pictures to make this film. The film has a dreamy touch . . . a visual poetry. I also used the music of my pianist friend David Ianni. I chose black and white to bring more melancholy to the ambiance.

—Vitùc

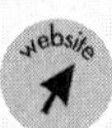 Visit the book's website to read the full interview.

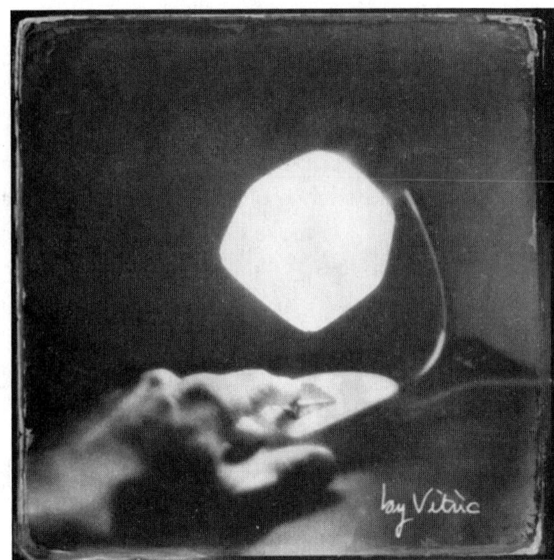

Fig. 4-9
Vitùc, *Chiaroscuro* (2012),
stop-motion animation,
1:49 minutes. Courtesy
of the artist.

Gaming

Balance can also applied in gaming situations. Take, for example, resources and strength in interactive competitive games. All players could have equal, or symmetrical, resources and abilities, lending the game a sense of fairness; many board games are set up like this. Asymmetrically balanced games give certain players different resources and skills. It is important to think carefully about how you will balance resources and abilities as a means of creating compelling game play.

Exercise

Form small groups. Each group will create a game that involves hats. This could be any type of game at all (racing, matching, hiding, passing, storytelling, etc.). Consider whether you want the game to be a measure of individual skill or a collaborative challenge. Brainstorm possibilities, and then use trial and error to arrive at the finished game. How will your game maintain *balance* among people who have different skills, while still keeping the game interesting and challenging?[5] Test the game on a group of people to see whether it feels balanced. Make adjustments as necessary.

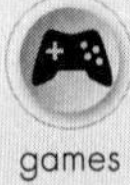

games

Altogether, balance of sound, movement, light, and other elements can play an important role in the participant's experience of a work, whether it is symmetrical, asymmetrical, radial, or imbalanced.

Contrast

Humans require changing stimuli to stay sensitive and alert. **Contrast** is another name for these changes or differences, which can be large or small. There can be contrast in nearly all of the elements and principles of four-dimensional art and design, as well as among the subject, content, and context of the work. Contrast can be strong or subtle, and it can be created out of any number of extremes:

- Bright/dark
- Closed/open
- Big/small
- Organic/geometric
- Somber/funny
- Smooth/rough
- Hot/cold
- Sweet/sour
- Stinky/fragrant
- Colorful/desaturated
- Loud/soft
- Quick/slow
- High/low or near/far (or any number of spatial relationships)
- Empty/full
- Harmony/dissonance
- Transparent/opaque
- Welcoming/repulsing
- Structured/unstructured

As in two- and three-dimensional art and design, contrast is often a key element in creating and maintaining the interest and focus of the viewer or participant. The artist must balance sameness with change to ensure engagement and to avoid **habituation**, which is the tiring of the nerves that occurs when a viewer experiences extended sameness or extended periods of rapid change (unless habituation is the artist's goal).

Exercise

Record two short (1 minute or less) audio descriptions of two favorite trips you've taken. They could be short of long trips, mundane or exotic, for fun or for work, and so on. Listen to each of your descriptions and analyze how the two trips contrast with each other, if at all. How can you heighten the contrast between these works? Re-record the descriptions, and think about contrast between tempo and energy dynamics. Once your revised version is complete, ask someone who has heard neither of the stories to listen and describe how they contrast with each other. Based on this feedback, how well did you convey contrast?

sound

In Zachary Zezima's animation *Cruising* (2014), a young introverted man moves from the still depths of a cruise ship through a variety of frenetic, colorfully vibrating, chaotic scenes of stereotypically scheduled cruise activities (Plate 2, color insert). His initial inability to accept his high-energy environment drives him to a scene of escapist fantasy, which is portrayed as a quiet blue calmness in direct contrast with the previous buildup of highly saturated frenetic movement and sound. Through this fantasy experience, the young man learns to cope with his discomfort and anxiety, and the animation ends. These strategic changes in color, movement, and sound help hold the viewer's attention from start to finish.

Exercise

Work in groups of three. One person will be in charge of a light source, another will be behind a camera, and the third will be the subject. Find a dark room in which to shoot, direct the light source at the subject to create high-contrast shadows, and then start shooting. Adjust the position of the light source and the distance from the subject, and compare and contrast the variety of shots. Figure out which positions are most effective at conveying various moods or emotions. Switch roles until each of you has had a chance to do all three tasks. Share your findings with the class.

 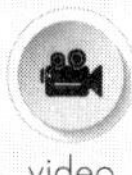

light   video

In any work, if all the elements and principles are directed toward evoking the same result, they will cancel each other out.[6] In *Baldessari Sings LeWitt* (1972), John Baldessari sings some of Sol LeWitt's statements from exhibition catalogs for the camera as a tribute to LeWitt. By adding musicality to these statements, he is creating contrast between the seriousness of the statements and the lighthearted nature of the songs. If he had simply read the statements in a serious tone for the camera, the piece would not have been nearly as compelling, and would not have reached as wide of an audience, because the seriousness of the text would have matched the seriousness of his tone. Contrast is a key ingredient for creating interest, if that is your intention.

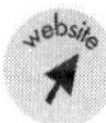 Visit the book's website to read an interview with John Baldessari.

A similar example is Pipilotti Rist's *Ever Is Over All* (1997). Two videos are projected on adjacent walls: one features a beautiful flower, and the other features footage of Rist in a blue dress smashing car windows along a city street with a flower-like prop (fig. 4-10). Everything in the work, from color to movement to sound, is harmonious—aside from the window smashing. She contrasts a stereotypically feminine character with a very nonstereotypical violent action. This single piece of contrast makes the piece more interesting.

Exercise

Brainstorm a list of things that describe you (creative, runner, lazy on beautiful days, etc.). Within your list, make sure there is *contrast*. For example, make sure your list is honest, and not just a list of all the positive things about you. Use this list to create a video self-portrait. This work could be an amalgamation of clips, or just one

(continued)

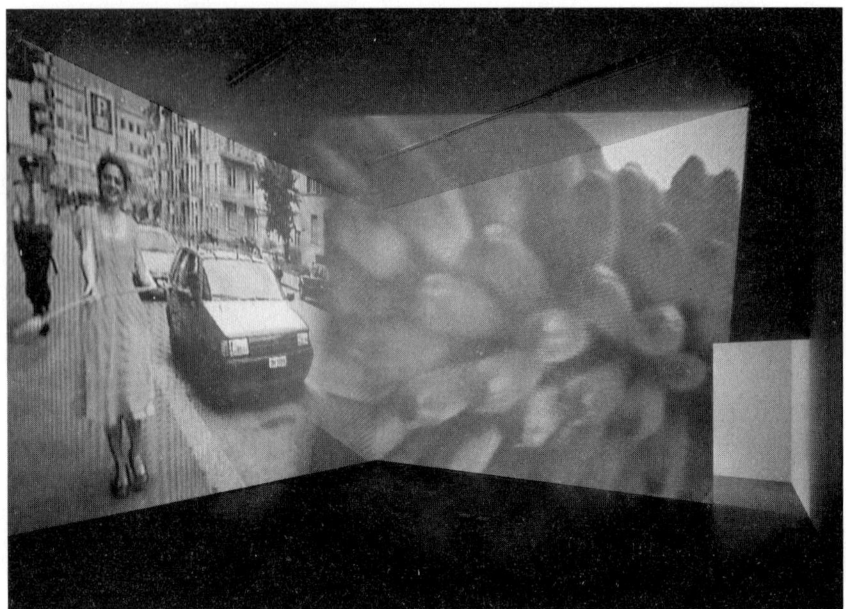

Fig. 4-10
Pipilotti Rist, *Ever Is Over All* (1997), audio/video installation, installation view at Kunsthalle Zürich, Zurich/CH. Photo by Alexander Troehler. © Pipilotti Rist; Courtesy of the artist, Luhring Augustine, New York, and Hauser & Wirth.

Exercise (*continued*)

clip, but it must include contrast and be an accurate self-portrait. At critique, compare and contrast your work with the work of others. What worked, and what could be improved?

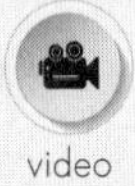

video

Using contrast to maintain interest does not always have to be the artist's or designer's primary intention. In Andy Warhol's film *Empire* (1964), the viewer sees a single, continuous shot of the Empire State Building. It remains virtually unchanged, aside from the passage from daylight to darkness throughout the film's 8 hours. Warhol is not concerned with holding the viewer's attention; instead he wants to create a situation in which viewers can "see time go by."[7] The work still has brief moments of contrast when a light on a neighboring building blinks or a bird flies by, but these elements are not central to the work's content.

Exercise

Go online, search for, and view a clip of Andy Warhol's *Sleep* (1963). After watching the work, write down what you think are the subject, form, content, and context for this work. Analyze how the artist used contrast. Compare and contrast your answers with others'. How are your answers similar and different from those around you? Were there any trends in the answers?

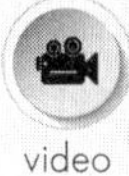

video

Altogether, contrast is an important principle that affects all the elements of art and design. It is a pivotal part of gaining and holding onto participants' attention in any work.

Direction/Reflection

The **direction** of a light, sound, or movement is the course along which it moves. Direction makes a significant difference in how light, sound, or movement is distributed, and how the viewer or participant experiences a work. For example, *verticality* of light, sound, movement, or architecture in a work can express dominance, security, and splendor. *Horizontality* in a work can express calmness, serenity, and a sense of being immovable. Use of *diagonal* directionality can express tension and dynamism. *Circular* directions can express balance, peace, and bliss.

Movement

In terms of movement, direction—and how much it varies—can help determine whether participants will want to continue, slow, or stop at various junctures. In the video game *Dark Souls II* (2014), directed by Tomohiro Shibuya and Yui Tanimura, a boss battle with the Duke's Dear Freja illustrates this phenomenon. *Dark Souls II* is a continuous, open-world exploration game of fighting enemies and bosses while collecting defeated souls. During the encounter, the enemy fires a projectile beam, which steadily tracks counterclockwise across the playfield. The direction of the beam drives the movement choices of the player within the environment (fig. 4-11). If the player stops or attempts to move against the direction of

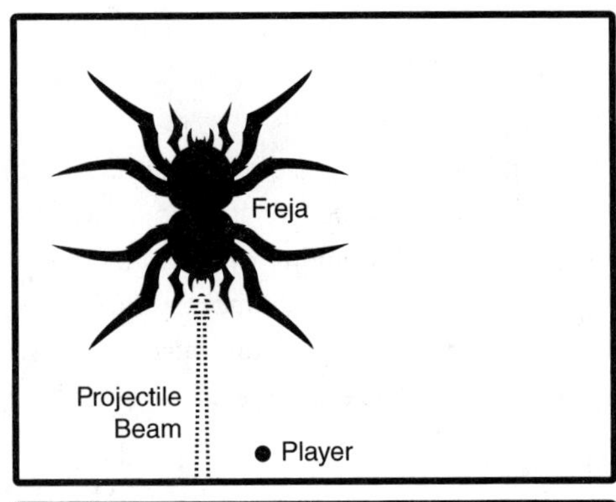

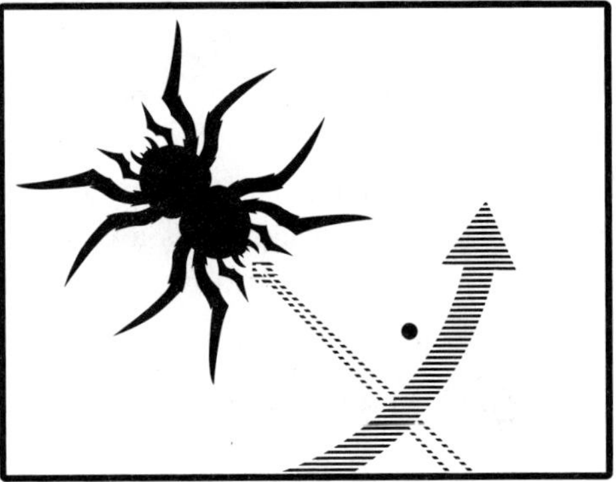

Fig. 4-11
Illustration of a boss battle with
the Duke's Dear Freja in *Dark
Souls II.* © Phil McCollam.

the beam, the player's character will likely die and the encounter will have
to be restarted. In this example, a clear path of motion is presented to the
player, who will have to follow this direction in order to continue playing.

Exercise

Select a first-person video game. (Examples include—but are not
limited to—*Elder Scrolls: Skyrim, Portal, Metroid Prime, The Stanley
Parable,* and *Titanfall.*) Analyze a section of the game for direction
of movement. Notice how various moving obstacles affect the direction of your movement choices. Write about these occurrences
and share with the class. Notice additional ideas that others
picked up and that you may have overlooked.

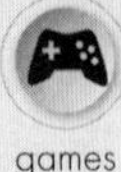

games

Light and Sound

The direction of light or sound can help establish the parameters of an environment depending on how the light or sound is reflected back towards the participant. Light and sound bounce, or reflect, off of different surfaces in different ways; walls will create a different reflected effect than water or fabric. Some sound or light may also be **absorbed**, or soaked up, by a surface rather than reflected elsewhere, or it may simply pass through an object.

Exercise

Create a dynamic (meaning it changes in some way) light installation that physically surrounds the participant. This means you will have to carefully select your installation space. If there are no walls in the space you choose, how will you create boundaries for your work? Are boundaries necessary? Use your knowledge of direction and reflection of light to help establish the parameters of your work. What causes the changes in this installation? Is it when people arrive at a certain point or complete a specific action? Or are the changes ongoing and continuous? How do participants enter and exit this work? Once you have created your installation, invite participants to enter, experience the work, and provide feedback.

light   installation

The direction and pitch of a sound will affect how well a listener can identify the location of its source. The direction of higher pitched sounds are very easy to sense, while lower pitched sounds tend to fill space and surround the listener, making it more difficult to discern directionality.

In Steve Roden's *Bird Forms* (2001), speakers were strategically placed throughout courtyard trees at UCLA's Hammer Museum, with attention to the placement and direction of the sound (fig. 4-12). Each speaker played recordings of birds that had been slightly manipulated, bringing attention to the preexisting birdsong occurring in the space. If the artist had placed the speakers on the ground or walls instead of in the trees, the direction of the sound would not have best imitated the placement of real birds. Through this precise use of direction, the work was strengthened.

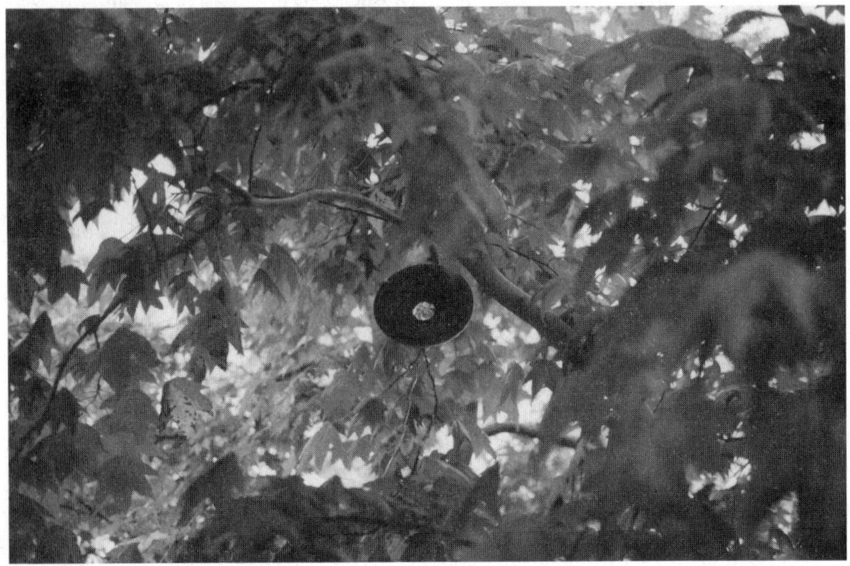

Fig. 4-12
Steve Roden, *Bird Forms* (2001), audio installation, dimensions variable. Courtesy of the artist.

Interview: Steve Roden

Bird Forms was an early site-specific sound installation. It was created for a courtyard with trees at the center of the Hammer Museum in Los Angeles. I was interested in the fact that these trees were usually filled with birds and birdsong. I have always felt that if sound is going to play in a public space, the artist must be conscious of the existing sonic landscape, so I am interested in creating works that integrate, rather than segregate. I used several recordings of birds on 78 rpm records from the 1930s as a kind of shadow or memory of those anonymous singers who passed away long ago, in an attempt to allow them to sing again in the trees. I manipulated many of the recordings, via guitar pedals and other analog devices, so that the sounds seemed to be birds but not quite. (I am not a fan of work that is too literal.) I worked without a

(continued)

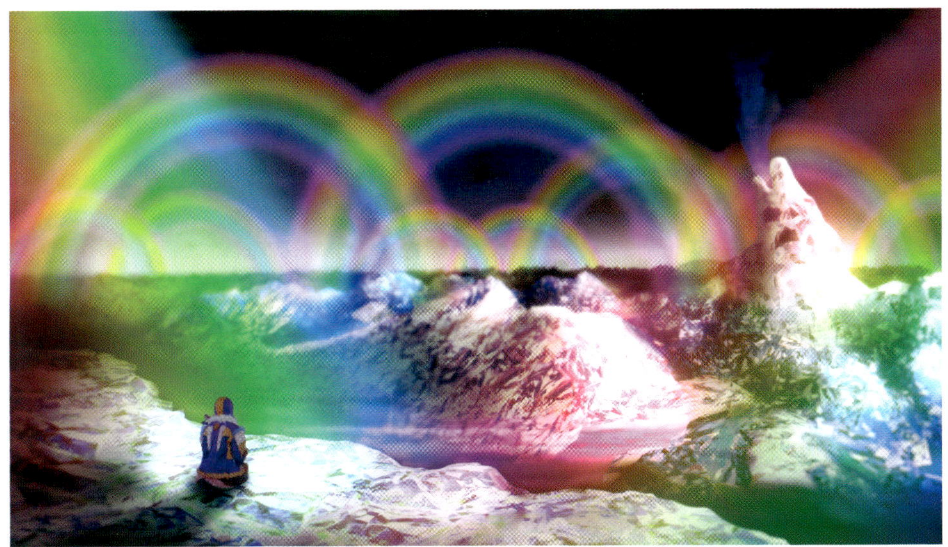

Plate 1

Rachel Maclean, *Over the Rainbow* (2013), digital video, 41:28 minutes. Courtesy of the artist. Commissioned by The Banff Centre, Canada and The Collective Gallery, Edinburgh. Funded by Creative Scotland.

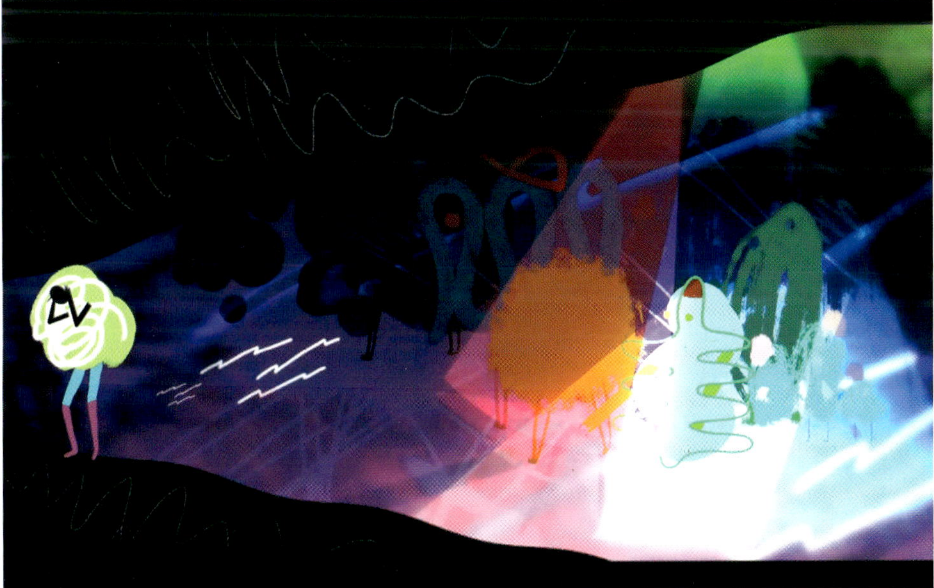

Plate 2

Zachary Zezima, *Cruising* (2014), animation, 3:21 minutes. Courtesy of the artist.

Plate 3
Paul Pfeiffer, *Morning After the Deluge* (2003), video still from projected video installation, running time: 20 minutes, looped. © Paul Pfeiffer. Courtesy Paula Cooper Gallery, New York.

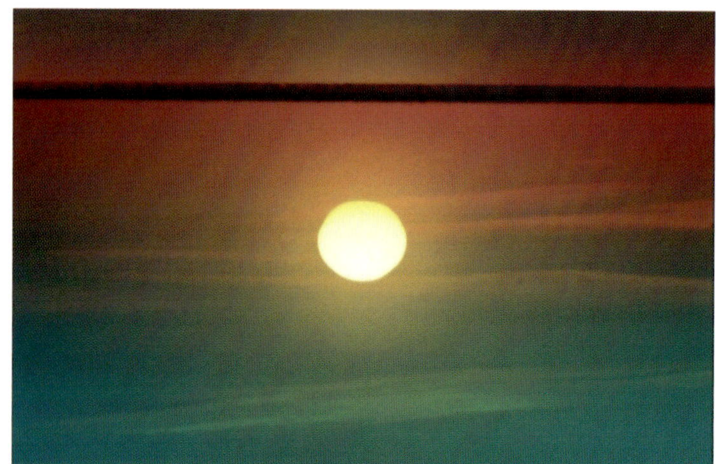

Plate 4
Ernesto Neto, *Walking in Venus Blue Cave* (2001), stocking, Styrofoam, buttons, incandescent lights, 13.1′ × 25.7′ × 27.6′ (3.96 m × 7.77 m × 8.12 m). Installation view, Tanya Bonakdar Gallery, New York, 2001. Collection Denver Art Museum. Courtesy of Tanya Bonakdar Gallery.

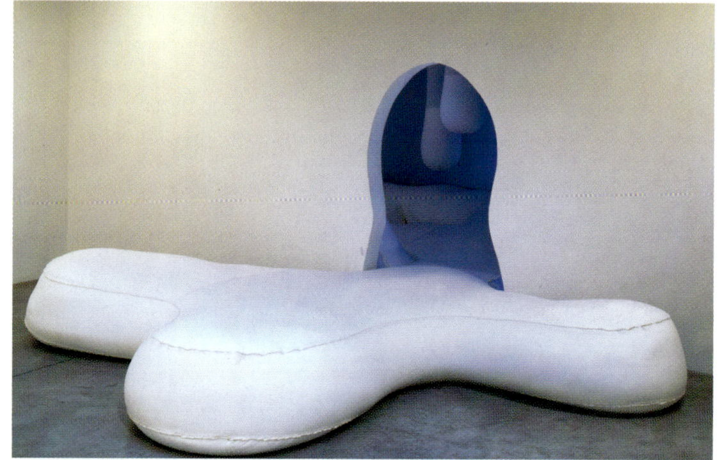

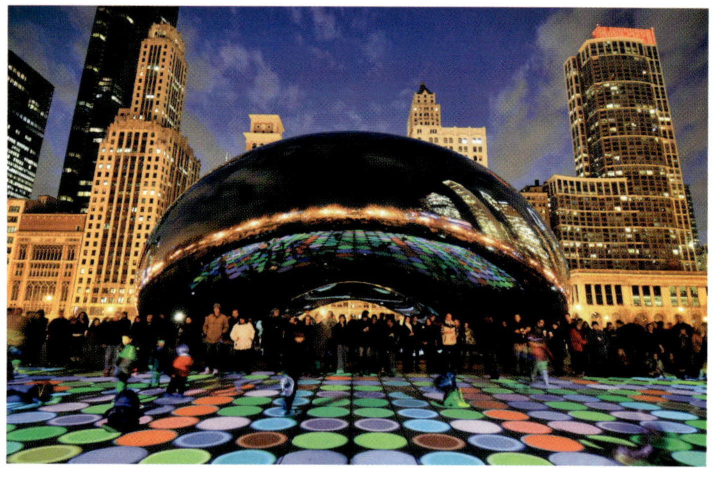

Plate 5
Luftwerk, *Luminous Field* (2012), interactive light and sounds installation and projection field 80′ × 30′. © Luftwerk.

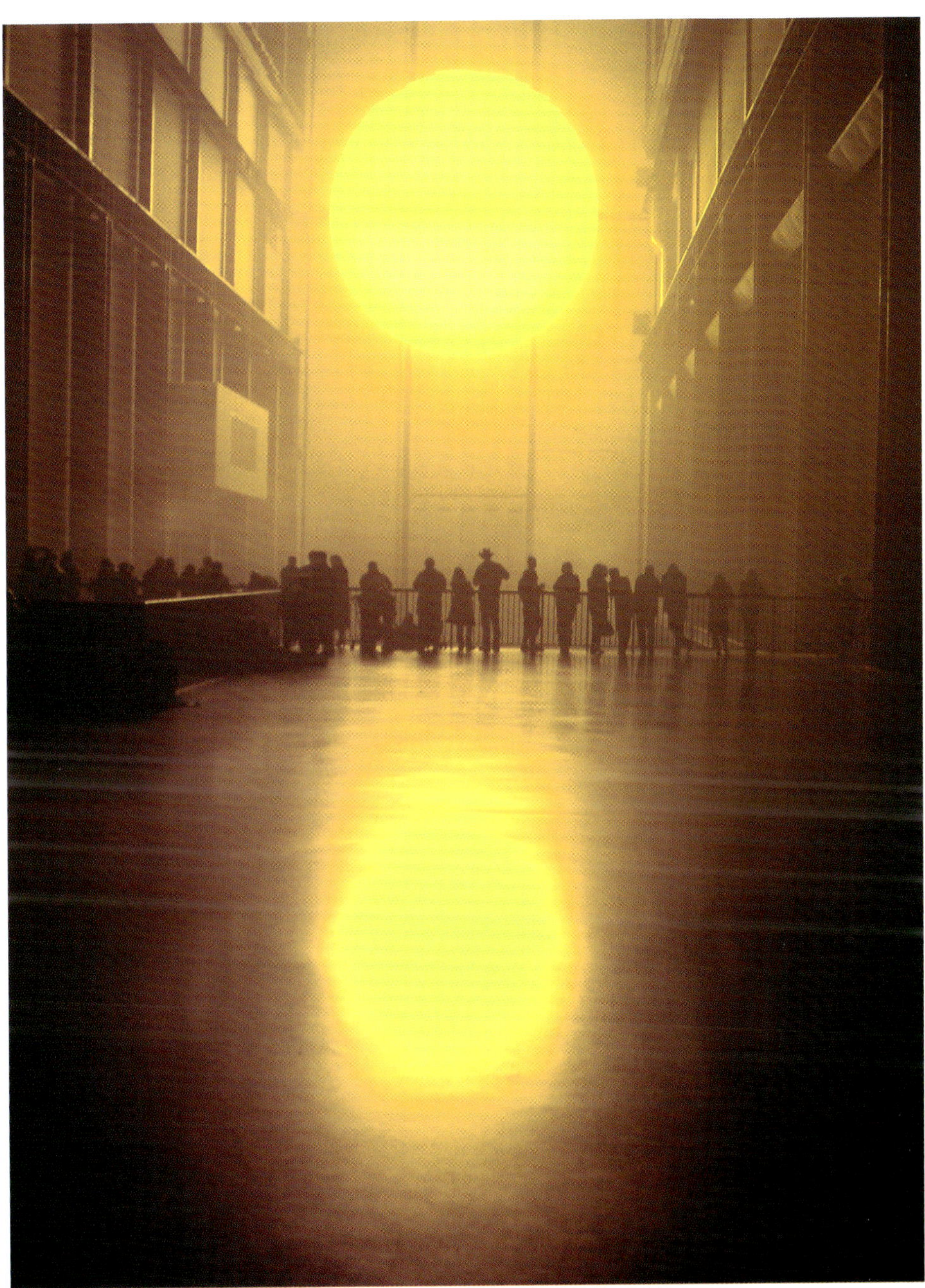

Plate 6
Olafur Eliasson, *The Weather Project* (2003), monofreqency lights, projection foil, haze machines, mirror foil, aluminum, and scaffolding, 26.7 m × 22.3 m × 155.4 m, installation in Turbine Hall, Tate Modern, London. Photo: Studio Olafur Eliasson, Courtesy the artist; neugerriemschneider, Berlin; and Tanya Bonakdar Gallery, New York, © Olafur Eliasson 2003.

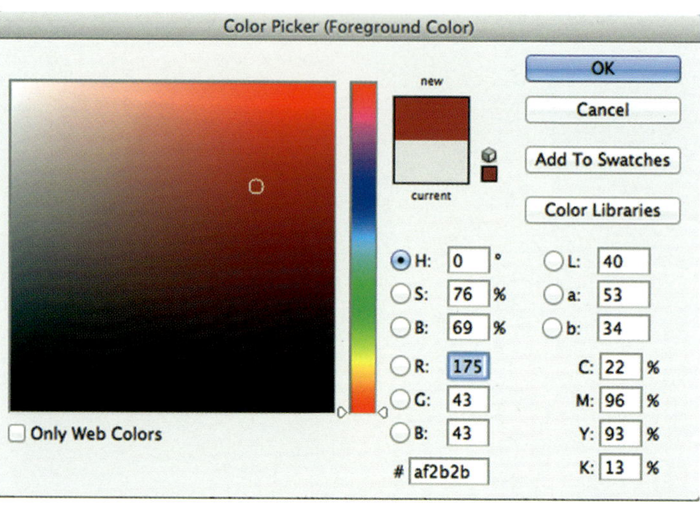

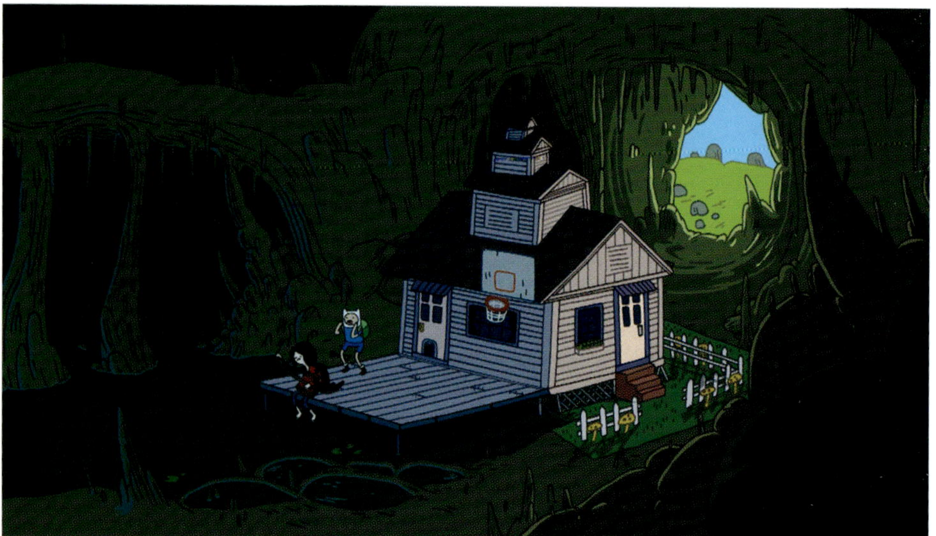

Plate 8

Adventure Time (season 2, episode 1). Notice a variety of hues across the frame, with shifts in both saturation and value as space transitions from outside to inside the cave setting. *Adventure Time* and all related characters and elements are trademarks of and © Cartoon Network.

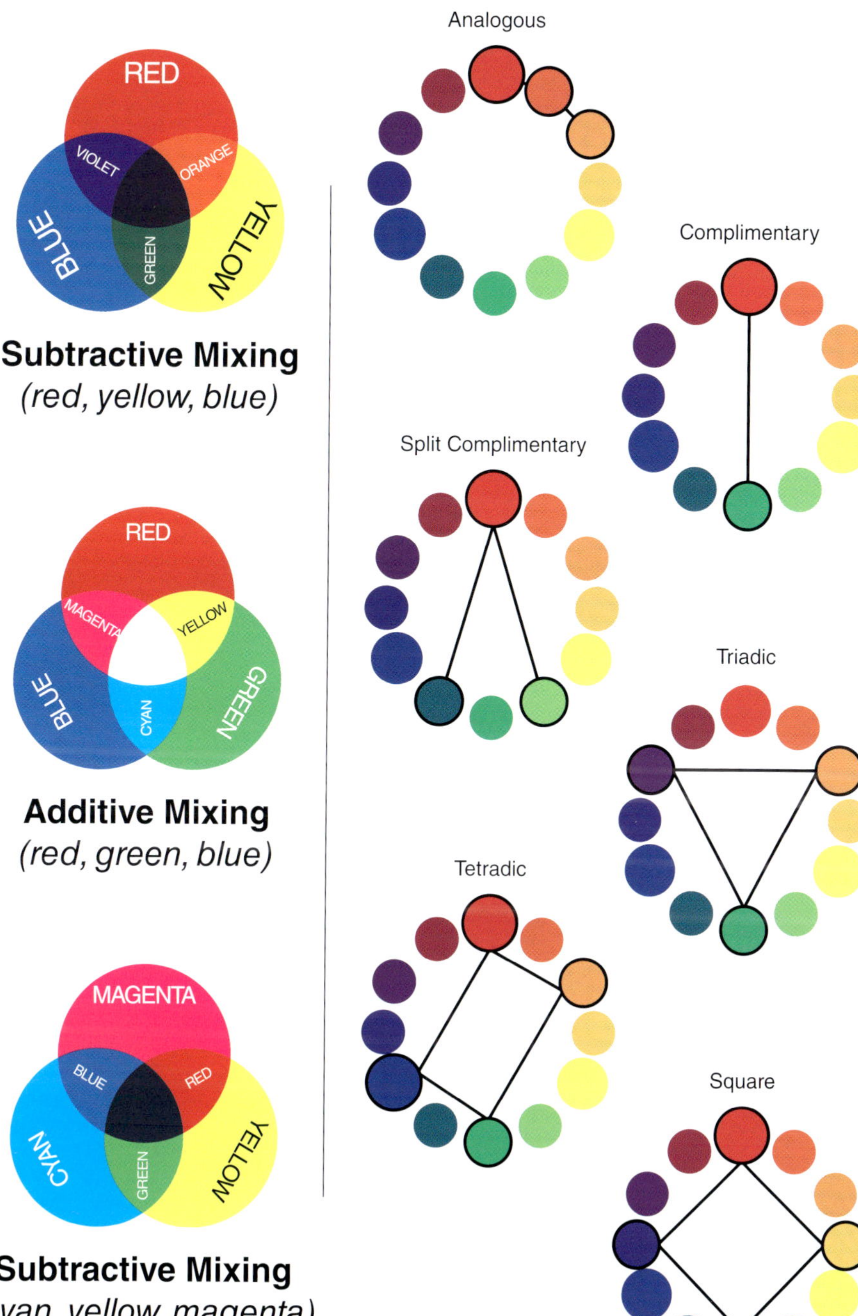

Plate 9
Various color schemes © Phil McCollam.

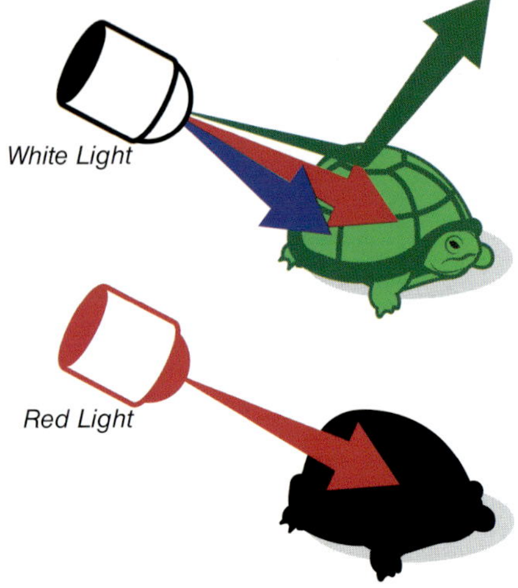

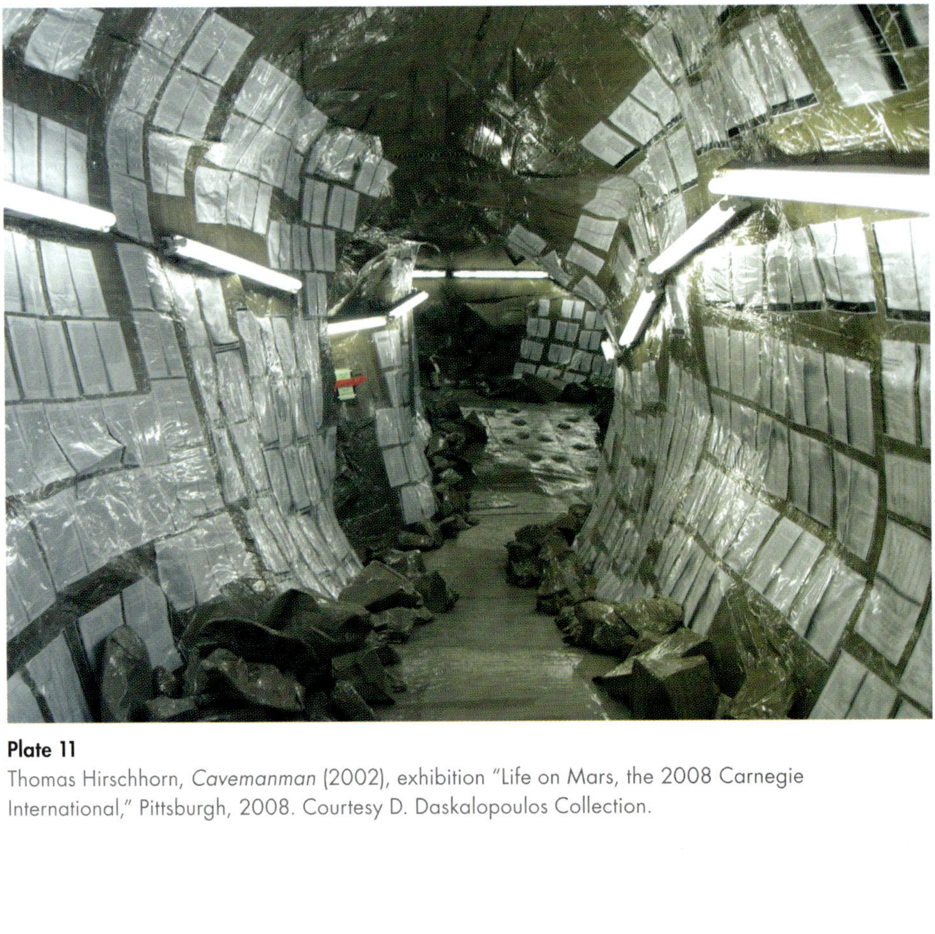

Plate 11
Thomas Hirschhorn, *Cavemanman* (2002), exhibition "Life on Mars, the 2008 Carnegie International," Pittsburgh, 2008. Courtesy D. Daskalopoulos Collection.

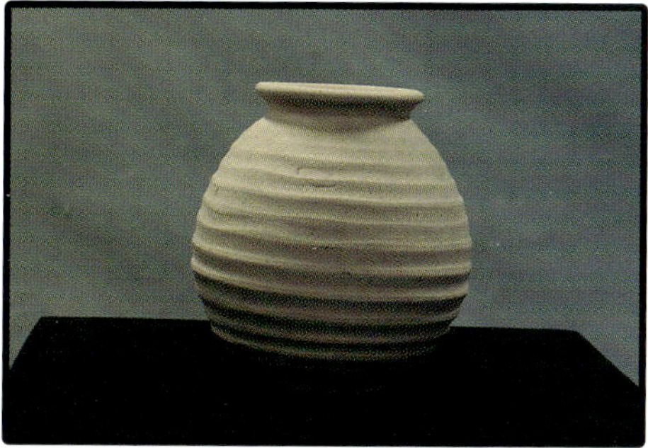

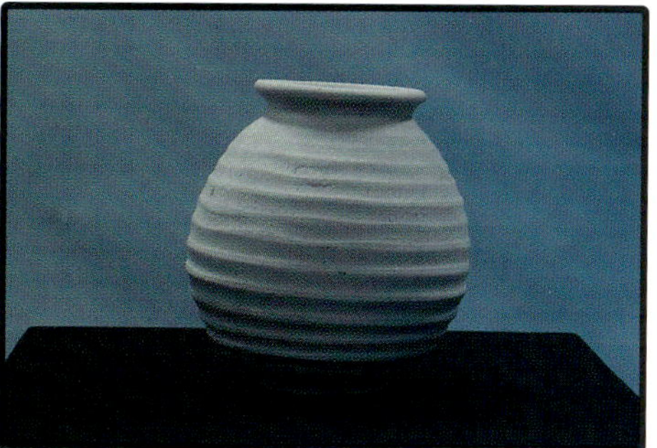

Plate 12
Notice the difference between the un-white balanced image on the left and the white balanced image on the right. © Phil McCollam.

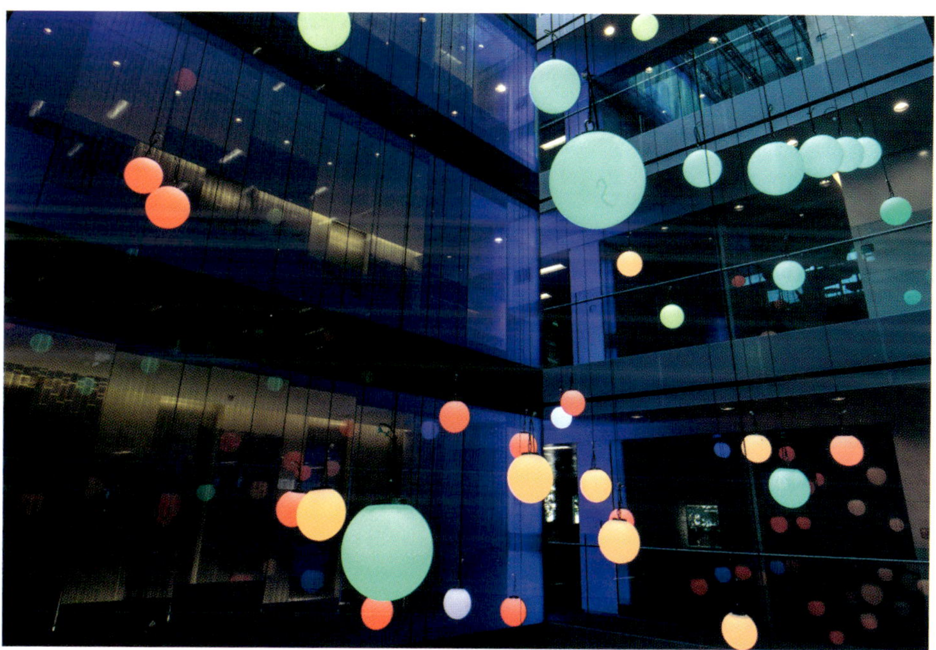

Plate 13
Ruairi Glynn and Alma-nac, *Balls!* (2014), light installation, dimensions variable. Courtesy of the artists.

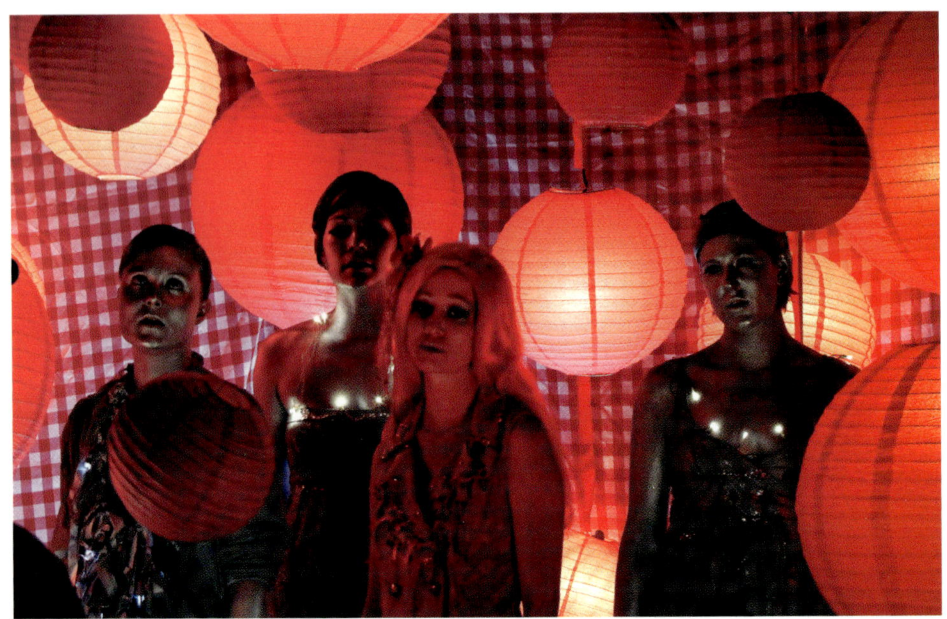

Plate 14

Glitter Chariot, *Should Have Been Blonde* (2012), music video, 4:15 minutes. Photographer: Robert Howard.

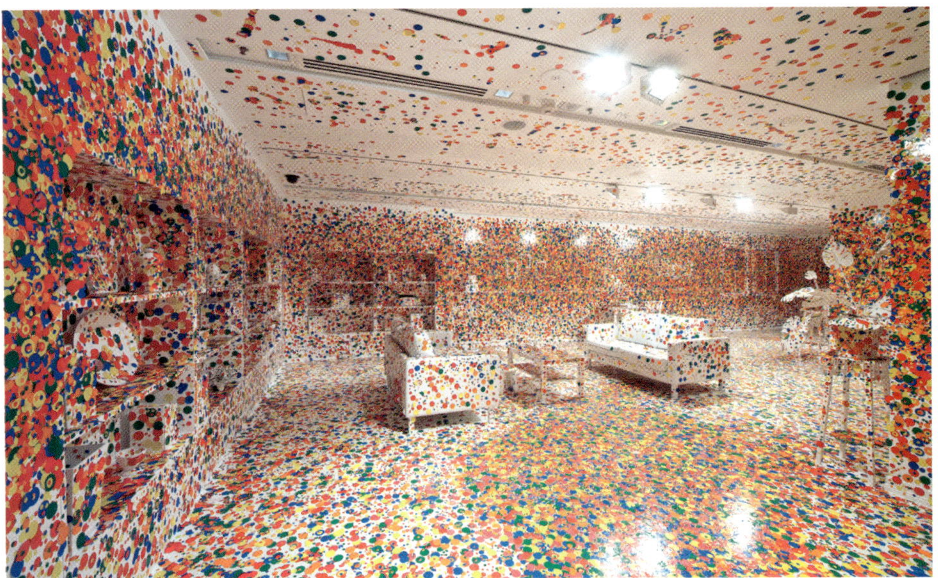

Plate 15

Yayoi Kusama, Japan, b. 1929, *The Obliteration Room* (2002 to present), furniture, white paint, dot stickers, dimensions variable. Collaboration between Yayoi Kusama and Queensland Art Gallery. Commissioned by the Queensland Art Gallery, Australia. Gift of the artist through the Queensland Art Gallery Foundation (2012). Collection: Queensland Art Gallery. Image © Yayoi Kusama. Courtesy David Zwirner, Victoria Miro Gallery, Ota Fine Arts, Yayoi Kusama Studio Inc.

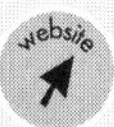

Interview: Steve Roden (*continued*)

computer or digital tools—as I like objects, situations, or sounds that aren't cleaned up. When I work with any tools, I tend to gravitate towards the artifacts of the medium—whether it be a cassette tape or guitar pedals or electricity. It's kind of like allowing your face to age naturally, as opposed to having plastic surgery simply to look younger . . . it isn't real.

—*Steve Roden*

Visit the book's website to read the full interview.

When working with light, there is a wide range of well-practiced directional approaches developed for theater, film, and television that can create a variety of feelings. For example, **sidelight**, or light aimed at the side of a subject, will expose the dimensions of your subject, while **backlight**, or light that is aimed at the back of an object, will often create a glowing outline—or halo effect—around the subject. Sometimes backlight is also passed through a diffusion material such as fabric or plastic, to create silhouettes (fig. 4-13). **Down-lighting**, light from directly above a subject or work surface pointed straight down, is a type of directional light associated with interior design because it is common in office and living spaces where it is not distracting and often sets occupants at ease. Stereotypically, we expect light to come from above because that is how we are generally illuminated in nature. **Up-lighting** is the opposite; it is pointed up at the subject from a location below and creates an accent on your subject. Having light come up from below can even be disarming because it places shadows in areas that are the exact opposite of where we see them on a daily basis. In Glitter Chariot's music video set in a bar, *Should Have Been Blonde* (2012), a combination of sidelight and up-light help reflect red from the lead female singer onto the silver-clad backup singers (Plate 14, color insert). The red tones are further enhanced by light diffused through red paper lanterns hanging all around the performers.

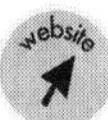

Visit the book's website to read an interview with Ryan Berg, who created the video for *Should Have Been Blonde*.

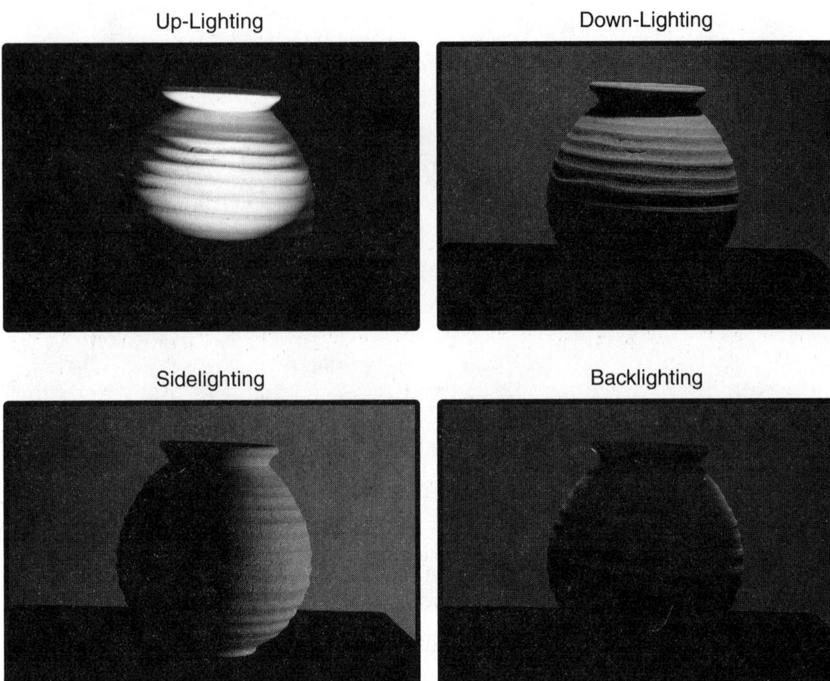

Fig. 4-13
Illustration of the different effects produced by sidelight, backlight, down-light, and up-light. © Phil McCollam.

Exercise

Ryan Berg cites Disneyland as one of his favorite 4D works, explaining, "It's [a] perfect design with sound, reality and fakeness all wrapped into one." Write down what you think are the subject, form, content, and context for Disneyland. Analyze how it uses direction or reflection in movement, light, and/or sound. Compare and contrast your answers with others'. How are your answers similar and different from those around you? Were there any trends in the answers?

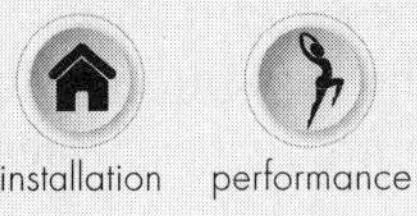

installation   performance

With any of these directional lighting techniques, it is important to be aware of **glare**, which is strong light directed or reflected into the participants' eyes. Generally, glare is to be avoided. However, in some cases, the

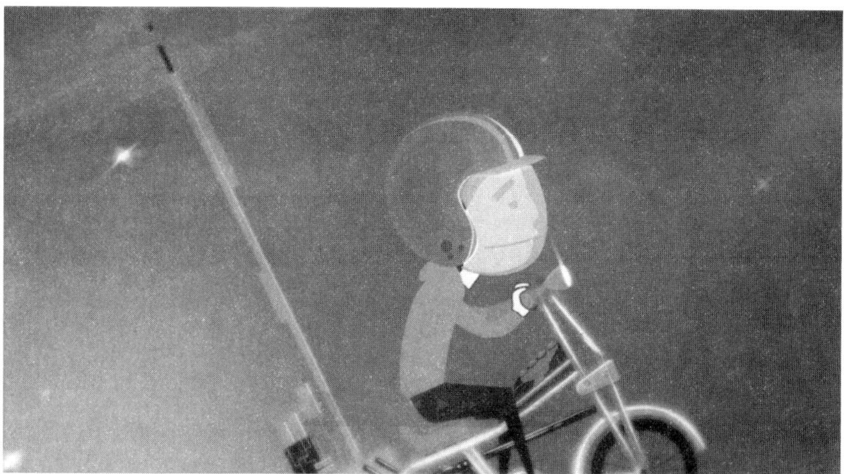

Fig. 4-14
Cesar Martinez, *A Rather Lovely Thing* (2014), animation, 3:47 minutes. Courtesy of the artist.

artist or designer may be seeking this particular effect for a conceptual reason. It is difficult to eliminate reflection altogether, although it can be reduced depending on the surfaces involved and the direction of the light.

Horizontal Orientation/Dutch Tilt

Another use of direction is the orientation of the horizon line or subject in screen-based works. In a film, a camera may tilt to make the horizon line or subject diagonal rather than horizontal or vertical. This change in direction, also known as a **Dutch tilt**, is an effective way to disorient, stress, or excite the viewer. Humans want the horizon line to always be horizontal, thereby anchoring us to the surface of the earth. Cesar Martinez's *A Rather Lovely Thing* (2014) is a fantastical short animation about a man seeking to reconnect with his girlfriend who has passed away. Martinez uses a diagonal orientation at a climactic moment to create anticipation as the protagonist shoots up into the atmosphere on a machine that will get him to heaven (fig. 4-14).

Interview: Cesar Martinez

I'm an illustrator and art director from Mexico City based in Vancouver. I've been a graphic designer for 8 years now but I'm aiming to do more personal projects nowadays to explore new styles and techniques, but mostly to create projects with true passion involved. [*A Rather Lovely Thing*] is a story about love and adventure. It started as a personal story to tell and a chance to do animation

(continued)

Interview: Cesar Martinez (*continued*)

without a team involved. During the production of this video, it became more like a universal feeling and a universal story to tell.

Can you describe a work by another artist that also uses the element of direction quite well?

I love how the villains were portrayed in the Batman TV show during the 60s. It was over used but it's definitely what it makes it so unique storytelling-wise.

—*Cesar Martinez*

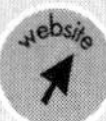 Visit the book's website to read the full interview.

Exercise

Brainstorm the premises for three different imaginary action-adventure films. For example, one might be about a woman who traverses the Sahara desert in search of treasure. Create a storyboard for the opening titles of one of these films. Use a combination of words and directional lighting to set the tone for the film. Show the work to a partner, and take note of his or her reactions. Did your partner feel like the titles supported the genre of action-adventure, and how or how not? Make revisions as necessary before final critique.

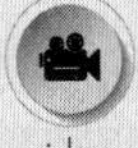 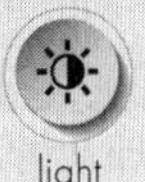

video   light

Architecture

One last element affected by direction is architecture, which can have a vertical or horizontal direction, or a combination of the two. Each direction conveys different ideas or feelings. For example, horizontal architecture—such as Frank Lloyd Wright's Prairie School of architecture, which consisted of low, long buildings—can imply steady, placid dependability, whereas vertical architecture—such as that of a skyscraper—suggests dynamism, power, and excitement.[8]

Overall, the direction of movement, light, sound, and architecture will affect how your work is understood and experienced. Your choices regarding direction should be weighed carefully.

Repetition

Repetition is the appearance of an element of art and design more than once within a work. Repetition can help bind a work together, creating a sense of cohesion. In 4D art and design, repetition can take the form of series, sequences, scenes, loops, rituals, habituation, rhythm, and pattern.

Series, Sequence, and Scene

A **series** describes multiple artworks that are linked by a repeating element such as a central concept, narrative, or visual element. For example, Matthew Barney's *Cremaster Series* (1994–2002) consists of five feature-length films, each with its own host of fantastical characters, exploring a variety of concepts and subjects such as sexual differentiation and maturation.

A **sequence** is a film term for a collection of related scenes. It could also refer to a collection of light or sound cues, or a collection of movements. Any light or laser show is an example of a light and sound sequence. While a **scene** is "defined by the unity of time, space, and action . . . a sequence, on the other hand, maintains one or more of these unities while introducing a discontinuity."[9]

Loop

A **loop** is the repetition of the same material over and over, and is commonly found in video, although it could also be found in lighting, sound, or movement sequences. Jonathan Rattner's *End, End, End* (2013), a durational video work dealing with loss, plays as an endless loop (fig. 4-15).

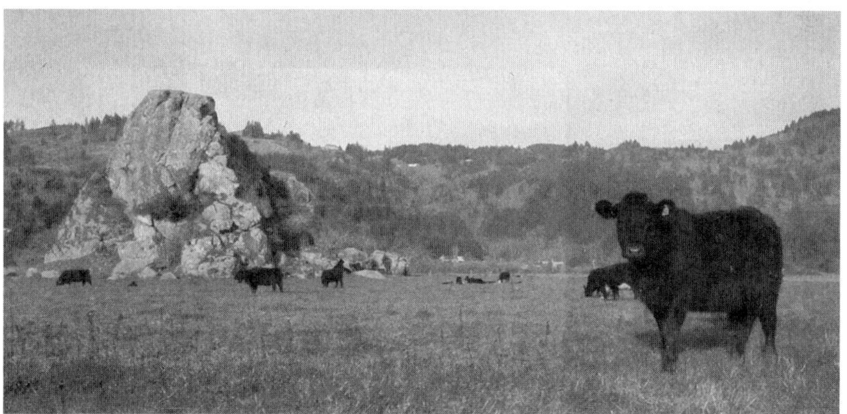

Fig. 4-15
Jonathan Rattner, *End, End, End* (2013), digital video, 8:46 minutes. Courtesy of the artist.

Participants are welcome to step in and watch a portion of the work, and then step away as they feel motivated to do so.

Interview: Jonathan Rattner

I consider the practice of time-based media as an opportunity to be reflective and mindful. I treat my process like a ritual, in which each step allows me to feel more present, active, and conscious of the world around me.

During production, I work very much like a photojournalist. I travel to locations, wander, observe, conduct interviews, and gather images and sounds. For the most part, I work alone, and I tend not to follow a script. I rarely use a tripod or lights, and I often shoot long durational shots without moving the camera (panning) or changing the focal length (zooming). While I'm recording sounds or images, I try to take in all of the sensory information around me; feel my body, listen to sounds, and look for visual patterns and rhythms in the environment. I'm interested in experiencing what I may have ignored without my camera.

In post-production, my approach is akin to that of a collage artist, juxtaposing images and sounds from different locations and times. My editing decisions are not preplanned, and a short work can take months to complete. Like production, editing is very much a meditative act in which I repeatedly review sounds and images as different constructions until a concept or story arises.

End, End, End is an experimental film that mimics the fragmentary nature of thoughts and memories. I made this work when someone in my life was dying. Reviewing it now, I think it has to do with my inability to know how to appropriately interact with losing a loved one. Conceptually, I was striving to make something meaningful out of a jumble of images, words, and sounds that are—on their own—(arguably) meaningless.

—*Jonathan Rattner*

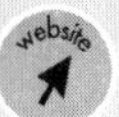
Visit the book's website to read the full interview.

Ritual

A **ritual** is a series of actions or a type of behavior regularly and invariably followed by someone. There are a variety of rituals, both public and private, but repetition is central to all of them. An example of art utilizing ritual is Miranda July and Harrell Fletcher's online project *Learning to Love You More* (2002–2009). It consisted of a website, a series of assignments or sets of instructions disseminated by July and Fletcher, and a collection of reports from people who chose to complete the assignments. The reports could consist of photos, text, videos, or other media. These assignments were ritualistic in that many people repeated them over time, following the artists' prescriptive directions. The collected completed assignments were then displayed in a variety of exhibitions, screenings, and radio broadcasts all over the world.

Exercise

Visit *Learning to Love You More* online, and execute one assignment that involves repetition. You must also use a time-based media to complete the assignment. As a class, critique each other's assignments for use of repetition and time. Whose work was most successful and why? What could others have done to improve their works?

 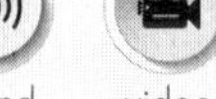 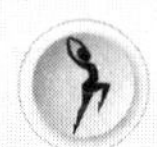  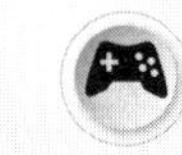 

sound   video   performance   installation   games   light

Exercise

Brainstorm a list of 10 rituals (for example, surprise birthday parties, first dates, getting up in the morning). Think about the role of repetition in rituals. Then create your own ritual. What is the motivation behind your ritual? Is repetition used in an expressive or utilitarian way? Be ready to demonstrate your ritual and explain your choices in critique.

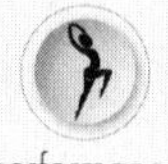

performance

Habituation

With any of these forms of repetition, an artist runs the risk of habituation, which is the tiring of the nerves that sense extended sameness or extended periods of rapid change. In some cases, an artist may actively seek out this result because once habituation is established, any changes to the repetition are amplified, which could help create focus within the work. In Joelle Dietrick and Owen Mundy's video *Anemophilous Formula for Computer Art*, the movement of the falling yellow-green dots creates the possibility of habituation for viewers who sit with the piece for its entire duration (see the book's website for a link to this work).

Exercise

As a class, stand up and scatter throughout an open space or room. Start moving around the space. Then select a person whose movements you are going to attempt to copy or repeat. Make sure the person you are repeating cannot tell you have chosen him or her. You do not have to repeat everything about this person; you could select just his or her tempo, direction, gestures, posture, and so on. Notice those around you, and see whether you can tell who they are repeating. Once you locate a pair, add yourself to their repetition. Continue until everyone is repeating the same person.

performance

Rhythm

Rhythm, a regularized repeating of movement or sound, is an element of musicality that has been borrowed by visual artists and designers. It can occur anytime repetition is present, and its opposite is *irregularity*. Humans embody rhythm in their heartbeats, breathing, and daily activities like walking. Human voices also tend to follow unique rhythms. Rhythm is utilized in animation and video as similar images, cuts, or types of shots repeat, and it can also be found in lighting and sound. It occurs in video games, which calculate and integrate how many times you can rapidly and rhythmically press a controller button. Rhythm can also help establish a sense of mood and timing in your work. For example, a very rhythmic soundscape could create a sense of calmness and reliability, or it could insinuate an oppressive environment. Meanwhile, irregularity in your work can keep participants on their toes, or it can leave them confused, scared, or amused.

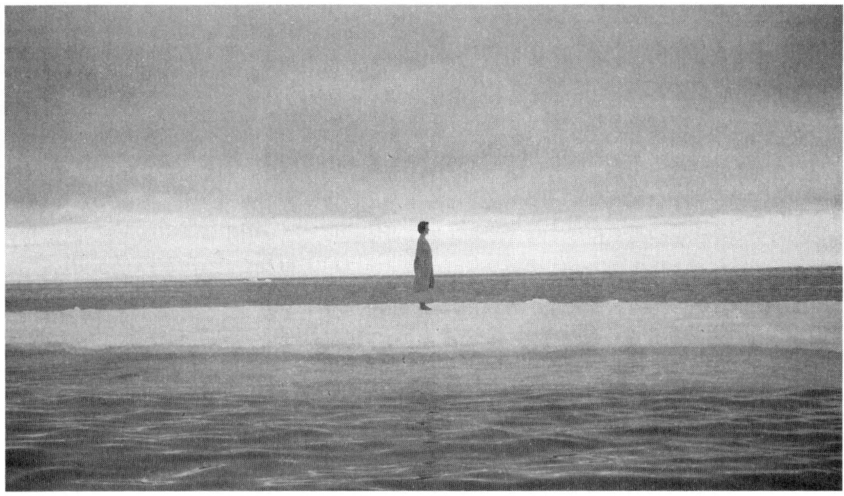

Fig. 4-16
Heidi Kumao, *Swallowed Whole* (2014), digital video, single channel, color, stereo,
4:07 minutes. Courtesy of the artist.

An example of rhythm in action is Heidi Kumao's single-channel video *Swallowed Whole* (2014) (fig. 4-16). This piece explores a feeling of isolation. It involves a rhythmic rolling of imagery from the top to the bottom of the screen. This movement simulates the crunching and compressing action of the sledding accident in which the artist broke her back. This traumatic experience inspired the work that in turn tries to convey the personal trauma through the manipulation of imagery.

Interview: Heidi Kumao

Swallowed Whole is a somber, animated, experimental film about surviving extreme isolation and physical limitations as a result of traumatic injury. After breaking my back in a sledding accident, I was forced to lie supine on the couch for 3.5 months during which my mind often descended into a desolate, disorienting dreamscape. Feeling stifled, I imagined that I was trapped under a frozen lake; life continued on above me while I looked up from below. This sensation became the kernel from which I created this film.

    Swallowed Whole draws a parallel between the exploration of this suspended state and Arctic exploration. The Arctic is a

(*continued*)

Interview: Heidi Kumao (*continued*)

completely foreign landscape to most people, a place in which time slows down, activity of daily life is transformed, and human capabilities are tested by its physical extremes. These characteristics could just as easily be used to describe the physical and psychological experience of recovering from a traumatic injury. Both journeys require the navigation of harsh new territories and possess unlimited blank space for thoughts, hallucinations, dreams, and nightmares. *Swallowed Whole* weaves together photos, animations, videos, and sound recordings and takes the viewer on an abbreviated journey through the physical and psychological landscapes of hospitalization and recovery. Some of the imagery and sounds were collected during The Arctic Circle 2013 Summer Solstice Expedition, an international research expedition for artists, writers, and scientists.

I edited the video to emphasize the physical impact of dropping, crashing, and slamming; repeated vertical frame-rolls from analog TV metaphorically replay the impact that literally broke my back. I wanted to create a video that viewers would feel; the bone-crushing sounds and jarring movement echo throughout the film mirroring the repetition of trauma, and the trauma of repetition, commonly associated with post-traumatic stress disorder. The recurring instability of the image reflects the fragility of my injured body while providing a palpable experience for the viewer. The piece is inspired in part by Joan Jonas' *Vertical Roll* (1972) which uses a common analog television set malfunction to create a shifting stage of activity. *Swallowed Whole* uses fragmentation to both tell and disrupt the story and serves as a window of empathy into PTSD repetition compulsion.

—*Heidi Kumao*

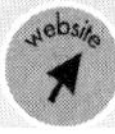
Visit the book's website to read the full interview.

Pattern

Pattern is a repeated set of organized elements. Human brains are wired to detect pattern even if no patterns actually exist. For example, many people search for familiar shapes in cloud formations. Pattern is inherent in music and architecture, and it is often purposefully utilized in lighting, movement, and sound. Pattern in a lighting design can help participants determine the physical form of the space as well as how they should function in it. *Silo 468* (2013), a light installation placed within an old silo and designed by Lighting Design Collective, is an excellent example of pattern at work (fig. 2-10). There are 2,012 holes drilled into the sides of the silo, and when the holes are illuminated, patterns form according to the light and wind patterns outdoors.

Interview: Tapio Rosenius of Lighting Design Collective

People tend to lose themselves within this work and begin to "see things." I find that brilliant because it allows something that has industrial scale and materiality to become subtle, sensitive, and personal. I believe the sole reason for that is the movement of the lights. If they were static I don't think we would get that response from people. The element of time is completely the central issue here. It also must be something about the frequency of the movement and the non-repeating nature of it. It feels familiar, natural, acceptable, calming.

   One very memorable event was when a Finnish couple requested to have their wedding inside the silo. We got a glimpse of the ceremony at the end of our movie about the project. It was amazing to see the piece transformed into a venue for all the rituals associated with a Finnish wedding.

   —Tapio Rosenius of Lighting Design Collective

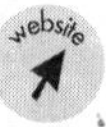
Visit the book's website to read the full interview.

Exercise

Go online, search for, and view a video of Jesús Rafael Soto's work *Blue Penetrable BBL* (1999). After watching the work, write down what you think are the subject, form, content and context for this work. Analyze how the artist used repetition. Compare and contrast

(continued)

Exercise (*continued*)

your answers with others'. How are your answers similar and different from those around you? Were there any trends in the answers?

 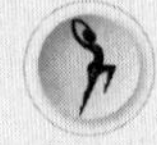
installation   performance

When something is repeated, it is never completely the same, because it is affected by the previous iterations or experiences of it. When a pattern of repetition is presented, viewers become more aware of breaks in the pattern. Participants become more alert to differences.[10] The placement of change—or its absence—within a stretch of repetition is often a pivotal part of a work and must be arranged carefully. For example, if you're dealing with a group of people in a performance, and you want each person to appear to the audience as a unique individual, simply ask them to all do the same thing. The differences in how each executes this similar action will immediately become clear, and they will all appear as individuals. If you ask them to all do something different, the audience will see only a collection of seemingly random actions and will not be scrutinizing each person for differences.[11]

Repetition, rhythm, pattern, and tempo can all reveal conceptual connections, or advance narratives. However, the artist must always question when and how to employ repetition.

Scale

Scale is the relative size of something in relation to its surroundings. It should not be confused with **proportion**, which is the comparative measurement of different parts of a whole. For example, proportions are exaggerated in the facial features of a caricature drawing, whereas scale is exaggerated when you compare dollhouse furniture to regularly sized furniture. Scale can refer to the size of a physical space, movements, the length or duration of a work, and so on. It can describe the size of an illuminated area or the size of a camera shot—wide versus extreme close-up. Scale can also describe the size of the overall project as it relates to the number of participants or steps involved; works that involve only a few people function on a much smaller scale than those projects that involve the interaction of an entire city.

Exercise

Try to make yourself as small as possible: don't think too much; just do it. Then relax. Now do the exact same thing, except this time *as you are attempting to make yourself as small as possible*, try to analyze the experience: how are you making yourself smaller, what are you physically doing with your body, how does it feel, and why are you doing it the way you are? Write down your observations. Then repeat the entire process, but now try to make yourself as large as possible. Share your findings with the group. Compare and contrast the group's findings. What are the commonalities? How could these observations help you create effective work? Why is it important to examine trends in human behavior?

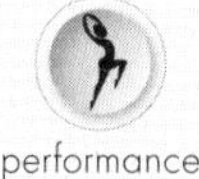

performance

Relativity

Relativity, or the comparison of a thing to its surroundings, is especially important to our understanding of scale. When people refer to something as small-scale, they are typically thinking of it as being smaller than they would expect to encounter. For example, if they say they saw a small house, we would generally interpret that to mean a house smaller than normally encountered. Similarly, if people refer to a project as living-room-scale or street-scale, they are comparing it to the relative size of each of those familiar spaces.

Exercise

Create two installations that can be entered physically. One should be the smallest possible scale while still allowing entry; the other should be the largest possible scale. The content of the works is entirely up to you. Take it to the extremes. Use light, color, movement, and sound to your advantage. At critique, determine which tactics were most successful and what could have been improved.

installation

Frame of Reference

Artists and designers can give their audiences clues about the scale of their projects by including familiar architectural objects (such as benches or doorways) or familiar systems of interaction to trigger scale comparisons. For example, a familiar system of interaction is patronizing a restaurant: when you arrive, you expect the forks to fit in your hand rather than be as tall as you are. Siqi Song's short animation *Food* (2014), which explores food sources and choices from a variety of viewpoints, immediately provides a frame of reference for the scale of the work when breakfast cereal is used in the opening scene (fig. 2-2). Most people know what size breakfast cereal is, and they therefore immediately understand the scale of the work.

Interview: Siqi Song

This is an animated documentary about food. I love food. I also love bringing stuff to life in stop-motion animation, so naturally combining the two loves was bound to happen. After speaking with different people about food and their preferences, I was surprised to find how different their opinions were and how much food affected their lives. I interviewed and recorded the statements of vegetarians, vegans, pescetarians, and meat eaters, and then edited the soundtracks and rebuilt the conversation using stop-motion animated foods that speak for themselves. The film brings in discussion about various topics in the food industry including factory farming, urban environments, and life choices.

—Siqi Song

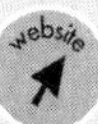

Visit the book's website to read the full interview.

Exercise

Create the largest possible sound you can, and the smallest possible sound. How will you present these sounds? For example, will you make the sounds live? Will you record the sounds and then present them through speakers? Will you have someone or something else make the sounds for you? As you make these decisions, also ask how context can help enhance the scale of the sounds. For example, if you just hold up your phone and play two clips, would that be as effective as creating a specialized installation for each sound, or creating a tour to hear the sounds in specific locations? Is it important to hear the two contrasting sounds in quick succession? At critique, determine which tactics were most successful, and what could have been improved.

sound   installation

Using Scale Effectively

Keep in mind that regardless of media, each artwork establishes its own scale and this should help direct artistic choices. A large-scale work may make a participant feel small and insignificant, while a small-scale work can feel intimate and empowering. In the independent video game *Jeff Koons Must Die!!!* (2011) by Hunter Jonakin, scale is a central factor in the participant's experience (fig. 4-17). The goal of the game is to wreak havoc in a simulated exhibit of artist Jeff Koons's work, which includes a variety of Koons's large-scale sculptures that are much larger than typical humans. Meanwhile, the housing for the game (when encountered in a gallery

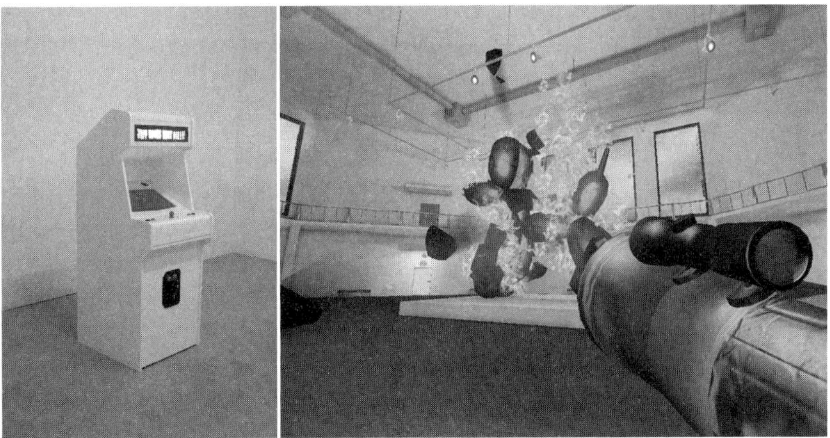

Fig. 4-17

Hunter Jonakin, *Jeff Koons Must Die!!!* (2011), video game and installation, dimensions variable. Courtesy of the artist

setting) is an intimate-scale, fabricated 1980s-style stand-up arcade cabinet, which accommodates only one participant at a time. This juxtaposition of large and intimate scales within the same work creates a compelling interactive experience.

Interview: Hunter Jonakin

Jeff Koons Must Die!!! came about in my last year of grad school when I was realizing that the art world was a complicated space to navigate. I wanted to create a piece that was conceptually layered and instill in it the possibility of shifting a viewer's ideological viewpoint while they were interacting with the work. Obviously, everyone reads art differently, but, at the very least, I wanted to create the space for that shift. The work is meant to seem didactic and polarizing, but I wanted to give viewers a chance to question their own destructive tendencies. In the end, all of us are implicated in the carnage, the struggle for power, overreaching ambitions, and need for acceptance.

What is one of your favorite 4D artworks, or pieces of design, and why?

I like Ryan Trecartin's *K-CorealNC.K (section a)* (2009) a lot because it perfectly mirrors popular culture, scrambles it, and serves it back up to you. It is mesmerizing. There is no narrative to speak of but it seems like there is a narrative. I feel like it is trying to tell me something very important but I just can't quite figure it out. In the end, I think it's telling me something I already know. The white noise of information is just repackaged in a new container and placed just out of reach. Interesting visuals, jump-cuts, and graphics overlays make this video difficult to stop watching.

—*Hunter Jonakin*

Visit the book's website to read the full interview.

Exercise

Go online, search for, and view Ryan Trecartin's video work *K-CorealNC.K (section a)* (2009). Write down what you think are the subject, form, content, and context for this work. Analyze how the artist used scale. Compare and contrast your answers with others'. How are your answers similar and different from those around you? Were there any trends in the answers?

video

Scale is also important in screen-based works, because scale can be ambiguous without a point of reference to judge it against. Viewers witnessing an object on-screen will judge the scale first by their general knowledge of the object and how large they imagine it should be. Then, they will compare the size of the object to the area it occupies on-screen, while also considering the specific environment it is shown in, including other recognizable objects. Finally, if available, they will compare the object to a human, or even just a part of a human, to determine the object's actual scale.[12]

Exercise

A *compulsion* is a fixation on behaving in a certain way. For example, you may have a compulsion to wear your pants a certain way. Brainstorm a list of 10 of your own compulsions. Then, create a time-based work that illustrates one of your compulsions. How can you use scale to heighten or improve this work? At critique, do not tell others what your compulsion is; see if they can guess based on your work.

    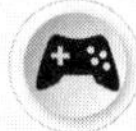 

sound   video   performance   installation   games   light

Altogether, scale is a powerful tool for creating the emotional environment of your work. Whether you are trying to amuse, scare, comfort, or impart wonder, using scale effectively will be central to your success.

Summary

In this chapter, we examined the principles of art and design borrowed from 2D and 3D analysis that are integral to our understanding of 4D art and design:

- Value/brightness, including how using different intensities of light (from low to high) can be used effectively in 4D artworks
- Balance and its role in movement, sound, lighting, and the gaming environment
- Contrast and how it can be effectively used in 4D works
- Direction/reflection as related to movement, light and sound, horizontal orientation, and architectural space
- Repetition, including distinguishing between a series and sequence, understanding ritual and habituation and their role in artworks, and recognizing the roles of rhythm and pattern in creating art
- Scale, including understanding relative scale, frame of reference, and how to use scale effectively

Applying these elements to our own work will lead to more effective and successful creations.

Key Terms

absorb   To soak up

asymmetrical balance   A type of balance in which parts are different on either side of a midline and feel like they could easily be thrown off balance

backlight   A light that illuminates the subject from behind, often creating a glowing outline—or halo effect—around the subject

balance   The measure of the relationship among different elements in an artwork

brightness   The relative intensity of a light as it grows to full luminance

contrast   The state of being different

diffused light   Light that passes through a material that scatters the light (clouds, haze, diffusion plastic, etc.)

direct light   Light pointed at a specific object or location

direction   The course along which something moves

down-lighting   Light from directly above a subject or work surface pointed straight down

Dutch tilt   A diagonal tilt of the camera; it is an effective way to disorient, stress, or excite the viewer

glare   Strong light directed or reflected into participants' eyes

habituation   The tiring of the nerves that sense extended sameness or extended periods of rapid change

high-key lighting   Brighter lighting situations

imbalanced   A condition of not being balanced

loop   The repetition of the same material over and over; it is commonly found in the presentation of video

low-key lighting   Darker lighting situations

pattern   A repeated set of organized elements

proportion   The comparative measurement of different parts of a whole

radial balance   A type of balance in which parts radiate out from a central point

reflected light   Light bounced off of one surface onto an intended object or location

relativity   The comparison of a thing to its surroundings

repetition   The appearance of an element of art and design more than once within a work

rhythm   A regularized repeating of a movement or sound

ritual   A series of actions or a type of behavior regularly and invariably followed by someone

scale   The relative size of something in relation to its surroundings

sequence   A film term for a collection of related scenes, although it could also refer to a collection of light or sound cues, or a collection of movements

series   Multiple artworks that are linked by a repeating element such as a central concept, narrative, or visual element

sidelight   Light aimed at the side of a subject

symmetrical balance   At type of balance in which parts are the same on either side of a midline and feel very stable

up-lighting   Light pointed up at the subject from a location below

value   Relative lightness or darkness (can refer to color or light)

visual weight   The weight your eyes assign to an object based on its dimensions, shape, location, and color

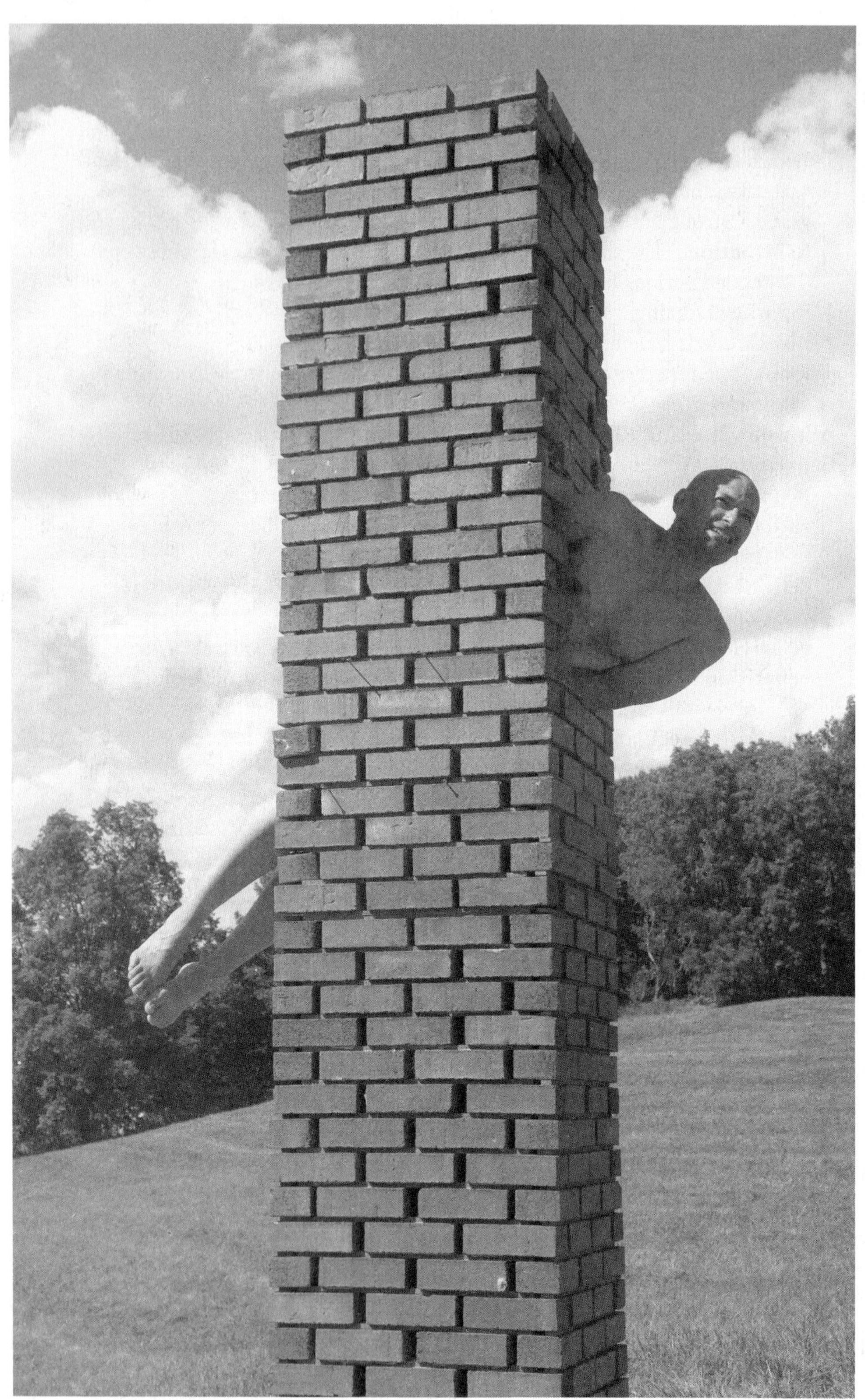

Courtesy of the artist. Photographer: Felicity Hogan.

5

Elements of 4D Art and Design

aving examined the elements and principles that carry over from 2D and 3D art and design, we will now more closely examine the elements of 4D design: time, architecture/topography, light, movement, and sound. These elements are the building blocks of any time-based work and can be infinitely rearranged to support your intentions as an artist or designer.

Time

The three dimensions—height, width, and depth—are augmented in 4D design by time. It is the fourth dimension. Although we all have a basic understanding of time, there are many different definitions of this term depending on the field from which one approaches it. For our purposes, we will say that **time** is the progression of events and existence from the past, through the present, and into the future. One could even simply say that time refers to change. All interactions take place over time and can range from nearly instantaneous, as in the case of a mouse click on your computer, to longer durations, such as days, months, or years. Humans often work to manipulate or control time: many work to lengthen their lives through diet, exercise, medicine, technology (such as traveling by plane rather than car), and more. Time can also be a potent tool for artists and designers: it reminds us of the limits on our own existence.

Categories of Time

There are several categories of time. **Measured time**—which is also known as *actual*, *objective*, or *clock time*—is time quantitatively measured by regularly recurring events or intervals, such as the passage of minutes, meals, seasons, or years. Because they can be measured, the length of cast shadows can also represent measured time, as can a variety of regularly recurring sounds in any given location. Live durational performances and events rely on actual time.

MEASURED TIME. Christian Marclay's 24-hour-long video piece *The Clock* (2010) uses time as its subject. It is also a clear example of measured time: footage from popular films showing different times throughout the day are edited together to form a clock that runs for 24 hours in real time (fig. 5-1). When the work is screened at a given location, the piece is purposefully aligned with the local time so that time as depicted in *The Clock* passes in unison with the viewer's actual time. A clock on-screen displays 8:00 when it is actually 8:00 in the gallery.

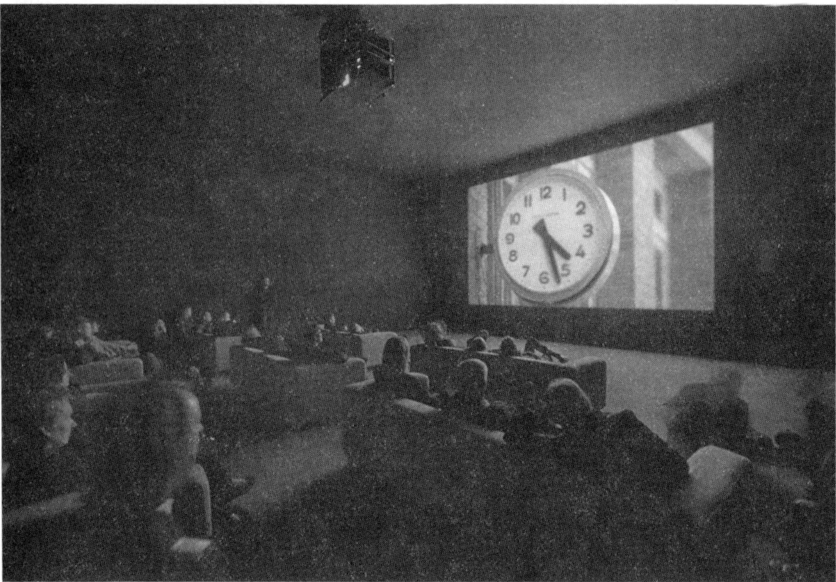

Fig. 5-1

Christian Marclay, installation view of *The Clock* (2010), single-channel video with sound; 24 hours. White Cube Mason's Yard, London (October 15–November 13, 2010). © Christian Marclay. Courtesy Paula Cooper Gallery, New York and White Cube, London. Photo: Todd-White Photography.

Another work shot in actual time, Paul Pfeiffer's *Morning After the Deluge* (2001), combines a sunrise and sunset by joining the two halves of the sun at the horizon line (Plate 3, color insert). Because the work utilizes actual time, the projection looks like a still image unless the participant stays with the work for the full 22 minutes of its duration. When utilized purposefully in this way, actual time can demand extreme patience from the audience.

Exercise

Create a 1-minute video that expresses clock time. Although Christian Marclay's *The Clock* (2010) is an example of this type of time, it is not necessarily the only method for presenting clock time in a project. At critique, compare and contrast your work with others'. Which works are most successful and why?

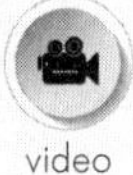

video

EXPERIENCED TIME. Experienced time—also known as *subjective, psychological, implied*, or *perceived time*—refers to the perceived of time passing. In the words of sound designer David Sonnenschein, it is "measured by the psychological disposition and attention of the participant. Whether [participants] are bored, excited, amused, or in pain will influence their subjective sense of time."[1] Experienced time is qualitatively measured and takes into consideration the significance of an event to a given individual. Therefore, by altering the other elements and principles of design, an artist or designer can effectively manipulate the participant's sense of experienced time by creating an engaging experience or environment.

In Tim Hawkinson's installation *Überorgan* (2000), he creates a massive, all-encompassing instrument out of inflatables, similar to an organ (fig. 5-2). The scale of this work and the elaborate nature of all the working parts can create a sense of excitement and interest for the participants, affecting their sense of experienced time. An actual hour spent with this work might feel as if only 10 minutes had passed because audience members' minds and bodies are so engrossed in the experience. This example also illustrates how subjective time is easily manipulated by using music due to its use of rhythm and tempo. A work with a speedy tempo can produce the sensation of time speeding up, while a slower piece might lull the participant into feeling that time has slowed down.

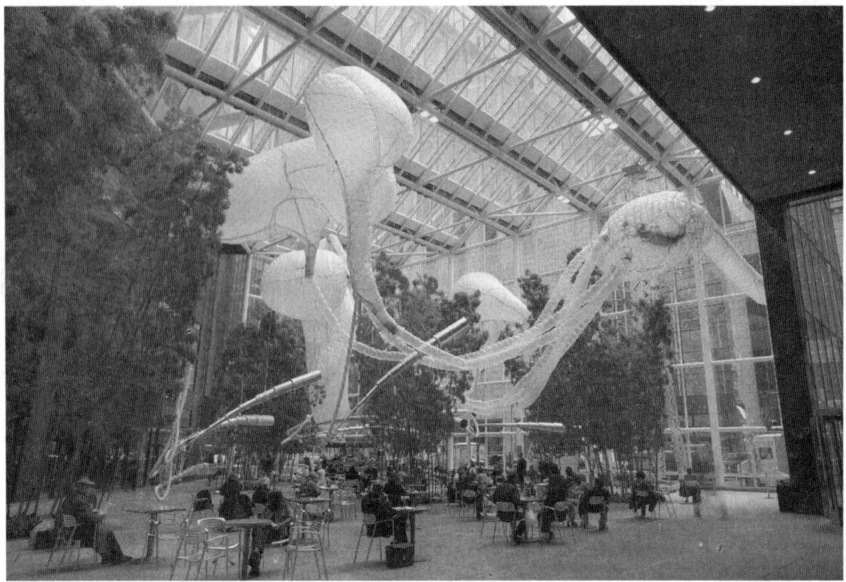

Fig. 5-2
Tim Hawkinson, *Überorgan* (2000), woven polyethylene, nylon net, cardboard tubing, various mechanical components, dimensions variable, installation view. Tim Hawkinson: Überorgan, 590 Madison Avenue, New York, March 26–June 1, 2005. © Tim Hawkinson, courtesy Pace Gallery. Photography by G.R. Christmas, courtesy the artist and Pace Gallery.

Exercise

PBS's series *Art21* has an episode on time (season 2, available online) that features Tim Hawkinson's *Überorgan* (2000) (fig. 5-2). This episode also features the work of Paul Pfeiffer, who creates videos such as *Morning After the Deluge* (2001) (Plate 3, color insert), which examine the importance of the passage of time. Write a comparative analysis of two of these artists' works, focusing specifically on their differing or similar usage of time. Discuss the subject, form, content, and context. Identify and explain the use of any elements or principles you feel are central to the works.

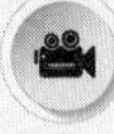

video   installation

EDITED TIME. **Edited time** is time that has been cut up and rearranged. It is a familiar term in film and video studies. Edited time can be linear or non-linear. **Linear time** (also known as *chronological time*) is mapped out in the order of past, present, and then future. **Nonlinear time** can reveal parts of the future mixed in with the past and present; there is no required order of events. For example, most people are familiar with the **montage**, which is a series of clips edited together to explore a piece of action, space, or time in greater detail or as an overview. A famous montage that has been parodied many times over is the physical training montage from the film *Rocky* (1976), which is set to the motivational song "Gonna Fly Now." In this montage the main character trains for a highly publicized boxing match. Here the director changed the order, or chronology, of a sequence to amplify the perceived meaning. Scenes from a training run are interspersed with scenes at a gym, leaving the viewer excited for Rocky's upcoming contest.

Another technique that manipulates our perception of time is **time-lapse photography**. Here, images are taken at regular intervals over a period of time, and then edited together to "speed up" a process that we normally don't experience. For example, it may take several days for a flower to bloom; by editing together pictures taken over the entire growth period, the bloom cycle can be condensed and becomes visible. This often has a surreal effect as time is collapsed in this process.

Exercise

Create a time-lapse video (edited time) of destruction or decay. To generate ideas, go online and research examples of this type of work, such as Sam Taylor-Johnson's *Still Life* (2001) in which a basket of fruit slowly decays, or Gustav Metzger's *Auto-Destructive Art* (1965) in which he paints with hydrochloric acid on stretched nylon, thereby slowly melting the material as he paints. Go through the steps of setting your camera to take photos at regular intervals, or work with a partner to manually photograph the work. In critique, ask what subjects were most powerful and why. Explain how the passage of time created or enhanced the meaning of the works.

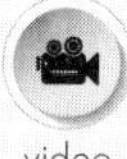

video

RUNNING TIME. Running time refers to the total length of a live event or a video piece (also known as *play time* when describing gaming). For example, most feature-length films have a running time between 90 minutes and 2 hours. **Plot time** (also known as *story time* or *scope [of a narrative]*) represents the span of time the plot covers within the work. For example, a film might have a running time of 90 minutes; however, its plot time may cover the history of the civil rights movement, which spans decades. It is possible for running time and story time to be the same duration, but it takes precise editing or a single continuous shot to align these two measurements. For example, each season of the television show *24* (2001–2010) consists of 24 one-hour episodes, which correspond to the 24 hours in a day. In this case, the running time and story time of the show have the same duration.

In video games, the total length of the game is often referred to as *play time*, although the play time of many games may be longer (or shorter) depending on how the player chooses to engage with the game. For example, some players might choose to thoroughly explore the game world, while others might engage in *speedrunning*, which is playing a game with the intent to finish as quickly as possible.

Exercise

Create a new game with an empty plastic bottle (any size or shape) in which anything can happen to the bottle during the game. Brainstorm at least 15 ways to engage this bottle in a game. It could be a physical competition, a board game, a card game, a video game, and so on. Figure out how many players there will be, and pay special attention to how long the game will last. Will it be short or long? Will participants potentially lose interest? Will the game end because of a preset time limit, or will it end when a certain goal is achieved? You will be forced to do some testing and changing until you arrive at a good length for your game. Once you have finalized the game, test it by having others play it, and ask for feedback on the timing.

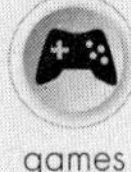

games

BIOLOGICAL TIME. Biological time is a measure of time related to bodily functions, such as when we feel awake, tired, or hungry. It is important to take biological time into consideration when constructing a time-based work because participants could be distracted by their bodies' sleeping or eating rhythms, depending on the time at which they experience the work. In Melissa Haviland's *White Gold* (2012), an interactive performance exploring parallels between sugar and fine porcelain, participants can eat cookies that have been freshly screen-printed with buttercream frosting (fig. 5-3). The success of the work can partially depend on whether or not participants' biological time is aligned with the presentation of the work. If the participants were not hungry when they encountered the work, and they did not take the cookies, the interactivity—and overall experience— would be less successful.

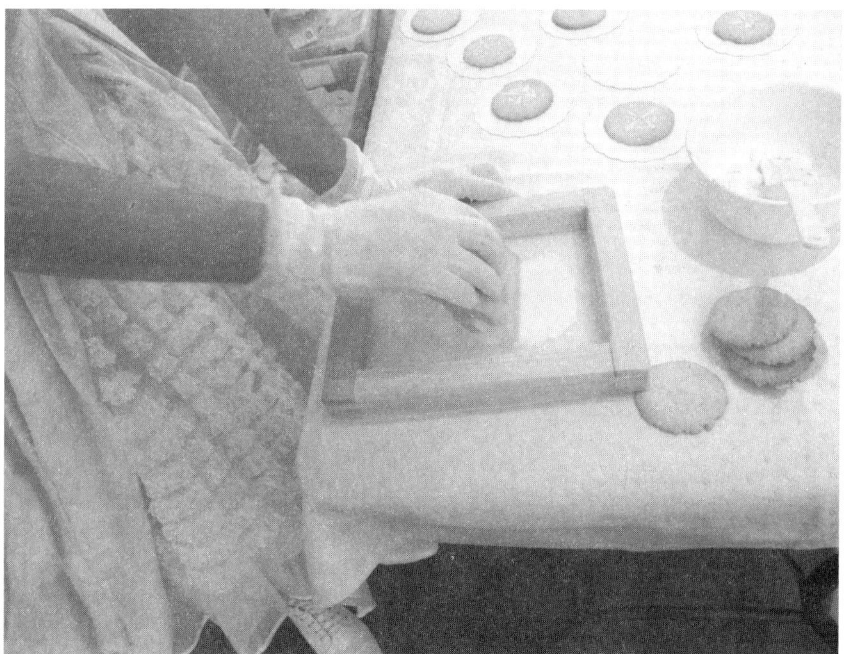

Fig. 5-3
Melissa Haviland, *White Gold* (2012), cookies, frosting, interactions, dimensions variable. Courtesy of the artist.

Interview: Melissa Haviland

Currently there have been two reiterations of a *White Gold*—the first in what I hope is a long series of pieces that compare sugar and fine porcelain.

Both pieces include me dressed in an all white dress serving cookies made or decorated through a printmaking process. In the first reiteration, I screen print icing on the cookies before serving them. In the second, I pre-made the cookies using cookie press plates that I made in the shape of teacups.

The goal with the *White Gold* series is to explore the conceptual and aesthetic relationships between fine china/porcelain and sugar and high-end sweets. Both sugar and porcelain have both been referred to as "white gold" in their history and have symbolized extreme luxury and indulgence. This quote from *Sugar: A Bittersweet History* by Elizabeth Abbot exemplifies the decadence that I am interested in examining: "In 1566, when Maria de Aviz married Alessandro Farnese, the Duke of Parma, the sugar platters at their wedding feast held a stunning array of sweets that guests devoured in sugar dishes and glasses, cutting larger bonbons with sugar knives and forks, mopping up syrupy ones with sugar bread."

—*Melissa Haviland*

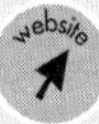 Visit the book's website to read the full interview.

Exercise

Go online, search for, and view *NUB* (it was performed multiple times/years) created by artist duo Dutes Miller and Stan Shellabarger. After watching the work, write down what you think are the subject, form, content, and context for this work is. How did the artists use time within the work? Compare and contrast your answers with others'. How are your answers similar and different from those around you? Were there any trends in the answers?[

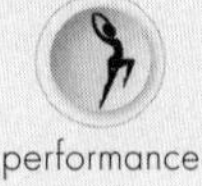

performance

DIGITAL TIME. **Digital time**, which is measured in milliseconds and often associated with technology, elicits an intense awareness of time. Think about how long it takes for a webpage to appear in your browser, and how you feel when it takes longer than expected. Think about watching an online discussion unfold before your eyes, as in Ed Fornieles's *Dorm Daze* (2011), which took place entirely on Facebook as a series of messages and posts among a group of fictitious people (fig. 6-8). If the communications had been revealed all at once, rather than as a series of quickly unfolding conversations, the work would have elicited a much different response from its audience. Digital time is also a factor in sporting events, such as swimming or running, where competitors may win by a fraction of a second. **Battery life** can create a similar hyper-awareness of time by highlighting the length of time a given battery allows you to complete a task on a piece of electronic equipment. Remember a time when you were nearing the end of the battery life of your device and you needed to quickly complete a task; at that moment you were hyper-aware of the battery life and how it could affect your experience.

There are many different types of time, and it is up to you as the artist or designer to decide which will most benefit your work. Although all humans experience time, conscious choices made while developing a work can cause the audience's experience of that time to change.

Architecture/Topography

Architecture

According to author and video game designer Jesse Schell, "The primary purpose of architecture is to control a person's experience." Nearly all principles of design play a part in the creation and analysis of architecture, and nearly all 4D artworks involve architecture unless they are executed away from any built structures. Artists and designers can deal with architecture in terms of both physical and virtual spaces based on their chosen medium.

Depending on your role, if you have the luxury of selecting the architectural space in which you will create a work, be sure to consider all available possibilities, not just traditional choices. For example, just because a traditional stage or a gallery space is available, it doesn't mean it is the best choice for your work. Instead, take into consideration the various components of your work, and seek out an architectural space that is the most effective choice for displaying or executing your specific work.

Exercise

From you current location, take note of the space you are situated in. We always position ourselves in relation to architecture such as walls, areas for sitting or standing, pieces of furniture within architecture, and so on. Take note of where your feet are and the nature of the topography. How near or far are you from various forms? How are light and sound behaving within the space?[2] Write down your observations.

installation

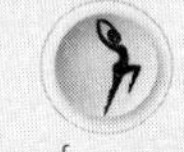
performance

Scale

Scale is a defining principle of architecture, whether we discuss it in terms of the size of the total volume of a space, or in terms of the partitioned volumes of individual rooms or spaces. Differently scaled spaces will affect viewers and participants in various ways depending on how full or empty they are. In your work, ask yourself if small spaces open into larger ones, or vice versa. Are there transitional spaces like hallways, or are different-sized spaces adjacent? How are these transitional spaces scaled? The scale of objects within an architectural space, such as furniture or other objects, also contributes to the overall feeling of a space and will help direct focus.

Video artist Isaac Julien uses large-scale projection screens to alter the architecture of the gallery in his work *Ten Thousand Waves* (2010) (fig. 5-4). He arranges the nine hanging screens irregularly throughout the central area of the space, rather than hanging them on the four walls in a more traditional fashion. This unexpected arrangement of large-scale screens deviates from viewer expectations, thus creating architectural interest and a meandering path for viewer interaction. Additionally, this piece is about memory, narrative, and point of view; the formal choice to scatter the large-scale screens showing a variety of points of view throughout the architectural space enhances these concepts by allowing the audience to experience the work in their own ways.

There are also regularly recurring elements of architecture that have an expected scale, such as doors, windows, floors, ceilings, and walls. People expect to see these elements because they regularly encounter them. Artists and designers can choose to alter their scale—or even not use them at all—according to their intentions. An example of an artist using scale and the

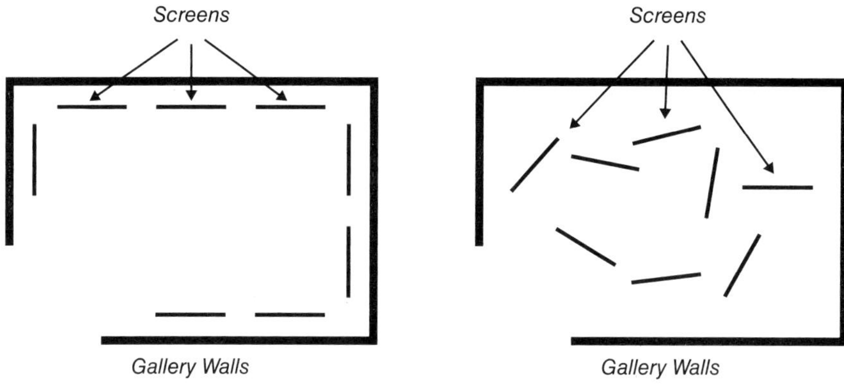

Fig. 5-4

The layout for Isaac Julien's *Ten Thousand Waves* (2010) involves screens that are hung irregularly throughout the central area of the space, rather than stereotypically hanging them on the four walls. © Phil McCollam.

absence of these stereotypical architectural elements is *Public Sculptor* (2010) by Cesar Cornejo (fig. 5-5). As part of the work, he diagonally inserted his body into an ambiguous and unadorned brick tower that was significantly taller than the onlookers. With no doors or windows, little is left to draw attention besides the intersection of the body and large stark architectural structure. During the performance, he interacted with the public, who also fed him, gave him water to drink, and talked with him about public sculpture and art related subjects. This work was an effort to redefine the relations between the public and the sculptural object through the use of architecture, performance, and scale.

Exercise

Brainstorm a list of 20 regularized architectural features of a contemporary space (such as windows, floors, and ceilings). Then, in a medium of your choice, purposefully alter the scale of one of these architectural features and invite participants to experience your alteration. Be creative in your alterations and work without damaging these architectural features. Observe participants' reactions to your alteration. Can you heighten their reaction? How?

 sound
 video
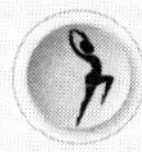 performance
 installation
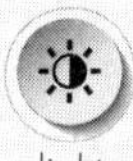 light
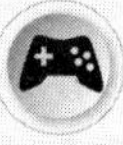 games

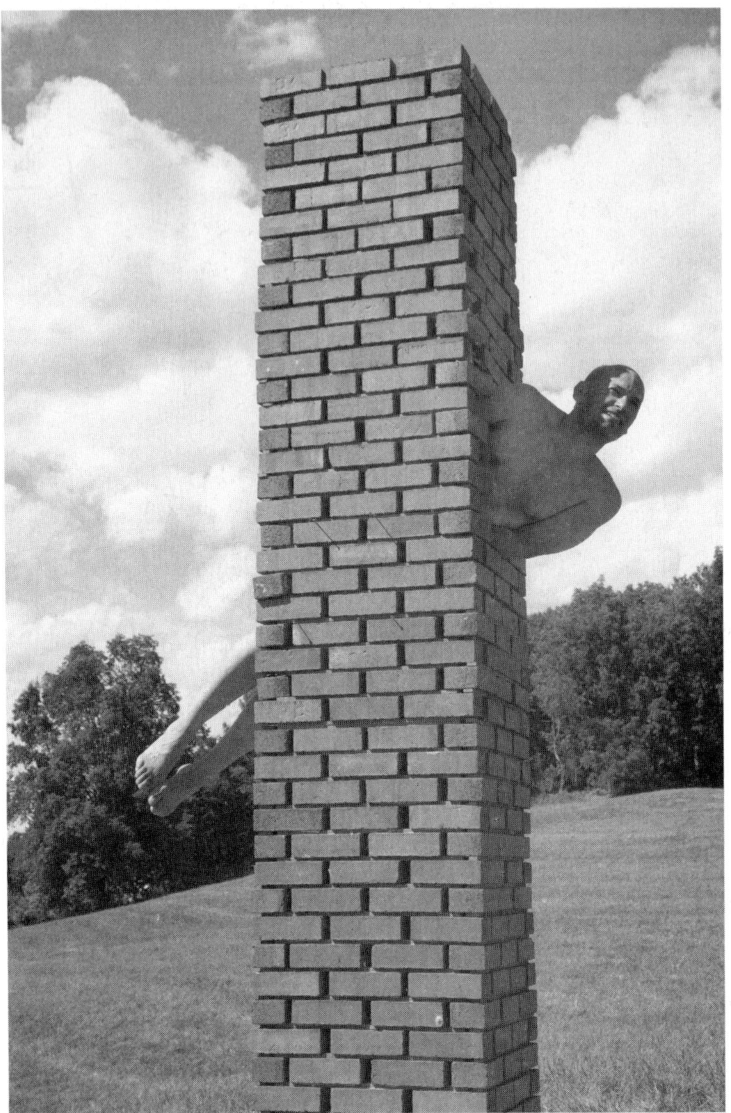

Fig. 5-5
Cesar Cornejo, *Public Sculptor* (2010), bricks, cement, wood, sculptor, 2 hours. Courtesy of
the artist. Photographer: Felicity Hogan.

Interview: Cesar Cornejo

Public Sculptor was created as a specific response to my experience working at the residency Art Omi. In that place there is a sculpture park, although because of its location it is hardly visited, so the whole site could be seen as an abstract installation piece. I wanted to comment on that situation by creating a piece that was interactive in a way that the distance between the artist and the work was reduced to its minimum expression, so the visitors when seeing the work would literally also seeing the artist.

Besides the interactions with the visitors and their responses which were somehow expected, something that I was touched by were the reactions of my fellow artists at the residency, they gathered around the piece and just stood or sat down there sharing the time with me, somehow becoming also part of the piece. The next morning I was congratulated by several of them; this was particularly rewarding to me. There is something about placing a vertical structure on a hill that touches our deepest zones, and even more if someone is inside it.

—*Cesar Cornejo*

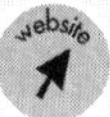
Visit the book's website to read the full interview.

Exercise

Go online, search for, and view Bruce Nauman's video work *Bouncing in the Corner, No. 1* (1968). After watching the work, write down what you think are the subject, form, content, and context for this work. How did the artist use architecture within the work? Compare and contrast your answers with others'. How are your answers similar and different from those around you? Were there any trends in the answers?

video

In contrast to Cornejo's unadorned tower, installation artist Ernesto Neto's immersive interactive work *Walking in Venus Blue Cave* (2001) utilizes recognizable architectural features such as floors, ceilings, and a door, while employing unfamiliar, highly tactile materials including nylon stocking fabric filled with Styrofoam beads to create large squishy forms (Plate 4, color insert). This pairing of the recognizable and the unfamiliar creates an environment that encourages participants to slow down, enter the work, and feel their own bodies in contact with the architecture. As you create your own 4D work, whether designing a game or plotting out a performance, you will have to consciously choose whether or not to embrace architectural elements that are most familiar.

Sound

Sound, and its behavior in architectural spaces, is also vital to the participants' experiences. By paying attention to hard surfaces and the echoes they can create, artists can decide whether or not to mute the room, to create the desired aural experience within the architecture. Sound can also mark a place in the same way one can recognize a landmark. The location may have radiator noises, a hum from air ducts, and so on. These phenomena lead to the concept of **room tone**, or the unique, subtle sounds of an empty room. Every architectural space has a different room tone, which must be considered during the planning and execution of a work. For example, if an artist or designer is going to add additional sounds to a recorded audio clip, he or she must have a sample of the room tone to help the recording sound cohesive and realistic—as if the combination of sounds is truly occurring in the same space. In this way, sound and architecture are tightly intertwined.

Similar to room tone, **ambient sounds**, or sounds from the immediate surroundings, can affect a viewer's experience at a live performance. For example, sounds such as traffic and passersby in outdoor settings can either distract from or enhance a piece depending on the nature of the work and the artist's or designer's intentions. An example of integrating ambient sounds and architecture is Max Neuhaus's piece *Times Square* (1977–1992 and 2002–present), which is a sound piece installed just underneath the sidewalk grates in Times Square, New York City. The work consists of speakers projecting a series of sounds up through the sidewalk grates on the pedestrian island located at Broadway between 45th and 46th Streets. Due to the work's architectural and topographic location, it has an intrinsic relationship to ambient sounds, including passersby and any number of other sounds bouncing off the tall buildings surrounding Times Square.

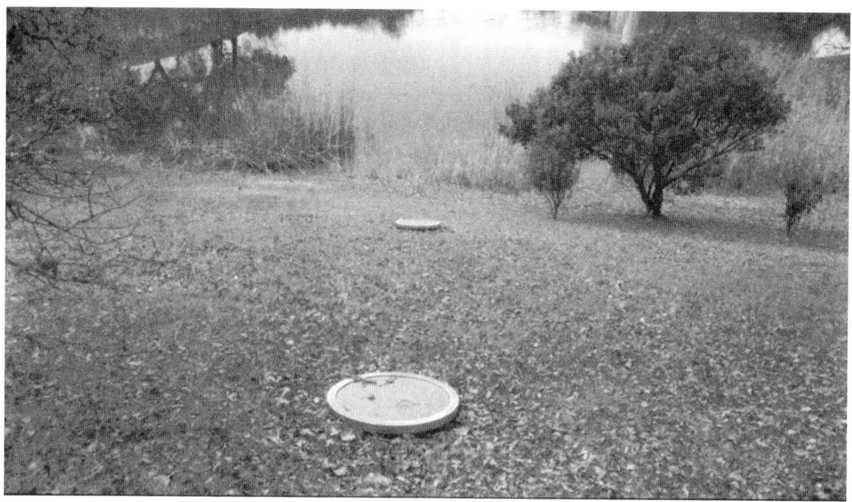

Fig. 5-6
Bill Fontana, *Earth Tones* (1992), six large, low-frequency loudspeakers buried at the Oliver Ranch in Northern California. Courtesy of the artist.

In this case, ambient sound becomes integral to the work; even though the installation features its own audio, the participant's experience would not be as strong without the surrounding sounds of the city.

Exercise

Go online and research the work *Earth Tones* (1992) by Bill Fontana, in which he buried six large, low-frequency loudspeakers around a lake in Northern California, and then played low-frequency sounds from the Pacific Ocean through the speakers (fig. 5-6). Create a work that utilizes the relocation of sound. While planning the work, consider that the sounds may contrast or harmonize with their new locations. Use architecture and topography to your advantage in this relocation. In critique, ask which works are most successful and why. Did contrasting sounds or harmonious sounds create stronger reactions?

installation   sound

Relative Location

Aside from the interactions of sound, architecture is also affected by the concept of **relative location**, which is the relationship between a location and other markers of space. For example, a work may address a nearby piece of architecture, such as a local restaurant, or it may address architecture or topography that is far away, such as a monument on the other side of the world. In each example, the relative location of these architectural landmarks changes how participants interpret the work—in one, a sense of familiarity could be generated, whereas the other could introduce a sense of the unknown or the mysterious.

Land artists of the 1970s used architecture and topography in remote locations. Nancy Holt located her concrete tube installation *Sun Tunnels* (1976) in the Utah desert away from any other architectural elements (fig. 5-7). Each of the concrete tubes is 9 feet in diameter and 18 feet

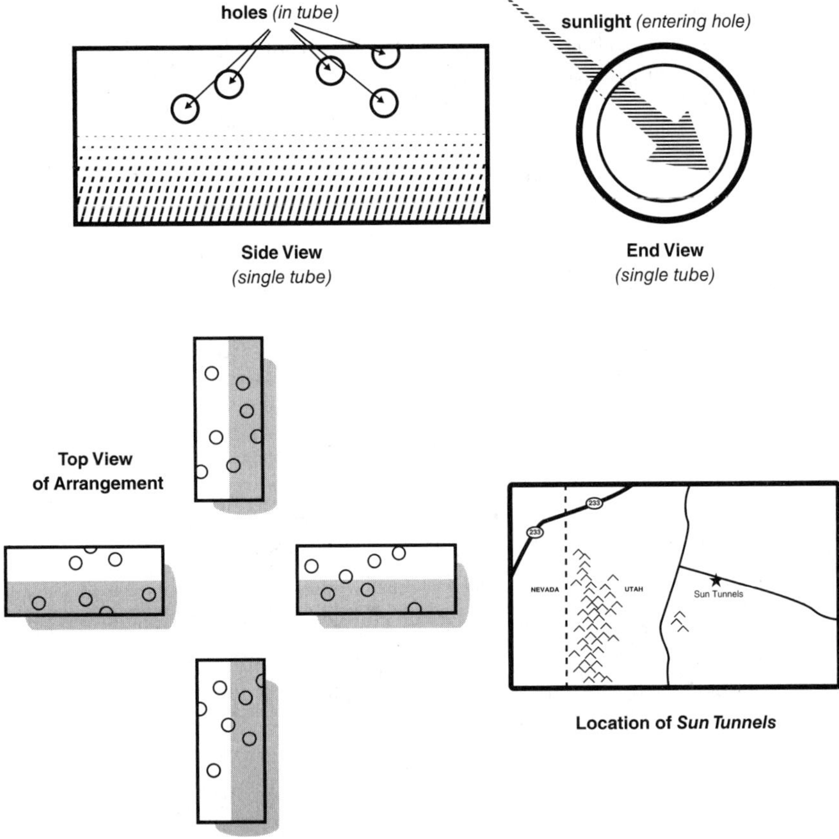

Fig. 5-7

The layout for Nancy Holt's *Sun Tunnels* (1976) is in an X-formation in alignment with selected celestial constellations. © Phil McCollam.

long—large enough to walk through standing upright; they are arranged in an X-formation in alignment with selected celestial constellations. The tubes also align with the rising and falling of the sun during the summer and winter solstices. The relative location of the piece emphasizes its connection to natural phenomena with relationships to constellations, solstices, and a remote setting, far away from any cityscape.

Similarly, *Prada Marfa* (2005), a site-specific, permanent land art project by artist duo Elmgreen and Dragset, is a sealed mockup of a Prada boutique located in the vast desert landscape off Highway 90 near Valentine, Texas (figs. 5-8 and 5-9). The installation is illuminated and displays a variety of wares from Prada—similar to a typical Prada store; however, this "store" is never open to the public. Typically, one would find a Prada boutique in a city center because the products are directly related to consumerism and high fashion; by placing the store n an empty, nonurban environment, relative location becomes a central element of the concept of this work.

Movement

Movement is also a central consideration within architecture, in that an artist or designer must think about how participants will pass through the work. Movement can affect a sense of community, or a lack thereof, depending on how open or closed the architectural space is. For example, basic architectural structures such as entrances and exits—whether physical or implied—help promote movement. In Holt's *Sun Tunnels*, it is clear that participants are invited to inspect the entrances to the tunnels

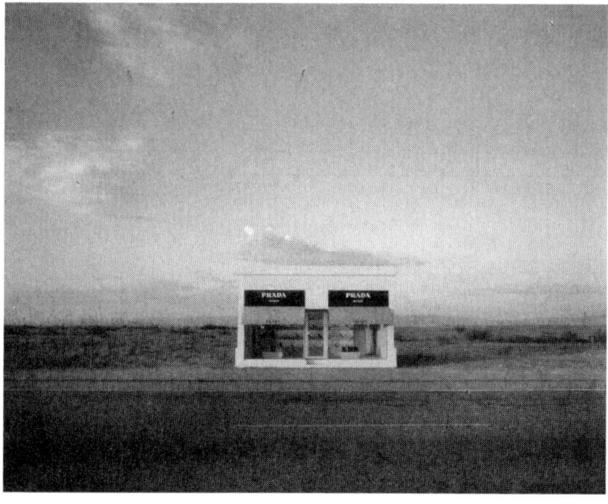

Fig. 5-8
Elmgreen and Dragset, *Prada Marfa* (2005), adobe bricks, plaster, aluminum frames, glass panes, MDF, paint, carpet, Prada shoes and bags, 760 cm × 470 cm × 480 cm. Courtesy: Art Production Fund, New York; Ballroom Marfa, Marfa; the artists. Photograph by James Evans.

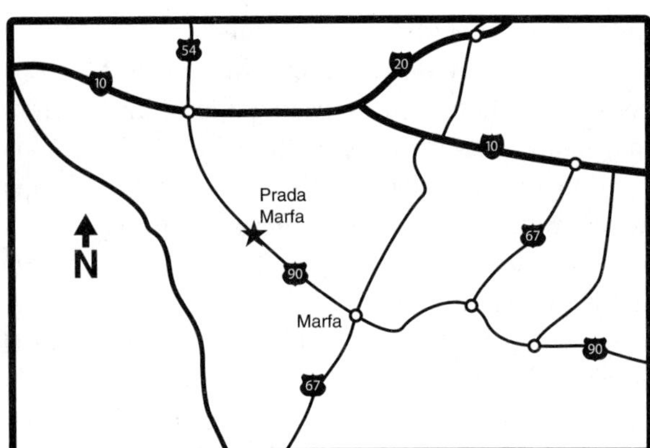

Fig. 5-9
Prada Marfa (2005) is located in the empty countryside off Highway 90 in Texas. © Phil McCollam.

because each tunnel has a door-like entry point. In Elmgreen and Dragset's *Prada Marfa*, the only movement possible is simply walking around the work because the entry to the store is sealed. This decision to limit movement through the architecture could be intended to reinforce ideas of exclusivity associated with an expensive brand like Prada, whereas in Holt's *Sun Tunnels*, participants are encouraged to walk through and around the installation.

Topography

Similar to architecture, the topography of a space is central to defining the space of your work. **Topography** is the physical nature or quality of the surface on which the work takes place. When beginning a new project, consciously establish the topography of your piece by making specific and purposeful choices. Avoid falling into easy options that do not necessarily serve the concept of the work. For example, in Thomas Hirschhorn's installation *Cavemanman*, he created his own cardboard topography, rather than simply using the floor of the gallery space (Plate 11, color insert). Similarly, your topographic choices should have a meaningful purpose, rather than defaulting to the topography of a space as you find it.

Another example that makes good use of topography is the video game *Shadow of the Colossus* (2005), in which the topography of the virtual world is integral to the game play (fig. 5-10). Each battle the player wages against the massive beings, called colossi, revolves around the use of environmental features—such as sand, water, and architectural structures—to the player's advantage. Even the colossi have their own topographic qualities, as their fur allows the protagonist to climb them while stone protects them from the player's attack.

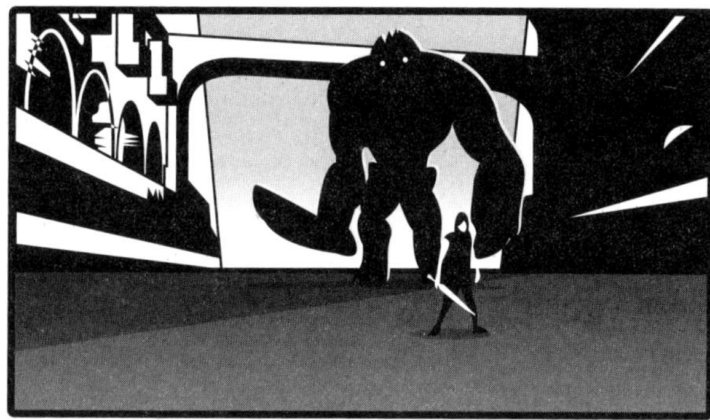

Fig. 5-10
Illustration of a moment
from the video game
Shadow of the Colossus
(2005). © Phil
McCollam.

Exercise

Find a location where you can create a site-specific game that
reacts to the space's specific architecture or topography. For this
exercise, no two people can use the same location. The game
should be simple enough that players can become quickly engaged, but it must also rely on the architectural and topographic
features of your specifically chosen site. The class will take turns
playing each game. After playing, consider what about this game
is site-specific. The most basic question could be: Why could this
game not exist anywhere else? Does the architecture or topography make the game stronger or weaker?

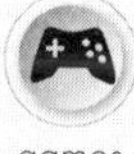

games

Another example of the importance of topography to a 4D work is Anne
Teresa De Keersmaeker's *Violin Phase from Fase: Four Movements to the
Music of Steve Reich* (1982) (fig. 5-11). This piece consists of De Keersmaeker
dancing on a thin layer of sand coating the topography of the dance space.
This specific topography allows for the revelation of a circle and diagonals
traced onto the ground by the movements of the performer over the course
of the dance. By actively tracing this geometry into the topography, the
artist is creating a physical representation of the amount of space one occupies over a specified amount of time, while also proposing a different way
to measure the earth through human movement.[3] This work would not be
the same dance without the malleable, sandy topography of the floor.

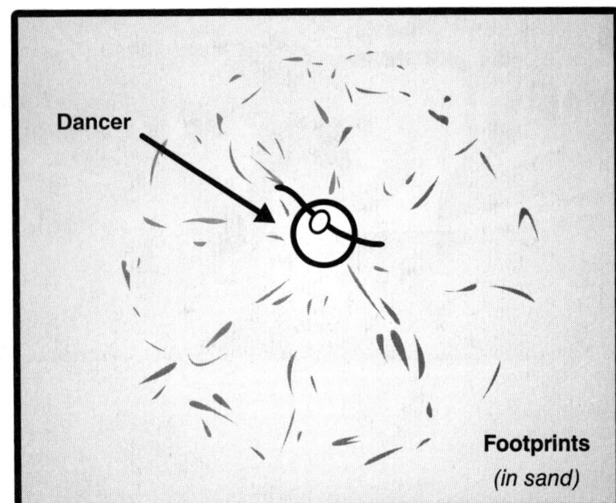

Fig. 5-11
Diagram of Anne Teresa De Keersmaeker's *Violin Phase from Fase: Four Movements of the Music of Steve Reich* (1982). © Phil McCollam.

In conclusion, architecture and topography are vital elements of all four-dimensional works, whether influencing the actions of a performance and interaction of the audience or affecting how the work is presented to or viewed by the audience. Both architecture and topography will affect all the other four-dimensional elements including sound, light, movement, and the perceived passage of time.

Light

Light is a form of radiant energy that reflects off the world around us and into our eyes, allowing us to see our environment and color. The number of light sources, their color, their direction, and their relative brightness all contribute to **visibility**, or the extent to which a participant can see within the space of a work.[4] Light is also one of the most immediate ways to create focus while also establishing mood. Light allows for visibility within the space of a work, and reveals three-dimensional forms through light and **shadow**, which is an area of darkness created when light is blocked.

Shadow, whether physical or digital, is one of the most immediately understood ways to manipulate light—or its absence—because we see and evaluate shadows all day long. There are two types of shadows: attached and cast. An **attached shadow** is directly fixed to an object, revealing its

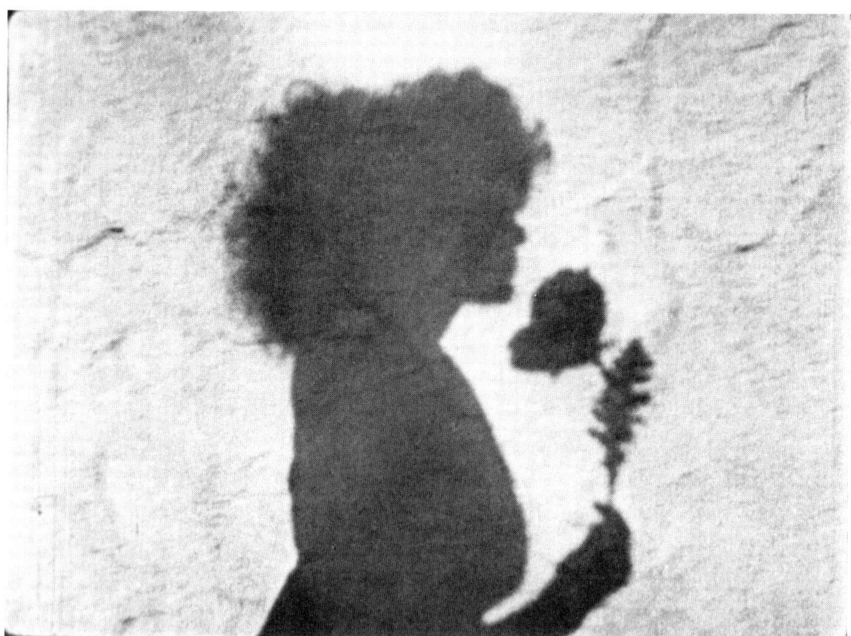

Fig. 5-12
Maya Deren, *Meshes of the Afternoon* (1943), film, 18 minutes. Photo Courtesy of Anthology Film Archives.

basic form. Take for example the nostrils in your nose. There are always shadows attached to the interior of your nostrils; they may shift as the light source changes, but these shadows are always attached to your nose. A **cast shadow**, in contrast, is independent of the object creating the shadow, and it reveals the object's relationship to its environment. A cast shadow may or may not be physically connected to the object; it will also be sharper and smaller when the object is close to the environmental surface, and fuzzier and larger when the object is farther away. In Maya Deren's surrealist film *Meshes of the Afternoon* (1943), in which a woman has premonitions of her own death, long cast shadows of her figure are used to signal the entrance of different versions of her dream self (fig. 5-12).

Ambient Light versus Specific Light

In general, there are two categories of light: ambient and specific. **Ambient light** fills and articulates the overall space. It could be natural light provided by the sun or moon, or it could be artificial lighting provided by light sources that generally fill a space, such as overhead fluorescent lights. For example, in *The Stanley Parable* video game, much of the environment is filled with ambient light from stereotypical fluorescent lights often found in office buildings (see fig. 2-11). Ambient light is always present unless a work takes place in total darkness, or darkness with specific lighting. Ambient lighting is usually used as a benchmark for the overall brightness of a work, and it should be taken into consideration before adding additional specific light sources. Ambient light is sometimes affected by uncontrollable sources such as **daylight**—light from the sun that changes color and brightness throughout the day and year, and is affected by weather. When working with daylight, take note of the intensity and direction of light throughout the day to help predict how it will interact with people, architecture, or other forms in the space. Direct sunlight is much brighter and causes harsher shadows than indirect daylight that has been changed by clouds or fog, which diffuses (scatters) the light, causing softer shadows. Sunlight will also be different according to the seasons: winter sun is weaker and cooler, while summer sun is stronger and warmer. Keep in mind that ambient light can alter the mood of a work, reminding participants of these seasons and feelings. Once the goals of a project are articulated, you can determine how to best work with or alter the ambient light.

Specific light, or *task light*, provides illumination for a specific task, or helps to draw focus to specific forms. As mentioned before, specific light is added to ambient light unless a work takes place in total darkness. Therefore, specific lights are added to a work with a purpose in mind. An example of a specific light is a **key light**, or *spotlight*, which is a focused light that draws the eye to a single point or location. As an example, in figure 5-18, you can see that a specific light has been focused on Einstein in the lower left corner. A medium or wide spotlight beam will provide moderate focus, while a narrow beam will provide higher contrast and more specific focus.[5] **Fill lights** are used to soften the key light and to illuminate areas of shadow cast by the key light. **Backlights** illuminate the subject from behind, often creating a glowing outline—or halo effect—around the subject. See figure 5-14 for a diagram of a key light, fill light, and backlight as used in three-point lighting. **Sidelights** are lights aimed at the side of a subject, creating highlights on one side of the subject's form and shadow on the other. The use of sidelights can be seen in the still from *Love's Shadow* (figure 1-18). **Accent lights**, or lights used to create patterns within the work by means of contrast, also fall under the umbrella of specific lighting. The small lights attached to the performers' dresses in Glitter Chariot's music video for *Should Have Been Blonde* could be considered accent lights because they create subtle accenting contrast in the scene (see Plate 14, color insert).

Exercise

Watch one of your favorite films and select one scene to analyze. First identify the subject, form, content, and context. Then examine the lighting: is it even or uneven? How many light sources are implied? It is not usually possible to know how many sources were truly used, so you will have to guess based on visual evidence. In what ways were ambient and specific lighting utilized? How were shadows used or not used? What else do you notice about the use of light? Write down your answers and then share them with a small group of your classmates. Did anyone else in the group notice different or similar light usage within their clips? Did clips that were more impactful utilize light differently than the other clips?

 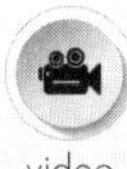

light   video

Shadows, Projections, and Projection Mapping

Projections involve purposefully cast light and shadow; **they** can range from the very rudimentary, such as basic shadow puppetry, to technology-intensive, utilizing mapping software to project onto three-dimensional surfaces.

In more rudimentary projections, an object such as a puppet is placed between a light source and a screen in order to cast a shadow or **silhouette**. There are a few factors to take into consideration. The sharpness of the imagery can be increased by bringing the object closer to the screen, or reduced by moving it closer to the light source. For example, if you watch a video clip of Eleanor Antin's *Love's Shadow*, you can see the effect of the ballerina's arms becoming more or less sharply defined as she moves them toward and away from the screen (fig. 1-18). Another example that uses silhouettes is *Beast* (2013), an animation by Constantinos Chaidalis (fig. 2-4). In this work there are moments when the main figures are shown in silhouette, such as when a stag stands alone on a hill. This type of shadow play and high-contrast imagery helps emphasize the drama and emotional struggles of a child who wrestles with being different from everyone else.

Visit the book's website to read an interview with Constantinos Chaidalis.

Similar to shadow puppetry and silhouettes is the use of cut metal stencils, or **gobos**, placed in front of lighting instruments with focusing lenses. In this case, the metal stencil is cut to form a specific shape or pattern, and when the focused light passes through this stencil, that same shape or pattern is projected onto a particular area. This type of projection is often used in theatrical or interior design settings as an effective way to add implied texture or depth to a work.

Front projection involves pointing a projector, connected to a computer or other device, at a screen designed to reflect light back at the viewer. This type of projection is used in most movie theaters and many classrooms. This type of projection can also be used with **projection-mapping**, which involves using software to map complex surfaces on which to project various imagery. These surfaces could include buildings, objects, bodies, and even smoke or fog. In Luftwerk's *Luminous Field* (2012), the projection is mapped onto the space around and below Anish Kapoor's public sculpture *Cloud Gate* (2006) (Plate 5). In this case and others, projection mapping can be used to create surrealist situations in which unexpected imagery is juxtaposed with live action or objects.[6]

Exercise

Brainstorm 20 answers to this question: What does the word "stealth" mean? Using one of the answers to that question, create a time-based work that illustrates or explores your definition, using only a single light source. The light source could be a window, a lamp, a flame, a flashlight, and so on. Experiment with the shape of the light and the shadows it casts. At critique, ask if people's choices feel purposeful or accidental. Which choices are most effective and why?

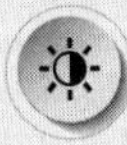

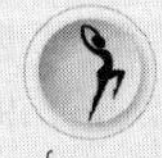

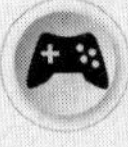

Light can also be considered in relationship to the materials with which it comes into contact. When light strikes a **transparent object**, it is transmitted or allowed to pass through the object, allowing us to see what is beneath it. Similarly, when light strikes a **translucent object**, much of the light passes through the object, but some is reflected, which causes a blurred or somewhat obstructed effect. When light strikes an **opaque object**, it reflects back into our eye, and does not pass through the object. Light can also pass through a material and be **refracted light**, which means it still passes through the material but changes direction upon exiting. Think of a prism: when light hits the prism, it appears to bend as it moves through the prism and a spectrum of colors is visible exiting the other side. These light phenomena of transparency, translucency, opacity, and refraction can be used to heighten or subdue concepts central to your work.

Using Light and Shadow in Your Work

As you manipulate the use of light and shadow in your work, take your audience, context, and any acts of participation into consideration. Keep in mind that human eyes see light in terms of contrast, and this ability changes as people age. Contrast can be enhanced or reduced by the number of objects or spaces you choose to illuminate. If too many objects or spaces are lit, participants will lose focus. Additionally, the brightest area within a work or environment will likely attract the most attention—use this brightness to your advantage.

Exercise

Brainstorm a list of 20 products for which you would like to create a commercial. Select one product and create a 15-second commercial that sells the product based on emotion rather than the practicalities of the product. For example, you might sell a tooth-whitening service because it will make the customer feel more attractive, rather than emphasizing how many shades whiter the product makes the customer's teeth. Use light to alter the mood accordingly. Keep your final goal in mind: if you are trying to make the consumer feel good about the product, the lighting used within the commercial may be different than if you are trying to make the consumer feel depressed. Hold a screening of all the commercials and ask how the use of lighting could have been improved, or how it succeeded.

 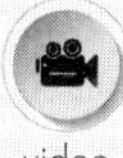

light   video

On a practical level, humans expect illumination from above, which produces shadows below—as with the sun (see Chapter 4 for discussions of value/brightness and direction/reflection). If that pattern is reversed, by moving the light source below the subject with shadows cast upward, it creates an unsettling or eerie effect; imagine someone telling ghost stories with a flashlight held under his or her face. Humans also subconsciously notice illuminated vertical surfaces, such as walls, first, because these surfaces generally guide us in day-to-day life. If the goal of your work is to direct participants through a space, some form of vertical illumination will help reduce distraction and improve focus on moving through the space. If the goal is to illuminate walls but de-emphasize the ceiling area, use long light sources close to the corner junctions between ceiling and wall. A more dramatic environment can be created by illuminating specific surfaces instead of the overall architecture of the space. Given this result, artists and designers should consider what their intentions are before deciding on surface and architectural illumination.

Dynamic Lighting

Thinking about surface and architectural illumination will also help you determine whether your lights will be static, meaning they stay the same, or dynamic, meaning they change over the course of the work. If you choose to have dynamic lighting, you will have to decide not only on the type of light sources that will be included, but also when the changes—or light **cues**—will occur. Unexpected dynamic choices—such as striking a single match within a dimly lit environment, fireworks juxtaposed with a dark night sky, light leaking around an opening door, and so on—can help hold a viewer's focus.

Francis Picabia's surrealist ballet *Relâche* (1924) used this dynamic method by creating unexpected moments of unbearable brightness via flashing lights covering architectural arches surrounding the stage. The surprising dramatic brightness of the lights added to the chaotic and absurd nature of the work by agitating the audience, which was a common goal of early surrealism (fig. 5-13). To further enhance these ideas, the ballet also involved seemingly unrelated film clips, dancing, and random actions such as pouring water from one container to another and pacing the stage.

Three-Point Lighting

One of the most commonly used lighting setups is called **three-point lighting**. It consists of a key light, a fill light, and a backlight (fig. 5-14). The key light is in front of the subject, slightly off to one side, and aimed at the front of the subject. The fill light is not quite as intense as the key light and is

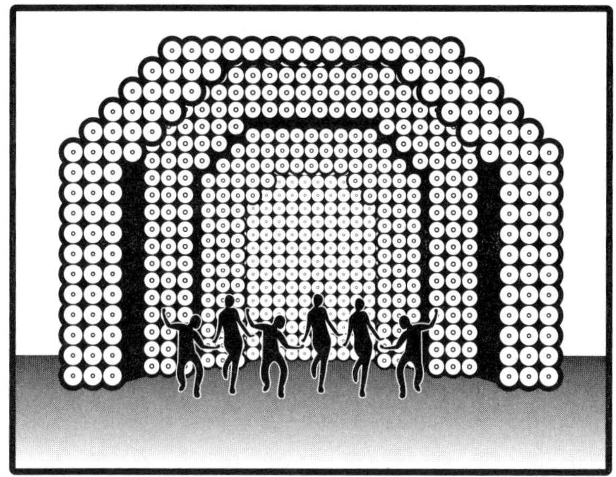

Fig. 5-13
Illustration of lighting plan for Francis Picabia's ballet *Rêlache* (1924) © Phil McCollam.

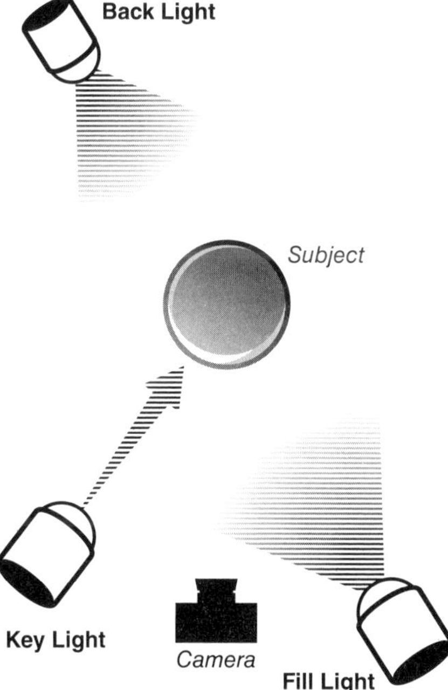

Fig. 5-14
Three-point lighting consists of a key light, a fill light, and a backlight. © Phil McCollam.

placed opposite the key light in front of the subject. The backlight is behind the subject and is used to help create separation between the subject and the background. Often the backlight is less bright than the key light. It might be a reflected or diffused light.

Exercise

Set up three-point lighting on a human subject, using whatever lights you have at your disposal such as lamps, flashlights, projectors, studio lighting, and so on. Play with your three lights to create three distinctly different effects or looks on your subject. For example, you might experiment with moving the three lights up or down and left or right, to create different looks. Take a photo or a video clip of your subject in each of these lighting setups, and compare with the rest of the class. Be ready to explain how you might use each of these lighting setups for different purposes, such as creating specific moods or effects.

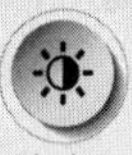
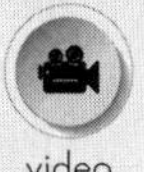

light   video

Light can be arranged in a number of different ways to create the expected, such as three-point lighting, or the unexpected, such as silhouettes and projection-mapping. Through careful manipulation, dynamic lighting can add contrast to a work through the use of change, while ambient and specific light can set a mood or draw focus. 4D works will either be strengthened or weakened through your use of light.

Movement

Movement is a shift or variation in the location of an object, light, or sound. It is a very effective way to direct the focus of a composition. Shape, space, levels of space, balance, energy dynamics, weight, and gestures affect movement. By utilizing these elements and principles, movement can serve any number of descriptive or expressive intentions, from physical to emotional reactions.

Successional movement leads the eye in one direction. For instance, a group of performers all pointing their fingers in the same direction is a successional movement. **Oppositional movement** contrasts this with a clash of forces that lead the eye in a different direction. An example of oppositional movement would be two characters in a video game attacking each other; their movements illustrate opposing forces moving toward or away from each other, and cause the participant's eyes to move back and forth between the fighters. Meanwhile, the absence of movement, or **stillness**, is also important to any 4D work, allowing for contrast within a work. For example, a character in a film may stop in the middle of a busy walkway; this lack of movement will cause him or her to stand out compared to everyone else in motion.

Exercise

Edward Muybridge was a famous photographer who studied the movement of both animals and humans. Do an online image search for a photo series by Muybridge. Then rotoscope a short animation of a person's or animal's movements in the photo series you found. **Rotoscoping** is the process of tracing single frames of film or video and then animating those traced frames. You can create this animation entirely by hand by printing out the images, tracing them on clean sheets of paper, and then binding them together into a flip-book; you can alternatively do the entire process on a computer using Photoshop, After Effects, or any of a number of free, open-source software applications of your preference. As you complete the work, examine how the figure or animal moves. Think about successional and oppositional movement, as well as stillness. If you were creating a long-form animation, how would an exercise like this enhance your understanding of movement and its impact on your work in general?

video

Movement in time-based works can be either observed or participatory. In Sara Holwerda's video performance *Chair Dance II* (2012), the audience members are not directly involved with the performance. Instead, they observe both the chair and the performer moving through space while Holwerda addresses concepts of femininity and societal expectations through her execution of traditional chair dancing combined with self-defense maneuvers (fig. 5-15).

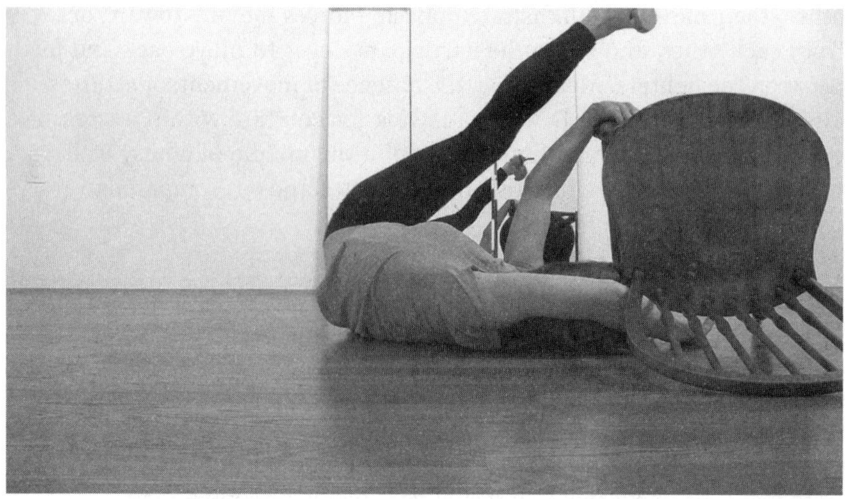

Fig. 5-15
Sara Holwerda, *Chair Dance II* (2012), video, 6:33 minutes. © Sara Holwerda 2012.

Interview: Sara Holwerda

When I made my first *Chair Dance* with the webcam on my
computer, I had a simple idea of doing a violent chair dance. The
chair dance is one of those hyper-feminine and often theatrical
forms of sexualized performance that I am often drawn to, with
appearances in movie musicals, burlesque, and strip tease
routines. I wanted to take the idealized relationship modeled by
this kind of performance—with the chair as the stand-in for the
male spectator—and extend the metaphor to include some of my
own experiences with violence and spectacle. I taught myself both
the chair dance as well as stage fighting movements from YouTube
videos, and incorporated some improvisation and self-defense
movements. I constructed a movement narrative with the chair that
begins with a classic chair dance and quickly devolves into a
strange and violent interaction with the chair. I am in constant
physical contact with the chair the entire time, and at the end I kick
the chair as far away from my body as I can.

—Sara Holwerda

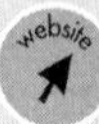

Visit the book's website to read the full interview.

Exercise

Go online, search for, and view a video of Nick Cave's *Soundsuits* in motion. After watching the work, write down what you think are the subject, form, content, and context for this work. Analyze how the artist uses movement. Compare and contrast your answers with others'. How are your answers similar and different from those around you? Were there any trends in the answers?

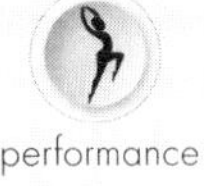

performance

In contrast, a first-person video game, such as Channel TWo's *FIND EACH OTHER. Begin There.* (2012), requires direct participation from the player, simulating the experience of moving through space (fig. 5-16). This two-person game presents an extensive cornfield with the occasional presence of wind turbines, a plane passing overhead, picket fences, ponds, and

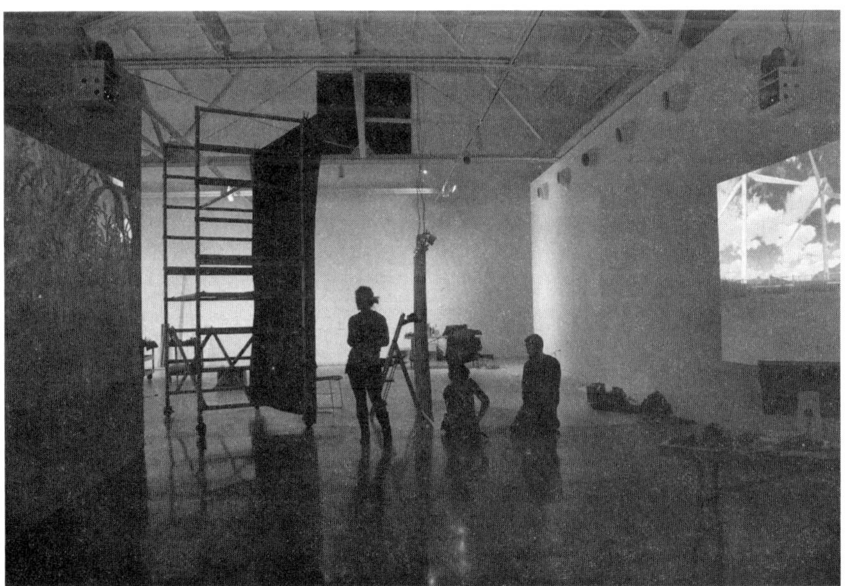

Fig. 5-16
Channel TWo, *FIND EACH OTHER. Begin There* (2012), two-channel, networked, interactive landscape, dimensions variable. © Channel TWo.

jewels embedded in the ground. The game conveys an underlying sense that things are not what they seem to be, motivating players to move through the field while trying to find one another. Because the players control movement within the game, they may also choose to remain still, electing to stay in one static location in hopes of being found by the other player.

Interview: Channel TWo

FIND EACH OTHER. Begin There. (2012) is a two-channel, networked, interactive landscape. Conceptually the work integrates a bucolic representation of farmlands, the promises of sustainable energy, time and space for wandering/leisure, and an underlying sense that things are not what they seem. *FIND EACH OTHER. Begin There.* is social. Using wireless game controllers, players can run through the virtual landscape in search of each other, or they can stay put and wait. Players must negotiate, communicate, and collaborate with each other in real space/time in order to orient themselves, and find each other in the game space. When players find each other, the game generates a low level rumble and a quick flash, flooding the space and players in green light. *FIND EACH OTHER. Begin There.* is an aesthetic, sensory, and critical experience intersecting the complexities of conflict and space, psychology of will, collaboration/exchange, and the individual's relationship to power and control. The title *FINE EACH OTHER. Begin There.* was borrowed from a chapter in *The Coming Insurrection, The Invisible Committee* (2008).

The staff for the Contemporary Art Museum (CAM), Raleigh 2012 exhibition, *Born Digital*, reported that the work was a noticeable favorite amongst children and young adults. *FIND EACH OTHER. Begin There.* was drawing crowds and repeat museum visits throughout the duration of the show. They also reported that gallery attendants and docents were keeping tallies on the number of times guests found each other. This additional level of access/engagement/play means the work took on more of a life than we had anticipated. This was a nice surprise.

—Channel TWo

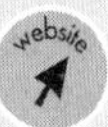 Visit the book's website to read the full interview.

Remember that participants experience the movement of an artwork—whether it is on a computer screen or in a physical space—through a frame of reference that includes where they have been and where they anticipate going, both mentally and physically.[7] Movement is a trigger for action: therefore the approach, entrance into the work, path within the work, and eventual exit from the work all contribute to an individual's response to a piece. Additionally, if participants themselves are encouraged to move as a part of the work, then the space of an artwork and the participant's mode of transportation should inform the movements utilized by the piece.

Movement, much like sound, has distinct parts: **attack** (onset, growth, birth); **sustain** (steady-state, duration, life); and **decay** (fall-off, termination, death).[8] During the onset of a movement, there is often a squashing or recoiling of the object/figure into its **base of support** (area beneath an object or person that connects with the supporting surface, such as feet or hands); think of a person's legs as he or she is about to leap. As the movement continues, the object will stretch out, eventually returning to its original shape, until it finally begins to stop by bouncing slightly before the complete end of the motion. These parts of a movement are central to planning movements, and are well articulated by animators Frank Thomas and Ollie Johnston in their book *The Illusion of Life*. If an object moves without using these three parts of movement it will look more artificial and less lifelike. For example, if a circle on a screen simply rises and falls without some squashing, stretching, and bouncing, it will not look as realistic as a circle that does follow these three parts of movement.

Additionally, the object's or figure's **center of gravity**, or the center of the mass in an environment of uniform gravity, affects movement. An object with a low center of gravity will often move steadily, while an object with a high center of gravity may often seem unbalanced. Keeping the parts of movement in mind while you develop a work will help you make decisions about elements such as timing, spacing, topography, and others.

Gestures and Isolations

Gestures, also known as *isolations*, are movements by a part of a whole, such as a single part of the body or a single part of a machine. Examples of gestures include flexing, extending, or rotating a person's arm. Gestures are routinely planned for and used in dance and video works. Imagine several dancers on a stage holding the same pose, and then imagine just one of them bending an arm. Your eyes will immediately be attracted to that movement, even if it is small. This is how gestures and isolations can be used to create focus within a work.

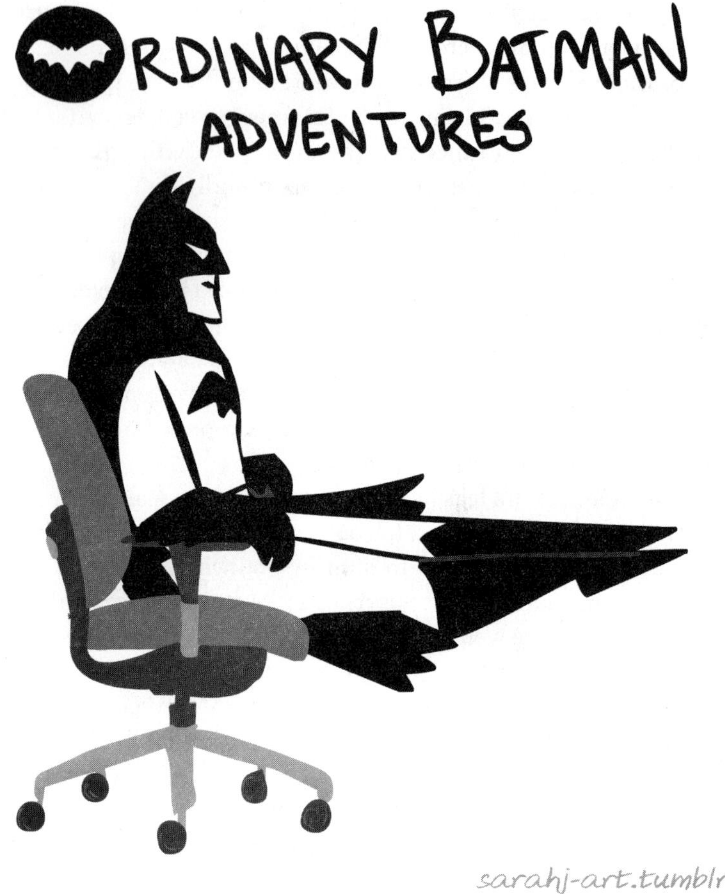

Fig. 5-17
Sarah Johnson, *Ordinary Batman* (2012–ongoing), animated GIF, 575 × 500 pixels.
Courtesy of the Artist.

Animated GIFs, which are digital image files that can display move-ment, and **cinemagraphs**, which are animated GIFs in which a minor and repeated movement occurs, are generally great at demonstrating isola-tions; repetition of movement is elemental to the form. Animator Sarah Johnson's *Ordinary Batman* series (2012–ongoing) uses GIFs to parody the comic book character Batman in a variety of mundane scenarios (fig. 5-17). These GIFs are studies in gestures and isolations that are used to create humor.

Interview: Sarah Johnson

I love animating. It's hard to make a digital illustration now without adding some kind of movement and turning it into a GIF. I try and loosen up with pencil and paper sketches before moving to a digital tablet or Cintiq. Making everything animated means everything I do ends up digital but getting back to something as tangible as paper makes the transition smoother.

Ordinary Batman Adventures began just as something quick and silly to break up some very tedious freelance animation I was struggling on. I wanted to do something simple and in less than 15 minutes. I still try to spend as little time as possible on *Ordinary Batman* GIFs as to keep with the idea of it as something relaxing and fun instead of another project.

—*Sarah Johnson*

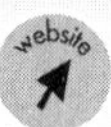
Visit the book's website to read the full interview.

Exercise

Brainstorm a list of 10 everyday gestures, and then invent 10 expressive gestures that relate to large-scale ideas such as freedom, war, chaos, love, and so on. How are these two sets of gestures similar to and different from each other? Are any gestures identical? Which parts of your body are you choosing to use and why?

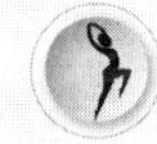

performance

Isolations can be everyday or behavioral motions we easily recognize, such as bringing a cup of coffee towards your mouth, or opening a door. Isolations can also be expressive and non-functional, such as swinging your arm in a circle to show joy, or repeatedly raising and lowering a shoulder to show unease. Expressive isolations can vary between **organic** and **angular** in the direction of their movement. Organic movement flows in rounded shapes, while angular movement involves more straight geometric shapes.

Movement in Film and Video

Movement also has a unique role in film and video. Not only can the subject being filmed move, but the camera can move in any number of directions, affecting how the viewer perceives the work. Some common camera movements are the **pan**, which consists of pivoting from side to side, and the **tilt**, which is pivoting up and down. Both of these camera movements allow participants to see more in the horizontal or vertical direction, and they contribute to a sense of expansiveness, reminding us that the world of the work continues beyond the current viewing frame. For example, in an old melodramatic film, the camera might be focused on a person tied to train tracks, and then pan to the side to reveal a train approaching in the distance. A **tracking** or **dolly shot**, in which the camera moves parallel to the ground (often on a rolling track), allows viewers to identify with the camera's point of view as it moves. For example, a tracking shot might be used to show a crowded sidewalk during a parade, helping the viewer to better understand how a performer in the parade (or the camera, in this case) would see and experience the parade from the performer's point of view. Cameras can also use a **zoom** movement, which is used to make the image larger or smaller by adjusting or changing the lenses. When a camera zooms in, objects appear larger and closer to the camera. Zooming in can draw attention to important details, such as a key bit of evidence in a murder mystery. When a camera zooms out, objects appear smaller and farther away from the camera, revealing the larger context of the scene. For example, at the end of the film *The Wizard of Oz* (1939), the camera slowly zooms out to reveal that Dorothy has finally made her way home and is surrounded by her family. All of these camera movements are borrowed by other 4D media such as video games, motion graphics, and interactive kiosks, and they contribute to the overall expressiveness of a 4D work.

Exercise

Get a copy of a favorite film, find a scene you know, and watch it, paying close attention to camera movements. List each movement of the camera after you notice it. Were any movements among those listed here, were they combinations, or were they something entirely different? Which movement attracted your attention the most/least? Do you notice any patterns?[9]

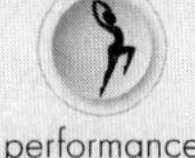

video   performance

Whether movement is acted out by a performer, acted out by a participant, or simply observed, or whether the movement is on behalf of a camera or an element on-screen, movement is central to the effectiveness of nearly all time-based works.

Sound

Sound is vibration that can be perceived by the ear. It is an integral part of communication and our social framework as it is used for speaking, singing, and musical expression. Public spaces are often regulated through sound, such as overhead announcements at airports and bus stations, or the use of a bell tower in a town center. Many human rituals involve sound, such as birthday parties or religious services. Sound can also act as a warning by alerting humans of danger in the distance: think of an explosion in the distance, or the sound of water rushing before a flood arrives on scene.

Exercise

Observation helps us to become more aware of our own artistic choices. Watch 5 minutes of a movie, television show, video game, or video work. Make a list of the sounds you hear: people, objects, actions, environmental ambiance, clues to emotions, anything accompanying a transition in scene or psychology. At the end of the clip, review your list. What surprised you about the sounds that you noticed? Were there any differences between was expected and what you actually heard?

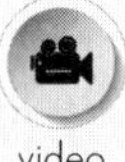
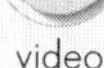

sound   video   games

Equally important is sound's opposite, **silence**, or the perceived absence of sound. As artist John Cage pointed out, there is no such thing as true silence. In this regard, silence may also be referred to as perceived silence. For example, if you sealed yourself in a soundproof room, you would still hear your body's heartbeat and breathing. Therefore, silence is implied despite relatively small or distant sounds, such as insects or a breeze through a window. Depending on the context, silence can serve to amplify sound or can be a tool for expression due to its own connotations. For example, because humans are social animals and often like to be surrounded by sounds, silence is sometimes associated with loneliness or death. As artists and designers explore sound, it is important to not forget the power of perceived silence within a piece.

Exercise

Brainstorm a list of 30 places you have never been. Then, select one location and storyboard a short video about your imagined first encounter with the location. Be sure to plot sound onto the storyboard. How will you use sound to tell this story? Show your storyboard to a partner and ask for his or her interpretation of your storyboard. Use that feedback to revise the work and improve it.

video   sound

Characteristics and Parts of Sound

In this section, we will examine the three basic parts of every sound, which are similar to the parts of a movement: an attack (onset, growth, birth); sustain (steady-state, duration, life); and decay (fall-off, termination, death). More technical analysis would break down the parts of a sound further, adding a first and second decay and so on. For our purposes, however, we will examine sounds in terms of only these three basic parts.

The attack of a sound is the time between the start of the sound and when it reaches its peak. The attack on some sounds is very fast, such as slamming a window closed; whereas the attack on other sounds can be much slower, such as the sound of a car approaching from the distance. Once a sound reaches its peak, the sustain is the amount of time before it decays or falls off. Bells often have a long sustain, whereas the click of a door latch has very little sustain. The decay is the amount of time it takes a sound to diminish to silence from its sustain state. The decay of a sound will be slower and have more reverberation, or echoing, in a space with hard surfaces off of which sound can bounce. In contrast, the decay of a sound will be much faster in a room with curtains, soundproofing, or other elements to absorb sound. The attack and decay of a sound communicate important information to the listener, such as distance from and speed of the source of the sound. Understanding and using these variations in sound and silence are an important way to aurally direct focus in a work. For example, using the sound of a train approaching, and making a point of using a long attack, can imply that the approaching train is far away yet important for our understanding of future events.

Categorizing Sounds

Sound can be arranged into a variety of groupings depending on your point of view. Here we will focus on the categories of synchronous, nonsynchronous, asynchronous, diegetic, and non-diegetic.

Synchronous sounds are those that are timed to their source on-screen or within a designated performance space. An example would be dialogue we see spoken by two people on-screen, or a teapot whistling onstage.

Exercise

Create a sound artwork that must be paired with a physical object or objects. The sound can come out of the object(s), surround the object(s), address the object(s), and so on. For example, if you selected an apple and a banana as your objects, what sound(s) would you select to pair with these objects? Why? At critique, see if participants can discern the relationship you were trying to communicate between the sounds and objects.

sound   installation

Nonsynchronous sounds play on-screen or onstage while their source is *not currently visible* but their source has been, or soon will be, visible. Video games often take advantage of this type of sound, such as the cyclical game *Shadow of the Colossus* (2005), in which participants seek out and defeat colossi. In this case, while moving through the game space the player can often hear the ocean off-screen; this sound indicates that the player is approaching the coast (fig. 5-10). Here ambient sound is a key to game play and identifying one's location within the game's environment. A **sound bridge** in film is another example of a nonsynchronous sound. This occurs when sounds from one shot continue into the next shot or vice versa. For example, we might hear a car approaching in one scene before cutting to a shot of the car making the sound. Our brains are trained to listen for these bridges because they are used constantly to connect multiple scenes together in film, video, and television.

Asynchronous sound is sound we hear that does not match what we see. For example, on-screen or onstage we may see a child in a detention room while we hear the sound of other children playing outside. We never see the children outside, but we hear them. Even more extreme asynchronous sound is to juxtapose an on-screen or onstage visual with a completely different sound, such as a person who appears as if on the verge of screaming, but then an entirely different sound comes out of his or her mouth, such as the sound of phone ringing. Asynchronous sound can be a useful way of illustrating an array of internal emotions.

Diegetic (sometimes called literal) **sounds** are "actual" sounds and **non-diegetic** (sometimes called nonliteral) **sounds**, are "commentary" sounds. These two categories of sound can be used in nearly all four-dimensional media. The distinction between diegetic and non-diegetic sound depends on each particular work and our understanding of the conventions or established reality of the piece in terms of viewing and listening. We know that certain sounds are represented as coming from the world of the work (diegetic), while others are represented as coming from outside the world of the work (non-diegetic). These two types of sounds can create atmosphere, determine time and place, communicate emotion, help create continuity, and herald the start or end of an event.[10]

Diegetic sounds include the voices of performers or characters, sounds made by objects within the work, or ambient sounds, which are the sounds created by the environment of the work. Ambient sounds are often the result of "movement, weight, size, solidity, resistance, contact, texture, temperature, impact, release, etc."[11] For example, in video games, the voices of the characters and the sounds their clothes make as the character moves are diegetic sounds. Diegetic sounds may also be connected to sources off-screen: when viewers hear relevant or expected sounds out of frame, it helps to create the sense of a three-dimensional world rather than just a two-dimensional screen.

Non-diegetic sounds include commentary, narration, and nonrealistic sound effects such as those in cartoons. This also includes music that is not being performed live within the world of the work. In a video game, a musical instrument is probably not creating the game's soundtrack on-screen at all times; this music would be considered a non-diegetic element of the environment. Non-diegetic sounds can be added to a work to create any

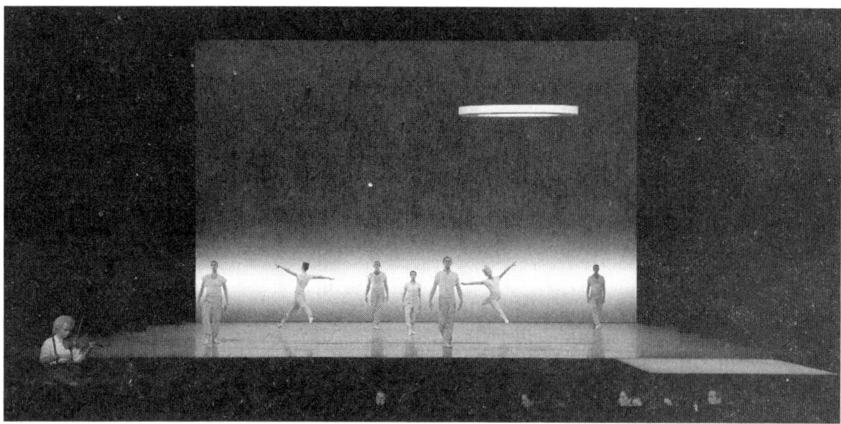

Fig. 5-18
Robert Wilson, *Einstein on the Beach* (2012), performance, 5 hours. Photo Credit: Lesley Leslie-Spinks.

number of emotions or impressions. Additionally, non-diegetic sounds, especially music, can add energy to a work, which is why music is routinely used in film, animation, and video games as a way to maintain interest between higher intensity moments.

Sometimes non-diegetic sound morphs into diegetic sound as we gain more knowledge of the piece. In the video game *Bioshock* (2007), Patti Page's "(How Much Is) That Doggie in the Window?" begins playing unexpectedly as the player enters a room in a later level. At first this music seems to be non-diegetic, as the audio appears to be triggered by no action of the player. However, inspecting the environment reveals that a jukebox has turned on, and the sound quickly becomes diegetic.

Keep in mind that the terms diegetic and non-diegetic come from the world of film sound studies, and they therefore assume a number of ideas about distinct separation between the viewer, the narrative, and the director's vision. However, not all contemporary works separate neatly into these defined boxes. *Einstein on the Beach* (1976), Robert Wilson's non-narrative opera, contains several gray areas where it is difficult to discern diegetic from non-diegetic sounds (fig. 5-18). There is a section in which the person performing the role of Einstein is playing a violin, and at the same time an orchestra is accompanying him. Is the violin operating strictly as a diegetic sound or as a non-diegetic sound? This phenomenon is neither good nor bad, and perhaps this aural ambiguity is what makes these moments in the work more interesting.

Interview: Robert Wilson

Einstein on the Beach has a classical formal structure in four acts
and three themes. It is an opera based on theme and variation and
is a time-space-construction. I started with the concept of light.
Without light there is not space. Einstein said light is the measure of
all things. I divided the three themes, A, B, and C, in the traditional
way that painters have measured space. Portraits, close-ups, still
life, a bit further away, and landscapes, a view from a great
distance. It is a work with which you can freely associate. It is
non-narrative.

—*Robert Wilson*

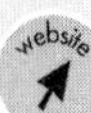
Visit the book's website to read the full interview.

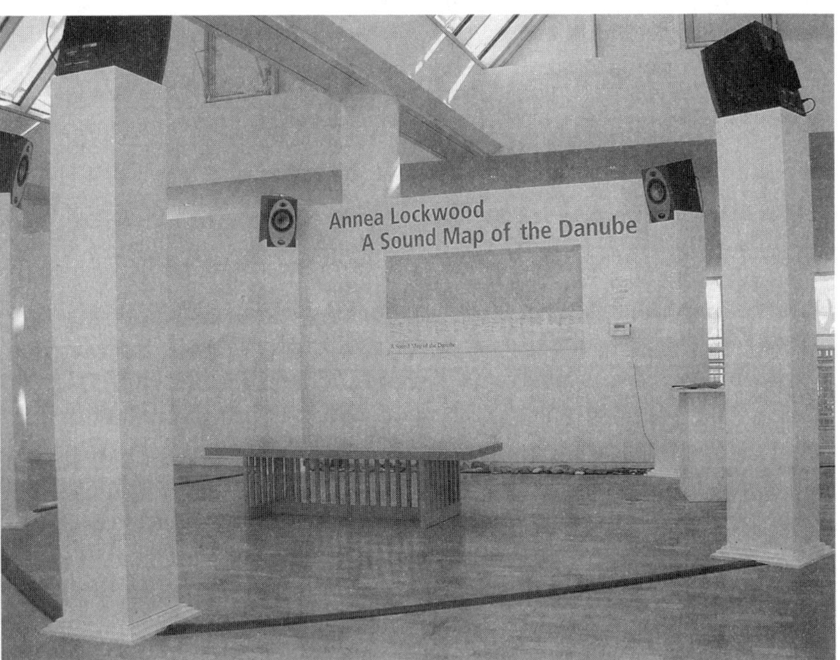

Fig. 5-19
Annea Lockwood, *A Sound Map of the Danube* (2005), six-channel surround sound
installation, 2:47:00 hours. Courtesy of the Artist.

There are also works that are purely sound, with little or no synchronized visual accompaniment. Annea Lockwood is a sound artist who has created a variety of "sound maps" of rivers all over the world, including *A Sound Map of the Danube* (2005) (fig. 5-19). These sound maps consist of recordings of not only different locations along particular rivers, but also human and animal interactions with the rivers. There might be a map of the river hanging on the wall where the sound map is installed, but there are no specific visuals assigned to particular parts of the sound composition.

Interview: Annea Lockwood

This work with rivers arises from my desire to sense their nature, the way they create their environments and, through immersion in their sonic energies, a deep integration with them. This extended listening and the close attention to detail, which is central to all my work, is a real joy to engage in. I love the process, love recording, editing, deciding, sensing and then seeing how others experience those sounds too.

For me one of the most beautiful experiences of sound, and a favorite artwork, in large part because of its unfathomable quality, has come from listening to sound artist Liz Phillips' *Wave Table* (2003). This is a deep black aluminum tank filled with water. You can't see beneath the water and initially the stillness of the surface makes it hard to discern where the water's edges or even the surface are—pure blackness. Then as you approach it becomes activated. Wave movement begins, deep sounds and tones emerge and change quality in response to your movement and distance from the tank. Essentially you are dancing with it. Here is her own description of the work: "As the sound plays through the water table, the low frequency notes create a wave-like movement in the water and the aural experience is modulated by the viewer. . . . Tuned resonant filters and compressors listen to the audience and respond in phrases, volumes and pitches in surprising relationships and with waves. [It can be seen at https://vimeo.com/92985533.]" This is all clear to me, and yet, there is something deeply mysterious here, compelling.

—Annea Lockwood

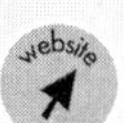
Visit the book's website to read the full interview.

Exercise

Go online and view *Wave Table* (2003), by artist Liz Phillips. After watching the work, write down what you think are the subject, form, content, and context for this work. Analyze how the artist used sound. Compare and contrast your answers with others'. How are your answers similar and different from those around you? Were there any trends in the answers?

sound   installation

It is important to recognize the parts of a sound for their usefulness in creating atmosphere and emotion within your work. Whether sounds are synchronous, nonsynchronous, asynchronous, diegetic, non-diegetic, or none of these, sound is a powerful tool at your disposal as an artist or designer.

Summary

In this chapter, we've defined and examined the basic elements of 4D art and design:

- Time, including various different types of time
- Architecture/topography, including how scale, sound, relative location, and movement effect our experience of architectural space
- Light, including projections and projection mapping; how to use light effectively in your own work; and dynamic, ambient, specific, and three-point lighting
- Movement, including using gestures and isolations to enhance your work, as well as an examination of movement in film and video
- Sound, including its characteristics and the different types of sound

These elements are important when we are preparing, creating, and eventually critiquing our own time-based works.

Key Terms

accent light   Light used to create patterns within the work by means of contrast

ambient light   Light that fills and articulates the overall space

ambient sound   Sound from the immediate surroundings

angular   Consisting of straight lines and corners

animated GIFs   Digital image files that can display movement

architecture   Buildings and other built structures through and around which an individual can move

asynchronous sound   Sound we hear that does not match what we see

attack   The onset, growth, or birth of a movement or sound

attached shadow   A shadow fixed to an object, revealing the basic form of the object

backlight   A light that illuminates the subject from behind, often creating a glowing outline—or halo effect—around the subject

base of support   The area beneath an object or person that connects with the supporting surface, such as feet or hands

battery life   The length of time a given battery allows you to complete a task on a piece of electronic equipment

biological time   A measure of time related to bodily functions

cast shadow   A shadow independent of the object causing the shadow, revealing the object's relationship to its environment

center of gravity   The center of the mass in an environment of uniform gravity

cinemagraph   Animated GIF in which a minor and repeated movement occurs

cue   Planned changes in lights or other elements

daylight   Light from the sun that changes color and brightness throughout the day and year, and is affected by weather

decay   The fall-off, termination, or death of a movement or sound

diegetic sound   "Actual" sounds, linked to the world of the artwork

digital time   Time measured in milliseconds; it is often associated with technology

dolly shot   Camera movement parallel to the ground, often on a rolling track

edited time   Time that has been cut up and rearranged

experienced time   The perceived speed of time passing (also known as *subjective time, psychological time, implied time,* or *perceived time*)

fill light   A light that softens the key light and illuminates areas of shadow cast by the key light

front projection Pointing a projector, connected to a computer or other device, at a screen designed to reflect light back at the viewer

gestures Movements by a part of a whole (also known as *isolations*)

gobo A cut metal stencil placed in front of a lighting instrument with focusing lenses

key light A focused light that draws the eye to a single point or location

light A form of radiant energy that reflects off the world around us and into our eyes, allowing us to see our environment and color

linear time Time that is mapped out in the order of past, present, and future (also known as *chronological time*)

measured time Time quantitatively measured by regularly recurring events or intervals, such as the passage of minutes, meals, seasons, or years (also known as **actual time, objective time, clock time**)

montage A series of clips edited together to explore a piece of action, space, or time in greater detail or as an overview

movement A shift or variation in the location of an object, light, or sound

nondiegetic sound "Commentary" sound, presented to enhance the world of the artwork

nonlinear time An arrangement of events to reveal parts of the future mixed in with the past and present; there is no required order of events

nonsynchronous sound Sound that plays on-screen or onstage while its source is not currently visible but has been, or soon will be, visible

opaque object A material off of which light reflects back into our eye, and does not allow light to pass through

oppositional movement Movement that leads the eye in a different direction

organic Rounded and soft (describes shape or movement)

pan A camera movement that consists of pivoting from side to side

plot time The span of time a plot covers within a narrative work (also known as *story time*, or *scope* [of a narrative])

projection Purposefully cast light and shadow; examples include basic shadow puppetry, film or video projection, and projection mapping on 3D forms

projection-mapping Using software to map complex surfaces on which to project various imagery

reflected light Light bounced off of one surface before hitting the subject

refracted light Light that strikes an object and passes through, but changes direction upon exiting

relative location The relationship between a location and other markers of space

room tone The unique subtle sounds of an empty room

rotoscoping   The process of tracing single frames of film or video and then animating those traced frames.

running time   The total length of a work, whether it is a live event or a video piece (also known as *play time* when describing gaming)

shadow   An area of darkness created when light is blocked

sidelight   Light aimed at the side of a subject

silence   The perceived absence of sound

silhouette   An example of a specific kind of accent light that places an object between the viewer and an area of light creating a shadow in the shape of the object

sound   A vibration that can be perceived by the ear

sound bridge   Film transition in which sounds from one shot continue into the next shot or vice versa

specific light   Light that provides illumination for a specific task, or to draw focus

stillness   Absence of movement

successional movement   Movement that leads the eye in one direction

sustain   The steady-state, duration, or life of a movement or sound

synchronous sound   Sound that is timed with its source on-screen or within a designated performance space

three-point lighting   A lighting setup consisting of a key light, a fill light, and a backlight

tilt   A camera movement that consists of pivoting up and down

time   The progression of events and existence from the past, through the present, and into the future

time-lapse photography   Images are taken at regular intervals over a period of time, and then edited together to "speed up" a process that we normally don't experience

tone   The quality of a sound vibration

topography   The physical nature or quality of the surface on which the work takes place

tracking shot   Camera movement parallel to the ground, often on a rolling track

translucent object   A material that allows much of the light to pass through, but some is reflected, which causes a blurred or somewhat obstructed effect

transparent object   A material that transmits or allows light to pass through, allowing us to see what is beneath it

visibility   The extent to which a participant can see within the space of a work

zoom   Utilizing camera lenses to make the image larger or smaller

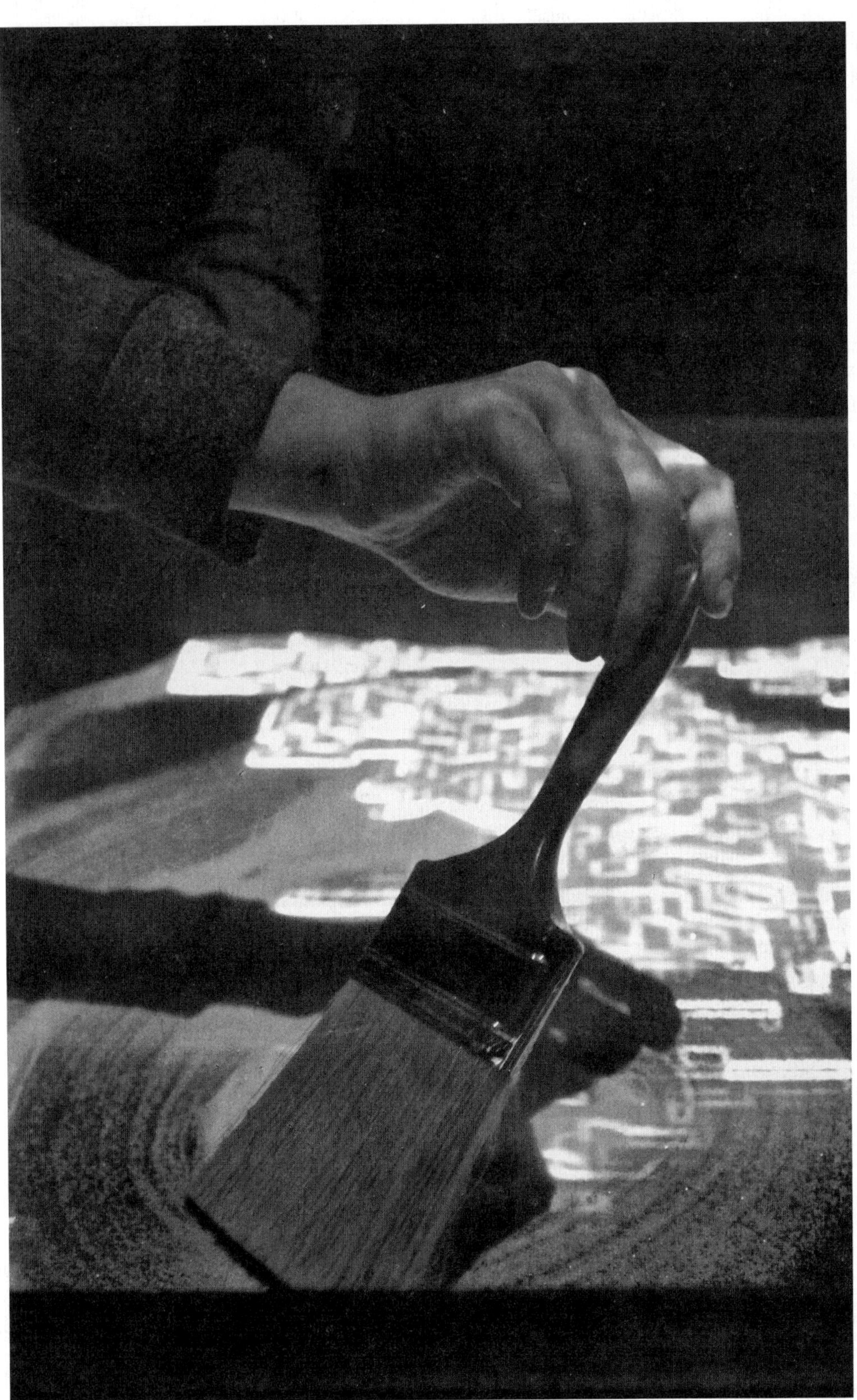

Courtesy of the Artist.

6

Principles of 4D Art and Design

Now that we understand the elements of 4D art and design, we can learn how to manipulate those elements using the principles of 4D art and design. In this chapter we will closely examine each of these principles: causality, duration, energy dynamics, interactivity, musicality, simultaneity/juxtaposition, spatial relationships, tempo/speed, and transitions. These principles are the guidelines for arranging the elements of any time-based work and can be infinitely combined to meet your needs as an artist or designer.

Causality

Causality is the principle that everything has a cause and effect. It is a key element of both **narrative**, which is an account of connected events (sometimes referred to as *story*), and non-narrative works.

Casey Scalf's non-narrative installation *The Sandbox of Life* (2014) allows participants to manipulate the sand in an elevated sandbox combined with a projector and computer. The projected imagery is affected by the arrangement of the sandbox and will change in response to changes in the sand (fig. 6-1). Manipulating the sand is a non-narrative action, yet there is clear cause and effect present between it and the projected imagery.

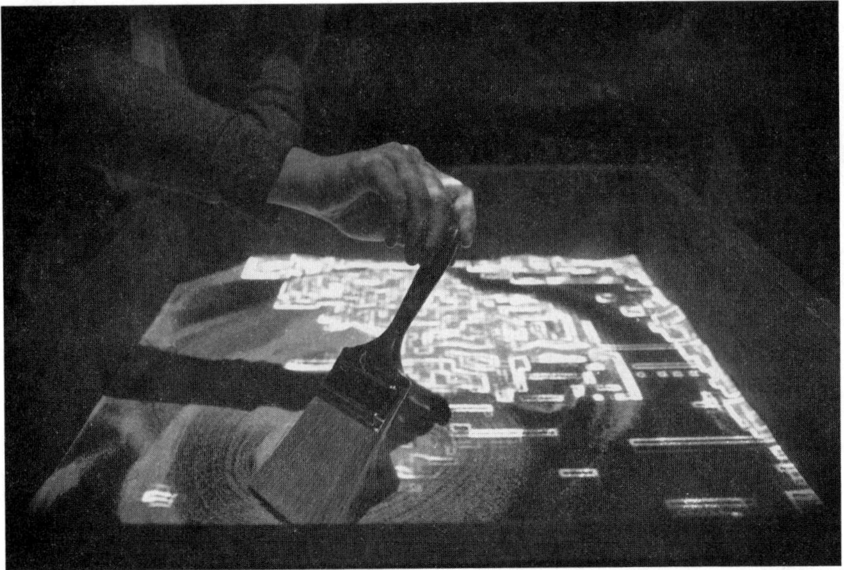

Fig. 6-1

Casey Scalf, *The Sandbox of Life* (2014), interactive installation, dimensions variable. Courtesy of the artist.

Interview: Casey Scalf

The Sandbox of Life represents the current culmination of many different scientific and artistic pursuits I've enjoyed. It takes some cellular automata, a bit of feedback, computer vision, projection mapping, and a few lines of code sitting on top of a little engineering, and out comes this multi-sensory, highly fluid interactive and collaborative experience anyone can use.

The Sandbox of Life is a black sandbox filled with sand. Upon this sand, and only the sand, patterns exhibiting lifelike growth qualities spread to all available space via projected light. Using your hands, or any other object, you can manipulate the contour of the sand and thus change the environment for the life forms. On top of this, the patterns can be "extinguished" via shadow and "ignited" via a handheld laser. You can also prevent the sand from growing life, as well as purposely populate previously vacant areas. It is all very natural with no specific rules. There are many different possibilities within the system.

I see this type of interactive experience and installation as a catalyst for conversations on new forms of computing. The current computer experience is a vestige of the typewriter and the printed page. Just as the first movie theaters displayed only still images, the current computer paradigm exhibits dependencies on previous platforms that limit the full potential and use of this new technology. *The Sandbox of Life* is step in a new direction. I see many things coming from it.

—Casey Scalf

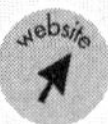 Visit the book's website to read the full interview.

Exercise

Think about the relationship between symptoms and causality. Physical illnesses certainly have symptoms, but so do other problems, such as poverty, social and religious conflicts, climate change, hunger, homelessness, mass shootings, gentrification. Brainstorm a list of 10 symptoms, and note the causes of the symptoms. Now, make an interactive installation based on one of these symptoms. Determine who your audience will be. How will you reach this audience and communicate causality? At critique, determine how well causality is communicated and how the experience could be altered to make the work more successful.

installation

Causality and Expectations

Causality implies expectation, and artists can use this sense of anticipation or suspense to establish any number of situations with expected or unexpected outcomes. In the moving light installation *Light Barrier* (2014) by collaborative duo Kimchi and Chips, participants first see a glowing fog hovering above an array of mirrors, followed by the appearance of various moving arrangements of geometric forms (fig. 6-2). In this case, participants first observe the effect, the glowing fog, and then the cause, the

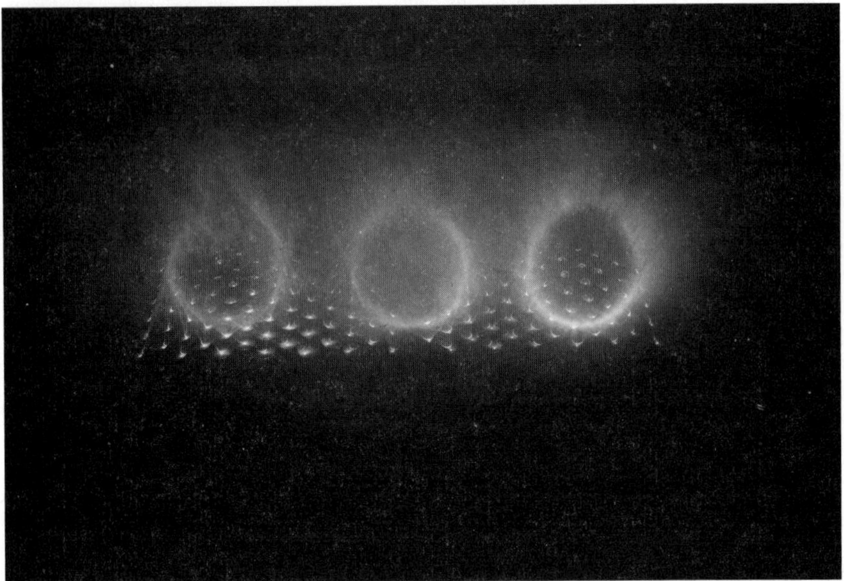

Fig. 6-2
Kimchi and Chips, *Light Barrier* (2014), convex mirrors, projection, scanning, dimensions variable. Courtesy of the artists.

arrangement of mirrors. Using cause and effect logic, viewers continue to expect further action above the mirrors rather than other locations within the piece. In this way, causality can be central to the success of many four-dimensional works by helping direct focus.

Exercise

Go online, search for, and view *Line Segments Space* (2013) by Kimchi and Chips. After watching the work, write down what you think are the subject, form, content, and context for this work. Analyze how the artists used causality to create expectation within the work. Compare and contrast your answers with others'. How are your answers similar and different from those around you? Were there any trends in the answers?

sound   installation   light

Artists and designers can also purposefully avoid using any clear causality as in Jonathan Rattner's video work *End, End, End* (see fig. 4-15). The excerpt on the book's website shows shots of cattle interspersed with a blank screen and a male voice repeating phrases about the end of a tape. The work has no clear cause and effect, which can affect the viewer in a number of ways, from intrigue and curiosity to frustration and boredom depending on the viewer's attention span and willingness to engage.

Causality can also affect participants' experiences if their expectations—based on perception—are not met. For example, if you present a video work as a documentary about dogs, but the entire video is nothing more than a long, still shot of a single flower, your audience might be confused and irritated that their expectations were not met. Artists and designers can purposefully choose to not meet expectations, but there should be a good reason for doing so. Otherwise, you are simply alienating your audience and risk losing them as audience members in the future.

However, if the expected is always delivered in a work, there will not be enough contrast to hold participants' interest. Artists and designers must strike a balance between meeting and denying expectations. Remember that in some situations when one expectation is not met, it can make meeting the fulfillment of the next expectation all the more satisfying. This concept relates to the elements of surprise and pleasure derived from the unexpected.

Causality and Narrative

If an artist or designer decides to create a traditional, **linear narrative**—with a plot containing a beginning, middle, and end that unfolds in that order—the causality will be easy to track. Usually, the first event causes the second event and so on. This is because humans experience time in one direction, moving from the past, to the present, and then to the future.[1] This narrative causality is clear in city-building games such as the *SimCity* series (1989–2008), *The Settlers* series (1993–2010), or an independent video game like *Dwarf Fortress* (fig. 2-8). In *Dwarf Fortress*, one of the primary ways to play is "Fortress Mode," in which the player selects a site and takes control of a group of seven dwarves to begin building a fortress. Each event or choice is recorded as a narrative, which can then be explored in "Legends Mode," in which the player is allowed to view a detailed history of the world from beginning to end. Narrative causality is central to this complex game.

Interview: Tarn Adams

The idea behind *Dwarf Fortress* is to make a fantasy world generator and simulator, and to allow you to take up a role in the world for a time and then move on to another role—right now that can be a single traveler or a colony of dwarves. We've tried to make the game as detailed as possible, and we also try to have the game generate as many parts of itself as possible, so that every experience will be different and complex.

—*Tarn Adams*

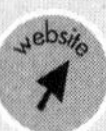
Visit the book's website to read the full interview.

Exercise

Brainstorm a list of 20 products for which you would like to create a commercial. Select one product and create a 15-second commercial that promotes only the practical aspects of the product, not the emotional connection. For example, you might sell a toothbrush and emphasize that it is less expensive than other toothbrushes. Think about causality and presenting as clear of a narrative as possible. How did your opening moments create expectations? How were those expectations handled? Was the ending clear, and was it necessary or successful?

video

However, an artist can also work with a **nonlinear narrative**, thereby jumbling the narrative, or presenting the beginning, middle, and end out of chronological order. Working with nonlinear narrative can enhance or detract from the meaning of the work by making causality more or less difficult to track. In the classic film *Citizen Kane*, we follow a news reporter through a series of nonlinear flashbacks as he tries to discover the meaning of a publishing tycoon's final words. The flashbacks sometimes return to the publisher's childhood, while others review more recent events. The nonlinear arrangement of the scenes adds to the building tension of the film.

Additionally, the way **conflict**, or struggle, is represented in a work will help causality become more apparent. Inner conflict includes emotional and moral challenges within the characters, while outer conflict includes struggles between characters, environments, external forces, and so on. The portrayal of inner and outer conflict in Eleanor Antin's *Love's Shadow* reveals causality between the rejection of a lover's advances and the ballerina's murder (figure 1-18).

Exercise

Go online and research Natalie Jeremijenko's *Environmental Health Clinic*, which creates solutions for environmental concerns. Select your own environmental concern to solve. Then, through a time-based work, create a solution for your environmental concern. Think about causality: what causes the problem, and how can you address that (even if it is simply drawing attention to it)?

  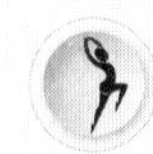  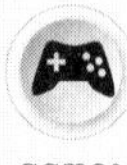 

sound   video   performance   installation   games   light

Causality and Sound

Sounds are often indicators of causality, and artists can exploit this attribute according to their needs. A viewer or participant who hears a car pull up and a door slam will expect to hear footsteps or some other indication of a person getting out of the car. This idea is closely tied to the use of sound bridges, discussed in Chapter 5, which are also an indicator of causality. In the opening titles of *Dawn of the Dead*, for instance, the voice of a newscaster begins during a shot of the actors' names smearing across the screen (figure 1-16). The voice continues into the actual shot of the newscast and the newscaster who is speaking. This sound bridge helps clarify that the zombie outbreak that the newscaster is discussing is causing the bloodshed.

Causality is a foundational principle that helps determine the flow of any time-based work by managing participant expectations. Artists and designers can use both narrative and sound to help enhance participants' sense of causality.

Duration

Duration is the overall length of time a work—or a portion of a work—lasts. This definition applies to all 4D media. Selecting the duration of your work is vital to its effectiveness and can help develop focus. If a work continues for too long, or if it is squeezed into too short of a time span, it will lose its power to affect the participant. Duration can be divided into smaller segments by changing a specific element, such as light or sound. One light cue can end a work and another can be used to start the work. Artists and designers must be aware of the amount of time viewers will need to comprehend the work and then make adjustments accordingly.

Exercise

Brainstorm a list of at least 20 events that last about 10 seconds. For example, eating a cookie in two bites might last 10 seconds. To help you brainstorm, also imagine things you wouldn't want to watch/hear/taste/feel/smell (experience) for 10 seconds, and things you would want to last longer than 10 seconds but don't. What would engage you for 10 seconds? Create a 10-second performance that is inspired by an item from your list. When creating your performance, you might think not only about things that last 10 seconds, but also about things that cannot last 10 seconds.

Repeat the above process of listing and creating a performance, but replace the time frame of 10 seconds with 10 minutes. Then, repeat the process again, replacing the time frame with 1 hour. At critique ask if it felt like works had an appropriate duration. Ask how performances shifted or changed when they became longer. Were there any physical challenges to the longer performances?

performance

Exercise

Brainstorm a list of 25 historical events. Create a storyboard for a
1-minute video or animation inspired by one of these events. How
do the actual duration of the historical event and the duration of
your video work compare? What strategies can be used to expand
or compress time? Could you expand or compress the duration of
your video to add meaning to your work? Ask for feedback on
your storyboard and make revisions accordingly.

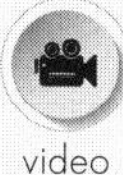

video

Duration can range from milliseconds to years, seeming nearly instantaneous. Ken Goldberg's work *Telegarden*, which lasted 9 years (1995–2004),
consisted of a soil bed and a robotic arm capable of watering, planting, and
viewing a garden via online controls (fig. 6-3). The work purposefully highlighted the contrast between the speed of the Internet (humans went online
to control and view these robotic gardening actions) and the much slower
pace of growing plants.

A work with a much shorter duration is Bas Jan Ader's 19-second performance *Fall II* (1970), in which the artist rode his bike into a waterway,
exploring the boundary between art and life. In contrast, Pippin Barr's
browser-based video game *Don't Drown* (2014) has an indefinite duration
based entirely on the participant's patience and endurance (fig. 6-4). The
objective of this game is to keep the avatar's head above water by clicking
the screen rapidly. Technically, this action could go on for a very long time—
or a very short time, depending on the participant's ability and will.

Interview: Pippin Barr

I'm a game maker and critic living and working in Malta. I have a
PhD in computer science from Victoria University of Wellington in
New Zealand, with the dissertation focusing on the value systems
promoted by popular digital games. I teach game design and

(continued)

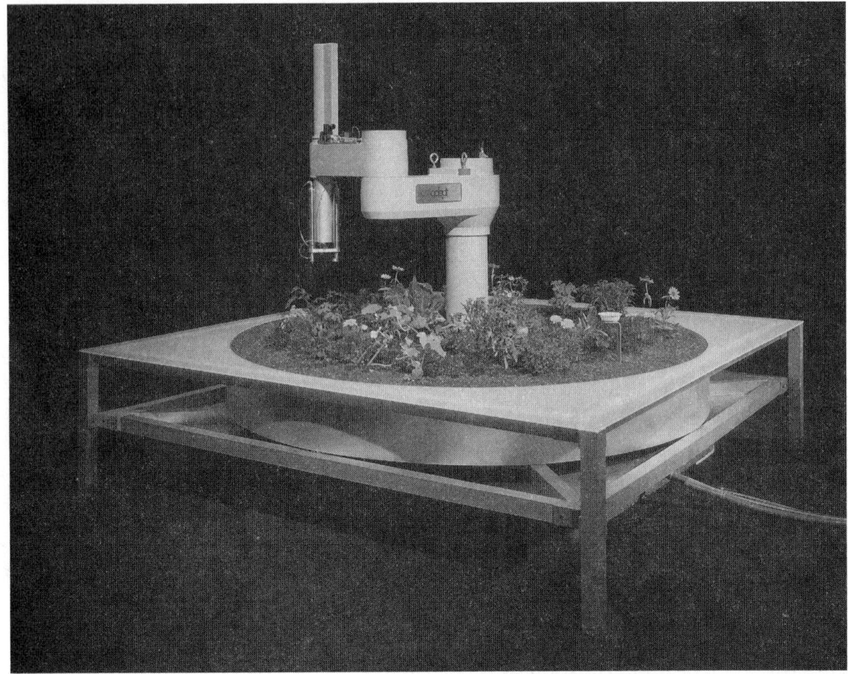

Fig. 6-3
The Telegarden (1995–2004), networked art installation at Ars Electronica Museum, Austria. Co-directors: Ken Goldberg and Joseph Santarromana. Project team: George Bekey, Steven Gentner, Rosemary Morris Carl Sutter, Jeff Wiegley, Erich Berger. Photo by Robert Wedemeyer. http://goldberg.berkeley.edu/garden/Ars/.

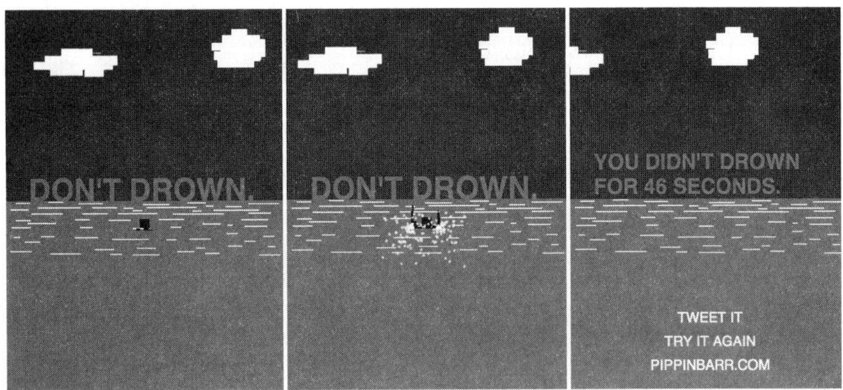

Fig. 6-4
Pippin Barr, *Don't Drown* (2014), browser-based video game. © Pippin Barr.

Interview: Pippin Barr *(continued from page 217)*

prototype at the university here, but spend most of my time working on various game projects, usually solo, but occasionally in collaboration with others (e.g., Marina Abramovic, @seinfeld2000).

I've focused on making games for the last three years, after spending time on various other media (comics, illustration, short stories). My essential practice boils down to having an idea I find entertaining ("What if there was a game version of the safety instructions on an airplane?") and then immediately beginning to make a game. Having a degree in software engineering, I'm familiar enough with code that I do all my own programming, and as I grew up in an art-loving household (my parents are art collectors) I've always been confident about (if not necessarily good at) creating my own visual art, so I do that for my games too.

—Pippin Barr

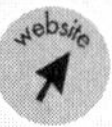

Visit the book's website to read the full interview.

Exercise

Go online, search for, and view performance artist Marina Abramović and Ulay's *AAA AAA* (1978). After watching the work, write down what you think are the subject, form, content and context for this work. Also analyze how duration affected the quality of the work. Compare and contrast your answers with others'. How are your answers similar and different from those around you? Were there any trends in the answers?

performance

Duration and Narrative

While not all time-based works include narrative, those that do can utilize many familiar literary terms. For example, **plot** refers to the action that happens within the duration of a given work, while **story** refers to the overarching description of the situation, including what happens before and after a particular plot. An example is William Shakespeare's play *Romeo and Juliet*. The plot lasts 4–6 days, while the story of the feud between the Montagues and Capulets lasted years. In film/video, the plot's duration is also referred to as **reel time**.

Duration and Media

Duration can also affect an artist's or designer's choice of materials. Take for instance a performance in which chocolate spoons are served with coffee. The spoons are meant to last a very short time—only until they melt away in the coffee. An example with a longer duration could be an installation work of paper sculptures embedded with wildflower seeds (sometimes called seed bombs). Although the sculptures themselves may be viewed as having artistic qualities, the work is not complete until the paper has deteriorated into the ground and flowers grow from the seeds. In either example, the duration of the work is influenced by the choice of materials and how they are used.

Exercise

Create a game involving a ball that lasts no longer than 30 seconds and can be played over and over in rapid succession. Then create a game using the same ball that lasts at least 5 minutes. Recruit players to experience both the short game and the long game. After they have played both games, ask them about their experience of the duration: Did they find one game more enjoyable than the other? Why? Is there anything they would change about either game? Do they prefer longer or shorter games? Try testing the two games on people who are hungry versus people who have just eaten. How do their answers to the interview questions differ? How does the context of hungry or nonhungry affect duration?

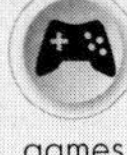

games

Motivated Duration

The goal of some spaces is to motivate the audience to spend more time within them. For example, some office spaces are designed to get workers to spend more time brainstorming, creating, working, and collaborating.

These spaces could employ a variety of approaches, from creating an open and fun, playful atmosphere, to defining quiet spaces for focused creative work free of distractions (see fig. 3-8, *Susan Cain's Quiet Spaces*).

Retail or merchandisable spaces, such as the window displays at department stores, are meant to entice potential shoppers to not only spend more time looking at the display, but then to go inside the store to shop. Interactive kiosks in exhibits are similar in that they invite participants to spend more time investigating a subject in further depth through touch-screens, engaging visuals, and other interactive features. If motivated duration is a part of your work, take into consideration the various ways the elements of 4D art and design can be arranged to create and maintain focus, thereby holding your participants' attention longer.

Managing duration is pivotal in controlling participants' experience of a 4D work. It is a key component of narrative and can influence an artist or designer's choice of media. Motivated duration is also central to directing and holding participants' focus.

Energy Dynamics

Energy dynamics, also known as *intensity*, refers to the amount and type of energy felt by the viewer or participant at any given moment. Participants will bring their own energy to an artwork, but they are also deeply affected by the energy dynamics of the work itself.

In Noelle Mason's *Mise-en-Scene* (2004), she submits her body to the energy dynamics of those who happen to interact with her work (fig. 6-5). She stands inside a closed box with electrodes attached to her body, which are controlled by buttons outside the box; the box has no windows but includes screens attached to the outside walls that display the performer inside. If a participant were to press the buttons and administer a shock, the energy dynamics of the performance would be drastically different than if people were concerned about her well-being. In the actual execution of the project, the gallery visitors collectively decided to not push the buttons. By asking the audience to administer—and view—physical pain, this work highlights the concept of **antagonism**, which is the goal of creating constructive debate around a serious topic while running the risk of alienating some individuals. The level of aggression in an antagonistic work must be appropriate to the content and subject matter of the work. If the aggression is too extreme, the work will alienate too many individuals and fail to provoke meaningful conversation. (For further reading on this type of activism, see the "Activism/Protest" section in Chapter 2.)

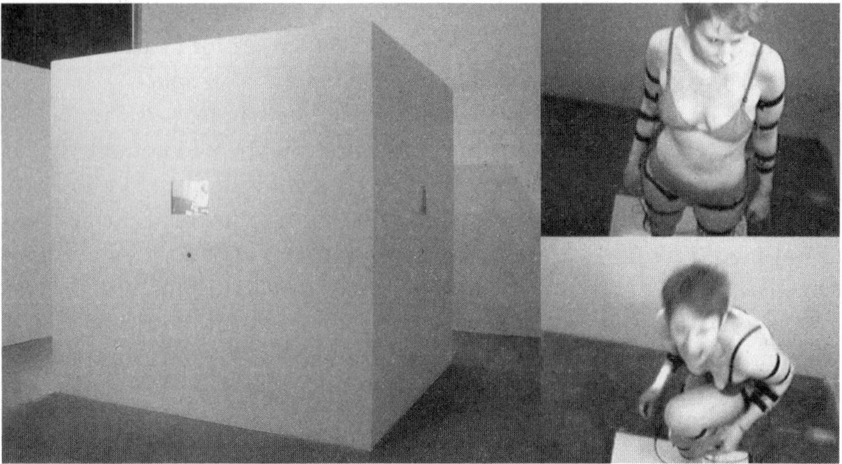

Fig. 6-5
Noelle Mason, *Mise-en-Scene* (2004), performative installation, duration variable.
Courtesy of the artist.

Interview: Noelle Mason

Early on it was all about Chris Burden for me. I was introduced to
his work in undergrad at UC Irvine where he had gone to graduate
school and formalized his minimal performance style. I came from
a background in physical theatre with an emphasis in Grotowski's
brand of Theatre of Cruelty . . . so early works like *Shoot* and *TV
Hijack* appealed, both for their shocking austerity and for their
bold intervention into the real. Burden is also very childish in a
way . . . his early work is not so different from *Jackass* and his
work from *B-Car* on literally uses toys . . . toys for children like
matchbox cars, train sets, and erecter sets and toys for adults,
sports cars, and tractors.

Daniel Joseph Martinez was also a huge influence on my
work. He was a professor of mine and his belief in art as a radical
social practice has had a profound effect on my continued interest
in the importance of making art. His museum tag piece for the
1993 Whitney Biennial "I can't imagine ever wanting to be white"
remains an enduring mark of institutional critique . . . that is
political but escapes being didactic through poetry and rhetoric.

His animatronic self-portraits reinterpret the nature of live performance through the dead meat of the automaton.

William Pope. L is an artist who really challenges the boundaries of absurdity and political correctness . . . he is fearless in both his confrontational strategies and in his choice of medium . . . he is mostly known for his "crawl" pieces in which he crawled across the island of Manhattan in a superman costume with a skateboard tied to his back.

—*Noelle Mason*

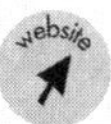
Visit the book's website to read the full interview.

Exercise

Go online, search for, and view *Shoot* (1971) by Chris Burden. After watching the work, write down what you think are the subject, form, content, and context for this work. How did the artist use energy dynamics within the piece? How might have the energy dynamics been different viewing the work in person rather than watching it on a screen? Compare and contrast your answers with others'. How are your answers similar and different from those around you? Were there any trends in the answers?

performance

Sound, light, movement, time, and architecture all contribute to the energy dynamics of a work. Energy can be high or low intensity. For example, low-intensity energy can make a typically vigorous movement such as jumping look feeble, while high-intensity energy can make jumping look chaotic. Movement is the element of 4D art and design that most clearly illustrates energy dynamics because it requires some sort of force or effort to sustain it, and humans can easily differentiate between a weak movement and a more forceful movement. However, a sound or light can also have high or low energy by changing its attributes to be louder and higher pitched, or brighter and more colorful, and so on. All of the elements and principles of 4D art and design can affect how participants perceive energy dynamics.

Energy can also be heavy or light depending on where or whom the energy is coming from.[2] Works that have serious content will often have energy that feels or is perceived to be heavy, such as Mason's potentially violent *Mise-en-Scene*. In contrast, works with more joyful content, such as Yayoi Kusama's *The Obliteration Room* (2011), have much lighter energy. In *The Obliteration Room*, participants received sheets of colorful dot stickers to apply anywhere they liked in a white room (Plate 15, color insert). This work is less emotionally challenging than deciding whether or not to electrically shock a human being, as in *Mise-en-Scene*, and therefore would be described as having lighter energy.

Exercise

Seek out two architectural spaces with completely different or contrasting energy dynamics; your class must be able to easily walk to both of the spaces. Write about what makes the energy dynamics of the spaces different. How does architecture affect the energy dynamics? Be specific, and be ready to explain your reasoning to the group as you tour from space to space, examining the energy dynamics of each one.

 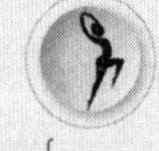

installation   performance

Energy Dynamics and Contrast

Contrast is closely tied to energy dynamics because the energy of a work can change over its duration. An artist or designer has to determine how and why the work will transform over the work's duration, and what this transformation will reveal or add to the work.

An example of contrasting energy dynamics is Kate Gilmore's *Through the Claw* (2011) (fig. 6-6). Gilmore directed a group of female performers who are faced with a large cube of clay. They slowly tear it apart, throwing handfuls of clay against the walls and floor until the cube is completely dispersed. The contrast in energy dynamics from the first frenetic actions to the later, slower, and more exhausted actions makes the performance interesting to watch.

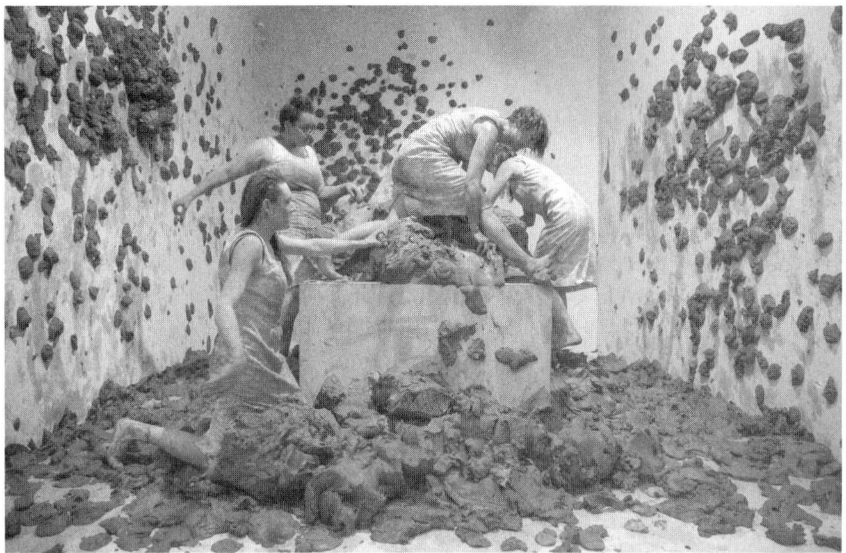

Fig. 6-6
Kate Gilmore, *Through the Claw* (2011), performance still taken at Pace Gallery, New York.
Courtesy of David Castillo Gallery.

Interview: Kate Gilmore

I am a video, performance, sculpture, and installation based artist.
I work in lots of different mediums all depending on the project
that I am developing. Coming from a pretty traditional sculpture
background, I am drawn to construction-based materials such as
wood, plaster, paint, clay. I create large scale sculptures and
installations and then do a performance for camera in which these
installations are altered, destroyed, transformed through a very
physical action of the main character (myself).

Through the Claw was a live performance made at Pace
Gallery in NYC. In this piece, 5 performers attack a 7,500 pound
cube of unfired clay. They tear it apart in whatever way they
choose, throwing it on the floor, walls, etc. The goal of the piece
was to completely eliminate the cube of clay through this intense
physical action of these five women.

—*Kate Gilmore*

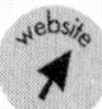 Visit the book's website to read the full interview.

Exercise

Brainstorm a list of 20 words or phrases that describe you as a person. Create a brief performance that acts as a self-portrait. Consider the energy dynamics throughout the piece with attention to where they change, if they change, and why they do or do not change. How do you communicate this change in energy? Ask your audience what they found exciting during the event and why. What did they pay attention to and why? When did they disconnect from the event and why?

performance

Another, less hectic example of contrasting energy dynamics is the work of artist Stelarc, who completed a series of performances in which he hangs from hooks through his skin. These performances, such as *Sitting/Swaying: Event for Rock Suspension* (1980), have minimal movement aside from the initial lifting of the artist into the air, a slight swaying of the counterweights, and the eventual lowering of the artist to the ground. However, the contrast in energy dynamics between the application of the hooks to the lifting of the body, and the eventual release to the floor, make this work engaging for viewers (fig. 6-7).

Interview: Stelarc

For *Sitting / Swaying: Event for Rock Suspension*, the insertions [of the hooks] were done sitting down on the gallery floor. We had already suspended a ring of rocks from the ceiling above the body, held in place by slip-knots. The cables were then connected to the hooks. When all the rigging was done I quickly pulled at the cables, releasing the slip knots and as the rocks came down, the body went up. It was not a static suspension. In fact the body was gently swaying from side to side generating random oscillations of the rocks. The performance duration was approximately 20 minutes. I stopped the performance when the telephone rang in the gallery.

—*Stelarc*

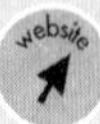 Visit the book's website to read the full interview.

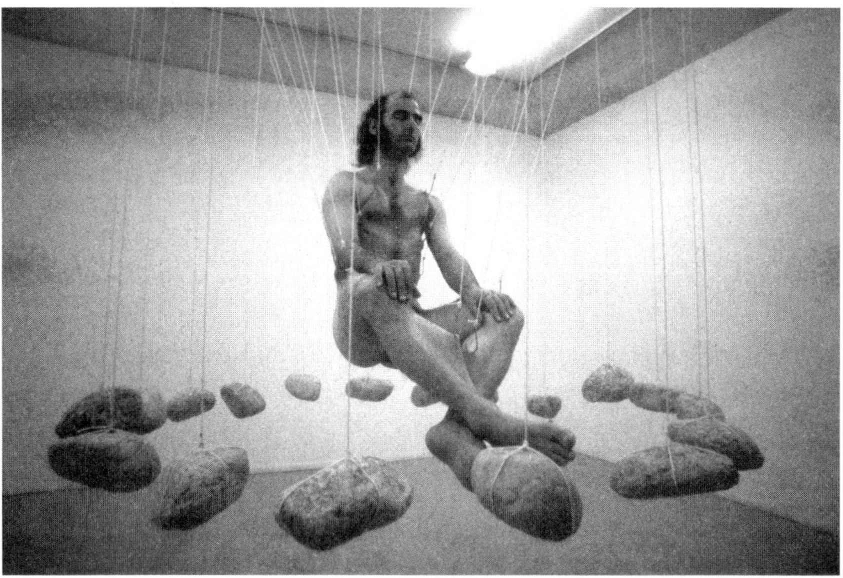

Fig. 6-7
Stelarc, *Sitting / Swaying: Event for Rock Suspension* (1980), performance still, dimensions variable. © Stelarc. Photographer - Keisuke Oki.

Exercise

Brainstorm a list of 10 pop songs to act as the inspiration for your work. You will create a game inspired by one of these songs. The game has to have at least two different energy levels. How are you able to engineer energy levels into a game? Think about quiet games and frenetic games—how are they similar and different? How can you apply those elements to your game? Test your game on people and make changes based on their feedback.

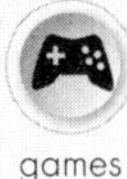

games

Altogether, energy dynamics and changes in them will help determine the mood and atmosphere for any work. The artist or designer must consciously choose where and how to direct the intensity of the work in order to communicate the desired concept.

Interactivity

Interactivity is the exchange of information between two or more entities. Those entities could be people, places, or things. Interactivity allows participants to react, respond, and communicate with one another and with the work itself.

Interactivity via Text

One of the most basic interactions is reading. Text requires active participation in order to understand its meaning. We find text throughout our daily activities in books, video games, advertisements, and more.

Many artists and designers have relied on text to enliven their 4D works. Jenny Holzer's work is nearly exclusively text installed in a variety of spaces, whether it is running on LED signs or projected. Carolee Schneemann's 1975 performance *Interior Scroll* would not have been nearly as effective without the written scroll she unraveled after removing it from her vagina. Text-based video games—such as Emily Carroll and Damian Sommer's choose-your-own-adventure game *The Yawhg*—are entirely dependent on text to propel the work forward.

Interactivity via Choice

Interactivity often involves the presence of choice, in which an action has an outcome with meaningful consequences. Choices can be obvious or subtle, rational or irrational, random or planned, or open-ended or specific. Katie Salen and Eric Zimmerman break down the anatomy of a choice in their book *Rules of Play: Game Design Fundamentals* as having five parts:

1. What happened before the choice?
2. How is the possibility of choice conveyed to the participant?
3. How did the participant choose?
4. What is the result and how will it affect future choices?
5. How is the result conveyed to the participant?

The answers to these questions can lead participants to develop strategies or tactics for further interaction, creating a feedback loop that can build or diminish depending on the nature of the work you have developed. **Feedback loops** push people toward specific behaviors. They consist of people providing information about their actions in real time, then providing some sort of immediate information about that action, and finally allowing time for an appropriate reaction to that feedback. It is clear that artists and designers have to plan and make very purposeful decisions regarding interactivity and choice in their work in order for feedback loops to effectively function.

Although it is found in some form in nearly all participatory works, this interactivity feedback loop is most evident in video game design where the development of rules for interaction is a way of establishing the boundaries of a game's world. Rules or guidelines for interaction and choice give participants something to react to and play against. Without carefully developed and calibrated guidelines, a work may fail to engage.

Exercise

Work in groups of three. Create a cooperative game in which players must work together toward a common goal. There are no media restrictions on the execution or creation of the game. Develop rules for play. Determine how many players are in the game. Does every player start out equal, or do they each have special abilities/roles? Do all the players work from the same information, or is some information exclusive, meaning that only certain players get to benefit from the information? (Think of the board game *Clue*: information is slowly revealed to single players as the game progresses.) Does the game restrict the freedom of participants, or do they feel overwhelmed by too much freedom? How can you strike a balance? Test the game on players and make any necessary changes.

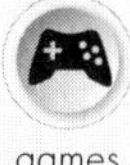

games

As you execute, research, and plan interactivity, consider your audience by paying close attention to trends in behavior and personality. There are many reasons a person may feel compelled to interact: competition, collaboration, shared experience, self-examination, the urge to be destructive, the influence of others, debate, or the search for a sense of belonging. You can use these and other reasons to help instigate and facilitate various forms of interaction in your work.

Exercise

Brainstorm to arrive at an everyday task that involves interaction and that you would like to improve. For example, maybe you would work to come up with a better way to store your keys so you don't lose them. Design a solution, try it out, make changes, and test it again. Do this revision process at least three times, and record your changes. Afterward explain your choices and process to the group.

performance

Who, What, Where, Why, When, and How

As you are creating a work, consider the who, what, where, why, when, and how of the interactions you are about to facilitate:

- *Who* is your intended audience for this interaction?
- *What* do you want them to do or experience?
- *Where* will this interaction take place? Will the interaction be surrounded by chaos or stillness? Reflect on how public or private your want the space to feel. The elements of light and sound in your selected location also will affect how inclined participants are to interact when you are determining where the interactions will take place. An environment with a higher degree of visual and aural contrast might make participants more active, depending on the task, whereas less light and sound might help create a more relaxed atmosphere.
- *Why* should people participate in this interaction? Ask yourself if the participants should trust you. Keep in mind that interactivity can be much easier within a relationship of safety and trust.
- *When* will the interaction take place?
- *How* will participants interact? Are they actively or passively engaging, and how much agency will you give them? Determine whether participants will have a multitude of overwhelming choices, or if there is a specific task you want them to undertake. Think about how long you would like the interaction to last. Deliberate on whether participants will be touching anything. If they will be, consider the weight, texture, and proportions of those physical interactions.

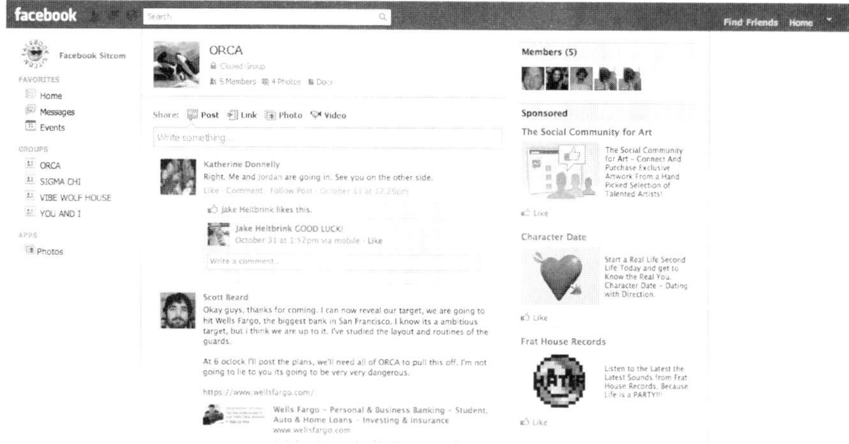

Fig. 6-8
Ed Fornieles, *Dorm Daze* (2011), screen capture, dimensions variable. © The artist, courtesy of Carlos/Ishikawa, London.

Participant-Artists

Taking all these variables into consideration, sometimes the boundary between artist and participant becomes blurred as interactivity increases. In many cases the audience becomes the artist. Ed Fornieles's interactive work *Dorm Daze* (2011) illustrates this idea (fig. 6-8). The work began with Fornieles inviting friends to take on roles of various stereotypical campus personas on Facebook. While the interaction was limited to those Fornieles invited, the work advanced exponentially as each of the participants posted as their character and interacted with one another, thereby blurring the line between artist and audience.[3]

Interview: Ed Fornieles

So *Dorm Daze* was a performance played out over three months on Facebook using 34 scalped profiles from Berkeley students. Participants inhabited the profiles, developing their character, relationships and storylines through interacting with each other. My role was to produce the context and set the tone and allow the environment to generate itself. For me success is the tipping point

(continued)

Interview: Ed Fornieles (*continued*)

where I lose control, it's a point when the performance moves away from one person's vision to a more complex place, where the end result is the outcome of participants pushing and pulling against each other.

—*Ed Fornieles*

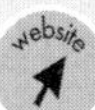
Visit the book's website to read the full interview.

Another online interactive work, Craig D. Giffen's *Human Clock* (2001–present), opens up interactivity even further by inviting anyone in the world to submit images with certain times on them (fig. 6-9). Every minute there is a collection of new images telling the current time.[4] Allowing participants to contribute to the creation of the work can allow for exciting and unexpected results; however, it also introduces risk to the work because you cannot always predict or control how participants will contribute.

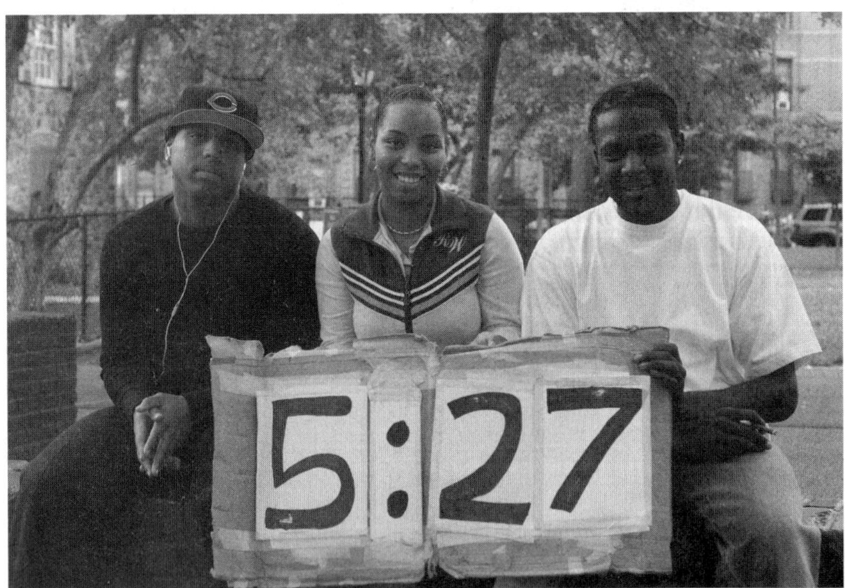

Fig. 6-9
Craig D. Giffen, *Human Clock* (2001–ongoing), performance still, dimensions variable. Courtesy of the artist.

Interview: Craig D. Giffen

When I first started *Human Clock*, I felt every "time" had to be numbers with a colon. It has been interesting to see how people react to the site. Some people absolutely hate the clock photos of people holding up the time, they prefer just to see random numbers occurring in real life (like a house address). On the other hand, some people don't like those photos at all because there is no colon in the photo. I've actually written all the code to make both camps of people happy so they can filter just the photo types they want, but I haven't gotten around to going through the 25,000 photos describing what is in each photo so the filters could work.

—Craig D. Giffen

Visit the book's website to read the full interview.

Exercise

Consider the use of crowdsourcing in Craig D. Giffen's *Human Clock*. Create your own crowdsourced, time-based work. Think about a concept that is important to you. What would you like the outcome to be? How could the crowd alter and change your intentions? How much freedom will you give participants? What constraints will you implement? Afterward, analyze how the project met or did not meet your intentions. If you had limited the interactions of the audience, would that have made the work stronger or weaker?

 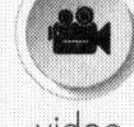 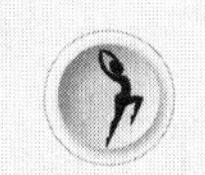 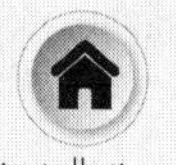 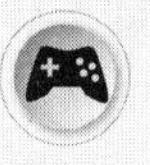 

Categories of Interactivity

Some individuals argue that all works of art and design are interactive because the viewer must actively engage with the work, whether it is a painting, video game, sculpture, or website. However, there are different types of interactivity. It is important to be aware of how these types differ so you can evaluate each work's effectiveness. Different practitioners from various fields define interactivity in their own unique way, and these categories will often overlap and combine in a multitude of ways.

For example, interactivity could be divided into cognitive, social, and contextual interactivity. **Cognitive interactivity** engages participants' minds with sight, sound, smell, touch, and taste sensory input.[5] **Social interactivity** engages participants with one another as they experience the work. **Contextual interactivity** facilitates interaction with the context of the work and lends attention to affecting and changing the contextual circumstances.

Another way to categorize interactivity is described in interaction designer Dan Saffer's four approaches to interaction design: participant-centered, activity-centered, system-centered, and artist- or designer-centered.

In **participant-centered interactivity** (also known as *user-centered design* [*UCD*]) the entire experience is focused on participants' needs and inclinations. We see this method in social or community-based practices in

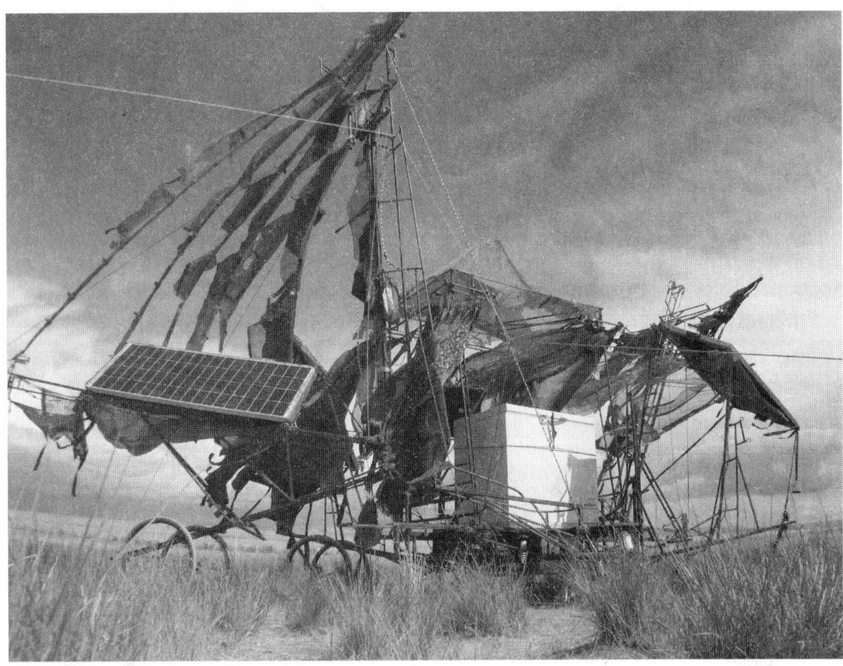

Fig. 6-10
Duane McDiarmid, *Trickster Project* (2009–2010), solar-powered ice cream cart in remote locales; max length 26', max width 24', and max height 20'. Courtesy of the Artist.

which artists or designers will go into the field to interview and observe their participants in order to ensure the work is aligned with the participants' requests and behaviors rather than solely those of the artist or designer. In *Trickster Project* (2009–2010), artist Duane McDiarmid created a traveling, solar-powered ice cream cart that visited remote locations in the southwest United States, providing cool treats to whomever encountered the work (fig. 6-10). In this work, McDiarmid physically transformed outdoor spaces to facilitate participant-centered interactivity of diverse groups of people at remote locations. (For more information on *research* as it relates to participant-centered interactivity, see Chapter 2).

Interview: Duane McDiarmid

I am the *Trickster Project*'s initiator. I dreamt it out of my expectations to have ice cream in the desert and the recognition that this marked my culture and me as laden with un-guided privilege enabled by often frivolous uses of technology. I began construction with significant help from the Russ College of Engineering at Ohio University—and especially electrical engineers Pat Dunham & Jonathan Blackenhorn. We cobbled together night vision, touch-activated computing, sensor activated video, GPS mapping, thermographic imaging, and of course a method of keeping the ice cream frozen, into a massive solar powered object that could slip between fiction and physical presence. I did the primary object construction and sewed the adorning garments. The real work of making the *Trickster Project* was solicitation involving a lot of email writing and phone calls to negotiate obstacles—practical, legal, and bureaucratic.

Once "launched," the project traveled with field crews inserting the work into land and social scapes. I was a circus ringmaster—showman, administrator, docent, and protagonist. But my main role in making the piece surprised me—I became the recipient of human kindness and good will and a central figure in an odd community of shared experience—one in which our differences and differing walks of life were not barriers.

—*Duane McDiarmid*

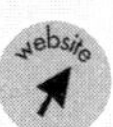

Visit the book's website to read the full interview.

Activity-centered interactivity makes the completion of a specific activity or task the primary goal of the work. On a daily basis, we encounter activity-centered interactivity anytime we browse an online shopping website or play a video game with a quest or specific problem to solve. An installation artist who has used activity-centered interactivity is Yayoi Kusama. Her *Obliteration Room* (2011) at the Queensland Art Gallery focused on the activity of collectively coating a white, furnished room in brightly colored dot stickers over the duration of 3 months (Plate 15, color insert). Kusama provided the dots and the room, and participants were tasked with placing the dots anywhere they wanted within the room. This work shows that interactivity can be playful: participants can enact a sense of freedom and experimentation without consequences within the structures of a specific activity.

In contrast to participant- or activity-centered interactivity, **system-centered interactivity** has as its primary goal the maintenance of a system. A system could be technology-centric, such as an industrially designed experience like a moisture-sensitive lawn sprinkler system. It could also be a less tangible system, like a chain of command within a company. Systems of interactivity will often include some sort of sensor to collect feedback and determine whether the goals of the system are being met, or if elements of the system need to be adjusted. These sensors could be mechanical or human. Consider a server at your favorite restaurant. His or her job is to maintain a pleasurable dining experience and to make adjustments to the system as necessary based on your feedback: adjusting lighting, refilling water glasses, bringing food, and so on.

An example of this type of interactivity occurs in Mary Mattingly's environmental installation *The Waterpod Project* (2009) (fig. 6-11). This work has a very specific context: a 30′ × 100′ docked barge that acts as a space to study a system of self-sufficient, water-based living for four artists who lived on it for 5 months. Viewers and participants visited the barge and observed the artists' activities while conversing with them about the project. Artists grew vegetables, raised chickens, and generated electricity, all in an effort to maintain this system of living and interaction.

Interview: Mary Mattingly

Touch Sanitation by Mierle Ukeles is a piece of 4D artwork that I find very important. Ukeles met and shook the hands of 8,500 sanitation workers in 1977. "I'm not here to watch you, to study you, to analyze you, to judge you. I'm here to be with you: all the shifts, all the seasons, to walk out the whole City with you." I face each worker, shake hands, and say: "Thank you for keeping NYC alive."

At an event for the *Waterpod*, curator Sara Reisman led a panel that Ukeles participated in. She told the story of *Touch Sanitation* to a full house, and her presentation was moving. In the late 70's the sanitation workers in NYC were on strike. News stories reported New Yorkers being rude and disrespectful towards sanitation workers as their garbage piled up. Ukeles gained such a reputation among the workers that when she notified a crew to let them know she would arrive the following day, even the workers who were sick or on disability arrived to shake her hand. To me, this illustrated two things that I'll always be conscious of: The waste we make is first our own responsibility. And, a simple gesture, empathy, and dedication can reach so many people. To me the stories she told became fable.

—Mary Mattingly

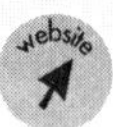 Visit the book's website to read the full interview.

Exercise

Go online and research *Touch Sanitation* by Mierle Ukeles. Write down what you think are the subject, form, content, and context for this work. Analyze how interactivity was used within the work, and how the work's impact may have been affected by the element of participation. Compare and contrast your answers with others'. How are your answers similar and different from those around you? Were there any trends in the answers?

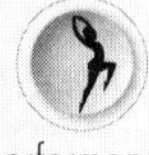   

performance   installation

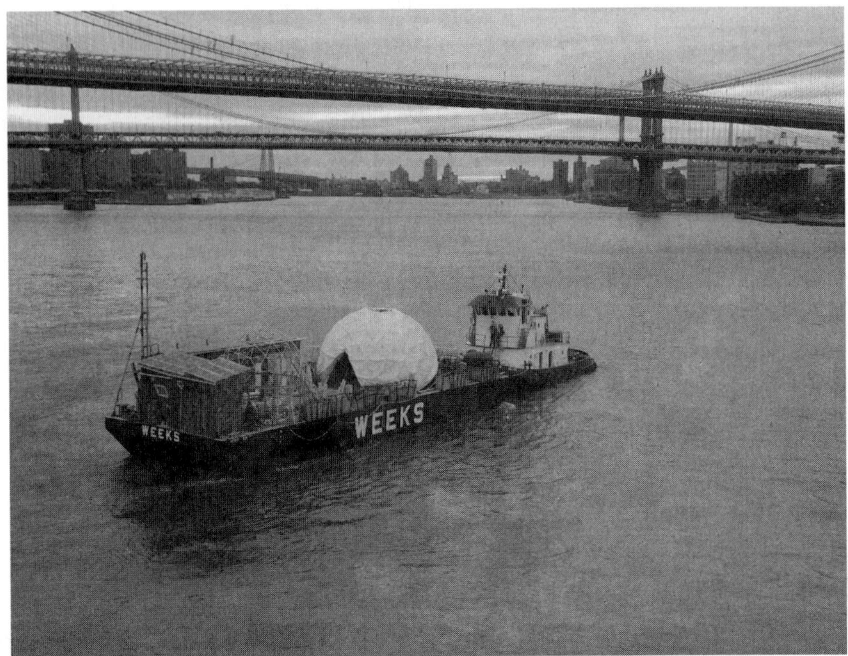

Fig. 6-11
Mary Mattingly, *The Waterpod Project* (2009), 100-foot-long floating sculptural living structure. Courtesy of the artist.

According to Saffer, the fourth type of interactivity is **artist- or designer-centered interactivity**, which is driven solely by the skills and interests of the artist or designer. Alicia Eggert's work *It's Nice to Meet You!* (2007–2008) is an example of work that was created purely from the artist's intuition (fig. 6-12). The playful piece consists of an inflatable self-portrait of the artist that is activated when a motion sensor detects the presence of another person. After 30 seconds it deactivates and falls to the floor, which is the amount of time the artist approximates it would take for a viewer to lose interest and walk away. In this example, the interactivity of the work is purely driven by the whims of the artist, not the desires of the participant.

Interview: Alicia Eggert

I received a bachelor's degree in Interior Design from Drexel University in Philadelphia, and then practiced at an architectural firm in New York for several years before earning an MFA in

Sculpture from Alfred University in New York. My artwork remains strongly rooted in design, and focuses on the relationship between language, image, and time.

My work is driven by concept as opposed to process, and my practice is extremely collaborative and interdisciplinary. Many artists enjoy working in solitude, but I prefer making work in conversation. I think ideas only get better when they're bounced around a bit. Plus, collaboration allows me to share the experience, the excitement, the responsibility, and the success with another person.

Although my work primarily takes the form of kinetic, electronic, and interactive sculpture, I often explore the same ideas in many different mediums, including drawing, photography, video, installation, and performance. My work's most common recurring theme is an exploration of the aesthetics of time. I believe that art can and should be affected by time, as opposed to frozen in it. So, like everything else in the world, my work often moves, changes, deteriorates, and in some cases even dies.

—Alicia Eggert

Visit the book's website to read the full interview.

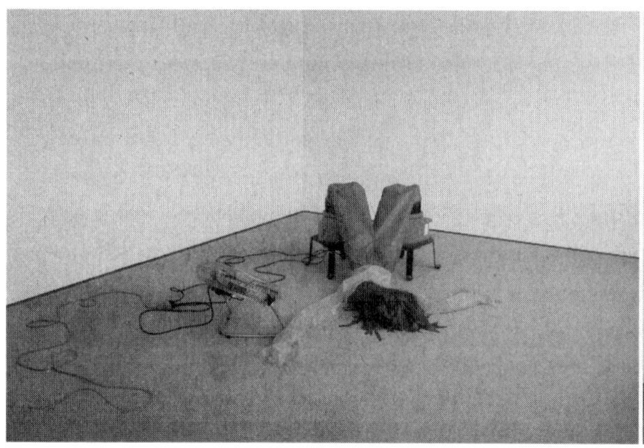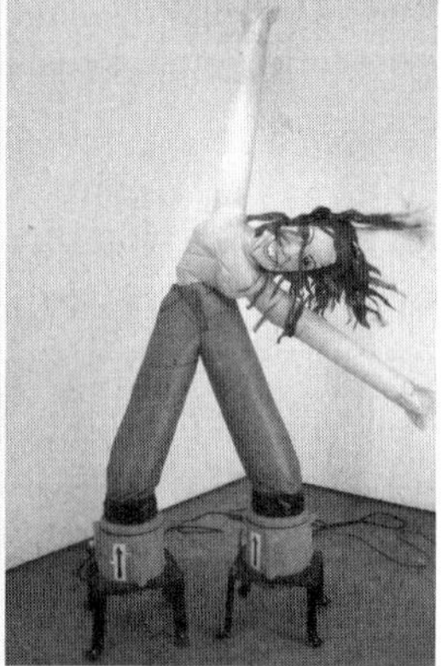

Fig. 6-12
Alicia Eggert, *It's Nice to Meet You!* (2007–2008), motion sensor, inflatable self-portrait, blower fans, industrial fan, Arduino microprocessor, electrical components, 83′ × 78′ × 20′. Courtesy of the artist.

Levels of Interactivity

Pablo Helguera, a socially engaged artist, writes about four other types of interactivity or participation in his book *Education for Socially Engaged Art*. Helguera's levels of interactivity include nominal, directed, creative, and collaborative participation. He also identifies three categories of interactivity or participation: voluntary, nonvoluntary, and involuntary participation.

Nominal participation involves reflection, as in the basic participatory experiences of encountering an artwork, such as viewing a painting, attending a lecture, or viewing a traditional theatrical play. **Directed participation** consists of participants completing a single task created by the artist or designer. Anna Anthropy's video game *Dys4ia* consists of a series of singular puzzle tasks directed by the artist (fig. 1-1) with the sole intention of having the player advance through the game by solving the puzzles.

Creative participation involves participants creating original content within a structure established by an artist or designer. Ed Fornieles's *Dorm Daze* is an example of this type of interactivity (fig. 6-8). His participants developed personas within the constructs put in place by the artist.

Collaborative participation exists when participants work together with the artist or designer to create both the structure and content of the work. An artist could arrive at a community, hold discussions on their particular interests and concerns, and together they might decide to plant a community garden. Then, the artist and the community work together to build and maintain the garden. Because the community collaborated with the artist to arrive at the form and content of the work, this piece would be considered collaborative participation.

Voluntary interactivity is an experience in which participants are knowingly engaged. Kusama's *The Obliteration Room* would fall into this category of interactivity, because it is a clearly defined and voluntary activity in a gallery space (Plate 15, color insert). **Nonvoluntary interactivity** is an experience in which participants discover they are engaged with a work without prior consent. Steve Roden's *Bird Forms* installation falls into this category because listeners may have wandered into the space of the work and not immediately realized they were hearing recordings and not the sounds of real birds (fig. 4-12). **Involuntary interactivity** consists of participants willingly engaging in an activity or situation that later turns out to be the work of an artist or designer. The work of the Yes Men often fits into this category (fig. 1-12). With involuntary interactivity, the artist or designer must carefully plan when to reveal the reality of the constructed situation, and what actions to take if this false reality is revealed prematurely, as was the case in the Yes Men's *US Chamber of Commerce Goes Green*.

Many individuals have analyzed and categorized interactivity. Through the careful use of interactivity in conjunction with purposeful research and planning, an artist or designer can orchestrate the most impactful interactive situation for participants.

Musicality

Sound—and specifically music—is a powerful addition to a work. It can be used to communicate important information about the context of a work or a specific point of view. For instance, if you enter an installation and hear spooky organ music, it will change the way you interpret and experience the work. The characteristic parts or principles of music and sound are called **musicality**. Every sound has three basic characteristics: **pitch** (the frequency of a sound vibration), **tone** (the quality of a sound vibration), and **amplitude** (volume in decibels).[6]

The musicality of a sound can be used as a tool for setting up a joke, warning of a threat, or establishing a particular emotional atmosphere. In Nikki Pike's installation *Ice Bellows* (2011), she explores the sound of coldness by creating an interactive musical instrument that plays sounds recorded from ice in various stages of cracking, popping, and creaking (fig. 6-13). Participants can push buttons on a control pad to play a selection of sampled ice sounds synchronized to illuminate the ice bellows in a variety of patterns. In this work, musicality creates an atmosphere of playfulness by allowing participants to create their own combinations of sound and light.

Interview: Nikki Pike

I consider myself a cultural agent. My work is motivated by a need to engage people by creating artistic platforms where only upon interaction does the work come to life. My driving force comes from a belief in the power of the arts to shift the participants' perspective and take an action in the community—even if ever so slightly. The most powerful forces that drive my concepts are tied to our basic needs as human beings: Food, Water, Shelter, and Love.

In my most recent works, I have found myself using strategies that surround the idea of PLAY to create curiosity or mystery to expose a playfulness that exists all around us. It is my attempt to relieve the audience of stress that comes from the unhealthy parts of our social system where we frequently reside. I aim to steer the public away from materialism, capitalism, stereotyping, discrimination, and excessive entertainment. My hope is to provide a sort of social well-being through the arts.

—*Nikki Pike*

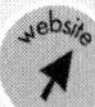 Visit the book's website to read the full interview.

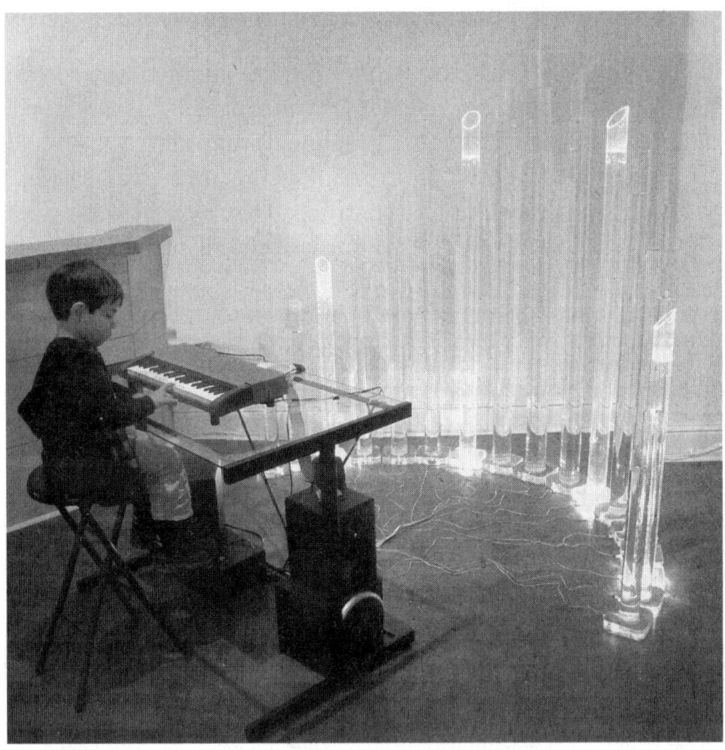

Fig. 6-13
Nikki Pike, *Ice Bellows* (2011), interactive sound installation, dimensions variable. Photography: Nikki Pike.

Pitch

Pitch, volume, and rhythm are the principles of musicality most commonly used in contemporary art and design. Pitch is a measure of frequency; high frequency equals high-pitched sounds, while low frequency equals low-pitched sounds. Some higher pitches, such as the voice of a child or a small animal, can evoke sympathy in the listener. Lower pitches, such as a lion's roar or the sound of an explosion, can be more powerful or threatening because they fill space uniformly, surrounding the listener.

Exercise

Find a copy of a film you enjoy and watch your favorite 10 minutes (time yourself). Write down what you hear, and describe those sounds in terms of pitch. Share your findings with the class. As a group, identify any trends that may appear.

sound

Volume

Volume is the amplitude or **loudness** of any given sound, and is sometimes characterized by **crescendos** and **decrescendos**, which are increases and decreases in loudness. Volume is affected by real or perceived distance. For example, a quiet conversation between two people in a restaurant may seem softer than a person yelling outside, but if you were to actually measure the volume while sitting at the table, the conversation would be louder because the person yelling is farther away. Volume is also influenced by how important a sound is to the listener. Because the human brain can effectively process only a limited amount of information at any given time, many sounds are deemed unimportant unless they are central to the listener's well-being. For example, if you hear a dog barking outside, you may think nothing of it, unless it might be *your* dog.

Volume can also be used to direct a listener's attention in much the same way a close-up shot is used for important visuals. For instance, by raising the volume of a particular sound, much like zooming in on a particular image, the listener is directed to focus on the loudest sound. John Cage's composition *4'33"* (1952) may be one of the best executions of this aspect of volume. In this work, Cage presented 4 minutes and 33 seconds of "silence" as a musical composition. However, the actual sounds of the composition include all the random sneezes, throat clearing, and readjustments of seats by the audience. Because there are no "musical" sounds to focus on in this work, these extraneous sounds produced by the audience become the loudest, and therefore most important, sounds of the artwork.

Exercise

Other artists beyond John Cage use silence in their work. Go online, search for, and view the directions for Yoko Ono's *Tape Piece I*. After considering this work, write down what you think are the subject, form, content, and context for this work. Analyze how you could use volume to execute this work. Compare and contrast your answers with others'. How are your answers similar and different from those around you? Were there any trends in the answers?

sound

Rhythm, Timbre, Melody, and Harmonics

Of rhythm, timbre, melody, and harmonics, the most frequently used principle is rhythm. Rhythm, as discussed in Chapter 4, is the regular repetition of a given element, sound or otherwise. It can be applied not only to sound, but also to other elements of art and design, such as movement, light, or architecture. In contrast, timbre, melody, and harmonics are tied only to sound, and most frequently to music. **Timbre** is the quality of sound. It is affected by the shape, size, and substance of any instrument used within the work, including the human voice. Every person has a slightly differently shaped throat, vocal cords, and head, which explains why everyone has a slightly different sounding voice. A sound's timbre can range from tonal to noisy: **tonal** sounds have sound waves that pulse at regular intervals, while **noisy sounds** are made of overlapping frequencies, producing complex waveforms. **Melody** is a procession of tones that create a tune. We often recognize melodies in popular songs. **Harmonics** are a selection of tones played simultaneously to create a chord. An easy example of harmonics would be the synchronized chords sung by barbershop quartets.

Exercise

Brainstorm a list of 10 human vocal sounds (yelling, whispering, etc.), a list of 10 sounds various objects can make (a pencil dropping to the floor, etc.), and a list of 10 environmental ambient sounds (wind through a window, etc.). Create your own recordings selected from your lists of a human voice, an object in action, and environmental ambiance. Then, alter the musical qualities of each recorded sound: pitch, volume, rhythm, and so on. Edit these altered sounds together to create a soundscape no longer than 30 seconds. Listen to each other's finished works and evaluate which works are most interesting and why.

sound

Exercise

Listen to Hugo Ball's sound poem *Karawane* (1917) on the book's accompanying website. It lacks any subject matter or narrative, and relies on rhythm and variations in loudness to engage the listener. Write your own 30-second sound poem in the spirit of *Karawane*. Use the elements of pitch, timbre, harmonics, volume, and rhythm to keep your listeners engaged. Make sure to include at least one example of each of the elements of musicality.

sound

Whether the emphasis is on pitch, volume, timbre, harmonics, or rhythm, the principles of musicality are useful for analyzing and fine-tuning the use of sound in any 4D work. Without consciously adjusting these characteristics of a sound, you may find that your work sounds less intentional or purposeful and can lack a sense of emphasis or focus.

Simultaneity/Juxtaposition

Simultaneity describes two or more things happening at the same time. **Juxtaposition** describes the comparison of two or more possibly contrasting elements or subjects to create a new meaning. Both concepts are present in time-based art and design and can greatly alter the meaning of a work. Juxtaposed elements can also be simultaneous. Simultaneous elements do not necessarily juxtapose one another.

The human brain cannot effectively process many similar sources of information simultaneously. Therefore, participants in your 4D work will either switch back and forth between the simultaneously presented elements or they will look for overall patterns on which to focus. However, if two sounds or visual elements contrast with each other, or are juxtaposed, such as speech versus music or low- versus high-pitch sounds, then participants will be better able to consider both simultaneously. This clashing of simultaneous elements creates tension and causes the participants to actively seek resolution. In this way, simultaneity and juxtaposition are good ways to draw your audience into the work and hold their attention.

The stop-motion video created for the band Air Review's song "Young" (2014), by artist Joseba Elorza, utilizes extreme juxtaposition of scale to create bizarre surrealist sequences such as giant figures looming among mountains while a young boy runs across the screen (fig. 6-14). This

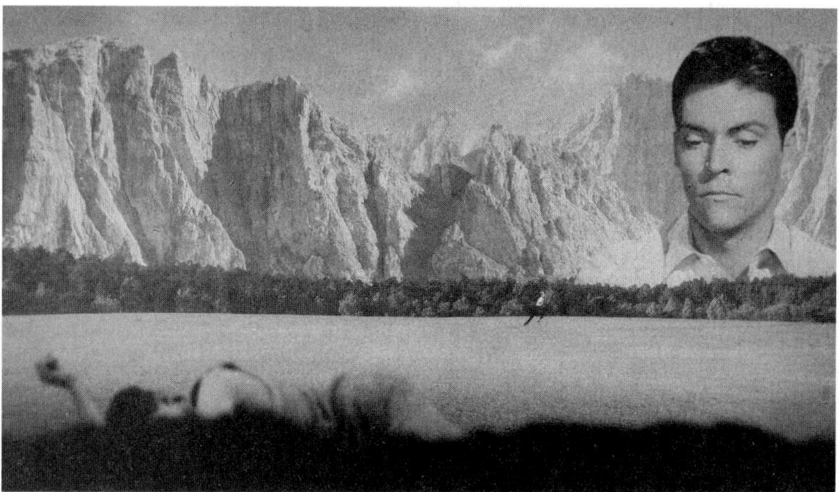

Fig. 6-14
Joseba Elorza, *Air Review—Young* (2014), digital animation, 3:50 minutes. Courtesy of Joseba Elorza.

purposeful juxtaposition of scale creates a more engaging experience for the viewer, as it affects perceived and actual expectations in a creative manner.

Interview: Joseba Elorza

I received the order on behalf of a member of the band that also makes collages, so in that sense there was a very good feeling throughout the process. They asked me to try to represent the road to maturity of a child and I thought that we could make that path literal and see a child running toward an uncertain future.

The theme of childhood gives you a lot of freedom to represent dream elements, and surrealism usually works very well in my work, so I tried not to limit myself and let that the process of searching for the footage lead me without a specific horizon or end goal.

—Joseba Elorza

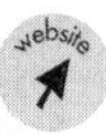
Visit the book's website to read the full interview.

Exercise

Go online, search for, and view Gergely Wootsch's three short videos for the *Penny Dreadful* series. After watching the works, select one of the three and write down what you think are the subject, form, content, and context for this work. How were simultaneity and juxtaposition used within the work? Did either affect the experienced impact of the video? Compare and contrast your answers with others'. How are your answers similar and different from those around you? Were there any trends in the answers?

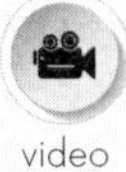
video

In film and video, simultaneity can be shown by alternating cuts between two events, also known as **crosscutting**. A **cut**, in which one shot ends and another one immediately begins in the same space and time, is the simplest transition and can be most abrupt depending on when it takes place.

Crosscutting purposefully cuts back and forth between two events. When viewers see crosscutting occurring, they are able to make the connection that these events are simultaneously happening. A famous example of crosscutting is the baptism scene from *The Godfather* (1972), directed by Francis Ford Coppola. The scene alternates between the baptism of a baby and the murder of the heads of the five families, creating a powerful juxtaposition.

Another way to create simultaneity is **superimposition**, in which two images are shown simultaneously on top of one another. The opacity on one or both images is reduced so the viewer can see through the image, thereby seeing them both at once. For example, an image of an X-ray of your head could be superimposed with an image of your face, allowing the viewer to see both your face and your skull simultaneously. This effect can add a sense of complexity or suggest relationships between unrelated subjects. View Glitter Chariot's music video *Should Have Been Blonde* on the book's website to see examples of superimposition used in several of the transitions.

Exercise

Brainstorm a list of at least 15 isolated sounds that are meaningful to you, such as an animal sound, a human body sound, a specific machine, and so on. Select two sounds from your list to juxtapose. Include these two juxtaposed sounds as inspiration for a short video work. The work must be no shorter than 30 seconds and no longer than 1 minute; it must also successfully hold the viewer's attention for the duration of the work. Ask for feedback on the finished work. Was the juxtaposition successful? Did it have a noticeable impact on success (or failure) of the whole piece?

sound   video

An additional way to create a sense of simultaneity is to juxtapose two or more clips within the same frame—also known as a **split screen**—or by showing the work on multiple channels (screens) at a single moment. Natalie Bookchin's work *Now He's Out in Public and Everyone Can See* (2012), utilizes multiple channels to create a compelling work (fig. 6-15). It consists of 18 channels of video clips taken from hundreds of online vlogs, or video blogs, commenting on a variety of viral media scandals involving famous African American men. The 18 channels are shown on 18 monitors hanging from cables at various heights and depths; participants move

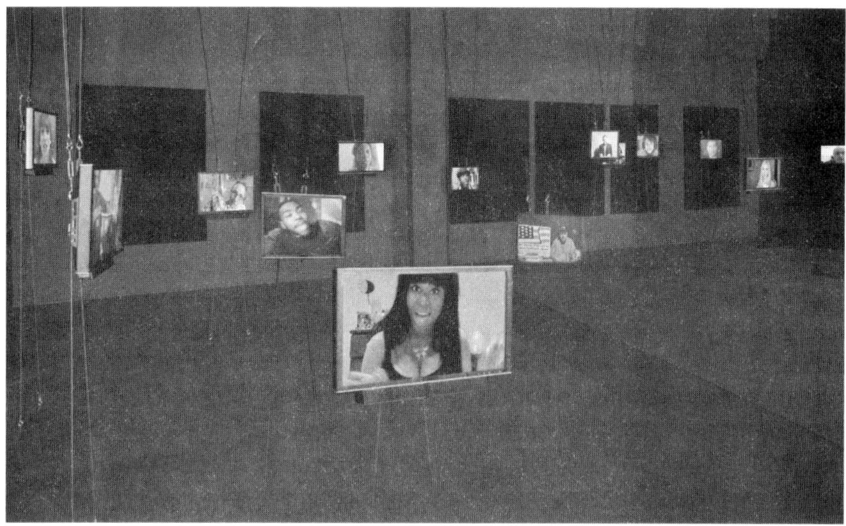

Fig. 6-15
Natalie Bookchin, *Now He's Out in Public and Everyone Can See* (2012), 18-channel video installation, 16-minute loop. Courtesy of the artist.

through the space while experiencing a variety of fragmented bodies and gazes, and attempt to piece together a story that is never complete. Split-screen and multichannel works are considered somewhat more interactive because the viewers are allowed to focus their attention where and when they like, rather than being guided linearly through the work.

Exercise

Brainstorm a list of at least 10 exciting stories you know without needing to reread or experience them. For example, you might know a story about rescuing someone from a sinking boat, or a story about climbing a mountain. Select two of the stories to occur simultaneously in a proposed animation, video, or game. Then create a storyboard expressing this simultaneity. Show the finished storyboard to others and ask whether they can understand the proposed simultaneity and how it affects the overall concept or form of the piece. Make changes as necessary.

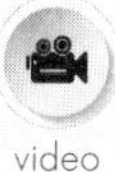
video

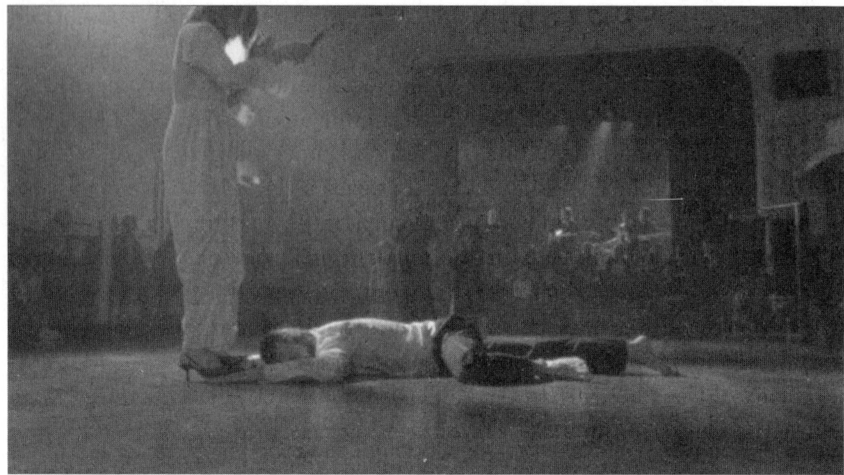

Fig. 6-16
Wim Vandekeybus, *Blush* (2005), film, 55 minutes. Courtesy of Wim Vandekeybus.

Another example of simultaneity is found within Wim Vandekeybus's short dance film *Blush* (2005), which explores emotions that can cause a person to blush (fig. 6-16). In this film, there is performative simultaneity when a group of dancers contorts on the floor as a second group steps on their hands and feet while executing mundane activities such as combing hair or buttoning shirts. This juxtaposition of actions creates an interesting power dynamic between those being stepped on and those who are doing the stepping. This juxtaposition of different points of view adds interest to the piece as the viewer is asked to consider the viewpoints and experiences of both sets of performers.

Exercise

Watch Wim Vandekeybus's *Blush* (2005). Analyze the work in terms of simultaneity and juxtaposition, and write at least five sentences explaining the work's relationship to these concepts. You will need to find and explain examples other than the ones included within this text.

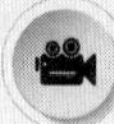 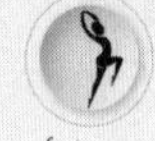

video   performance

Juxtaposition is also a vital ingredient in manufacturing humor. By juxtaposing a situation, person, or idea with its logical extreme—also known as **satire**—the subject's flaws are humorously exposed. In Cayla Skillin-Brauchle's performance in Mumbai, India, titled *Certifying the Truth* (2013), she offers to certify examples of the "truth" presented by participants (fig. 2-3). This piece manufactures humor through references to the continuous bureaucratic procedures necessary for a foreigner to maintain visas and affiliations. She juxtaposes these absurdly humorous procedures with the trust foreigners in India must give to others as they navigate daily interactions. Her work is a humorous and poignant satirical exaggeration of the situation a foreigner actually encounters in India.

Interview: Cayla Skillin-Brauchle

Certifying the Truth was inspired by the number of hoops that I had to jump through to get this or that document stamped and/or officially copied during my time in Mumbai, India. From an outsider's perspective, the situation was so absurd: Who is that guy with the stamp? Is he really that important or is he just the guy with the stamp and the seal? So I started thinking, "Hey, I could make my own stamp. I could approve documents."

From there I started to think about what I might certify, and, as a foreigner living abroad, the idea of truth came to mind. I faced numerous situations where my version of the truth and others' versions of the same truth did not align; yet as a newcomer living in one of the world's largest cities, I depended daily on the various versions of the truth that neighbors and strangers provided me.

As with many of my performance pieces, I craft them to a specific point and then leave them open-ended. Through performance, I continue researching ideas rather than making a hard-and-fast statement of how things are. I like to have the participants tell me how things are and then hopefully that gets shared with a wider audience. In that respect, I suppose as an artist-cum-historian-cum-sociologist, I tend to value primary sources over book research. I spend time thinking, meditating, and doing some book research but at some point I crave real interaction with my subject matter and that's when I meet with reality.

—*Cayla Skillin-Brauchle*

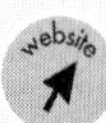

Visit the book's website to read the full interview.

Because they are able to create or emphasize contrast effectively within a given experience across any media, simultaneity and juxtaposition are important factors in creating interest and tension within a 4D work.

Spatial Relationships

We can identify spatial relationships in the elements of architecture, topography, lighting, space, sound, and movement. Some of the most basic spatial relationships are described by the ideas of high, middle, low, far, and near, which we previously discussed when exploring the ideas of contrast and movement. These spatial relationships are **relative**, meaning that they are determined in relationship to other factors. What might be considered "high space" in one set of circumstances might be considered "low space" in a different set of circumstances. For example, Stefan Prosky's installation *Partisan* (2014) is a relatively *low* work in terms of spatial relationships (fig. 2-7). This piece consists of two equally equipped robots in the form of the White House and the Capitol competing to push each other out of a ring-shaped space on either a floor or table. This work visually represents ideas of political battle. Whether the work is displayed on the floor or on a slightly elevated table, it appears below most people's eye level, and would generally be considered a relatively low work. However, if you compare this piece to a work that is displayed at the bottom of a deep ravine, Prosky's work might seem to take place in relatively high level. Another example is aaajiao's projection mapped work *Time Refactoring* (2012) (fig. 6-17). In this work, which explores expressions of time through projected imagery, the entire piece appears on the façade of a multistory building, well above the heads of the audience. Many would consider this work to have relatively high spatial relationships. However, if you contrast this work with a piece that involves jumping out of a plane, the work will not seem nearly as high.

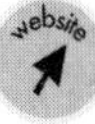
Visit the book's website to read an interview with Stefan Prosky.

Exercise

Go online to find an artwork/piece from Yoko Ono's book *Grapefruit*, and take note of the artwork's title. Based on what you can

(continued)

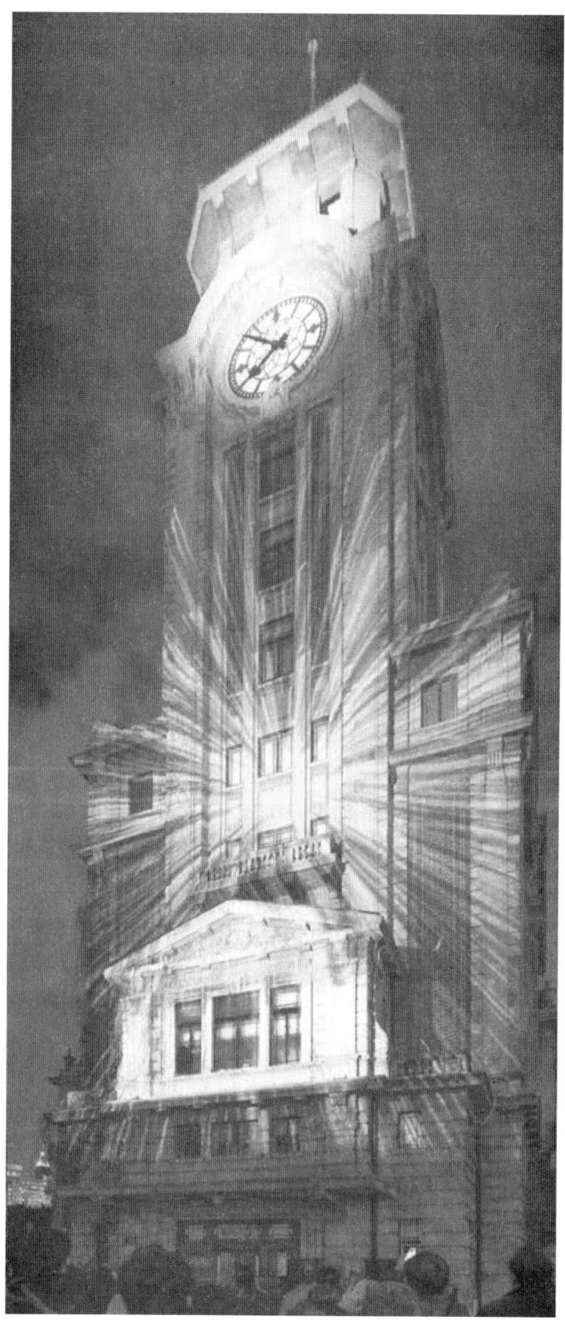

Fig. 6-17

aaajiao, *Time Refactoring* (2012), projection mapping for Shanghai Art Museum, 12 m × 38 m. © aaajiao.

> **Exercise** (*continued from page 252*)
>
> see and find about the work, write down what you think are the subject, form, content, and context for this work. Analyze how the work might use spatial relationships, especially between the forms and the audience or participants. Compare and contrast your answers with others'. How are your answers similar and different from those around you? Were there any trends in the answers?
>
>  
>
> performance   installation

The arrangement of various elements in a work help create focus. For example, in a traditional performing space with an audience facing a stage, there are established spatial relationships for directing focus. One possible arrangement would be moving the main character farther away from the audience on stage (also known as upstage). This forces other people onstage to turn their backs to the audience in order to interact with that main individual. This simple rearrangement of space automatically directs the audience's focus to the person upstage. Similarly, a performer who appears lower in space—perhaps sitting or lying down—may attract less focus than a performer who is still standing or is elevated on a platform. Other practiced spatial relationships include using diagonal and triangular arrangements—rather than straight, linear, or boxy arrangements—because they appear more dynamic to viewers. Additionally, if you add an obstacle between interacting elements—regardless of whether it is large or small, moveable or immoveable—it will create tension.

Organizing a Space

In addition to objects and individuals, architectural spaces can also occupy a variety of spatial relationships.[7] For example, in a work that encompasses multiple spaces, the spaces themselves can be organized in a variety of ways, much like you would arrange elements within a single space (fig. 6-18):

- *Linear spaces* are organized end to end—think of a strip mall where stores are side by side.
- *Radially organized spaces* extend out from a central space—think of the end of a cul-de-sac where all the houses point toward the same central point.

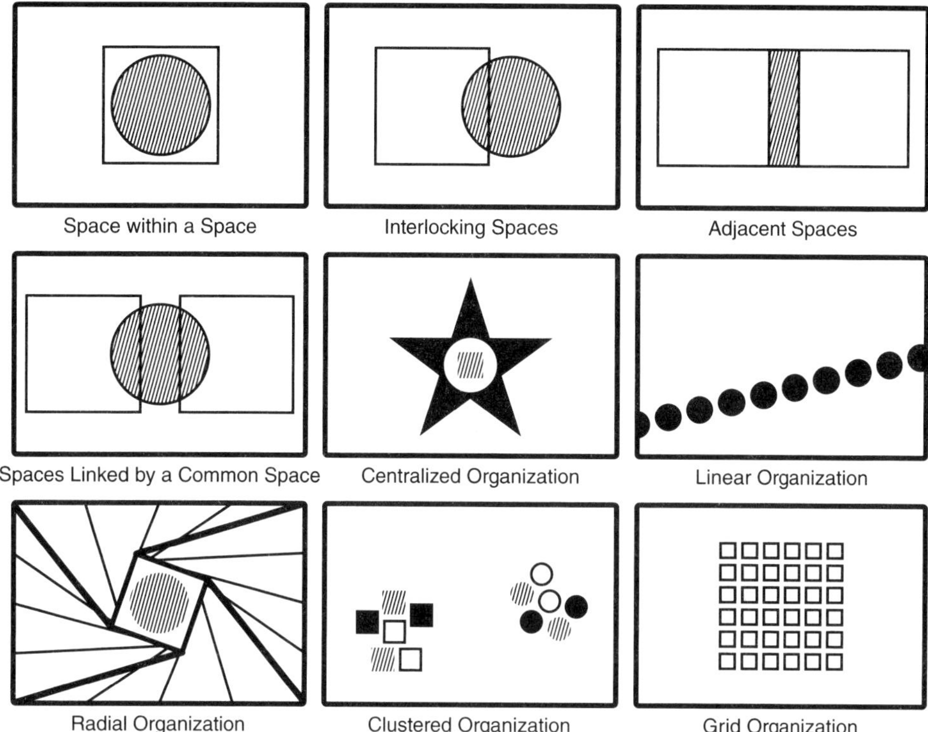

Fig. 6-18
Different types of spatial relationships. © Phil McCollam.

- *A space within a space* is the containment of one space within another, such as a webpage on a computer screen inside of a room.
- *Interlocking spaces* involve a field of space that overlaps a volume of another space—think of how a staircase interlocks with both the floors it connects.
- *Adjacent spaces* are two or more spaces that "share a common border," such as a master bedroom and a master bathroom.
- *Spaces linked by a common space* are exactly as they are described—imagine two stores across from each other in a shopping mall that are linked by the common concourse between them.[8]
- *Centralized spaces* have a dominant space surrounded by less important spaces; for example, the less sacred parts of a church generally emanate out from a centralized sanctuary space.
- *Clustered spaces or webbed spaces* are near to one another, but one space does not necessarily dominate the others, much like small towns clustered along a highway.

- *Gridded spaces*, similar to city streets laid out with rectangular blocks, follow the framework of evenly spaced, overlapping horizontal and vertical lines to arrange or divide the space.

Exercise

Taking a notepad and writing utensil with you, walk into a building through one entrance and exit the building through another. Take notes on the various spatial relationships as you move into, through, and out of the building. Do you encounter centralized, linear, radially, clustered, or gridded spaces? Are there any spaces that are a combination of two or more spatial relationships? How does each of these spatial relationships influence how you feel? Are there any changes in spatial relationships as you move through the building? How do those changes affect your mood or experience? How could you apply this use of space to a work you have already created? Compare your experiences with those in the group.

installation

Spatial Relationships on Screens

In 4D works on-screen, there are a variety of similar terms for spatial relationships. One might use the terms **background, middle ground,** and **foreground** to describe the different areas of on-screen space. These spaces are found in individual **frames,** which are single still images from a film or video.

Framing terms include close-up, medium, and long shots. In film and video works, a **shot** is the continuous footage between when you start and stop a recording camera. While the definitions of these shots are relative to any given project, we can generally discuss them in terms of human scale. A **close-up shot** usually includes shoulders and head, while a **medium shot** might include a view of knees or waist and the rest of the body, up to the head (fig. 6-19). A **long shot** shows the entire figure in its setting and better establishes a sense of environment. However, all of these shots are relative to the other shots in the film, so what might be a close-up in one film could be a long shot in another. When choosing shots, it is important to remember that the closer the subject is to the camera, the greater the emotional connection may be to the viewer.

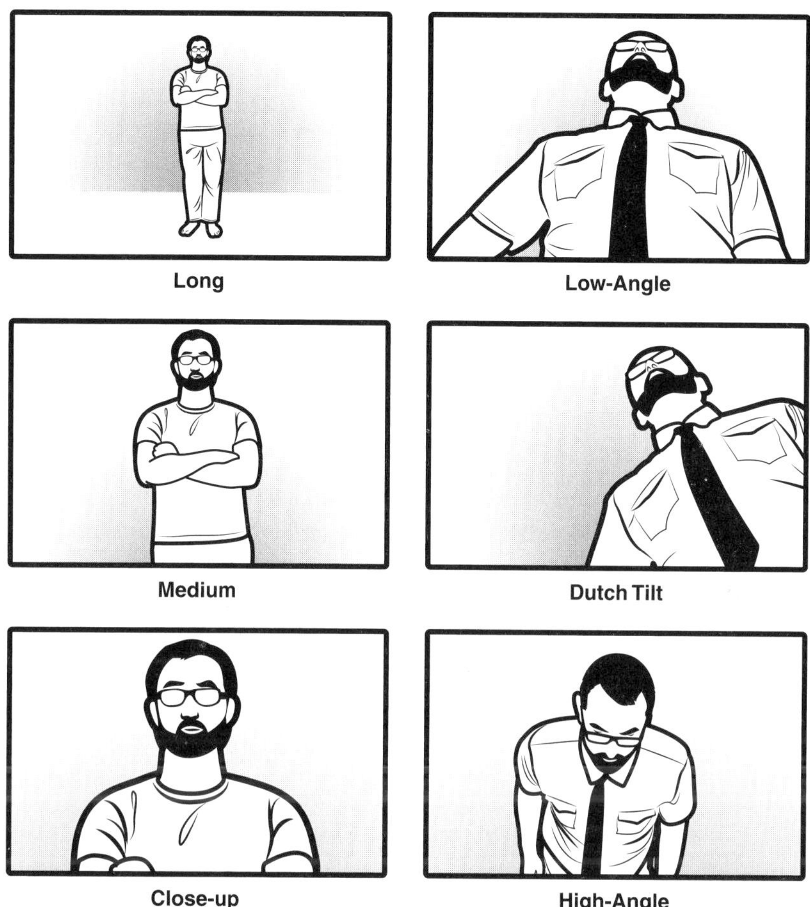

Fig. 6-19
A selection of common shots and framing choices. © Phil McCollam.

Another key decision is where within the frame you will place your subject. If you place your subject on the left side of the frame, it might seem as if it is entering or beginning, while moving it to the right may make it appear to be ending or leaving. The rule of thirds can also help you make decisions about where to place your subject within the frame (see Chapter 3). It states that you can divide any frame into thirds both horizontally and vertically; where those lines intersect are good locations to place your subject (fig. 3-9). In works that include a visually discernable third dimension, the depth of the frame can also be divided equally into thirds. The rule of thirds helps you avoid placing the subject in the physical center of the frame, which is visually less interesting or dynamic than placing it slightly off to one side or the other.

Exercise

Brainstorm a list of 10 fairy tales. Select one as the subject for a 30-second video work. This work does not necessarily have to be narrative, but it will be influenced by your selected fairy tale. Experiment with framing shots at different levels. Where do you use close-ups, medium shots, and long shots, and why? How many different ways can you position your subject, and how does each option affect your concept?

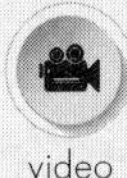
video

In addition to framing, camera angle is a basic part of spatial relationships in film. All of the shots that we've discussed assume a straight-on, eye-level camera angle. However, artists, designers, and videographers can shoot from below their subject, also known as a **low-angle shot**; above their subject, also known as a **high-angle shot**; or from very high above, which is called a **bird's-eye view** (fig. 6-19). They can also rotate the camera to shoot a diagonal composition, creating what's called a Dutch tilt (see Chapter 4). They also have to decide whether they will show the ground or the horizon. Each orientation will provide different information to the viewer, which can affect how the work is perceived.

Exercise

Create a hand frame by putting your hands out in front of you and arranging your fingers to form a rectangle (fig. 6-20). Use your frame to find at least 10 different, well-composed shots in the room in which you are sitting. Have a partner take a photo of each shot through your hand frame. Everyone should work in the same space.

Note: When beginning to work with spatial relationships, people tend to unintentionally limit themselves to comfortable spatial relationships. It is important to examine the full range of possible spatial relationships in any given work. Where should things be grouped or left separate? Are you looking for realistic or expressive arrangements? Would framing the same objects from above create the same sensation as framing them from below?

After everyone has finished, share with the class to find the most compelling shots from the entire collection.

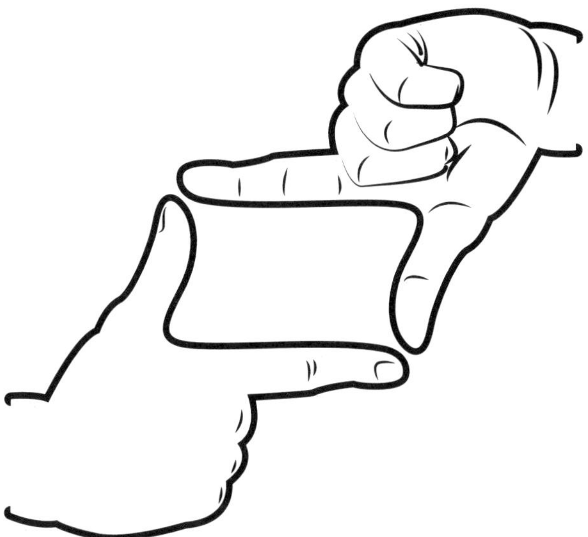

Fig. 6-20
Hand framing.
© Phil McCollam.

Depth of field is also an important film and video concern in terms of defining spatial relationships. **Depth of field** is the area that appears to remain in focus between the nearest and farthest objects in a scene. A shallow depth of field—in which the subject appears to be in focus but the background is blurry—can help draw the viewer's eye directly to the subject without much external distraction. A deep depth of field allows for nearly everything to appear to be sharply in focus, regardless of proximity, and can help give viewers a clear sense of the current environment.

Spatial arrangements, whether on-screen or in person, are vital to creating focus in your time-based work by creating purposeful divisions experienced by the viewer or participant.

Tempo/Speed

Tempo—also referred to as *speed*, *pace*, or *velocity*—is the rate at which time, sound, light, or movement passes. Tempo can range from slow to fast and can accelerate (speed up) or decelerate (slow down). Tempo is also relative to its setting. One snail can appear to move much faster than another snail, but it is likely quite slow in comparison to a flying insect. In this way, tempo can be integral to a participant's interpretation of the work. Thus, artists and designers must consciously ask whether a piece is too fast or too slow, and consider when and how tempo will change within the work.

Once a tempo becomes too fast or too slow, participants may struggle to stay engaged or may even become physically exhausted, which may or may not be your intention.

Tempo can also directly affect meaning: if you speed up or slow down the rate at which dialogue is moving, it can completely change the essence of what is being said. An example is John Cage and David Tudor's collaboration *Indeterminacy* (1959). In this work, Cage randomly chose different lengths for each segment, and then randomly selected a text that he would read and a score that Tudor would play simultaneously. Sometimes the text was very short but the time allotted was long; in this case, Cage had to speak very slowly. Other times, the text was very long and the time short and he had to do the opposite. Similarly, Tudor had to fit his own tempo into the time allotted regardless of the actual length of the music. Cage's texts were later published as part of his book *Silence* (1961), which allowed for a totally different understanding. The reader can spend any amount of time studying the texts, without being distracted by the speed of Cage's delivery or the unrelated piece of music playing simultaneously.

Exercise

Brainstorm a list of 10 actions you can make with your body, such as stepping, waving, chewing, and so on. Choose one action that can be exact and repeatable and which includes a clear beginning and end. Repeat it several times. Alter the tempo for each repetition: perform the action in a medium tempo, a fast tempo, and a slow tempo.[9] Ask a partner to watch the action at each of the three tempos and have him or her explain how meaning changes as the tempo changes.

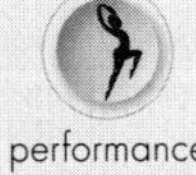

performance

Exercise

Research the work of William Kentridge by viewing some of his charcoal-and-eraser animations online. Create a 60-frame

(5 seconds at 12 frames per second) stop-motion animation in this charcoal-and-eraser style. Then, adjust the tempo to slow down the action by playing it at 6 frames per second and then speed it up by playing it at 18 frames per second. Reflect on the effect the tempo has on the project via verbal or written critique. Consider how quickly you want time to pass, and how quickly it actually passes.

video

In film, animation, and video games, the tempo can be manipulated by the actions on-screen, the timing of the cuts, and the number of cuts. Tempo can also be manipulated by slowing down a video sequence—**slow motion**— or speeding it up—**accelerated motion**. In slow-motion video, gravity might appear to be reduced and the direction of movement may become ambiguous. In accelerated motion video, everything feels more spastic and objects appear to move unpredictably. Time-lapse videos accelerate motion even more, essentially reducing motion to still frames taken at regular intervals and then stringing those stills together at normal viewing speed— usually about 24 or 30 frames per second. This technique explains how we can watch a seed grow into a plant or a car travel across the country over the course of a few seconds or minutes.

Exercise

Film a short narrative scene (example: Jane happily goes to work, John sleepily sews a shirt, etc.) in no more than 5 shots. Use the tempo of the cuts to reinforce the narrative. Where do you want the tempo to speed up or slow down, and why?

video

An example of tempo at work is Sparksight's animation for *International Recruiting with CollegeWeek Live* (2014), in which they use an upbeat tempo to convey the effectiveness of this company's international

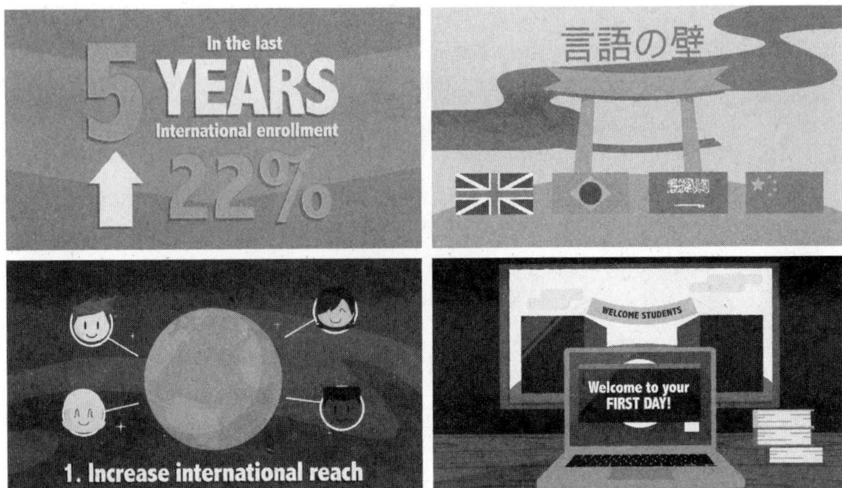

Fig. 6-21
Sparksight, *International Recruiting with CollegeWeek Live* (2014), motion graphics, 2:24 minutes. Courtesy of Sparksight and CollegeWeek Live.

recruitment services. The speed at which objects move across the screen affects the viewer's understanding and builds enthusiasm for the service (fig. 6-21). In contrast, Bill Viola's video installation *The Crossing* (1996) is reliant on a much slower tempo (fig. 6-22). This installation, split into two sides of a room, show an experience with water on one side and fire on the other. The extremely slow tempo at which a man walks toward the viewer and experiences water streaming onto him from above or fire engulfing him provides a mysterious mood to this video work. In both works, purposefully selected tempo is central to conveying the desired meaning.

Exercise

Create opening credits for an imaginary generic comedy film and an imaginary generic horror film. You can use motion graphics software, a stop-motion approach, or video. Use the exact same text and movements for both films, but use only tempo shifts to switch from comedy to horror. Where can on-screen elements be sped up or slowed down to create a sensation of humor or of fear and anticipation?

video

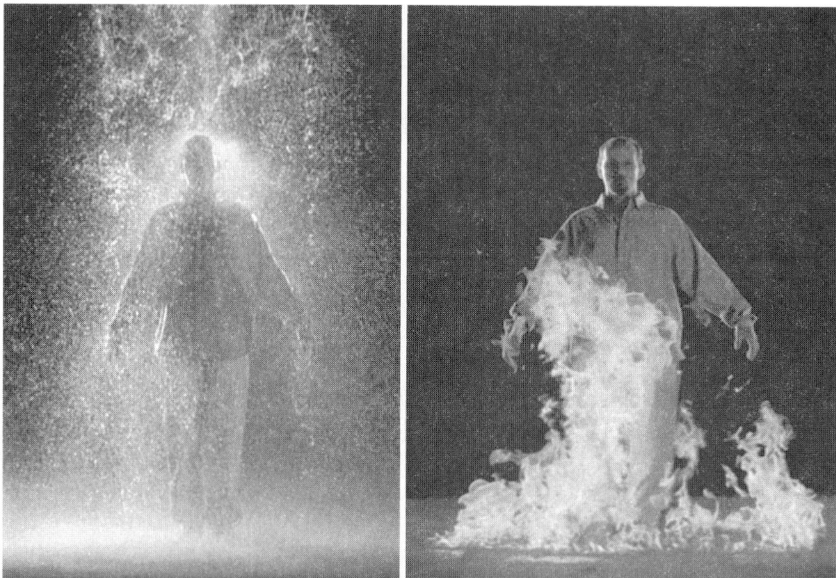

Fig. 6-22
Bill Viola, *The Crossing* (1996), Video/sound installation, 4.9 × 8.4 × 17.4 m. Two channels of color video projections from opposite sides of large dark gallery onto two large back-to-back screens suspended from ceiling and mounted to floor; four channels of amplified stereo sound, four speakers. Performer: Phil Esposito. Courtesy of Bill Viola Studio LLC.

Tempo is vital to participants' understanding of time, sound, light, or movement in your work because it will affect not only how they experience the work but also how they interpret its concepts.

Transitions

Transitions are well defined in film and video; however, they are equally important to movement, sound, light, and other media. Generally, **transitions** move participants from one energy dynamic to another, allowing for change and development over the course of a work. The speed of a transition can be very fast, occurring in less than a second, or much slower, occurring over the course of years. There are common transitions such as the passing of the seasons, the stages of life from birth to death, and the rise and fall of a story or narrative.

Pat Oleszko's *Odds at Sea Bahian Odyssey* (2008), a Brazilian parade performance and film, uses movement and sound to transition from mystical to joyous: performers walk 5 miles to the sea and continue to travel toward the horizon in a boat (fig. 2-6). As artists and designers select their transitions, they need to consider whether the transitions will be consistent throughout, or will transform over the course of the piece. It is also important for them to consider the space(s) in which the transitions take place, as Oleszko does in her work. In *Odds at Sea Bahian Odyssey*, the abandoned building where the performers begin is accompanied by sounds and music at a relatively slow pace. During the transition, when the performers are prompted to move away from the building and a young boy runs across an open field to greet them, faster tempo music is introduced. As in many successful 4D works, the sound changes rhythm, volume, and pitch to indicate an important shift is happening. The juxtaposition of spaces and sounds helps lend contrast and interest to the work, marking the subjective change from the solitary to communal.

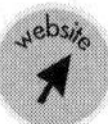

Visit the book's website to read the an interview with Pat Oleszko.

Exercise

Go online to search for and view Oskar Schlemmer's performance *Triadic Ballet* (you will likely find the rerecording of the ballet from the 1970s; this will work for this exercise). After watching the work, write down what you think are the subject, form, content, and context for this work. How did the artist use transitions within the ballet? Did the transitions of the filming create an experience that differs from how a live audience may have experienced the performance? Compare and contrast your answers with others'. How are your answers similar and different from those around you? Were there any trends in the answers?

Types of Transitions from Film Studies

There are also established transitions in film studies that can be applied to many 4D media. Remember, a cut is the simplest transition in screen-based works. Cory Arcangel's video work *Paganini Caprice No. 5*, uses only simple cuts, abruptly changing from one clip of a guitar tutorial to the next for every note in *Paganini's Caprice No. 5* (fig. 2-12). This use of a basic cut adds to the intricacy of the original musical work by creating a very choppy visual accompaniment to the complex and fast-moving score. In contrast to the simple cut, crosscutting is alternating cuts between two events. We sometimes see this effect played out in live theatrical productions: when a scene on one part of a stage is illuminated, and then the lights switch to another scene on a different part of the stage, it can be implied that the events are happening simultaneously or have some affect on each other. A **fade in** or **fade out** results in an on-screen image transitioning to or from black or white. A live fade involves a space gradually becoming illuminated or darkened. An on-screen **cross-fade** dissolves from one shot to blackness briefly that then dissolves to the next shot, whereas a live cross-fade simultaneously dims one set of lights as another illuminates. A **dissolve** allows one on-screen shot or scene to appear as the other disappears, and a **wipe** looks like one on-screen shot is sliding across the screen to reveal the next one. Although they seem very basic, these are some of the most commonly used transitions in screen-based media and some forms of live performance.

Exercise

Browse a newspaper to find a subject for a short performance. The performance must contain at least three transitions, which could be movements, lighting choices, sound cues, and so forth. Show your work to a partner, and ask him or her to examine the rhythm of your transitions. Do you need to speed up or slow down in any areas to create visual interest? Do the transitions add to or detract from the viewer's experience?

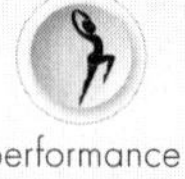

performance

In an **action-to-action transition**, the action in one shot continues into the next. The lobby scene from the feature film *The Matrix* (1999) demonstrates several action-to-action transitions as the characters Neo and Trinity storm a building to save Morpheus from the Agents. In an **eyeline transition**, in contrast, an individual looks in one direction, and then the next shot shows where he or she was looking. For example, in the classic film *Rear Window* (1954), a wheelchair-bound photographer watches his neighbors out his back window. The film features continuous eyeline transitions, reinforcing the fact that the main character is seeing events happen along with the audience.

In a **graphic matching transition**, one shot includes an object of a certain shape, color, or quality, and in the next shot there is a similar, but different, form. Alfred Hitchcock's *Psycho* (1960) has a well-known graphic matching transition following the famous shower scene in which a woman is stabbed to death. The camera follows the water and blood down the circular shower drain, which transitions to a similarly shaped woman's eye. Some **detail-revealing transitions** exist solely to show or emphasize detail, whether it is physical, emotional, or intellectual. In Sofia Coppola's *Marie Antoinette* (2006) there is a scene in which Marie and friends indulge in fashion and treats. There are a variety of detail-revealing transitions that help to emphasize the decadence and frivolity of the moment.

There is also the **non-sequitur transition**, which offers little, if any, logical connection between shots. Depending on how they are used, the connections made by transitions in film can help increase emotion, and can give viewers clues to the subject's motivation, or they can cause ambiguity and uneasiness by appearing illogical or mysterious. Transitions alter the way a work is perceived, visually and emotionally, by the viewer. Rachel Maclean's *Over the Rainbow* uses these non-sequitur transitions to help emphasize the pop-culture mash-up nature of her work. (Follow the link on the book's website to view this work.)

Exercise

Working with at least one partner—although more people in the group can lead to better solutions—find three short video clips online to connect together. Then, as a group, decide on the order in which the clips will appear. Now, without consulting each other, work individually to join the clips together using transitions of your choosing. Afterward, examine each person's transitions. Which transitions are most and least effective? Did more than one editor use any of the same transitions?

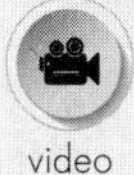

video

An artist or designer may also purposefully choose to omit transitions within his or her work. This approach can be useful in creating different subjective sensations such as time passing, emotions changing, or environments shifting. For example, an artist may want to lead viewers to believe that it is one point in time but then instantaneously imply that it is several years later. A simple example of this type of flash-forward occurs in Charles Dickens's *A Christmas Carol*, when the main character is taken forward in time to see his own death. Similarly, in dream scenarios, emotions and environments often change immediately and inexplicably. Matt Barton and Jacob Ciocci's video installation *Extreme Animalz: the Movie, Part 1* (2005) plays in this illogical dreamlike space and has a frenetic, pulsating quality that seems devoid of any sort of purposeful transitions (fig. 6-23). There is a

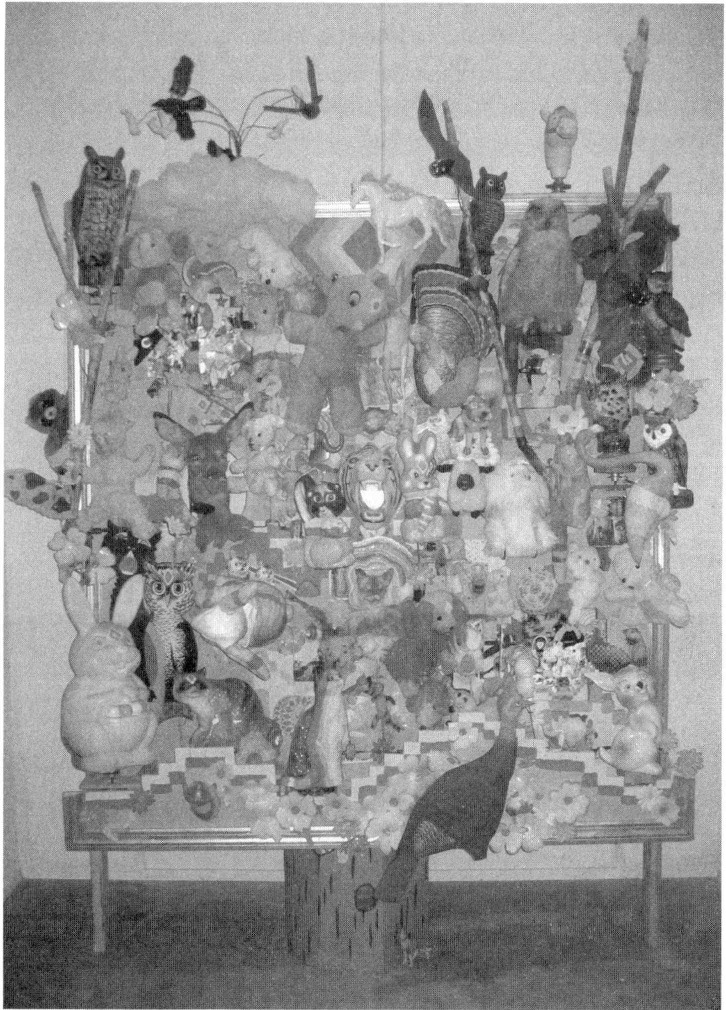

Fig. 6-23
Matt Barton and Jacob Ciocci, *Extreme Animalz: the Movie, Part 1* (2005), multimedia installation. Courtesy of the artist.

tremendous amount of movement in the mechanical spinning, bouncing, and shaking of various animal toys, while the video screens embedded among the moving toys flash a variety of animal imagery. The piece seems to pit the ordinary against the extraordinary, without any transitions at all. Keep in mind here that we are referring to the live experience of encountering this artwork, rather than the video documentation of the work, which indeed includes transitions such as dissolves.

Exercise

Brainstorm a list of 10 ideas connected with the concept of transportation, such as trains, planes, bicycles, and so on. Select one idea, and make a short film in which all edits are made in-camera, meaning that you will not be editing the footage after shooting and you must shoot in the order in which you want the viewer to see the shots. This forces precise planning of transitions—a storyboard is recommended. At critique ask each other whether better transitions could have been used and how those transitions could have been implemented.

video

Depending on the subject, form, content, and context of a piece, the presence or absence of transitions can feel natural or unnatural. It is the job of the artist or designer to determine what is appropriate for the work.

Summary

In this chapter, we examined these principles of 4D art and design:

- Causality, including how it builds certain expectations in viewers; its role in creating narrative; and how the use of sound can imply casuality in an artwork
- Duration was studied in terms of its effect on narrative, how different media can effect the duration of a work and thus its impact, as well as how artists try to motivate viewers to spend more time interacting with their work

- Energy dynamics and their effect on the audience's/viewer's experience of a work, as well as how an artist can use contrast and change in dynamics to structure a work
- Interactivity, including using text and individual choice as a basis for engagement; addressing basic questions (who, what, where, when, and how) when creating an artwork; transforming audience members into creators along with the artist; and the types and levels of interactivity that can be found in different artworks
- Musicality, including an examination of basic musical elements: pitch, volume, rhythm, timbre, melody, and haromnics
- Simultaneity/juxtaposition and the role that both play in creating and experiencing time-based artworks
- Spatial relationships, including how to organize a space and the way space is structured on-screen
- Tempo/speed and how it affects the performance and reception of an artwork
- Transitions, including some techniques taken from film studies

These principles can be used to describe and critique time-based works in various media. Now that you have studied the components of a work, the elements and principles borrowed from 2D and 3D art and design, as well as those elements and principles specific to 4D works, you will be better able to analyze and critique works in order to improve your own art and design practice.

Key Terms

accelerated motion   A speeded-up video sequence

action-to-action transition   A transition in which the action in one shot continues into the next

activity-centered interactivity   Interactivity in which the completion of a specific activity or task is the primary goal of the work

amplitude   Volume in decibels

antagonism   The goal of creating constructive debate around a serious topic while running the risk of alienating some individuals

artist or designer-centered interactivity   Interactivity driven solely by the skills and interests of the artist or designer

background   The area behind a subject

bird's-eye view   A shot from very high above the subject

causality   The principle that everything has a cause and effect

close-up shot   A shot that usually includes shoulders and head

cognitive interactivity   Interactivity that engages participants' minds with sight, sound, smell, touch, and taste sensory input

collaborative participation   Interactivity in which participants work together with the artist or designer to create both the structure and content of the work

conflict   Struggle

contextual interactivity   Interactivity that facilitates interaction with the context of the work and lends attention to affecting and changing the contextual circumstances

creative participation   Interactivity that involves participants creating original content within a structure established by an artist or designer

crescendo   An increase in loudness

crosscutting   In film/video, alternating cuts between two events

cross-fade   A transition in which one shot dissolves to blackness briefly and then dissolves to the next shot

cut   One shot in film or video ends and another one immediately begins in the same space and time

decrescendo   A decrease in loudness

depth of field   The area that appears to remain in focus between the nearest and farthest objects in a scene

detail-revealing transition   A transition that discloses detail, whether it is physical, emotional, or intellectual

directed participation   Interactivity that consists of participants completing a single task created by the artist or designer

dissolve   A film/video transition that allows one shot or scene to appear as the other disappears

duration   The overall length of time a work—or a portion of a work—lasts

energy dynamics   The amount and type of energy felt by the viewer or participant at any given moment

eye-line transition   A transition in which a character looks in one direction, and then the next shot shows where he or she was looking

fade in or fade out   The transition of an image to or from black or white

feedback loops   Consist of people providing information about their actions in real time, then providing some sort of immediate information about that action, and finally allowing time for an appropriate reaction to that feedback

foreground   The area in front of a subject

frame   A single still image from a film or video

graphic matching transition   A transition in film/video in which one shot includes an object of a certain shape, color, or quality, and in the next shot there is a similar, but different, form

harmonics   A selection of tones played simultaneously to create a chord

high-angle shot   A shot from above the subject

interactivity   The exchange of information between two or more entities

involuntary interactivity   An experience in which participants willingly engage in an activity or situation that turns out to be the work of an artist or designer

juxtaposition   Comparing two or more possibly contrasting elements or subjects to create new meaning

linear narrative   A narrative that advances chronologically, with a clear beginning, middle, and end

long shot   A shot that shows the entire figure in its setting and establishes a sense of environment

loudness   The amplitude or volume of any given sound

low-angle shot   A shot from below the subject

medium shot   A shot that might include a view of knees or waist and the rest of the body, up to the head

melody   A procession of tones that create a tune

middle ground   The area immediately surrounding a subject

musicality   The characteristic parts or principles of music and sound

narrative   An account of connected events (sometimes referred to as *story*)

noisy sounds   Sounds made of overlapping frequencies, which produce complex waveforms

nominal participation   Interactivity that involves reflection, as in the experience of encountering a painting, lecture, or traditional play

nonlinear narrative   A jumbled narrative that presents the beginning, middle, and end out of chronological order

non-sequitur transition   A transition that offers little, if any, logical connection between shots

nonvoluntary interactivity   An experience in which participants suddenly realize they are engaged with a work without prior consent

participant-centered interactivity   Interactivity in which the entire experience is geared toward participant needs and inclinations (also known as *user-centered design,* or UCD)

pitch   The frequency of a sound vibration

plot   The action that happens within the duration of a given work

reel time   The plot's duration (specific to film/video work)

relative   Determined in relationship to other factors

satire   The juxtaposition of a situation, person, or idea with its logical extreme

shot   The continuous footage between when you start and stop a recording camera

simultaneity   Two or more things happening at the same time

slow motion   A slowed-down video sequence

social interactivity   Interactivity that engages participants with one another as they experience the work

split screen   The juxtaposition of two or more clips within the same frame

story   The overarching description of the situation, including what happens before and after a particular plot

superimposition   Two images are shown simultaneously on top of one another

system-centered interactivity   Interactivity in which maintenance of a system is the primary goal

tempo   The rate at which time, sound, light, or movement passes (also referred to as *speed*, *pace*, or *velocity*)

timbre   The quality of sound

tonal sounds   Sound waves that pulse at regular intervals

tone   The quality of a sound vibration

transition   A progression that moves participants from one energy dynamic to another, allowing for change and development over the course of a work

volume   The amplitude or loudness of any given sound

voluntary interactivity   An experience in which participants are knowingly engaged

wipe   A film/video transition that looks like one shot is sliding across the screen to reveal the next one

Appendix

Technical Tips

Equipment

I would recommend all students work with a digital single-lens reflex (DSLR) camera with high-definition (HD) video capability and a digital audio recorder. In general, a DSLR camera will take a higher quality photos and video than most cell phones. It will allow for greater control over settings like the shutter speed, ISO or ASA (the rating of the film's sensitivity to light), and aperture opening. Of course, understanding these functions requires additional training and practice. However, this level of technology might not be available to all students, and so it is acceptable to substitute any available technology where necessary. Students could rely solely on their phones as long as they have video, photo, and audio recording capability. Phones are often less expensive and more portable than DSLR cameras, and in some cases a project might conceptually call for the look and feel that shooting with a phone provides. In a foundational setting, the mastery of concepts and principles is often more important to the success or failure of a project than the quality of tools used.

Software

None of the video exercises in this text requires professional grade editing software. The free video editing software on any Mac (iMovie) or PC (Windows Movie Maker) will be sufficient to complete any exercise listed in this text. Additionally, there are ample online sources for introductory tutorials on this software—such as Vimeo Video School—to help quickly acclimate students to basic editing tasks. Some departments may need to train students on a particular professional grade software in place of the free alternatives. This more in-depth software training is available online at a variety of locations including Lynda.com, which provides excellent online tutorials for individualized learning. Additionally, searching the Internet will yield a large volume of free video tutorials for most free or professional-grade software.

Some of the professional grade video editing software includes Final Cut Pro or Adobe Premiere Pro, which both allow for a great degree of control over the editing process. Adobe Premiere Pro runs on both Mac and PC machines and is compatible with After Effects (a video-compositing software included in the Creative Cloud). Final Cut Pro runs only on Mac computers. Both Adobe Premiere Pro and Final Cut Pro offer a collection of video effects, titles, animations, and audio presets similar to iMovie or Windows Movie Maker, but the professional applications offer a wider selection of options and will produce videos of superior quality. For example, Final Cut Pro and Premiere Pro have multi-camera support for syncing up to multiple simultaneous shots from different cameras, professional export options, as well as sophisticated color, video, and audio correction.

There is also a variety of free audio editing software available for download online. I recommend Audacity, http://audacity.sourceforge.net, which runs on both Mac and PC. Additionally, Audacity comes with an extensive and thorough help manual—complete with tutorials—upon download. This software is easy to learn and will allow students to execute basic editing tasks.

Processes

SHOOTING PHOTOGRAPHS. When you create an installation, performance, or other live ephemeral work, it is very useful to take high-quality photos to document the event. The following suggestions can help you take better photos of your work:

- Whether you are using a DSLR camera, a point-and-shoot camera, or your phone, be sure to set it to its highest size and quality settings. These settings will result in the largest possible image, which gives you more flexibility in the editing process. You can always make a digital photo smaller, but you can't make it bigger than the size at which it was originally shot without reducing image quality.
- If you have control over the lighting as you document the work, remember that indirect light is good and natural indirect light is even better. A room with windows can offer indirect sunlight, even on an overcast day. Avoid sunlight striking your work directly, as this can

cause glare (unless that is a conceptual part of the work). If you are working outdoors on a sunny day, you can hold up some type of screen between your subject and the sun to help disperse the direct light. The plastic covers for fluorescent lights in drop ceilings can work well for this purpose, and are inexpensively available at hardware or home improvement stores.

- If you are working with artificial light, try to use two or more light sources—preferably of similar wattage strengths. (See figure 5-14 for a description of three-point lighting.)
- If you need lights, visit a hardware or home improvement store, which often sells clip lights or construction site work lights for less than a photography store.
- Make sure to use a tripod to hold your camera as still as possible. You will produce sharper photos than if you were holding your camera yourself. If you do not have a tripod, you can try to minimize movement by using both hands to hold the camera, drawing both elbows in to your midpoint until they're close to touching, and then firmly holding your forearms as close to your torso as possible. Hold your breath just before and while hitting the shutter.
- If you are just starting to practice documentary photography, take many photos of your time-based work using different settings to get the best possible results. You will learn what works well in different scenarios with practice.
- Turn off your flash. Unless you know how to "bounce" the flash from your camera to a middle surface and then to your object, turn this function off. The flash will decrease contrast in the photo by eliminating shadows. In this way, flashes can dramatically alter the appearance of a work, and unless that is your intention, the flash should be avoided.

SHOOTING VIDEO. Whether you are shooting video for an original work or documenting a live performance, there are many things you can do to improve the quality of your footage:

- If you are documenting a performance piece, make sure to plan for the documentation from the beginning of the project—avoid letting it be an afterthought. This means setting aside time and resources such as camera equipment and funding to pay additional helpers to assist you if necessary.
- If you are documenting a performance piece, you must decide whether the documentation will simply be the most accurate representation of the work as possible, or a piece unto itself. Depending

on your answer, this could change how you shoot and edit your footage. Elements like voiceovers and dramatic close-ups may or may not be appropriate according to your intentions.

- Whenever possible, create a storyboard, list of shots, or other plans for shooting before you begin. See figure 1-15 for a sample storyboard. This will not only help you save time by being organized, but it will help anyone assisting you to understand your vision for the work.
- Charge your batteries and clear your memory card before you start shooting. If you have extra batteries or memory cards, bring them with you.
- Bring a tripod with you to help avoid shaky footage, or, if you don't have a tripod, set your camera on a steady surface. If there is no steady surface, you can hold the camera with both hands, keep your stance wide, breathe slowly, and keep your elbows close to your body.
- When you start shooting, remember to hold on your subject for at least 5 seconds to allow viewers to focus and to allow enough footage for editing. Try to place your subjects facing the light source, or, at the least, avoid having the light source directly behind your subject. If you cannot change your subject's position, you can use a reflective surface, like a white piece of paper or cardboard, to reflect light back onto your subject and eliminate harsh shadows.
- Generally, you will want to minimize camera movement and let your subject move within the video frame. However, there are a couple of simple camera motions that are commonly used: the pan, which is moving the camera horizontally, and the tilt, which is moving the camera vertically.
- When you are composing your shot, remember the rule of thirds, and avoid placing your subject in the dead center of the frame. Instead, if you divided the frame into thirds, both vertically and horizontally, you would want your subject to land at the intersections of those divisions.

RECORDING AUDIO. Here are some simple rules to follow when recording audio:

- Select a directional microphone rather than an omnidirectional microphone, which picks up all sound. For example, if you are in an amusement park, an omnidirectional microphone will pick up the sounds of people walking and talking, the sounds of the rides and vendors, and any other ambient sounds in the area. An omnidirectional microphone makes it more difficult for the listener to focus on a specific source of sound, such as a single speaker's voice, and instead conveys the overall feeling of a particular environment. A directional microphone is ideal for anytime you want to focus on a specific source of sound, such as the sounds of a single amusement vendor scooping ice, or a single person speaking.

- When recording, attempt to maintain a consistent environment just in case you need to go back and rerecord a sound. For example, try to use the same space under the same conditions and the same settings on your device.
- Take note of how far away the sound is from your recording device, and, if possible, use a screen to help avoid any popping and hissing from human speech.
- Try to reduce ambient noise. If you are indoors, unplug any humming machines, air conditioners, and so on, and make sure you are away from computers and other electronic fans.
- Record in a sound-dampened space. You can hang some sound-absorbing blankets or fabric to cover hard surfaces that will otherwise bounce sound.

STOP-MOTION ANIMATION. Stop-motion animation can be completed using a variety of free programs. Step-by-step video tutorial directions are easily found for each program via an Internet search. These tutorials will tell you exactly how to use your chosen software to create a stop-motion animation.

Here are some basic tips for shooting a stop-motion animation:

- Create a storyboard, and plan all the necessary movements in the animation.
- When you are setting up the camera, make all necessary changes and alter the settings, testing to ensure you have the look you want, before you begin your shoot.
- Establish all of your camera settings in advance. If you rely on software to correct a setting later, you will have to make that fix in all the frames, not just one. This will be extremely time-consuming.
- When you start to shoot a stop-motion animation, place the camera and then do your best to not move or bump the camera until you are finished. It is very helpful to have a remote shutter release, or work with a timer to avoid accidentally moving the camera.
- Once you start shooting, do not alter any of the camera settings. You want the images to feel continuous. If the exposure or focus suddenly changes, it will distract the viewer. For the same reason,

lighting should remain constant throughout the work, unless it is a purposeful change that supports the concept of the work.

- If you are shooting outdoors, work quickly to capture similar lighting throughout the work.
- Always work to complete the shoot in a single session if at all possible; this will help you avoid any of the inadvertent changes in position and lighting.
- As you shoot, try to shoot more frames than you think you will need. You can always remove frames, but it is nearly impossible to go back and shoot more.

EDITING. Here are some tips to follow through the editing process:
- Save your files and back them up regularly. Editing takes a lot of time, and losing those files can be particularly frustrating.
- Whether you are editing video or audio, you will want to start by organizing your files in a way that makes sense to you. Use folders or bins to help group clips together in a logical way. Most editing programs will have a window or space specifically designated for organizing your files.
- Editing programs also offer a timeline area where you can place your clips in order, trim them, and add transitions. The process of trimming and adding transitions will vary depending on the software you use, and therefore it is important to seek out tutorials specific to your chosen software.
- Another standard feature is a preview window of sorts, where you can see how your edited clips will look or sound.
- After you have made all the edits, export your finished work.

MOTION GRAPHICS. Here are some guidelines for creating motion graphics:
- Good motion graphics start with a compelling story. Before you start creating the piece, plan out your story. Simplify your message to its most basic and compelling parts. Ask yourself why anyone should care about this piece.
- Once you know your story, the choices about effects you will use, the direction of movement, color choices, and so on will become more apparent.
- Once you get to the point of executing the movement of your graphics in a program, remember to keep movement dynamic by engaging all three parts of a movement: attack, sustain, and decay (refer to Chapter 5 on movement).

- Other simple tips for making text and graphics appear more lifelike include using drop shadows to emulate a feeling of depth and motion blur to imitate the way the human eye perceives motion.
- As you are working, remember to take significant breaks, and then return to the work with fresh eyes. These breaks will allow you to see mistakes and changes that need to be made.

Resolution and Raster/Vector Files

Resolution is the degree of detail visible in an image or video (fig. App-1). Closely tied to the idea of resolution are two types of image files: raster and vector (fig. App-2).

High Resolution *(300ppi)*

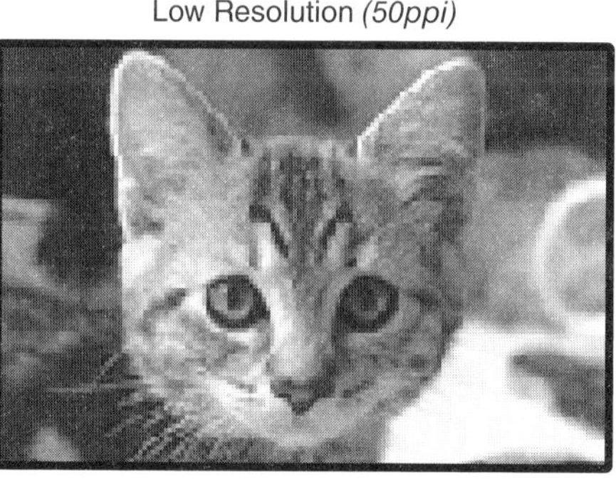

Raster File

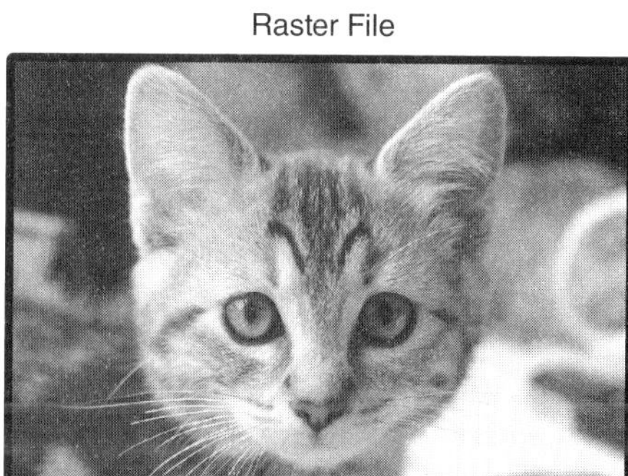

Low Resolution *(50ppi)*

Vector File

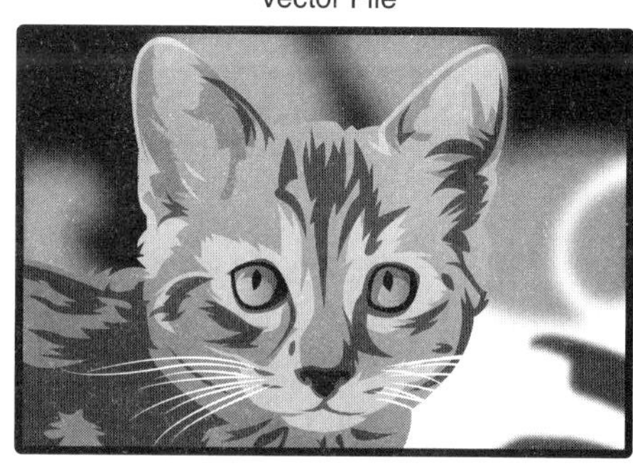

Fig. App-1
High-resolution photos provide a greater degree of detail than low-resolution photos. Original photo by Ryan Forsythe, used under the Creative Commons license (https:// creativecommons.org/licenses/by-sa/2.0/ legalcode).

Fig. App-2
Raster images are created using pixels, which limits their capacity to be resized. Vector images can be resized endlessly. © Phil McCollam.

Raster files are made of **pixels**, the smallest unit of digital displays. These are tiny squares of color designated a three-digit RGB number or four-digit CMYK number (refer to Chapter 3 for a discussion of RGB and CMYK). The most familiar raster files are digital photographs. Raster files (common types being .jpg, .tif, .png, and .gif) have a set resolution, or maximum number of pixels available, in height and width, when the file is opened. This resolution is measured in pixels per inch (ppi). To provide a sense of scale, images we view on screen are typically projected at 72 ppi, although many devices are now able to display images with a greater ppi density. Video, similar to digital photography, is also a raster-based medium. In video, the **aspect ratio**, or the height and width of the frame (in pixels), will determine the resolution of the work.

Raster files are best suited for producing and editing digital photographs or materials that are digitally scanned to the computer. Remember that digital video is a series of digital raster images shown in quick succession. Altering these raster files within raster-editing programs—such as Adobe Photoshop, PaintShop Pro, Pixlr, or GIMP for still images; Adobe Premiere Pro, Final Cut Pro, iMovie, or Windows Movie Maker for video— will provide better opportunities for creating seamless adjustments than using vector-editing programs such as Adobe Illustrator or Inkscape.

When working with raster-based media, you can always make your resolution smaller (the computer will calculate which pixels to remove in order to make the image smaller). However, you can never make the image larger than the original resolution because the computer will be forced to invent new pixels to fill in the gaps, which leads to a blurry, "jaggy," or pixilated appearance. This automatic process of removing pixilation, or "jaggies," from in image is referred to as **anti-aliasing**. It is always wise to create an image at the highest resolution possible to allow for any future use.

Vector files are made of vectors, which are points connected by angles or curves that can be endlessly resized without losing detail. Because vectors are essentially mathematical equations, they are resolution-independent, so you don't have to worry about pixels getting lost or invented. Any color number can be assigned to the curves in a vector file. Files commonly associated with vector are .dwg, .eps, and .ai.

Vector-based images are typically utilized when creating and editing imagery that includes text and/or sharply defined illustrative elements. Unlike raster images, vector images can be enlarged or shrunk without losing details due to pixel limitations; artwork produced for locations such as billboards, window or wall decals, signage, and apparel will often be built using vectors to allow for efficient resizing and repurposing across various media.

Keep in mind that some documents and applications will allow for the combination of raster and vector artwork in a single work. Three-dimensional modeling applications—such as Blender, Rhinoceros, 3D Studio Max, and SketchUp—will use vector-based processes to create 3D objects and raster-based imagery to add visual textures to the objects' surfaces. Similarly, printed materials such as posters or zines can combine raster images, such as photographs, with vector-based text to allow for greater flexibility in production and quality optimization.

Glossary

absorb To soak up

accelerated motion A speeded-up video sequence

accent light Light used to create patterns within the work by means of contrast

action-to-action transition A transition in which the action in one shot continues into the next

activity-centered interactivity Interactivity in which the completion of a specific activity or task is the main goal of the work

actual time *See* **measured time**

additive color mixing The process of mixing colors of light

afterimage A "ghost image" that is visible after a participant looks away from the original object

ambient light Light that fills and articulates the overall space

ambient sound Sound from the immediate surroundings

amplitude Volume in decibels

analogous color scheme Three colors that are directly next to one another on a 12-color color wheel

angular Consisting of straight lines and corners

animated GIFs Digital image files that can display movement

antagonism The goal of creating constructive debate around a serious topic while running the risk of alienating some individuals

antagonist The villain we root against

anti-aliasing The process of removing pixilation, or "jaggies," from an image

architecture Buildings and other built structures through and around which an individual can move

artist- or designer-centered interactivity Interactivity driven solely by the skills and interests of the artist or designer

aspect ratio   The height and width of the frame (in pixels)

asymmetrical balance   A type of balance in which parts are different on either side of a midline and feel like they could easily be thrown off balance

asynchronous sound   Sound we hear that does not match what we see

attached shadow   A shadow fixed to an object, revealing the basic form of the object

attack   The onset, growth, or birth of a movement or sound

audience   The people with whom you are communicating through your work

background   The area behind a subject

backlight   A light that illuminates the subject from behind, often creating a glowing outline—or halo effect—around the subject

balance   The measure of the relationship among different elements in an artwork

base of support   The area beneath an object or person that connects with the supporting surface, such as feet or hands

base plane   The horizontal field of space on which action takes place

battery life   The length of time a given battery allows you to complete a task on a piece of electronic equipment

biological time   A measure of time related to bodily functions.

bird's-eye view   A shot from very high above the subject

brainstorming   An active approach to producing ideas and solutions in a noncritical environment with emphasis on quantity over quality

brand   To distinguish an entity from others by creating specific narratives and designs to describe its identity

brightness   The relative intensity of a light as it grows to full luminance

cast shadow   A shadow independent of the object causing the shadow, revealing the object's relationship to its environment

causality   The principle that everything has a cause and effect

center of gravity   The center of the mass in an environment of uniform gravity

character   A person portrayed in a performance or work of writing

chroma keying   A technique for compositing two images or video clips together by masking a particular color range

chronological time   *See* **linear time**

cinemagraph   Animated GIF in which a minor and repeated movement occurs

clock time   *See* **measured time**

close-up shot   A shot that usually includes shoulders and head

CMYK   Acronym for cyan, magenta, yellow, and black: the primary colors for printing processes

cognitive interactivity   Interactivity that engages participants' minds with sight, sound, smell, touch, and taste sensory input

collaborative participation   Interactivity in which participants work together with the artist or designer to create both the structure and content of the work

collage   A specific collection of sketches and imagery

color   The perception of different wavelengths of visible light

color schemes   Specific, pleasing groupings of color

complementary color scheme   Pairing of two colors that are directly across from each other on a color wheel

composition   The arrangement of the elements and principles of art and design

conflict   Struggle

concept   The message the artist or designer intends to communicate

content   The meaning or impact of the work created through the intersection of subject, form, and context

context   The set of factors surrounding the creation and display of the work

contextual interactivity   Participation that facilitates interaction with the context of the work and lends attention to affecting and changing the contextual circumstances

contrast   The state of being different

craft   The skill with which media is manipulated

crane shot   The camera is mounted on a crane that can rise smoothly to a place far above the scene, or can lower down to ground level

creative participation   Interactivity that involves participants creating original content within a structure established by an artist or designer

crescendo   An increase in loudness

critique   The act of discussing an artwork

crosscutting   In film/video, alternating cuts between two events

cross-fade   A transition in which one shot dissolves to blackness briefly and then dissolves to the next shot

cue   Planned change in lights or other elements

cut   One shot in film or video ends and another one immediately begins in the same space and time

daylight   Light from the sun that changes color and brightness throughout the day and year, and is affected by weather

decay   The fall-off, termination, or death of a movement or sound

decrescendo   A decrease in loudness

depressed base plane   A horizontal field of space on which action takes place below participants

depth of field   The area that appears to remain in focus between the nearest and farthest objects in a scene

dérive   An unplanned experimental walk through an urban space

designer-centered interactivity   *See* **artist- or designer-centered interactivity**

detail-revealing transition   A transition that discloses detail, whether it is physical, emotional, or intellectual

diegetic sound   "Actual" sound, linked to the world of the artwork

diffused light   Light that passes through a material that scatters the light (clouds, haze, precipitation, diffusion plastic, etc.)

digital time   Time measured in milliseconds; it is often associated with technology

direct light   Light pointed at a specific object or location

directed participation   Interactivity that consists of participants completing a single task created by the artist or designer

direction   The course along which something moves

dissolve   A film/video transition that allows one shot or scene to appear as the other disappears

dolly shot   Camera movement parallel to the ground, often on a rolling track

down-lighting   Light from directly above a subject or work surface pointed straight down

duration   The overall length of time a work—or a portion of a work—lasts

Dutch tilt   A diagonal tilt of the camera; it is an effective way to disorient, stress, or excite the viewer

edited time   Time that has been cut up and rearranged

elevated base plane   A horizontal field of space on which action takes place above participants

emotional content   Content that causes the participant to have an emotional reaction

energy dynamics   The amount and type of energy felt by the viewer or participant at any given moment (also known as *intensity*)

event score   A series of instructions

experienced time   The perceived speed of time passing (also known as *subjective time, psychological time, implied time*, or *perceived time*)

eyeline transition   A transition which a character looks in one direction, and then the next shot shows where the person was looking

fade in or **out**   The transition of an image to or from black or white

fair use   A section of US copyright law that allows the use of published materials as long as a specific set of criteria are met

feedback loops   Consist of people providing information about their actions in real time, then providing some sort of immediate information about that action, and finally allowing time for an appropriate reaction to that feedback

fill light   A light that softens the key light and illuminates areas of shadow cast by the key light

filters   Generally placed in front of a white light source to alter the quality of the light

foreground   The area in front of a subject

form   The sensorial experience of the work; it encompasses the material or media used to create a work, as well as the organization of the elements and principles of art and design within a work

frame   A single still image from a film or video

frivolity   Indulgent in foolishness and idleness

front projection   Pointing a projector, connected to a computer or other device, at a screen designed to reflect light back at the viewer

gels   Filters made of thin transparent plastic sheets placed in front of a white light source to absorb all the colors of light except the color they are supposed to transmit

geometric shape   Linear and angular

Gestalt theory   visual illusions created to highlight the human tendency to establish continuity between various arrangements of objects or partially obscured objects

generative art   Computer-generated artwork that is algorithmically determined

gestures   Movements by a part of a whole (also known as *isolations*)

glare   Strong light directed or reflected into participants' eyes

gobo   A cut metal stencil placed in front of a lighting instrument with focusing lenses

graphic matching transition   A transition in film/video in which one shot includes an object of a certain shape, color, or quality, and in the next shot there is a similar, but different, form

habituation   The tiring of the nerves that sense extended sameness or extended periods of rapid change

hand-held shot   A video shot that is intentionally unstable and shaky

harmonics   A selection of tones played simultaneously to create a chord

high-angle shot   A shot from above the subject

high-key lighting   Brighter lighting situations

hue   The name of a color (blue, red, green, yellow, etc.)

identity   The set of characteristics that define a person

identity politics   Taking political action to promote the interests of an ill-treated or repressed group

imbalance   A condition of not being balanced

implied time   *See* **experienced time**

intellectual content   Content that engages the participant's thought process

intensity   *See* **energy dynamics**

interactivity   The exchange of information between two or more entities

involuntary interactivity   An experience in which participants willingly engage in an activity or situation that turns out to be the work of an artist or designer

isolations   *See* **gestures**

juxtaposition   Comparing two or more possibly contrasting elements or subjects to create new meaning

key light   A focused light that draws the eyes to a single point or location

light   A form of radiant energy that reflects off the world around us and into our eyes, allowing us to see our environment and color

linear narrative   A narrative that advances chronologically, with a clear beginning, middle, and end

linear time   Time that is mapped out in the order of past, present, and then future (also known as *chronological time*)

long shot   A shot that shows the entire figure in its setting and establishes a sense of environment

loop   The repetition of the same material over and over; it is commonly found in the presentation of video

loudness   The amplitude or volume of any given sound

low-angle shot   A shot from below the subject

low-key lighting   Darker lighting situations

measured time   Time quantitatively measured by regularly recurring events or intervals, such as the passage of minutes, meals, seasons, or years (also known as *actual time*, *objective time*, or *clock time*)

medium (media = plural)   The material and process used to create a work

medium shot   A shot that might include a view of knees or waist and the rest of the body, up to the head

melody   A procession of tones that create a tune

message   Your stance on a particular issue; relating to activism and protest

metaphor   A comparison that does not use "like" or "as"

middle ground   The area immediately surrounding a subject

monochromatic color scheme   A grouping of colors that consists of only one hue and its tints and shades

montage   A series of clips edited together to explore a piece of action, space, or time in greater detail or as an overview

movement   A shift or variation in the location of an object, light, or sound

musicality   The characteristic parts or principles of music and sound

narrative   An account of connected events (sometimes referred to as *story*)

negative space   The area surrounding the form or area of focus

noisy sounds   Sounds made of overlapping frequencies, which produce complex waveforms

nominal participation   Interactivity that involves reflection, as in the experience of encountering a painting, lecture, or traditional play

nondiegetic sound   "Commentary" sound, presented to enhance the world of the artwork

nonlinear narrative   A jumbled narrative that presents the beginning, middle, and end out of chronological order

nonlinear time   An arrangement of events to reveal parts of the future jumbled in with the past and present; there is no required order of events

nonrepresentational   When a work does not depict a recognizable person, place, or thing, and the subject is purely the quality of arranged sensory elements, such as shape, sound, color, light, and so forth

non-sequitur transition   A transition that offers little, if any, logical connection between shots

nonsynchronous sound   Sound that plays on-screen or onstage while its source is not currently visible but has been, or soon will be, visible

nonvoluntary interactivity   An experience in which participants suddenly realize they are engaged with a work without prior consent

objective time   *See* **measured time**

opaque object   A material off of which light reflects back into our eye, and does not allow light to pass through

oppositional movement   Movement that leads the eye in a different direction

optical color mixing   The process whereby the human eye mixes two or more colors together because they are close to each other

organic   Rounded and soft (describes shape or movement)

overhead plane   A horizontal field of space that occurs above the base plane and further defines the boundaries of the space

pace   *See* **tempo**

pan   A camera movement that consists of pivoting from side to side

participant-centered interactivity   Interactivity in which the entire experience is geared toward participant needs and inclinations (also known as *user-centered design*, or UCD)

pattern   A repeated set of organized elements

perceived time   *See* **experienced time**

photomontage   A specific collection photographs arranged by an artist or designer

physical content   Content that affects one's body or biological functions

pitch   The frequency of a sound vibration

pixels   The smallest unit of digital displays tiny squares of color designated a three-digit RGB number or four-digit CMYK number (refer to color chapter for discussion of RGB and CMYK)

plot   The action that happens within the duration of a given work

plot time   The span of time a plot covers within a narrative work (also known as *story time*, or *scope* [of a narrative])

point of view   A facet of context answering the question "Whose story is this?"

positive space   A form or area of focus within a larger space

primary colors   The irreducible colors that can be mixed together to create additional colors; there are different primaries for light, pigment, and ink printing processes

privilege   An unearned benefit or advantage due to an aspect of your identity, such as race, religion, gender identity, sexual orientation, class/wealth, citizenship status, and so on

projection mapping   Using software to map complex surfaces on which to project various imagery

projection   Purposefully cast light and shadow; examples include basic shadow puppetry, film or video projection, and projection mapping on 3D forms

proportion   The comparative measurement of different parts of a whole

protagonist   The hero we root for and who undergoes transformation

psychological time   *See* **experienced time**

radial balance   A type of balance in which parts radiate out from a central point

raster files   Files made of pixels

recontextualization   Juxtaposition of a familiar element, such as an image, movement or sound, and so on, in contrast with a context that is not typically associated with the element

reel time   The plot's duration (specific to film/video work)

refracted   Light that strikes an object and passes through, but changes direction upon exiting

reflected light   Light bounced off of one surface onto an intended object or location

relative   Determined in relationship to other factors

relative location   The relationship between a location and other markers of space

relativity   The comparison of a thing to its surroundings

repetition   The appearance of an element of art and design more than once within a work

representational   When a work depicts a recognizable person, place, or thing

resolution   (1) In a narrative, when the problem is solved or the story ends; (2) the degree of detail visible in an image or video

reverberation   Prolonging a sound

RGB   Acronym for red, green, and blue: the primary colors of light

rhythm   A regularized repeating of a movement or sound

ritual   A series of actions or a type of behavior regularly and invariably followed by someone

room tone   The unique, subtle sounds of an empty room

rotoscoping   The process of tracing single frames of film or video and then animating those traced frames

rule of thirds   A guide stating that you can divide any space into equal thirds, by height, width, and depth, and where those thirds intersect are good locations to place your subject

running time   The total length of a work, whether it is a live event or a video piece (also known as *play time* when describing gaming)

RYB   Acronym for red, yellow, and blue: the primary colors of pigment-based mixing

satire   The juxtaposition of a situation, person, or idea with its logical extreme

saturation   Purity or intensity of a color

scale   The relative size of something in relation to its surroundings

scope (of a narrative)   *See* **plot time**

secondary color   The result of mixing two primary colors together to reach a hue exactly balanced between the two primaries

sequence   A film term for a collection of related scenes, although it could also refer to a collection of light or sound cues, or a collection of movements

series   Multiple artworks that are linked by a repeating element such as a central concept, narrative, or visual element

setting   The location where a narrative takes place

shade   The mixture of a pigment-based color with black

shadow   An area of darkness created when light is blocked

shape   The outline of a form

shot   the continuous footage between when you start and stop a recording camera

sidelight   Light aimed at the side of a subject

silence   The perceived absence of sound

silhouette   An example of a specific kind of accent light that places an object between the viewer and an area of light creating a shadow in the shape of the object

simultaneity   Two or more things happening at the same time

simultaneous contrast   The visual effect in which two complementary colors placed next to each other appear more intense

slow motion   A slowed-down video sequence

social interactivity   Interactivity that engages participants with one another as they experience the work

sound   A vibration that can be perceived by the ear

sound bridge   Film transition in which sounds from one shot continue into the next shot or vice versa

space   A continuous area or expanse within which a work can take place

specific light   Light that provides illumination for a specific task, or to draw focus

speed   *See* **tempo**

split-complementary color scheme   On a 12-color color wheel, this is a single color and the two colors on either side of the color's complement

split screen   The juxtaposition of two or more clips within the same frame

spotlight   *See* **key light**

square color scheme   On a 12-color color wheel, this is a collection of 4 colors that are connected by a square

stillness   Absence of movement

stop-motion animation   A series of still images shown in quick succession to imply movement

story   The overarching description of the situation, including what happens before and after a particular plot

storyboard   A series of sketches describing planned actions in a work

story time   *See* **plot time**

subject   What the artist or designer is attempting to portray; the depicted people, places, and things

subtractive color mixing   The process of mixing pigment-based colors

subjective time   *See* **experienced time**

successional movement   Movement that leads the eye in one direction

superimposition   Two images are shown simultaneously on top of one another

sustain   The steady-state, duration, or life of a movement or sound

symmetrical balance   A type of balance in which parts are the same on either side of a midline and feel very stable

synchronous sound   Sound that is timed to its source on-screen or within a designated performance space

system-centered interactivity   Interactivity in which maintenance of a system as its main goal

task light   *See* **specific light**

temperature   The relative warmth (a hint of red/orange) or coolness (a hint of blue) of white light

tempo   The rate at which time, sound, light, or movement passes (also referred to as *speed*, *pace*, or *velocity*)

testimonial   A statement referencing personal experience

tetradic color scheme   On a 12-color color wheel, this is a collection of 4 colors that are connected by a rectangle, and consist of two complementary pairs

three-point lighting   A lighting setup consisting of a key light, a fill light, and a backlight

thumbnails   Small, rough sketches to communicate general ideas; often they are completed in large batches as a brainstorming technique

tilt   A camera movement that consists of pivoting up and down

timbre   The quality of sound; it is affected by the shape, size, and substance of any instrument, including the human voice

time   The progression of events and existence from the past, through the present, and into the future

time-lapse photography   Images are taken at regular intervals over a period of time, and then edited together to "speed up" a process that we normally don't experience

tint   The mixture of a pigment-based color with white

tonal sounds   Sound waves that pulse at regular intervals

tone   The quality of a sound vibration

topography   The physical nature or quality of the surface on which the work takes place

tracking shot   Camera movement parallel to the ground, often on a rolling track

transition   A progression that moves participants from one energy dynamic to another, allowing for change and development over the course of a work

translucent object   A material that allows much of the light to pass through, but some is reflected, which causes a blurred or somewhat obstructed effect

transparent object   A material that transmits or allows light to pass through, allowing us to see what is beneath it

triadic color scheme   On a 12-color color wheel, these are three colors that form an equilateral triangle

up-lighting   Light pointed up at the subject from a location below

user-centered design (UCD)   *See* **participant-centered interactivity**

value   Relative lightness or darkness (can refer to color or light)

vector file   Files made of points connected by angles or curves that can be endlessly resized without losing detail

velocity   *See* **tempo**

viewpoint   A term from film and video studies describing how the composition of each shot can express facets of a point of view

visibility   The extent to which a participant can see within the space of a work

visual weight   The weight your eyes assign to an object based on its dimensions, shape, location, and color

volume   The amplitude or loudness of any given sound

voluntary interactivity   An experience in which participants are knowingly engaged

white balancing   Camera adjustment to record a true white according the temperature of a given lighting situation

wipe   A film/video transition that looks like one shot is sliding across the screen to reveal the next one

zoom   Utilizing camera lenses to make the image larger or smaller

Additional Resources

Architecture

Ching, Francis. *Architecture: Form, Space, and Order.* 3rd ed. Hoboken, NJ: John Wiley & Sons, 2007.
Wallschlaeger, Charles, and Cynthia Busic-Snyder. *Basic Visual Concepts and Principles for Artists, Architects and Designers.* New York: McGraw-Hill, 1992.

Color

Albers, J. *Interaction of Color.* New Haven, CT: Yale University Press, 1975.
Bankston, D. *The Color-Space Conundrum.* American Cinematographer, 2005.
Benson, J. L. *Greek Color Theory and the Four Elements.* Amherst: University of Massachusetts, 2000.
Birren, F. *Color Psychology and Color Therapy: A Factual Study of the Influence of Color on Human Life.* Whitefish: Kessinger, 2006.
Itten, Johannes. *The Art of Color.* New York: Van Nostrand Reinhold, 1974.
Munsell, Albert H. *A Grammar of Color: A Basic Treatise on the Color System of Albert H. Munsell.* New York: Van Nostrand Reinhold, 1969.

Composition and Gestalt

Barrett, Terry. *Making Art, Form & Meaning.* New York: McGraw-Hill, 2011.
Berger, Arthur Asa. *Seeing Is Believing: An Introduction to Visual Communication,* 3rd ed. New York: McGraw-Hill, 2007.
Eisner, Will. *Comics and Sequential Art.* Arlington: Poorhouse Press, 2001.
Luecking, Stephen. *Principles of Three Dimensional Design.* Upper Saddle River, NJ: Pearson Education, 2002.
McCloud, Scott. *Understanding Comics.* Northampton: Kitchen Sink Press, 1994.
Ocvirk, Otto G., Robert E. Stinson, Philip R. Wigg, Robert O. Bone, and David L. Cayton. *Art Fundamentals.* New York: McGraw-Hill, 2013.

Creativity/Ideation

Bohm, David. *On Creativity.* New York: Routledge, 2000.
Briggs, John. *Fire in the Crucible: Understanding the Process of Creative Genius.* Grand Rapids, MI: Phanes Press, 2000.
Gold, Rich. *The Plenitude: Creativity, Innovation, and Making Stuff.* Cambridge, MA: MIT Press, 2007.

Johnstone, Keith. *Impro: Improvisation and the Theatre*. London: Routledge, 1992.

Sweeney, John. *The Art of the Laugh*. Minneapolis: Aerialist Press, 2005.

Van Pelt, Peggy, ed. *The Imagineering Workout: Exercises to Shape Your Creative Muscles*. New York: Disney Editions, 2005.

Directing

Bartow, Arthur. *The Director's Voice: Twenty-One Interviews*. New York: Theatre Communications Group, 1988.

Bloom, Michael. *Thinking Like a Director*. New York: Faber and Faber, 2001.

Clurman, Harold. *On Directing*. New York: Macmillan, 1972.

Katz, Steven D. *Film Directing: Cinematic Motion*. Studio City, CA: Michael Wiese Productions, 1992.

Kazan, Elia. "On What Makes a Director." *Directors Guild of America Newsletter* (January 1990): 4–12.

Film and Video

Johnson, Lincoln F. *Film: Space, Time, Light and Sound*. Orlando, FL: Holt, Rinehart and Winston, 1974.

Pramaggiore, Maria, and Tom Wallis. *Film, A Critical Introduction*. New York: Laurence King, 2008.

Schroeppel, Tom. *The Bare Bones Camera Course for Film and Video*. New York: Allworth Press, 2015.

Zettl, Herbert. *Sight, Sound, Motion: Applied Media Aesthetics*. Belmont, CA: Wadsworth, 2004.

Games, Gaming, and Play

Callois, Roger. *Man, Play, and Games*. Chicago: University of Illinois Press, 2001.

Fullerton, Tracy. *Game Design Workshop*, 2nd ed. Burlington, MA: Morgan Kaufmann, 2008.

Iuppa, Nick, and Terry Borst. *Story and Simulations for Serious Games*. Waltham: Focal Press, 2007.

Schell, Jesse. *The Art of Game Design*. Burlington, MA: CRC Press, 2008.

Sutton-Smith. *The Ambiguity of Play*. Cambridge, MA: Harvard University Press, 2001.

Interactivity

Buston, Bill. *Sketching User Experiences*. Burlington, MA: Morgan Kaufmann, 2007.

Helguera, Pablo. *Education for Socially Engaged Art*. New York: Jorge Pinto Books, 2012.

Preece, Jennifer, Yvonne Rogers, and Helen Sharp. *Interaction Design: Beyond Human-Computer Interaction*. Hoboken, NJ: John Wiley & Sons, 2002.

Saffer, Dan. *Designing for Interaction: Creating Smart Applications and Clever Devices*. Berkeley: New Riders, 2007.

Light

Box, H. C. *Set Lighting Technician's Handbook*, 3rd ed. Waltham: Focal Press, 2003.

Brown, B. *Motion Picture and Video Lighting*, 2nd ed. Waltham: Focal Press, 2007.

Carlson, V., and S. Carlson. *Professional Lighting Handbook*, 2nd ed. Waltham: Focal Press, 1991.

Handell, L. T., and A. T. Handell. *Intuitive Light: An Emotional Approach to Capturing the Illusion of Value, Form, Color, and Space*. New York: Watson Guptill, 1995.

Motion Graphics

Art of the Title, Available at http://www.artofthetitle.com.

Braha, Yael, and Bill Byrne. *Creative Motion Graphic Titling for Film, Video, and the Web*. Waltham: Focal Press, 2011.

Design Museum London. *Saul Bass, Graphic Designer (1920–1996)*. Retrieved September 4, 2015, from http://design.designmuseum.org/design/saul-bass.

Krasner, Jon. *Motion Graphic Design, Applied History and Aesthetics*. Waltham: Focal Press, 2013.

Thomas, Frank, and Ollie Johnston. *The Illusion of Life: Disney Animation*. New York: Disney Productions, 1981.

Movement

Bogart, Anne, and Tina Landau. *The Viewpoints Book: A Practical Guide to Viewpoints and Composition*. New York: Theatre Communications Group, 2004.

Epstein, William, and Sheena Rogers, eds. *Perception of Space and Motion*. San Diego, CA: Academic Press, 1995.

Kepes, Gyorgy. *The Nature and Art of Motion*. New York: George Braziller, 1965.

Narrative

Glassner, Andrew. *Interactive Storytelling: Techniques for 21st Century Fiction*. Boca Raton, FL: AK Peters, 2004.

Meadows, Mark Stephen. *Pause and Effect: The Art of Interactive Narrative*. Berkeley: New Riders, 2003.

Sheldon, Lee. *Character Development and Storytelling for Games*. Independence, KY: Thomson Course Technology, 2004.

Performance Art

Goldberg, RoseLee. *Performance Art: From Futurism to the Present*, 3rd ed. London: Thames & Hudson, 2011.

Goldberg, Roselee. *Performance: Live Art Since the '60s*. London: Thames & Hudson, 2004.

Sound for Film, Music, and Editing

Alten, Stanley R. *Audio in Media*, 4th ed. Belmont, CA: Wadsworth, 1994.

Bordwell, David, and Kristin Thompson. "Fundamental Aesthetics of Sound in the Cinema." pp. 181–199. In Elisabeth Weis and John Belton (eds.), *Film Sound: Theory and Practice*. New York: Columbia University Press, 1985.

Chion, Michel. *Audio-Vision: Sound on Screen*. New York: Columbia University Press, 1994.

Sound (Non-film)

Russ, Martin. *Sound Synthesis and Sampling*. Waltham: Focal Press, 1996.

Voegelin, Salome. *Listening to Noise and Silence: Towards a Philosophy of Sound Art*. New York: Continuum International Publishing Group, 2010.

Shrivastava, Vinay. *Aesthetics of Sound*. Dubuque, IA: Kendall/Hunt, 1996.

Theater

Gillette, J. Michael. *Theatrical Design and Production*. New York: Mayfield, 2000.

Theory

Barrett, Terry. *Why Is That Art? Aesthetics and Criticism of Contemporary Art*. New York: Oxford University Press, 2011.

Kimmelman, Michael. *The Accidental Masterpiece: On the Art of Life and Vice Versa*. Westminster: Penguin Books, 2006.

Notes

Preface

1   Anne Bogart and Tina Landau, *The Viewpoints Book: A Practical Guide to Viewpoints and Composition* (New York: Theatre Communications Group, 2004).

Introduction

1   "Bauhaus 1919–1933," Bauhaus Dessau Foundation, accessed March 13, 2013, http://www.bauhaus-dessau.de/index.php?bauhaus-1919-1933.
2   Anne Bogart and Tina Landau, *The Viewpoints Book: A Practical Guide to Viewpoints and Composition* (New York: Theatre Communications Group, 2004).
3   "Tim Berners Lee (1955–)," BBC History, accessed August 19, 2015, http://www.bbc.co.uk/history/historic_figures/berners_lee_tim.shtml.

Chapter 1

1   Jason Persse, "From a Whisper to a Scream: Following Yoko Ono's Instructions," accessed July 14, 2010, http://www.moma.org/explore/inside_out/2010/07/14/from-a-whisper-to-a-scream-following-yoko-onos-instructions.
2   Dejan Todorovic, "Gestalt Principles," Scholarpedia, accessed August 19, 2015, http://www.scholarpedia.org/article/Gestalt_principles.
3   Todorovic, "Gestalt Principles."
4   Todorovic, "Gestalt Principles."
5   Elisabeth Ginsberg, Elisabeth. "Mining the Museum," *Beautiful Trouble*. Accessed September 12, 2015. http://beautifultrouble.org/case/mining-the-museum/
6   Jamie Utt, "How to Talk to Someone About Privilege Who Doesn't Know What That Is," accessed December 7, 2012, http://everydayfeminism.com/2012/12/how-to-talk-to-someone-about-privilege/.
7   Quoted in Allan Kozinn, "Maryanne Amacher, 71, Visceral Composer, Dies," *New York Times*, accessed July 13, 2013, http://www.nytimes.com/2009/10/28/arts/music/28amacher.html?_r=0.
8   Paul Schmelzer, "Insurgent Inquiry: The Art of Allora & Calzadilla," *Eyeteeth: Incisive Ideas* (blog), accessed July 13, 2013, http://eyeteeth.blogspot.com/2004/04/insurgent-inquiry-art-of-allora.html.
9   Pablo Helguera, *Education for Socially Engaged Art* (New York: Jorge Pinto Books, 2012).

Chapter 2

1   G. Lemons, "When the Horse Drinks: Enhancing Everyday Creativity Using Elements of Improvisation," *Creativity Research Journal* 17, no. 1 (2005): 25–36, doi: 10.1207/s15326934crj1701_3.

2   J. Michael Gillette, *Theatrical Design and Production* (New York: Mayfield, 2000).

3   John Sweeney, *The Art of the Laugh* (Minneapolis: Aerialist Press, 2005).

4   Jesse Schell, *The Art of Game Design: A Book of Lenses* (Burlington, MA: Taylor & Francis Group, LLC, 2008).

5   Schell, *Art of Game Design.*

6   Quoted in Michael Bloom, *Thinking Like a Director* (London: Faber and Faber: 2001), 25.

7   Ed Sikov, *Film Studies: An Introduction* (New York: Columbia University Press, 2010).

8   Doyle Canning and Patrick Reinsborough, "Think Narratively," in *Beautiful Trouble*, ed. Andrew Boyd and Dave Oswald Mitchell (New York: OR Books, 2012).

9   Terry Barrett, *Making Art, Form & Meaning* (New York: McGraw Hill, 2011).

10   Katie Salen and Eric Zimmerman, *Rules of Play: Game Design Fundamentals* (Cambridge, MA: Massachusetts Institute of Technology Press, 2004).

11   Canning and Reinsborough, "Think Narratively."

12   ACLU, "The ACLU and Citizens United," accessed June 21, 2013, http://www.aclu.org/free-speech/aclu-and-citizens-united.

13   Andrew Boyd and Dave Oswald Mitchell, eds., *Beautiful Trouble* (New York: OR Books, 2012).

Chapter 3

1   Anne Bogart and Tina Landau, *The Viewpoints Book: A Practical Guide to Viewpoints and Composition* (New York: Theatre Communications Group, 2004).

2   David Sonnenschein, *Sound Design: The Expressive Power of Music, Voice and Sound Effects in Cinema* (Studio City, CA: Michael Wiese Productions, 2002).

Chapter 4

1   Philip Gordon, *Principles & Practices of Lighting Design: The Art of Lighting Composition* (Woodside, CA: Blue Matrix Productions, 2011).

2   Gordon, *Lighting Design.*

3   Herbert Zettl, *Sight Sound Motion* (Belmont, CA: Wadsworth, 1999).

4   Anne Bogart and Tina Landau, *The Viewpoints Book: A Practical Guide to Viewpoints and Composition* (New York: Theatre Communications Group, 2004).

5   Jesse Schell, *The Art of Game Design: A Book of Lenses* (Oxford: Taylor & Francis Group, LLC, 2008), 176.

6   Bogart and Landau, *Viewpoints Book.*

7   "MoMA | The Collection," accessed July 2, 2013, http://www.moma.org/collection/object.php?object_id=89507.

8   Zettl, *Sight Sound Motion.*

9   Ed Sikov, *Film Studies: An Introduction* (New York: Columbia University Press, 2010).

10   Bogart and Landau, *Viewpoints Book.*

11   Bogart and Landau, *Viewpoints Book.*

12   Zettl, *Sight Sound Motion.*

Chapter 5

1   David Sonnenschein, *Sound Design: The Expressive Power of Music, Voice and Sound Effects in Cinema* (Studio City, CA: Michael Wiese Productions, 2002).

2   Anne Bogart and Tina Landau, *The Viewpoints Book: A Practical Guide to Viewpoints and Composition* (New York: Theatre Communications Group, 2004).

3   Ben Cocio, "MOMA 'On Line' Series: Anne Teresa De Keersmaeker," accessed August 19, 2015, https://vimeo.com/21823379.

4   J. Michael Gillette, *Theatrical Design and Production* (New York: Mayfield, 2000).

5   Philip Gordon, *Principles & Practices of Lighting Design: The Art of Lighting Composition* (Woodside, CA: Blue Matrix Productions, 2011).

6   Gillette, *Theatrical Design.*

7   Francis D. K. Ching, *Architecture: Form, Space and Order*, 3rd ed. (Hoboken, NJ: John Wiley & Sons, 2007).

8   Sonnenschein, *Sound Design.*

9   Sikov, *Film Studies.*

10   Aaron Copland, "Tip to Moviegoers: Take Off Those Ear-Muffs," http://www.americanmusicpreservation.com/TheHollywoodFilmMusicReader.htm.

11   Sonnenschein, *Sound Design.*

Chapter 6

1   Herbert Zettl, *Sight Sound Motion* (Belmont, CA: Wadsworth, 1999).

2   Anne Bogart and Tina Landau, *The Viewpoints Book: A Practical Guide to Viewpoints and Composition* (New York: Theatre Communications Group, 2004).

3   Carolina A. Miranda, "The New World of Net Art," ARTnews, accessed June 12, 2013, http://www.artnews.com/2013/06/12/the-new-world-of-net-art/.

4   Haroon Baig, "Top 10 Creative Ways to Display Time," *Smashing Magazine*, accessed August 15, 2008, http://www.smashingmagazine.com/2008/08/15/top-10-creative-ways-to-display-time/.

5   Katie Salen and Eric Zimmerman, *Rules of Play: Game Design Fundamentals* (Cambridge, MA: Massachusetts Institute of Technology Press, 2004), 59.

6   David Sonnenschein, *Sound Design: The Expressive Power of Music, Voice and Sound Effects in Cinema* (Studio City, CA: Michael Wiese Productions, 2002).

7   Francis D. K. Ching, *Architecture: Form, Space and Order*, 3rd ed. (Hobeoken, NJ: John Wiley & Sons, 2007).

8   Ching, *Architecture.*

9   Bogart and Landau, *Viewpoints Book.*